WOMEN IN WARTIME

WOMEN IN WARTIME

Dress Studies from Picture Post 1938–1945

GERALDINE HOWELL

BLOOMSBURY VISUAL ARTS
LONDON • NEW YORK • OXFORD • NEW DELHI • SYDNEY

BLOOMSBURY VISUAL ARTS
Bloomsbury Publishing Plc
50 Bedford Square, London, WC1B 3DP, UK
1385 Broadway, New York, NY 10018, USA

BLOOMSBURY, BLOOMSBURY VISUAL ARTS and the Diana logo are trademarks of Bloomsbury Publishing Plc

First published in Great Britain 2019

A catalogue record for this book is available from the British Library.

A catalog record for this book is available from the Library of Congress.

ISBN: HB: 978-1-350-00092-6
ePDF: 978-1-350-00093-3
eBook: 978-1-350-00094-0

Typeset by Integra Software Services Pvt. Ltd.
Printed and bound in Great Britain

To find out more about our authors and books visit www.bloomsbury.com and sign up for our newsletters.

CONTENTS

LIST OF FIGURES

ACKNOWLEDGEMENTS

My first thank you must be to Gale-Cengage Learning for having had the vision to digitize *Picture Post*. Without this online resource, research would have been far harder and involved endless days in libraries working with friable paper copies. The *Picture Post Historical Archive* is easy to access and to use, requiring only membership of any institution subscribing to it. I joined the Westminster Reference Library, which holds the *Picture Post* archive as part of its Newspapers and Magazines Collection, and I am grateful to the Library for both taking the Archive and offering free access to it.

From its inception this project has benefitted from the advice and guidance of a small, dedicated team at Bloomsbury Publishing. Thank you to Hannah Crump who piloted me through the proposal and commissioning stages and helped me to establish something of the parameters of the work at a crucial time in its early development. Thereafter, I have had the tireless support of Frances Arnold, Editorial Director for Visual Arts, whose encouragement and thoughtfulness have been so much appreciated, particularly during the period of reflection and reorganization following the project review. Thank you also to Editorial Assistant Yvonne Thouroude for listening to worries and talking things through. For the care, attention to detail and professionalism with which my text was prepared for publication, thank you to Vinu Vijayamurugan and the team at Integra.

I am especially indebted to Professor Lou Taylor for agreeing to read the manuscript in draft. She is always clear and candid and her thorough and meticulous review was the catalyst for some serious rethinking of both text and structure.

I would also like to thank Caroline Theakstone, Research Editor at Getty Images, for all her help in finding the images I wanted. Her time and energies on my behalf have meant I have been able to include a large proportion of the photographs on my wish list and deliver the sort of illustrated text I aspired to. Thank you also to Neil Stewart, Digital Library Manager at the London School of Economics, for permission to publish the 'Old Clothes Shop' from John Thompson's photographs from *Street Life in London*.

In a small number of cases it was not possible to establish or confirm image copyright for either individual photographs or whole photo-stories. This has meant some key articles are discussed without illustration. These include, for example, 'Enough of All This', 'ARP Warden to Glamour Girl', 'A Mayfair Girl Gets Married', 'Fashions for the Farm' and 'How to Run Your Dress Allowance'. All of these are, of course, readily available to view via the *Picture Post* Historical Archive which by curating and maintaining access to the magazine is keeping this wealth of material in the public domain. Such a resource is all the more valuable as it becomes the only way of seeing photographs whose primary provenance is now either lost or unclear.

INTRODUCING *PICTURE POST*

Dress, fashion and *Picture Post*

Picture Post magazine provides a unique archive of dress, fashion and fashionability covering a wartime period that witnessed unprecedented social upheaval and hardship. This book sets out to explore the many ways in which *Picture Post* stories reveal the sheer diversity of clothing and beauty culture practised during this extraordinary time and the ways in which the dress and accessories captured on camera narrated their own discrete histories. Women from many different backgrounds and of varying ages, often reflecting widely divergent aspirations and opportunities, can all be found within the pages of *Picture Post*. Close scrutiny of their clothing and accessories, hair and beauty ideas, and the nature of their association with the fashions and the fashionable of the period, all communicate much about the social fabric of individual lives and the cultural contexts which shaped them. *Picture Post* remains a still largely untapped resource for the dress historian, and it is the purpose of this book to highlight its contribution to the study of these evocative elements of material and social culture.

The chronological parameters have been determined by the dress history story of war being told. *Picture Post* was launched in October 1938. During its first year it charted much about how fashion and beauty culture were understood within different communities in the period leading up to Britain's declaration of war on 3 September 1939. Stories thereafter pursued these ideas further by investigating how wartime conditions brought about changing approaches to fashion consciousness, health and well-being. By 1944 news from France made it clear that a couture industry of sorts had survived in Paris and this, together with the tide of war having turned by the autumn and winter of that year, began a re-orientation of fashion thought away from war, the primary focus of this book, and towards peace. Articles reflecting these changing perspectives throughout the winter and spring of 1945 are, therefore, the last to be considered. After victory another set of stories arise based on the aspirations of peace and the economic priorities of the post-war era.

Picture Post illustrated both the broad reaches of fashion itself and the lifestyle choices that became fashionable during the wartime years. The different types of work and leisure patterns that arose were often responsible for promoting alternative style priorities that largely added to, rather than displaced, existing dress practice. *Picture Post* stories charted these continually evolving attitudes towards clothing, accessories and cosmetics alongside of new interests in health and body consciousness.

While each of the chapters that follow develops its own dress themes and issues, two areas of investigation are common to the work as a whole:

- the extent to which dress stories from *Picture Post* shape our understanding of women's lives.
- the distinctive use of the photo-story in facilitating an appreciation of the changing nature of fashion and female identities.

Central to the first is the sheer diversity of subject matter covered by *Picture Post* while the second highlights the unique quality of the historic record created by the many gifted photographers and writers whose work came to define the magazine's signature style.

Direct and indirect stories

Working with *Picture Post* as a dress history archive it becomes clear that the magazine offers information on clothing culture, fashion and beauty in two ways: either **directly** or **indirectly**.

Stories that took readers into fashion houses or beauty parlours, discussed a Utility wardrobe or a make-do-and-mend project, **directly** explored aspects of the wartime

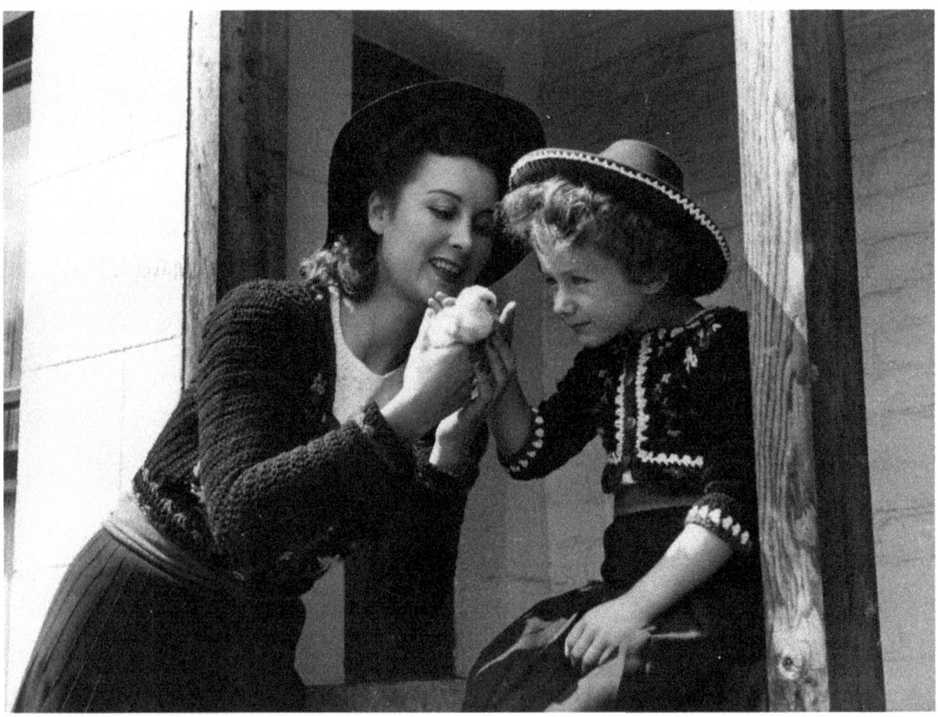

Figure 1 'Boleros for Mother and Daughter: Thick hand-knitted sweaters are becoming a rarity. This pair are grand for the country.' From 'Mother-and-Daughter Fashions', *Picture Post*, 30 August 1941, p. Kurt Hutton/*Picture Post*/Getty Images (3249576).

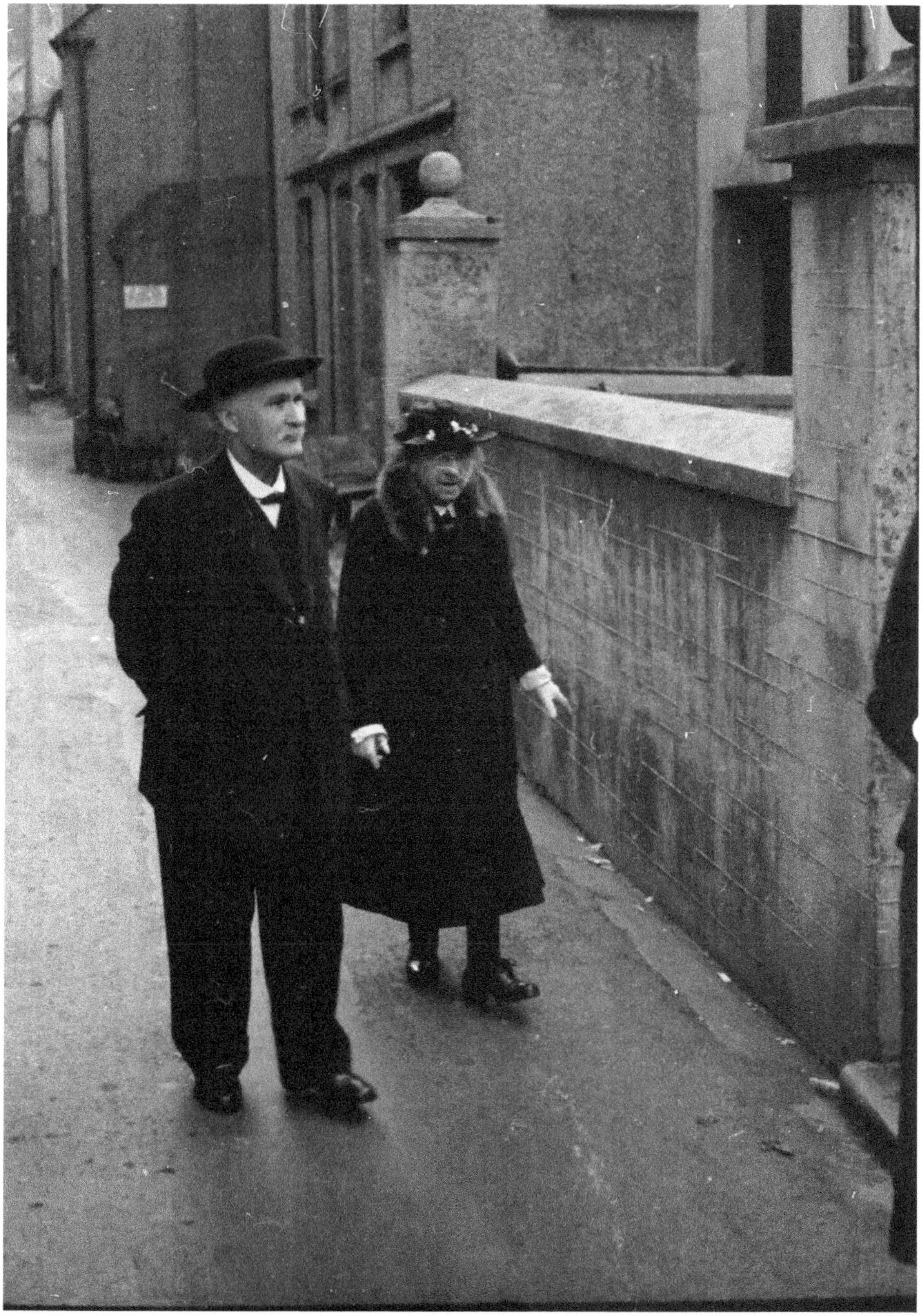

Figure 2 'Sunday Suits: We keep our own style of dress in the village. It's neat and dignified. It suits us. And you can always tell Sunday by the clothes we wear.' From 'Life of a Village', *Picture Post*, 1 October 1938, p. 48. Felix Man/*Picture Post*/Getty Images (3368569).

world of fashion as did features on health and well-being – increasingly associated with achieving the fashionable look and figure.

These stories often took an approach to the subject that was less predictable or unusual in some way. Readers were shown an insider's perspective or a behind-the-scenes view that became characteristic of the *Picture Post* method. Whether witnessing the backstage preparations for a couture show in Paris, the development and marketing of a new range of corsetry, watching beauty consultants being put through their training or observing some of the latest extraordinary treatments and techniques at work in the contemporary beauty salon, *Picture Post* provided a visual understanding of the modern world of fashion often considerably demystifying the more privileged and closed aspects of it in the process.

For every article directly on fashion there were many more that **indirectly** provided a view of dress and material culture through stories on the living conditions, lifestyles or life experience of a heterogeneous collection of people and communities. The visual narratives of these photo-stories indirectly recorded the way clothing and accessories were worn and used by individuals or social groups so establishing a relationship between appearance and the social context in which people worked or lived. Here are some of the most authentic illustrated records of individual lifestyles in Britain during the immediate pre-war and wartime period that we have and as such an extraordinarily rich set of narratives for the dress historian.

While *Picture Post* might chart the workings and evolution of many and varied elements of the ephemeral world of fashion, it is this unique collection of photo-stories revealing the everyday dress practices of people across the social spectrum that defines its particular significance as a dress history archive. Such a record is one of the less appreciated legacies of *Picture Post* that this book hopes to now fully recognize.

How reliable is *Picture Post* as a dress history archive?

Before beginning this exploration it is essential to establish that the information to be found in *Picture Post* can be accepted as both reliable and accurate by the dress historian. To what extent can *Picture Post* provide a genuine and dependable historical narrative? What type of truth does it offer and how is this arrived at?

At the heart of these questions lies the fact that the camera can never, of course, offer an entirely objective record because, as with any media communication, it is compromised in varying degrees by the humanity which informs it. The photographer will inevitably colour his or her work through approach, methodology or a combination of both. This clearly has the potential to affect the nature of the truth revealed. As the *Time Life* editors acceded, writing on photojournalism, 'Where people and events are concerned, there is no such thing as an objective photograph.'[1] The choice of subject, its treatment and the darkroom techniques brought to bear on the final photographs are all reflective of the variables at work in delivering the 'truth'.

The picture editor's selection and composition of photo-material creates the story he or she wants to tell, also opening up further possibilities for bias, emphasis or distortion. If any photographic narrative is to be accepted as truthful and reliable, all these factors have to be confronted.[2]

Questions about *Picture Post*'s authenticity can be approached in two ways:

- by looking at the **editorial policy** that was established by founding Editor Stefan Lorant and continued assiduously for ten years by his successor Tom Hopkinson;
- by considering something of the **attitude and approach** revealed by key photographic contributors to *Picture Post* whose photo-narratives provide so much of the information to be studied.

Early on in his career Stefan Lorant remembered recording how he wanted 'to print the truth, to enlighten readers of subjects on which they have scant knowledge, not to underestimate them or disregard their intelligence, but share with them a common knowledge, to learn together'.[3] In terms of how photography was to be used he believed that 'the camera should be as the notebook of a trained reporter, recording contemporary events as they happen without trying to stop them to make a picture; people should be photographed as they really are and not as they would like to appear'.[4] He also expressed the view that 'photo reportage should concern itself with men and women of every kind and not simply with a small social clique; everyday life should be portrayed in a realistic, unselfconscious way'.[5] Lorant wanted *Picture Post* to tell real stories about real life in all its diversity.

This could not be achieved without the support of photographers who shared this vision. In 1947, in his book *Speaking Likeness*, long-time photo-reporter for *Picture Post* Kurt Hutton described the philosophy behind his work:

> Human life is full of fleeting moments of beauty, fun, joy, humour and, yes, of tragedy. To catch these moments and preserve them is far more fascinating to me than posing artistic pictures of beautiful models in elaborate studios by clever lighting ... I do just one thing – I let my subjects express themselves naturally.[6]

The surroundings in which they found themselves were also not to be 'artificial in any way'.[7] He believed that his job 'is (or should be) to produce a true, objective picture of life as it is lived: of people in everyday life as they look and act, do and are done by, when no camera is anywhere near them'.[8] Hutton accepted that this was not always possible: 'Some things are as a rule staged – a fashion show, a photo-call at a theatre',[9] but where subjects could be encouraged to forget about the camera, perhaps through an interviewing journalist's ability to establish an engaging conversation, then staging, ideally, became much less obvious and the subject emerged with greater authenticity.

Hutton believed that people had to 'mean something to the photographer' if a 'speaking likeness' was to be captured on camera. Without this interest there was 'nothing at all to prevent his having a thoroughly enjoyable afternoon shooting the waxworks in Madame Tussaud's'.[10] This engagement with the subject, while subjective, had all the benefits of attempting to elicit a greater reality or truth.

On a similar theme *Picture Post* was not a fan of the Hollywood publicity photograph as an article from 1942 called 'Film Stills: Photography at Its Most Antiquated'[11] revealed. A selection of typical formulaic poses of Hollywood actress Carol Bruce – including the 'Quiet-Home-Loving Girl Still' and the 'Only-Go-By-Plane Still' – were considered stale and repetitive and as 'thrilling as cold porridge', provoking the caption writer to ask when Hollywood would 'employ some real photographers, and take some actual photographs'.[12] While *Picture Post* did not entirely avoid using conventional star images and star-lifestyle shots,[13] editorial policy in general tried to reveal the more individual or unexpected side of the celebrity life.[14]

Tim Gidal, another early *Picture Post* photographer, expressed the view that the 'good photo-reporter is also a good documentary director. He never poses something which has not happened just for the sake of photographic impact'.[15] In a similar way photographer Felix Man, who with Kurt Hutton was to work on *Picture Post* from its inception, prioritized the real, everyday elements that established the authenticity of his subject. Man and Hutton also worked, wherever possible, without the use of harsh and unnatural flash-lighting, so as to retain the naturalness of the photographic record.[16]

The philosophy underpinning the creation of *Picture Post*'s photo-stories was, therefore, to provide as genuine and authentic a record of the situation or subject the photo-journalist encountered as might be possible. The subjectivity of the photographer or writer was unavoidable. In so far as it might be used to offer others a better understanding of the reality in question it could be used positively.

The reality *Picture Post* wanted to share with its readers was one that would move beyond the activities of the rich or famous to provide what was, in its view, a fairer representation of the cultural diversity of British life. This included a desire to reveal social injustice and deprivation where it existed in the poorer and poorest areas of society to both raise awareness and provoke action. The magazine developed a culture of inclusivity and enquiry that defined its political and philosophical orientation and established the frame of reference within which contributors largely worked.[17]

Writing in November 1939, Lorant expressed the view that *Picture Post* 'firmly believes in the ordinary man and woman; thinks they have had no fair share in picture journalism; believes their faces are more striking, their lives and doings more full of interest, than those of the people whose faces and activities cram the ordinary picture papers'.[18] This interest in ordinary people created fresh, innovative journalism that explored a wide variety of social groups, communities and individuals. The result was a series of original, modern photographic stories that, today, provide us with such a unique and detailed archive of dress and material culture.

Lorant established an editorial strategy that would take *Picture Post* readers from, for example, couturier Norman Hartnell's gracious Regency home to the bleakness of tenement life in Stepney. In terms of social documentary its pages revealed the fascinating otherness of other people's lives with a visual emphasis rarely encountered in a British magazine before. Whether stories covered the marriage of a Mayfair girl or the make-over of an East End charlady, the experiences of a girl pilot or an unemployed man's wife, readers could open their copies and see, sometimes with an almost visceral clarity, what it meant to be in someone else's shoes.[19]

These stories also revealed as much about the common aspirations of communities – for health, happiness, well-being – as the economics that divided them, denying to some what it gave to others. In pursuit of a truth, both immediate and compelling that only this type of photo-report could offer, *Picture Post* brought readers new insights into both the lives they already knew and those they didn't. The pragmatic orientation to the real world that defined editorial policy opened up opportunities to expose the iniquity of life-sapping inequality and poverty of opportunity and to promote social responsibility and welfare reform. Here *Picture Post* became a radical exponent of the need both to confront unfairness and injustice wherever it discovered it and to promote fresh thinking on old and often entrenched cultural problems. It became a tireless supporter of the downtrodden and politically powerless, offering itself as a voice on their behalf and a champion for the changes necessary to create more humane, compassionate ways of living.[20] At the same time *Picture Post* also celebrated much that was uplifting, enriching and funny in human society.[21]

Lorant's social democratic platform would be achieved through this coverage of a comprehensive cross section of contemporary British life. *Picture Post* would also be a prominent medium for Lorant's passionate anti-fascist convictions born out of his own experiences in Nazi Germany where, in March 1933, he was imprisoned without charge for six months.

In the wake of Hitler's rise to power[22] and the spread of Nazi ideology many areas of freedom of expression – literary, artistic and political – became subject to severe repression and the risk of imprisonment. Lorant had been editing the well-known German picture magazine the *Munich Illustrated Press* since 1928. While the paper had a Catholic bias and a 'leaning away politically from the Nazis',[23] the precise nature of his political offence was never revealed. The Nazi paper *Völkischer Beobachter*, commenting on the arrest, reported that Lorant was 'under suspicion of [being involved in] Bolshevist intrigues'[24] and described him as an Hungarian Jew without German citizenship.

Lorant subsequently wrote of his experience in his book *I was Hitler's Prisoner*, published in Britain by Victor Gollancz in 1935.[25] His fear of Hitler, who he described as 'a tremendous danger, a very impressive demagogue',[26] and his deep distrust of Nazi aggression would provide a central anti-fascist focus for the political orientation of *Picture Post* from the outset. Journalist Kaye Webb described *Picture Post* as 'a campaigning' paper.[27] Capable of exposing the stark reality of extremism and its concomitants of persecution and brutality,[28] *Picture Post* also reflected, in balanced measure, those aspects of British life – its traditions, customs, landscapes, art and industry – that, while imperfect, represented a democratic and often precious heritage.

Picture Post turned the camera lens on locations both familiar and far-off. It featured stories of anthropological enquiry alongside of hard foreign news, the endlessly appealing antics of the affluent juxtaposed against the daily struggle for survival of the deprived. Webb recalls, 'It was wonderful to be part of something so good ... There wasn't a story that somewhere didn't have some social message.'[29]

Picture Post achieves an authenticity, therefore, born out of its desire to reveal and reflect cultural diversity and to explore real life with an unvarnished yet compassionate commitment to the truth. As an historical archive its social and philosophical orientation defines its distinctive vision without compromising its capacity to offer a valid and legitimate historical record. A product of the shared beliefs and sensibilities of its key photographers and writers and enriched by the contribution of its many guest writers, the photojournalism of *Picture Post* deserves to be considered as both an authoritative and a reliable witness to the times it set out to record.

Uses of photo-reporting prior to *Picture Post*

The photographic approach and methodology that contributed so much to the specific vision of *Picture Post* had developed from two particular photographic antecedents – **illustrated social documentary** and the **German illustrated magazine**. Both of these add to our understanding of the way photo-reportage emerged as a distinct picture-based form offering an accessible and compelling alternative to illustrated text. It is useful to explore these forerunners of photojournalism and to show that a desire to provide a visual and sometimes visceral depiction of the truth lies at the heart of both.

Illustrated social documentary

The British tradition of social inquiry and investigation that informs the illustrated social documentary has a history going back to the Victorian period. Writer and journalist Henry Mayhew was a pioneer in the field, publishing his *London Labour and the London Poor* in 1851 with an extended edition in 1861. Containing detailed descriptions of the life and work of many of London's poor and poorest communities and illustrated with line drawings, Mayhew's pen portraits were so well received that his book was reprinted four times by 1865.[30] There was clearly popular appeal in the subject. In 1877 the documentary photography of Scottish-born John Thomson[31] was published comprising thirty-six images of working-class London street life accompanying articles by Adolphe Smith.[32] In both cases the writers and photographer reflected a direct confrontation with a level of social deprivation often little understood by those not party to it.

Examples of photography used for the similar purpose of recording the necessitous lives and social circumstances of the poorer classes were also appearing in America. The early photo-reporting of Jacob A. Riis, for example, brought the shocking conditions of tenement living in New York to public attention in *How the Other Half Lives*, published in 1890.[33] The investigative photography of Lewis Wickes Hine would later publicize the endurance often required of immigrants arriving at Ellis Island and the appalling social injustice of child labour.[34]

By the mid-1930s photographs taken for the Farm Security Administration were capturing the living conditions of those most affected by the Great Depression. Operating under Roosevelt's New Deal programme, a number of photographers, including Walker Evans and Dorothea Lang, provided 'outstanding pictures' that 'shocked the conscience of America by their starkness'.[35] Margaret Bourke-White, one of the first photographers to be asked to join *Life* magazine, also contributed to this photographic record of poverty and destitution in *You Have Seen Their Faces*, written by Erskine Caldwell in1937.[36]

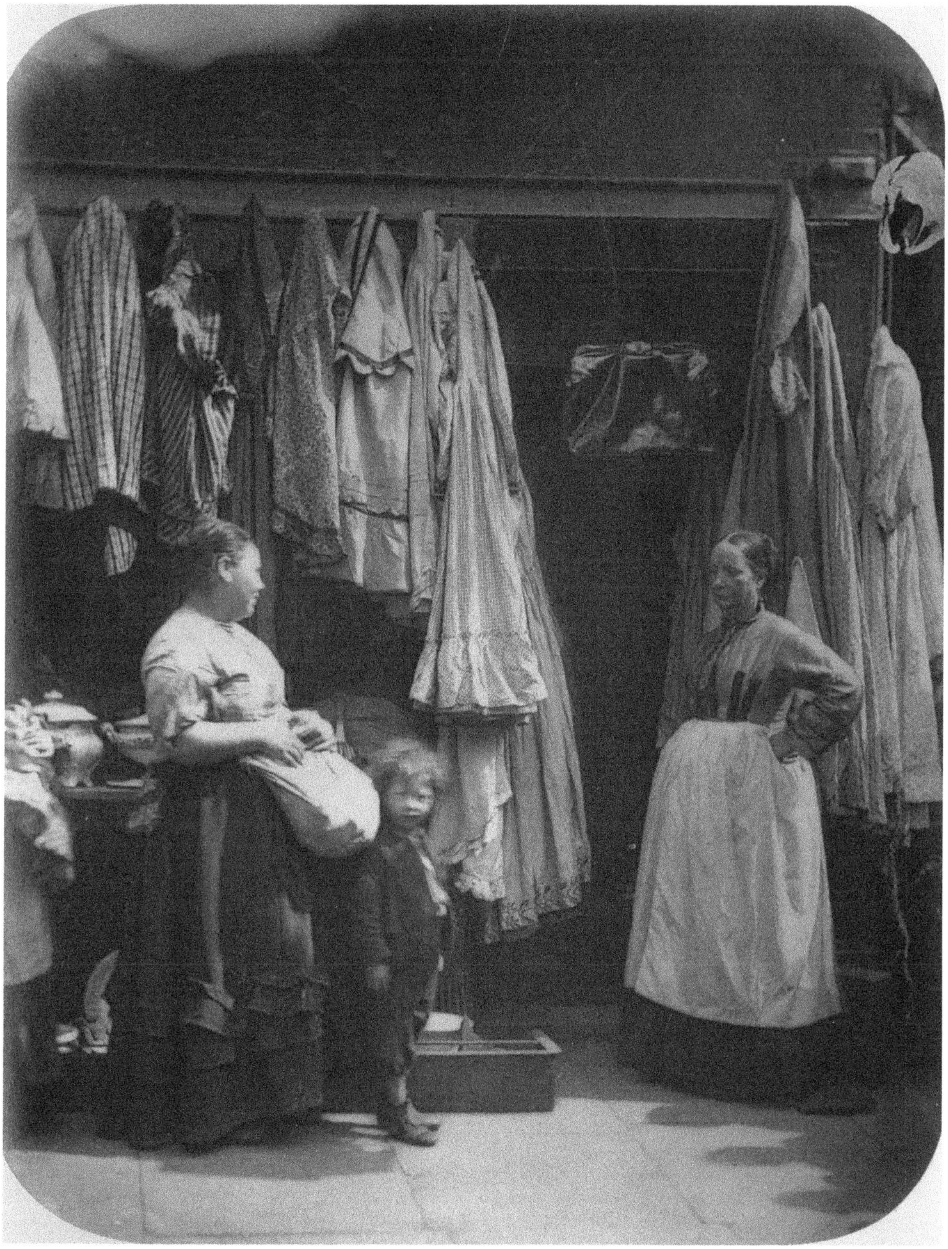

Figure 3 'Old Clothes Shop' from *Street Life in London*, John Thomson and Adolphe Smith, 1877. 'A second-hand clothes shop in a narrow thoroughfare of St. Giles .... It is here that the poorest inhabitants of a district, renowned for its poverty, both buy and sell their clothes.' LSE Library (lse-gos508mem).

The potential for photography to engage attention at both an intuitive and intellectual level made it an invaluable partner to documentary of any form. Photographs were increasingly creating awareness of how others lived and opening up new perspectives on social difference, arguably prompting harder questions about how and why social boundaries came to be drawn.[37] The camera thus became central to the process of recording cultural histories through the breadth of its vision as well as its capacity for close observation and attention to detail, features that would also underpin the photojournalism of *Picture Post*.

Mass observation, a form of social documentary

The desire to know more about, and engage with, the ordinary everyday at least as much if not more than the extraordinary or exceptional also lay at the heart of the Mass Observation (MO) organization. This was formed in 1937 to study and document aspects of British life and the British people. In much the same way that anthropology entailed the study of human society in all its variety, MO wanted to study real life as it was being experienced at home across Britain. Founders Tom Harrisson and Charles Madge believed too little was known about 'our next door neighbour and his habits ... ourselves'. Of 'conditions of life and thought in another class or another district our ignorance is complete'.[38] This offers something of a continuum with social documentary in the desire to reveal the less seen, undiscovered or avoided, under our noses.

One of the earliest projects undertaken by MO in 1937 concerned looking at working life in the mill town of Bolton, known as Worktown. Photographer Humphrey Spender was approached to take photographs of Bolton and its people, their homes, livelihoods and leisure interests. While still a student he had photographed the slums of Stepney, and he later accepted work from the *Left Review* to photograph the Jarrow Hunger Marches.[39]

Spender's main concern at MO was to 'allow things to speak for themselves'.[40] Recognizing that it was 'impossible to exclude the person in charge of the camera from most kinds of picture', photography was, nevertheless, in Spender's opinion 'often better' at gathering this type of information 'than any other medium'. The necessity for maximizing the photograph's potential to 'disclose information ... show people's faces, people's behaviour ... their clothing and other details'[41] placed constraints on both the choice and composition of the subject matter. This created a specific photographic discipline within which to work that Spender found helpful as it 'limited ... the extent to which you can manipulate the whole thing'.[42]

The resilience, strength and sense of character that emerged from Spender's Worktown people are communicated through an honesty of treatment that deepens our understanding of some of the grimmer realities of working-class life while also making us aware of the everyday things that brought pleasure, diversion or solace. In this lies Spender's discreet yet warm compassion. In his introduction to *Worktown People: Photographs from Northern England 1937–38* by Humphrey Spender, editor Jeremy Mulford remarked on what he saw as 'a strong discipline derived from a natural tact and empathy' informing Spender's work so that he 'engages with his subjects, and expresses his own sensibility, but not at their expense. Indeed that is at the core of his sensibility'.[43]

Spender was among the first photographers to be asked to work on *Picture Post*. His experience and approach to his work provided an excellent fit with the founding principles

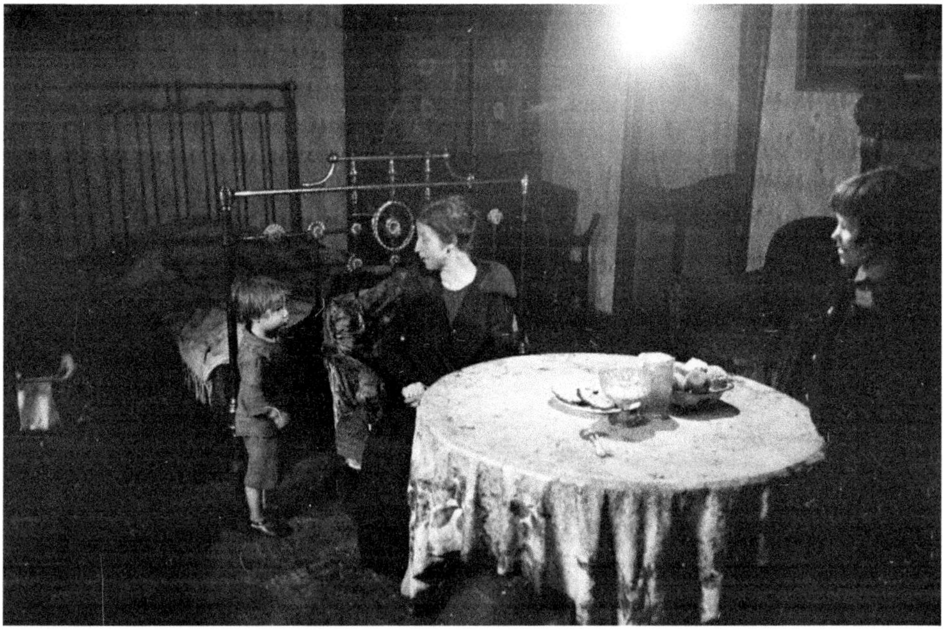

Figure 4 'In the Home of a Tynesider: A penny was produced. It was put in the gas meter. A broken mantle allowed just enough light for the picture to be taken. The room otherwise – a basement room – was permanently dark. The bread and cake on the table was all the food they had. There were other children not in the picture'. From 'Tyneside', *Picture Post*, 17 December 1938, p. 28. Humphrey Spender/*Picture Post*/Getty Images (3379700).

of the new paper. Recounting the difference between covering a story on Tyneside for both the *Mirror* newspaper and *Picture Post*, Spender described how for 'the *Mirror*, I'd been expected to make the industrial scene picturesque, including unemployment; whereas for *Picture Post* we were able to produce a feature of realism so harsh that we evoked a strong complaint from the mayor'.[44]

The use of photography within social documentary and social anthropology provided significant historical data in visual form. Individual images from Spender's *Worktown People* often revealed a whole story in themselves. A washing day, a parade, mill work, an election, placed people in the contexts of their homes, work or landscapes and in the process revealed much about the nature of their lives. Across the Worktown photographs as a whole, the details of social culture that became apparent – from dress style and home interiors to shopping practices and pub outings – established an authentic sense of the place and community of pre-war Bolton. Today the collection continues to embody a unique visual archive of local history.

German illustrated magazines

The other direct antecedent of *Picture Post* was the popular illustrated magazine genre that flourished in Germany from the late 1920s.

In a move that began to prioritize the photograph over the written text, media photographers in Germany had started to create sequences of photographs where, as photo-reporter Tim Gidal recorded, 'one photo leads into the next and the outwardly combined set of pictures add up to an inner reality and an inner combination'. These new photo-stories were 'conceived and executed as an inter-related unit of photographs, taken mostly on a single occasion by a single photographer and held together in a meaningful way ... by one underlying theme or idea'. This provided a fresh and modern way of reporting in contrast to the work of already well-known photographers such as Martin Munkacsi or Dr. Erich Salomon, who had largely provided single-picture reports. While Salomon also created picture collections, these had 'no appreciable inner connection apart from dealing with the same or similar objects'.[45] The photo-sequence was absorbing to look at and conveyed in two dimensions something of the frame-by-frame action of film.

By 1929, popular weeklies such as the *Berlin Illustrated Newspaper* (*Berliner Illustrirte Zeitung* or *BIZ*) and the *Munich Illustrated Press* (*Munchner Illustrierte Presse or MIP*) began to include picture-essays, recognizing the particular relevance of these new visual narratives in the context of contemporary life. Editor of *BIZ* Kurt Korff expressed the view that the public had become 'increasingly accustomed to receiving a stronger impression of world events from pictures than from written reports' and that it was 'no accident that the development of the cinema and the development of the *Berlin Illustrated Newspaper* run roughly parallel'. Editors, 'like film writers and directors', now had to be able to convey life 'in pictures'.[46]

Stefan Lorant's own background had included work in both the film and the magazine industry. As a young adult he had worked as a stills photographer in the film industry in Vienna, subsequently becoming a cameraman in Vienna and Berlin. After this he moved into magazine work, becoming editor of *Das Magazin*, one of the first German picture papers, and in 1929 he became editor-in-chief of the popular *Munich Illustrated Press*. Here he was responsible for the magazine's layout, selecting photographs and composing the sequences that would tell specific stories.[47]

Photographic material was often acquired from one of two Berlin photographic agencies: Weltrundschau (Worldview), begun in 1928 and selling largely to the *BIZ*, and Dephot (Deutscher Photodienst: German Photo Service), begun in 1929 and dealing mostly with the *MIP*. Both specialized in providing 'photo-reports and picture-essays in contrast to news photos'.[48] Photographers Felix Man and Kurt Hutton, who would become key members of the photography team at *Picture Post*, worked for Dephot at this time.

In many ways Lorant's work on the *MIP* provided a clear model for *Picture Post*. The primacy of the photo-report and the breadth of topics – contemporary and historic, fashion and fashionable, politics and leisure – reflected a desire to provide material that would be both informative and entertaining for a broad-based readership. In terms of its political orientation Magilow records that 'unlike the press affiliated with parties on the far Left or far Right, the MIP, BIZ and KIZ[49] generally sided with the rule of law and democratic institutions'.[50] In a similar way *Picture Post* would not espouse politically extreme views or principles but rather provide a platform for the development of a humanitarian philosophy with core beliefs in social justice and fairness.

The most direct connection between *Picture Post* and the German illustrated magazines was the fact that three of the founding participants of *Picture Post*, Lorant and photographers Kurt Hutton and Felix Man, had all worked on picture magazines in Germany.[51] An established pioneer in the field of photo sequencing and picture layout,[52] Lorant clearly saw the significance of the new narrative genre, while Hutton and Man had both supplied photo-stories for the *MIP*. These three would meet up again in England in 1934 but not before loss of democracy and the threat of persecution would have a life-changing impact on each of them as National Socialism increased its hold over Germany.

With the arrival of Hitler as German chancellor in 1933 the Nazi propaganda machine began its work of infiltrating the media publishing houses. After his spell in prison in this year there was no free press to which Lorant could return, and without a job or means of support he returned to his native Hungary. Here he edited a Sunday supplement of the daily magazine *Pesti Naplo* (*Pest Journal*) for just over three months during which time he was 'monitored by his Hungarian countrymen on behalf of the Nazis'.[53] Hoping to publish his account of being imprisoned in Germany and to warn the 'unsuspecting English people about the dangers of Hitler',[54] Lorant left Hungary and arrived in England in April 1934, a refugee from Nazi tyranny.

By 1933 Felix Man had become aware that his role as a photo-reporter would be compromised by conflict with Nazi ideology. He asked Illustrations Director at the *Berliner Illustrierte Zeitung*, Kurt Szafransky, to send him abroad on a world tour from where he could report freely without Nazi interference. Seven months later Szafransky was no longer in his job and the publishing house of Ullstein, which had published the *BIZ*, had been taken over by the Nazis.[55] By the time Man returned to Berlin, journalists 'had to join the Reichspressekammer, a Nazi organisation' and 'working connections with Jews were forbidden'. An old friend obtained Man the necessary exit permit and he, too, left for England. Here he met Lorant quite by chance – 'neither of us had known of the other's presence in London'.[56] The meeting was fortuitous and re-established professional ties. When Man's friend Kurt Hutton[57] also left Germany in 1934 and helped out temporarily on *Weekly Illustrated* – Lorant's first venture into picture magazines in Britain – a trio formed, united by a fear of Nazi ideology and oppression and a desire for a democratic way of life and freedom of expression.[58] These beliefs would be central to the meaning and method of *Picture Post*.

By 1941self-taught English photographer Bert Hardy[59] from Blackfriars in London joined the permanent staff at *Picture Post* having already sold photo-stories to the magazine through the General Photographic Agency.[60] At only twenty-eight years old he was considerably younger than Man and Hutton but had acquired an understanding of, and appreciation for, the quality and type of photojournalism for which *Picture Post* had become known. Revealing a remarkable capacity to find the extraordinary in the ordinary and capture the many faces of day-to-day life in wartime Britain, Hardy would become one of the best-known *Picture Post* photographers who, with Hutton and Man, would cover almost any subject from military action to fashion, domestic life to political drama.

Working in the tradition of the picture story as his colleagues had conceived it, Hardy invested his photography with humanity, warmth and compassion, achieving an immediacy and poignancy that were both thought-provoking and memorable. Here were authentic stories that narrated the diverse realities of everyday life in war.

Picture Post owed a good deal, therefore, to the working methods pioneered by the German illustrated press and to the expertise of a core staff who had been directly involved with both the growth and consolidation of photo-reportage as the next generation of magazine journalism. Recognizing the power of the visual image to engage, entertain and educate, the photo-story extended the medium of social documentary. The unified picture-feature presented readers with image sequences on everything from world events to local customs in a credible and often compelling format, revitalizing the everyday and opening up new perspectives on the unfamiliar. Here were stories that conveyed reality with a modern dynamism and potency.[61]

Writers at *Picture Post*

In investigating the specific photographic origins of *Picture Post* through the social documentary tradition and the German Illustrated magazines, much has been said of the photographers involved and the methodology and philosophy which underpinned their work. This has established how photographers aimed to capture truth and the extent to which they have therefore left a reliable historic record. Alongside these photographic narratives there were also captions and written articles. This section explores in brief the type of writers who worked for *Picture Post* and something of the values and beliefs which characterized their work and contributed to the philosophical orientation of the magazine.

Tom Hopkinson had certainly never experienced the life-changing threat of political oppression or racial hatred. His safe, middle-class upbringing had not, however, shielded him from understanding the grim and anxious lives that resulted from financial hardship. The son of a clergyman, he had witnessed needy and distressed parishioners calling on his father for help at a time of sorely limited social assistance. In an early job in advertising he became uncomfortable promoting products as better than they were, and in an effort to do something of more practical value he volunteered as a prison visitor. In this work he saw first-hand the often harrowing poverty of prisoners' wives and families. In his autobiography, Hopkinson wrote, 'Often a wife had no idea what assistance might be available nor of where and how to get it . . . There was then no welfare state, but I started to think that there ought to be one.'[62]

Picture Post reflected this desire for greater social understanding and responsibility through the social documentary journalism of writers like Sydney Jacobson, William Cameron and J. B. Priestley.[63] Their work sustained variously a belief in social justice, the need for greater equality and fairness across British society and the entitlement of all to a secure, healthy and happy future. The importance and significance of the ordinary man and woman, their lives and lifestyles and their hopes for the future beyond war were all themes that carried *Picture Post* writers – alongside their photographer-colleagues – into diverse communities throughout Britain.

In 1941 Anne Scott-James became *Picture Post*'s first women's editor. Scott-James came from *Vogue* where she had risen from helping out with publicity and knitting to becoming Beauty Editor. A 'convinced liberal' Scott-James had attended St Paul's School, 'an enlightened and liberal establishment' which had 'helped to finance a settlement in Stepney' in which she 'took a deep interest, visiting it whenever I could and making real friends'.[64] She had admired *Picture Post* from its inception and later wrote about it as 'young, spirited and provocative ... political and reformist ... its heart was with the poor, the unemployed, the wretchedly housed'.[65] She described Tom Hopkinson's approach in editing *Picture Post* as following on from Lorant's methods by 'making every issue a mix of features of varying mood, from blitz to the Windmill Girls, from the rough life of a deep-sea trawler to Tommy Handley and ITMA'.[66] She also expressed the view that Hopkinson 'made the paper increasingly political and controversial, gradually building up a campaign for a more equal Britain after the war'[67] while always including a balance of material 'to relieve the sense of social mission'.[68]

Scott-James was keen to establish her role as providing general interest features that would not just appeal to women and to always link her stories to current news or wartime events. Her range of topics for *Picture Post* was often thought-provoking and always timely and her commitment to photo-journalism both complete and easy. She was, as she said, a 'natural photographer's mate'.[69]

Other key members of staff were John Langdon Davis,[70] who contributed features on popular science and health issues, MacDonald Hastings,[71] a war correspondent who also reported on country matters and leisure pursuits, and Honor Balfour,[72] who would write the early series on great artists which included rare colour reproductions.

With different backgrounds and careers, interests and political and social affiliations, the writers and photographers on *Picture Post* each in their own way contributed to the outlook and philosophy upon which the magazine was based and brought with them a diversity of experience that reflected the broad-church appeal of the magazine. When Tom Hopkinson and Edward Hulton, for example, joined the politically mixed '1941' Committee, formed to champion greater efficiencies in war production and to promote a fairer post-war future, they not only became part of a creative forum for intellectual discussion but also connected *Picture Post* to a range of contemporary thinking on significant wartime controversies. This could only help in maintaining the magazine's currency and its capacity to, in turn, engender public awareness and social debate. The group was chaired by J. B. Priestley and included a number of socialist and liberal thinkers such as Michael Foot, Richie Calder, Kingsley Martin, Richard Titmuss, Violet Bonham-Carter and H. G. Wells, among others.[73]

The broad network of writers, photographers, analysts, commentators, politicians and other professionals who at one time or another contributed their expertise to *Picture Post* together sustained its ethos of enquiry and enlightenment, provided a spirit of confident engagement with the conversations and controversies of the day and actively sought to promote a fairer and safer future for all. It provides us today with an authentic social and philosophical voice and in doing so contributes a distinctive and singular historical narrative.

Picture Post establishes itself

When *Picture Post* was launched on 1 October 1938, all of its 750,000 copies had sold out by midday.[74] This immediate popularity was sustained as the weeks went by so that by February 1939 the print run had escalated to 1,350,000 copies.[75] In terms of its weekly content and the way photography was being used, *Picture Post* was offering something different from other similarly priced weekly magazines which included a range of sports, leisure and women's publications. As a weekly it was not competing with the hard or breaking news dealt with by the daily papers but offered reviews and discussion of news stories instead. Often developed through photo-reportage these features were designed to considerably enhance readers' appreciation of an event or topic. The political weeklies such as the *Spectator* and *New Statesmen* were not picture-focused while the weekly *Illustrated London News* provided illustrated features rather than image-based narratives.[76]

The only magazine to offer the photojournalism of *Picture Post* was its immediate predecessor the *Weekly Illustrated*, begun in 1934. This had been Stefan Lorant's first magazine venture after arriving in London and was the first picture paper ever to be published in Britain. Felix Man and Kurt Hutton both made substantial contributions to the early issues which 'at 2d. for twenty-eight large-format pages full of photographs ... represented good value for money'.[77] Lorant ran the paper for twenty-two issues during which time sales figures continued to rise reaching 285,000. The popularity of the picture paper was thus established, although Lorant's sure handling appears to have been crucial as circulation declined after his departure.[78] Hopkinson described *Weekly Illustrated* as being 'built around pictures' and remarked on how the size of the picture story as a concept expanded from rarely more than two pages in *Weekly Illustrated* to 'eight, ten – or at times even fourteen pages' in the larger pre-war issues of *Picture Post*.[79]

Weekly magazines for women or those catering for specific leisure interests were generally illustrated by line drawings or still photography. The *Radio Times* and *Film Weekly*[80] are only two of many publications representing the arts and leisure, while magazines such as *Woman, Woman's Own, Woman's Pictorial, Woman's World* and *Home Chats* reflected the popularity and buoyancy of papers for and about women and sold in a similar price range to *Picture Post*.[81] Both of these categories represented quite specific market interests which controlled the range of content and meant that while they shared the news stand with *Picture Post* they were not in direct competition with it.[82]

While the women's magazine sector in general was relatively prolific, sales of individual titles were limited. This was because, as wartime editor of *Woman* Mary Grieve pointed out, 'pre-war divisions of taste and income set a limit on the number of like-minded women it was possible to gather together. Habits of cooking and entertainment, uses of leisure, aesthetic preferences, standards of home-making, vocabulary and hygiene all had so many shades of acceptance that there was some excuse for the proliferation of magazines'.[83] *Picture Post* had no such specific demographic in mind. Its policy of reflecting cultural variety, as opposed to identifying with one social group or strata, arguably won it a broader readership as a result. Mary Grieve commented that by 1940 *Woman* had a readership of over a million but that this was 'less considerable in influence than *Picture Post* at its dynamic best' with its 'well-edited, well-produced pages'.[84]

The photo-sequence

The proliferation of photographic stories within *Picture Post* helped to create its signature style and was a method of communicating news and information that would remain popular with the British public throughout the war years. But exactly what was a photo-sequence and how did it work? In what way does it hold important information today as an historic narrative on the material culture of the period, a visual archive of dress and fashion history? A story that appeared in *Picture Post* in October 1940 provides an excellent example that answers these questions.

'The Taking of a Fashion Magazine Photograph'

Picture Post, 26 October 1940, pp. 22–25

Taking up two double pages this photo-sequence explored the various types of people and work involved in the taking of fashion photographs for the fashion magazine *Vogue*. Photography was by Zoltan Glass and the accompanying text by Anne Scott-James.[85] Stefan Lorant had, by this time, made a new home in America leaving his replacement Tom Hopkinson to oversee how the feature would appear in *Picture Post*. Eleven individual photographs were used. Each clearly told an aspect of the story while the content of each frame, the image size and its placement within the final composition provided additional levels of meaning to enhance and enrich the experience of the story by visual means.

Two themes emerge from the outset:

- The first is that Glass was recording a process of achieving images that was diametrically opposed to his own while working for *Picture Post*. The fashion magazine photograph was one where both the subject and the setting were artificially enhanced and contrived. This was quite different from the photojournalists' prime purpose to capture something real and truthful. Two ways of taking photographs are therefore seen working in parallel as Glass truthfully recorded a process designed to create a fantasy. Both, it emerges, required a good deal of thought if the final outcome was to be a success.
- The second theme is about looking and understanding more closely what we are seeing. Almost all of the pictures chosen for this story have a reference to looking at something, challenging the reader to inquire what that something is and why the photographer has drawn our attention to it. This leads to greater engagement with the subject matter and suggests that a story on fashion can be a vehicle for more thoughtful reflection. It is not entirely the light-weight subject it might seem.

In starting to look more closely at the photo-sequence it is important to note that the images can work without the text and have a flow and logic of their own. This is

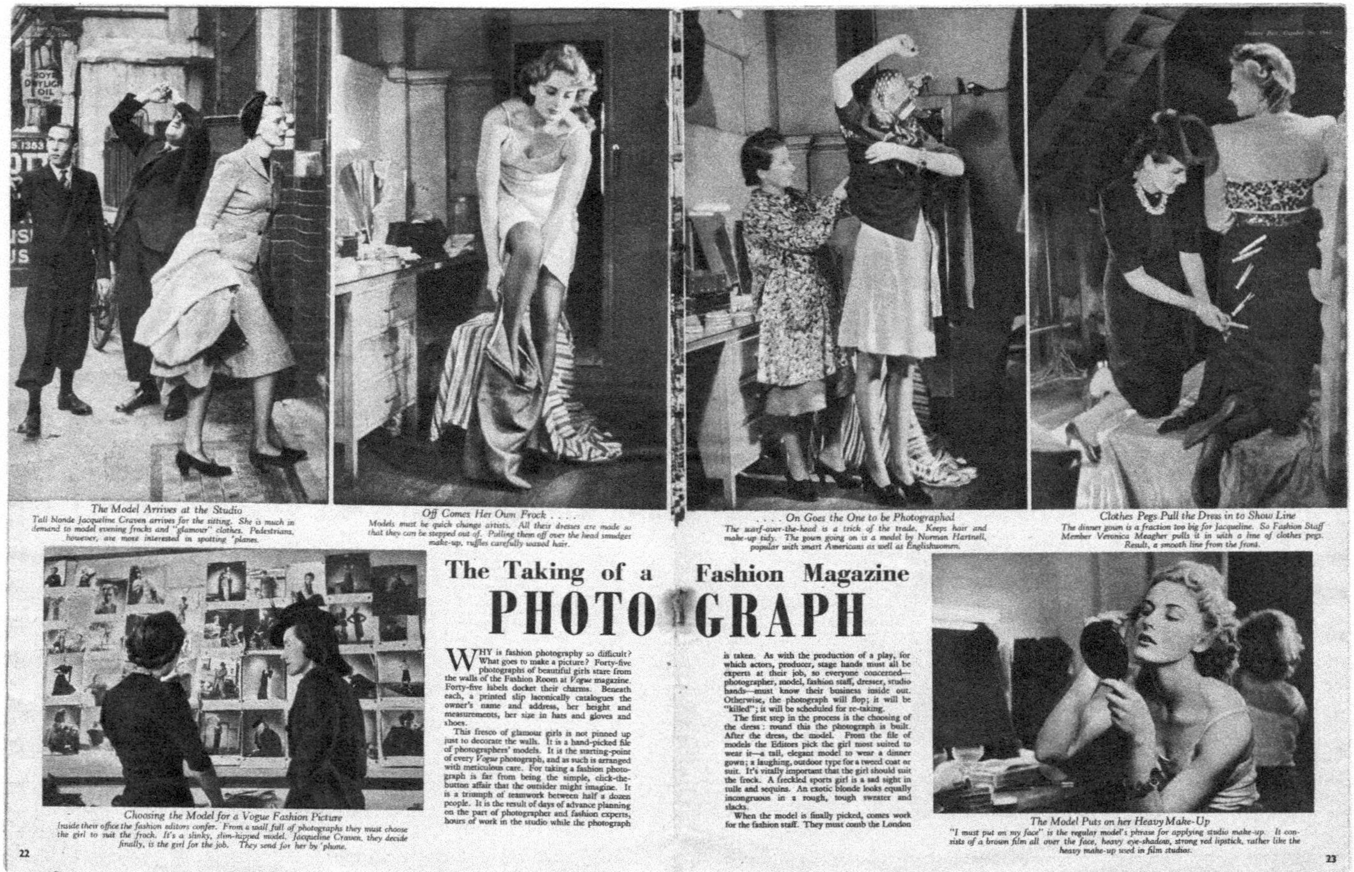

The Model Arrives at the Studio

Tall blonde Jacqueline Craven arrives for the sitting. She is much in demand to model evening frocks and "glamour" clothes. Pedestrians, however, are more interested in spotting 'planes.

Off Comes Her Own Frock . . . .

Models must be quick change artists. All their dresses are made so that they can be stepped out of. Pulling them off over the head smudges make-up, ruffles carefully waved hair.

. . . . On Goes the One to be Photographed

The scarf-over-the-head is a trick of the trade. Keeps hair and make-up tidy. The gown going on is a model by Norman Hartnell, popular with smart Americans as well as Englishwomen.

Clothes Pegs Pull the Dress in to Show Line

The dinner gown is a fraction too big for Jacqueline. So Fashion Staff Member Veronica Meagher pulls it in with a line of clothes pegs. Result, a smooth line from the front.

The Taking of a Fashion Magazine PHOTOGRAPH

WHY is fashion photography so difficult? What goes to make a picture? Forty-five photographs of beautiful girls stare from the walls of the Fashion Room at *Vogue* magazine. Forty-five labels docket their charms. Beneath each, a printed slip laconically catalogues the owner's name and address, her height and measurements, her size in hats and gloves and shoes.

This fresco of glamour girls is not pinned up just to decorate the walls. It is a hand-picked file of photographers' models. It is the starting-point of every *Vogue* photograph, and as such is arranged with meticulous care. For taking a fashion photograph is far from being the simple, click-the-button affair that the outsider might imagine. It is a triumph of teamwork between half a dozen people. It is the result of days of advance planning on the part of photographer and fashion experts, hours of work in the studio while the photograph is taken. As with the production of a play, for which actors, producer, stage hands must all be experts at their job, so everyone concerned—photographer, model, fashion staff, dresser, studio hands—must know their business inside out. Otherwise, the photograph will flop; it will be "killed"; it will be scheduled for re-taking.

The first step in the process is the choosing of the dress: round this the photograph is built. After the dress, the model. From the file of models the Editors pick the girl most suited to wear it—a tall, elegant model to wear a dinner gown; a laughing, outdoor type for a tweed coat or suit. It's vitally important that the girl should suit the frock. A freckled sports girl is a sad sight in tulle and sequins. An exotic blonde looks equally incongruous in a rough, tough sweater and slacks.

When the model is finally picked, comes work for the fashion staff. They must comb the London

Choosing the Model for a Vogue Fashion Picture

Inside their office the fashion editors confer. From a wall full of photographs they must choose the girl to suit the frock. It's a slinky, slim-hipped model. Jacqueline Craven, they decide finally, is the girl for the job. They send for her by 'phone.

22

The Model Puts on her Heavy Make-Up

"I must put on my face" is the regular model's phrase for applying studio make-up. It consists of a brown film all over the face, heavy eye-shadow, strong red lipstick, rather like the heavy make-up used in film studios.

23

Figure 5 *Picture Post*, 26 October 1940, pp. 22–23. Zoltan Glass/*Picture Post*/Hulton Archive/Getty Images (575717687).

not a random collection of shots loosely held together by the subject. The first double-page establishes the process of choosing and preparing the model while the second focuses on the work of the fashion photographer. Individual pictures reveal specific points of interest which across the story as a whole build to provide a greater range of ideas about the topic than might first be anticipated. These lines of thought identify something of the approach to the story's creation and the nature of the photojournalist's method.

The first image establishes the theme of looking as the reader looks at the photograph of two *Vogue* fashion editors, one looking at the other who is looking at a wall of model photographs. The stillness and sense of concentration within the image conveys something of the significance of the choice to be made, a theme that will develop as the sequence progresses. In contrast the four pictures above and across the double page then move along much more quickly as the model, once selected, arrives, changes and prepares to be photographed.

Model Jacqueline Craven first appears entering the studio from the street. Well dressed in a two-piece suit comprising a below-the-knee skirt and short revere-collared jacket with a button-finished pocket, she wears dark, low-heeled court shoes, a neat half-turban that keeps her hair in place and carries a heavier coat. This is smart fashion for the period. The classic British woollen suit seen here would form the basis of one of the subsequent wartime Utility styles which adopted the simplicity and elegance of the tailored two-piece as a wardrobe staple for all.

The photograph not only establishes the stylish chic of the model. Equally as important, perhaps, as her appearance are the two men immediately behind her. Attention is drawn to them because they are both looking pointedly up at the sky. Here again is the theme about looking. What were they looking at? By the time of this story Britain had already endured nearly two months of blitz conditions, including daylight air-raids during September, and although little is made of this – the caption alludes to the men being more interested in 'spotting planes' than in the model – it is a direct allusion to wartime conditions. Despite these, however, the fashion shoot goes on, incongruous though this might seem.

Picture Post was not averse to including images of women either in a state of undress or revealing underclothing. Sometimes this was intentional and sometimes, perhaps, unintentional. This low-key objectification of women will be returned to elsewhere.[86] In the next two photographs the theme of looking surfaces again as the reader becomes party to the private act of undressing and dressing, seeing what would generally not be seen.

Model Jacqueline can take off her own clothes but the value of a couture gown is emphasized by the apparent need for a dresser in putting one on. Not so valuable, however, that it can't be held in at the back with wooden clothes pegs because it is too big. The thought of the model looking glamorous and svelte from the front because she is held in with pegs at the back is funny and surely intentionally compromises the fashion fantasy being created. Will the model have to lie down on the pegs as she takes up the semi-reclining pose seen in later photographs? That the gown looks right appears to be more important than the gown itself. Here again is the theme of looking and understanding more about what we are seeing.

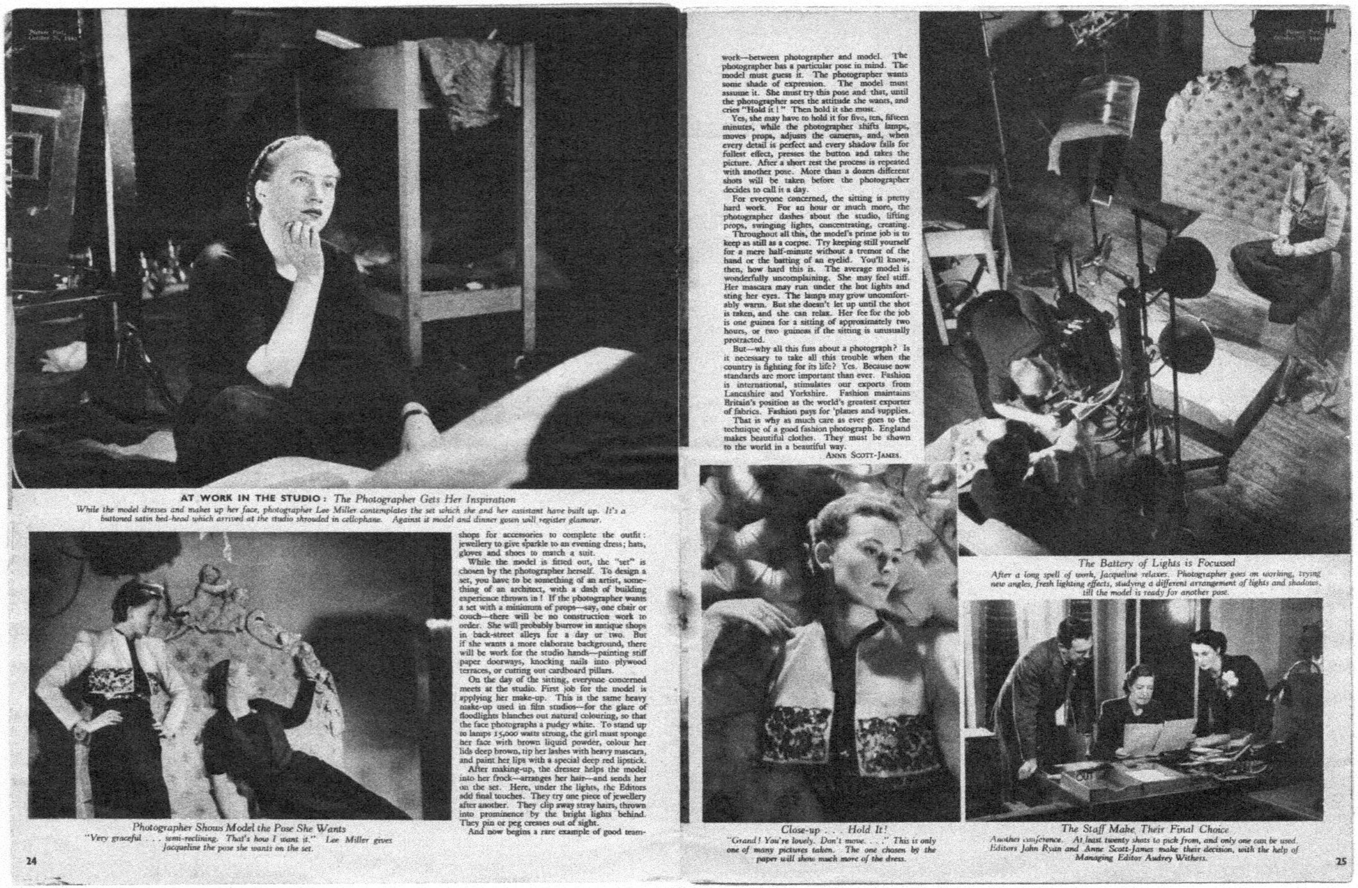

AT WORK IN THE STUDIO: *The Photographer Gets Her Inspiration*

While the model dresses and makes up her face, photographer Lee Miller contemplates the set which she and her assistant have built up. It's a buttoned satin bed-head which arrived at the studio shrouded in cellophane. Against it model and dinner gown will register glamour.

Photographer Shows Model the Pose She Wants

"Very graceful . . . semi-reclining. That's how I want it." Lee Miller gives Jacqueline the pose she wants on the set.

shops for accessories to complete the outfit: jewellery to give sparkle to an evening dress; hats, gloves and shoes to match a suit.

While the model is fitted out, the "set" is chosen by the photographer herself. To design a set, you have to be something of an artist, something of an architect, with a dash of building experience thrown in! If the photographer wants a set with a minimum of props—say, one chair or couch—there will be no construction work to order. She will probably burrow in antique shops in back-street alleys for a day or two. But if she wants a more elaborate background, there will be work for the studio hands—painting stiff paper doorways, knocking nails into plywood terraces, or cutting out cardboard pillars.

On the day of the sitting, everyone concerned meets at the studio. First job for the model is applying her make-up. This is the same heavy make-up used in film studios—for the glare of floodlights blanches out natural colouring, so that the face photographs a pudgy white. To stand up to lamps 15,000 watts strong, the girl must sponge her face with brown liquid powder, colour her lids deep brown, tip her lashes with heavy mascara, and paint her lips with a special deep red lipstick.

After making-up, the dresser helps the model into her frock—arranges her hair—and sends her on the set. Here, under the lights, the Editors add final touches. They try one piece of jewellery after another. They clip away stray hairs, thrown into prominence by the bright lights behind. They pin or peg creases out of sight.

And now begins a rare example of good team-

24

work—between photographer and model. The photographer has a particular pose in mind. The model must guess it. The photographer wants some shade of expression. The model must assume it. She must try this pose and that, until the photographer sees the attitude she wants, and cries "Hold it!" Then hold it she must.

Yes, she may have to hold it for five, ten, fifteen minutes, while the photographer shifts lamps, moves props, adjusts the cameras, and, when every detail is perfect and every shadow falls for fullest effect, presses the button and takes the picture. After a short rest the process is repeated with another pose. More than a dozen different shots will be taken before the photographer decides to call it a day.

For everyone concerned, the sitting is pretty hard work. For an hour or much more, the photographer dashes about the studio, lifting props, swinging lights, concentrating, creating.

Throughout all this, the model's prime job is to keep as still as a corpse. Try keeping still yourself for a mere half-minute without a tremor of the hand or the batting of an eyelid. You'll know, then, how hard this is. The average model is wonderfully uncomplaining. She may feel stiff. Her mascara may run under the hot lights and sting her eyes. The lamps may grow uncomfortably warm. But she doesn't let up until the shot is taken, and she can relax. Her fee for the job is one guinea for a sitting of approximately two hours, or two guineas if the sitting is unusually protracted.

But—why all this fuss about a photograph? Is it necessary to take all this trouble when the country is fighting for its life? Yes. Because now standards are more important than ever. Fashion is international, stimulates our exports from Lancashire and Yorkshire. Fashion maintains Britain's position as the world's greatest exporter of fabrics. Fashion pays for 'planes and supplies.

That is why as much care as ever goes to the technique of a good fashion photograph. England makes beautiful clothes. They must be shown to the world in a beautiful way.

ANNE SCOTT-JAMES.

The Battery of Lights is Focussed

After a long spell of work, Jacqueline relaxes. Photographer goes on working, trying new angles, fresh lighting effects, studying a different arrangement of lights and shadows, till the model is ready for another pose.

Close-up . . . Hold It!

"Grand! You're lovely. Don't move. . . ." This is only one of many pictures taken. The one chosen by the paper will show much more of the dress.

The Staff Make Their Final Choice

Another conference. At least twenty shots to pick from, and only one can be used. Editors John Ryan and Anne Scott-James make their decision, with the help of Managing Editor Audrey Withers.

25

Figure 6 *Picture Post*, 26 October 1940, pp. 24–25. Zoltan Glass/*Picture Post*/Hulton Archive/Getty Images (575717753).

The pegs are being applied by a stylish *Vogue* assistant wearing a svelte dark dress, chunky necklace and fur toque, all considered part of the smart, simpler elegance now establishing itself as appropriate for war. This look is in marked contrast to the simple floral overall of the dresser in the previous frame. Demographic conclusions can be drawn from these dress codes and the interesting variations of status they infer.

The final image on the double spread shows Jacqueline applying her eye make-up. The caption and text, though not essential, are helpful in explaining that heavier make-up was needed as the bright photographic lamps drained the model's face of natural colour. The image, in drawing attention to the artifice required for a fashion photograph, yet again underlined the fact that what would be seen was neither real nor natural – not that this necessarily compromised the beauty of the final image.

Turning over, if size of image reflects emphasis and importance, then the half-page picture of fashion photographer Lee Miller would signify recognition of her status and prestige in the field.[87] Staring abstractedly into the distance, as if lost in her own train of thought, she appears to be oblivious to the presence of Glass's camera. Or is this appearance of naturalness a bluff? A fashion model herself in the later twenties and early thirties, the dreamy expression seen here is certainly reminiscent of fashion images taken of Miller particularly by photographers Man Ray and Hoyningen-Huene.[88] Exactly what Glass is doing is elusive but his image would certainly seem to reference Miller's past as a model and, possibly, the unique perspective such experience has given her as a fashion photographer.

Through Glass's camera lens we are looking at someone who has been so much looked at and now considers how best to see others. The image exudes a stillness despite the bustle and preparation all around. The reader can pause to consider the effect of the portrait, born out of who this woman is and the sense of history that surrounds her. Is this image of the model-turned-photographer perhaps the most arresting of all for capturing Miller's natural beauty, possibly as if by chance, amid all the unglamorous behind-the-scenes paraphernalia of a busy studio?

Below this image a smaller picture shows Miller demonstrating to her model the pose she wants her to adopt. Here Glass reasserts the fashion focus as Jacqueline and the reader watch Miller recline against a satin-quilted bedhead replete with gilded cherubim. The pose is achieved in the image directly opposite on the facing page. The luxurious setting and languid charm of the model together create the desired cameo of a beautiful world where pale, beaded evening jackets and soigné dark evening dresses signify an opulence and serenity most can only dream of.

This is the first time also that the reader gets a better idea of the Norman Hartnell gown at the centre of all the activity. The short bolero jacket is collarless and decorated with a generous panel of floral-patterned beading around the lower edge. A similar panel appears just below the line of the jacket on the dark, full-length evening gown. The gown is interesting in itself. While it represents the chic and expensive elegance associated with couture and the skill in decoration for which Hartnell was noted, it also establishes that in the high fashion world at least gowns of this type were still being made.

Evening dress, particularly of the more glamorous and prestigious type, had increasingly become unfashionable after the outbreak of war. Not only was it impractical through the early blackouts, but wearing this type of clothing in the company of those now in uniform was considered inappropriate. Women were fashioning their own responses to both these difficulties by increasingly avoiding formal wear of this type. As more people got into uniform, evening wear met its demise. The only styles that remained tended to emerge from the wealthier fashion sector. These appeared in darker shades, often buttoned or closed modestly to the neck and were generally far simpler and less ornamented in appearance than before the war. Exactly this type of garment is seen here.[89]

Why was so much effort being expended over photographing a form of dress for which there appeared to be increasingly less demand? The text, in this instance, supplied a helpful answer. In the final paragraph of the story Anne Scott-James herself asked, 'Why all this fuss about a photograph? Is it necessary to take all this trouble when the country is fighting for its life?' The answer was a resounding yes, because now it was especially necessary in her view to maintain the highest standards because:

> Fashion is international, stimulates our exports from Lancashire and Yorkshire.
> Fashion maintains Britain's position as the world's greatest exporter of fabrics.
> Fashion pays for 'planes and supplies'.
>
> That is why as much care as ever goes to the technique of a good fashion photograph. England makes beautiful clothes. They must be shown to the world in a beautiful way.[90]

This impassioned rhetoric in defence of the British fashion industry now repositions how the story about a dress and a photograph is to be perceived. British women might have changed the way *they* were dressing in response to war, a fact that had already caused a downturn in the formal evening-wear sector of the home fashion trade, but Norman Hartnell was also 'popular with smart American women as well as Englishwomen'.[91] Here was a bigger economic picture. At this stage in the war, and before the arrival of Lend-Lease aid from America a little over four months later,[92] Britain needed to maintain her exports abroad in order to pay for the materiel of war. Fashion was one such export and America a target market. Taking the most glamorously persuasive photograph of this Norman Hartnell gown now becomes an entirely justifiable exercise in fashion marketing.

Glass is taking his photographs, however, to reveal the *process* behind the final fashion image, rather than the high purpose and validity accorded to it. Far from being in thrall to the lavish and fanciful world of the fashion shoot, he is there to demystify it and open up to readers its behind-the-scenes reality. The artifice of it all does not go unnoticed by his camera. In the second largest image on the final page, which again suggests its importance to the photo-story, model Jacqueline is pictured relaxing during a break. The photograph, taken from above the studio set, reveals that the luxury bedhead is not part of a bed and that Jacqueline has been sitting on what appears to be a rigid box covered with a length of fabric. Most of the frame is taken up by the tools of the photographer's trade – strident, industrial, complicated in appearance. Rows of lights, wires, spot-lights are being adjusted by Miller in readiness for other photographs using other effects. Here is the reality behind the fiction, the staging of 'lights and shadows' that deliver the final picture.

The penultimate frame shows one of the results. It is unclear who has taken this, Glass or Miller, as the caption states it is 'only one of many pictures taken'.[93] If it is by Glass, which is most likely, he has captured just the hint of a Mona Lisa smile from the model as she looks away vaguely into the distance. This is the type of photograph the whole process has been about achieving, beautiful, romantic, pensive. The close-up of Jacqueline's face rather than the dress around which the shoot primarily revolves might indicate that this is indeed the work of Glass and that, in the *Picture Post* way, the people involved are as interesting as the clothing being celebrated.

In summary, the fashion photographer has constructed an apparently glamorous setting in which to fully appreciate and convey the inherent opulence of a British couture garment. A broader purpose for this has been suggested via the text. The photojournalist has directly recorded the reality behind the fashion photograph, revealing both its artifice yet also its art. Indirectly the sequence has offered a narrative on various aspects of wartime fashion and the way women were choosing to dress and why. The reader has been invited to look carefully at what each photographer is seeing and doing, prompted by visual reminders within the frames that see others looking or being looked at.

The final frame is a last reminder of this theme as the *Vogue* editors are seen looking at the photographs produced and making their final choice for the magazine. Their selection is recognized now as being especially important given the photograph's task to promote British textiles and couture internationally as part of fashion's war effort.

Conclusion

Fashion stories in *Picture Post* reflect how women acquired, wore or used clothes during everyday life in a period of unparalleled turmoil and how hostile conditions impacted on style and health and beauty culture. Editorial policy prioritized truthful and genuine visual and written narratives that today provide authentic histories played out in real time. *Picture Post* caught on camera and in conversation much about the process and practice of dress and material culture across classes and communities, revealing the opulence and privilege enjoyed by some and the sad lack of material comforts experienced by a significant number of others. Its visual and literary commentaries offer today a uniquely detailed archive of dress and adornment while providing candid, often poignant and always thought-provoking histories of both ordinary and less ordinary women in extraordinary times.

1
BEAUTY'S BLUEPRINT

Introduction

In this first chapter the focus will be on what *Picture Post* can tell us about conceptions of female beauty and the faces and figures considered to comprise beauty's blueprint during the last year of peace and earliest years of war. If a blue print offers a plan or guide to the making of something, then fashion's blueprint starts with the underlying body contours around which the shapes and silhouettes of a season are styled. These contours reflect the types of figure most prized at any one time and, in concert with current fashions, inspire complementary hairstyling and grooming practices. As a picture magazine *Picture Post* was in an ideal position to capture these forms and their reciprocal fashions both directly, through features on fashion, and indirectly, through lifestyle stories.

Picture Post was not in the business of being a fashion magazine or of catering exclusively for women. It did not, therefore, contrive to dictate what the fashionable silhouette might be or attempt to lay down rules for beauty. The information that *Picture Post* gives us about these two aspects of fashion comes rather from photo-stories or illustrated advertisements that by design, or by the way, conveyed what was happening in the contemporary world of clothing and body culture. It visited fashion mannequins in training and glamour girls taking to the stage, reviewed trends in corsetry and carried advertising for contemporary slimming aids. It explored current treatments in beauty parlours and investigated developments in hair styling. All of these help to establish for us today the various elements of the beauty blueprint as they came together in the shadow of war and something of how they might be achieved.

The fashionable figure

The nature of bodily grace and beauty and the relationship between the two are well-established in an article from December 1938 when *Picture Post* visited a training school for young women wanting to become fashion models. The article called 'The Making of a Mannequin'[1] was photographed by Kurt Hutton, who followed a new pupil through the various stages of a three-week training course, for which she had paid the not inconsiderable sum of fifteen pounds. Some girls, readers were told, entered the field untrained because they had been 'noticed', serving in shops or in some other way demonstrating 'the instinctive poise and grace' required of a model. But for girls who chose to train, courses like this were the first step on a potentially lucrative career path where freelance earnings could reach as high as fifteen to twenty pounds a week.[2]

The new student was 'a good height' at 5 feet 9 inches in high heels[3] and was pictured undergoing a variety of exercises, all in a one-piece swimsuit and heels, to acquire the good posture, poise and elegance essential for the successful mannequin. No mention was made of an ideal weight or body shape, and readers were left to suppose that the model represented the right shape with her height and slender figure and without the 'unflattering curves' that no aspiring model must have.[4]

On a similar theme *Picture Post* returned to a modelling school in November 1940, this time in America.[5] As Britain descended into its second winter of war, and the first of open hostilities, readers were introduced to Mariana Smillie's New York Empire Mannequin School, Beach Unit, where young women learnt the art of outdoor modelling in response to a demand from beach clubs and private beaches. The girls, in a variety of fashionable swimwear, practised exercises that strengthened 'ankles and feet, limber[ed] the calves and reduce[d] over-abundant curves',[6] to achieve the correct balance of slender physique with graceful movement. Beach fashions ranged from a figure-hugging polka-dot-and-

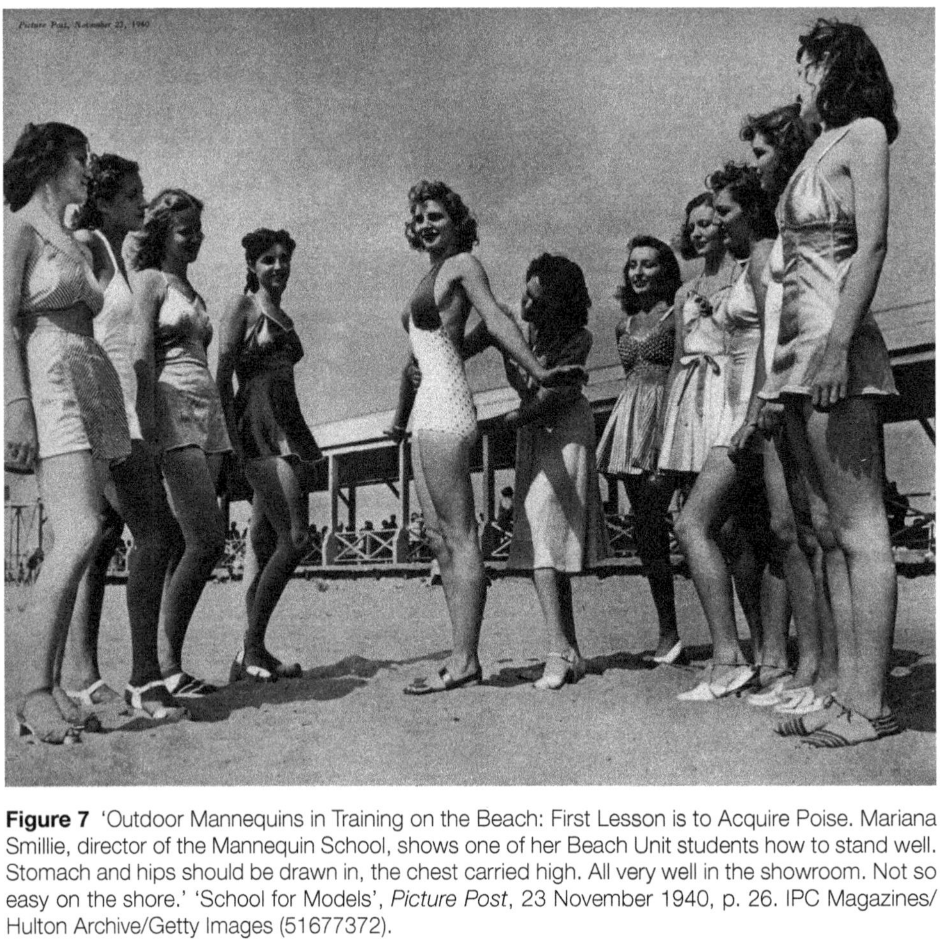

Figure 7 'Outdoor Mannequins in Training on the Beach: First Lesson is to Acquire Poise. Mariana Smillie, director of the Mannequin School, shows one of her Beach Unit students how to stand well. Stomach and hips should be drawn in, the chest carried high. All very well in the showroom. Not so easy on the shore.' 'School for Models', *Picture Post*, 23 November 1940, p. 26. IPC Magazines/ Hulton Archive/Getty Images (51677372).

plain halterneck swimsuit to various satin pleated bathing dresses and playsuits, while shoe choices included an espadrille, soft sneaker and open-toed sandal with ankle strap. Hair appeared mostly wavy or curled, to suit the windblown nature of al fresco modelling, and lipstick was revealed as the most essential make-up item to use when facing up to the sun. This successful combination of the sportif, lithe figure with good balance and poise might earn these sea-shore models around the equivalent of thirty pounds a week – rather more than the pre-war freelance British rate. Elegance and good posture were clearly essential attributes to make the most of the fashionable willowy figure.

The relationship between staying slim and diet was broached, if not with any great conviction, in an article on London's 'Workhouse' restaurant in the West End where professional models went to eat.[7] Photographer Kurt Hutton captured the informal, stylish atmosphere of the restaurant that was populated by well-dressed and well-groomed fashion models, businesswomen and actresses, all of whom placed a premium on looking good and eating to keep that way.

The 'Workhouse' was a 'new type of restaurant'[8] in offering figure-conscious food. Few details surfaced as to the type of dishes on offer, however, nor were there any helpful tips on nutrition for readers. What did emerge very clearly through the photo-story was the sense of style emanating from the diners and the careful attention to details of dress and

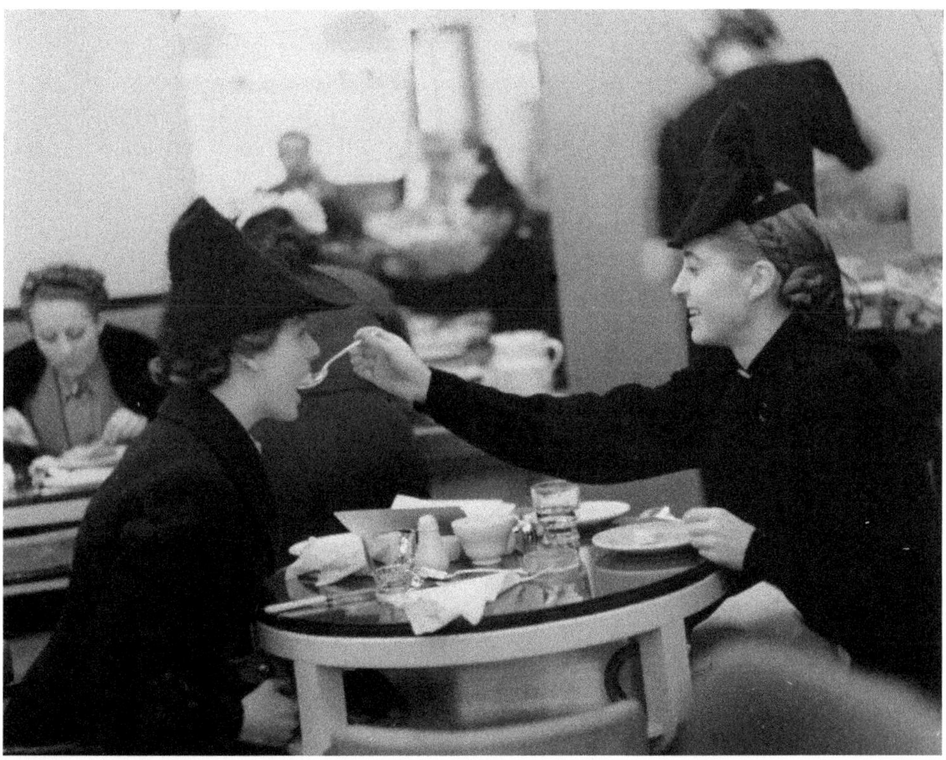

Figure 8 'Lunch-Time in the Bond Street Mannequins' Restaurant: 'Most of the girls who come to this little restaurant every day are mannequins. Here they get a meal with which everyone can be satisfied, and on which no one will get fat'. From 'Where The Beauties Go For Lunch', *Picture Post*, 3 December 1938, p. 33. Kurt Hutton/Getty Images (2669904).

accessories that were intrinsic to this. The photographer's eye captured smart tailored suits and coats, neat silk blouses and fashion hats ranging from pill box, soft brim and wide beret to gauze veiled, fur fascinator and miniature tricorn. Here was what it meant to be well turned out, to be part of a fashionable lifestyle. As far as the food was concerned the lemon cakes and devil chocolate cakes – mentioned as the house specialities – no doubt went some way towards explaining the restaurant's popularity although, in the absence of information on calories or portion sizes, not necessarily its capacity to keep customers slim.

The ideal figure and the nature of glamour

While mannequins of one sort or another identified the fashionable form as both svelte and graceful, *Picture Post* introduced another perspective on beauty in terms of its association with 'glamour'. The photo-story of 'A Glamour Girl's Day' followed the young Chester Hale American dance troupe through their normal daily routine, before appearing on stage in two evening shows at the Dorchester Hotel.[9] Considered to be the ideal height and weight for their work at five foot six and eight stone eight pounds, these girls offered a slightly different form of physical beauty and one closely associated with their intensely active life. Here glamour was fashioned from a light, athletic figure achieved through hard

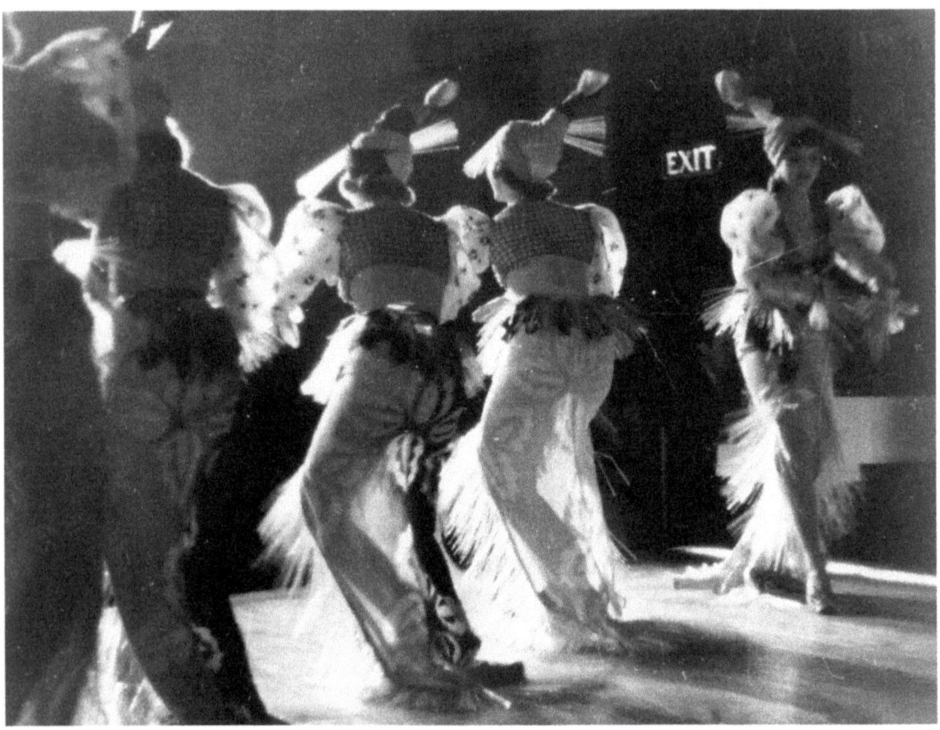

Figure 9 'Glamour Girls as the Audience Sees Them – With all their Glamour'. From 'A Glamour Girl's Day', *Picture Post*, 22 October 1938, p. 13. *Picture Post*/Getty Images (2636493).

work and dedication.[10] A glamorous stage lifestyle was the icing on the cake of physical endurance and professional rigour. In this case fit was an essential part of the beauty blueprint.

A rather different view of glamour emerged in a story from May 1939 entitled 'The Making of a Glamour Girl'[11] when *Picture Post* joined a group of young women hopefuls arriving to audition as glamour-girls for a new floor-show at the London Casino. Requiring no training or specific qualifications the work required a good face, a tall slim figure and the ability to wear clothes well. The girls could be seen auditioning mostly in swimwear, de rigueur for this type of selection procedure it would seem, and thereafter – for those offered work – attending costume fittings before appearing on stage in bespoke Paris gowns.[12]

Training seemed to largely focus on learning the movements required to parade on stage in extravagant and opulent costumes, for which the girls were able to earn 'not less than £5 per week'.[13] Largely young again, many 'only 16 or 17', and with past experience modelling or on the stage in common, few, we are told, had any other ambition than to continue 'to be just glamorous'.[14] The writer reminded readers that the job, however, only lasted as long as the good looks and figure.[15] The idea of glamour that emerged here, almost entirely based on the fortuitous possession of the right physical attributes, was in contrast to that reflected through the Chester Hale girls, where glamour was a hard-won accolade resulting from skill and ability.

Achieving the fashionable figure

Avoiding the extremes of the garcon look of the later 1920s or the curvaceous fashions of the earlier Edwardian era, the silhouette of the later 1930s reflected a balance between weight and height that produced a generically slender figure.[16] Beauty resided in physical grace, elegance of movement and a healthy vitality. Women who did not naturally possess the trimmer figure had familiar options for shaping up: to exercise and eat appropriately or to purchase figure-enhancing foundation wear. *Picture Post* ran stories on a variety of ways of staying fit and healthy through exercise and the enjoyment of an outdoor life and in doing so was reflecting the growing participation in sports and active pursuits that had been developing throughout the 1930s.[17]

The quick fix, however, in terms of achieving a more desirably svelte silhouette came from wearing a corset of one sort or another.[18] In *Picture Post's* article 'The History of the Corset',[19] two things were established. The first, as revealed through the sequence of photographs, was that foundation wear was big business – then worth 13 million dollars in America.[20] Corsets were shown being made, quality tested, launched and promoted, satisfying the demand from 'thousands of buyers from U.S. and Canadian cities' for the latest in figure-improving yet flexible corset design.[21]

Modern corsetry clearly allowed for more movement in a way the bones and busks of previous eras had not, and there was no doubt that huge numbers of women were still relying on these garments to achieve their best lines. While photographs showed aspects of the American corsetry industry, there was nothing to suggest that many British women were not similarly disposed to depend on artificial rather than natural methods of figure correction.

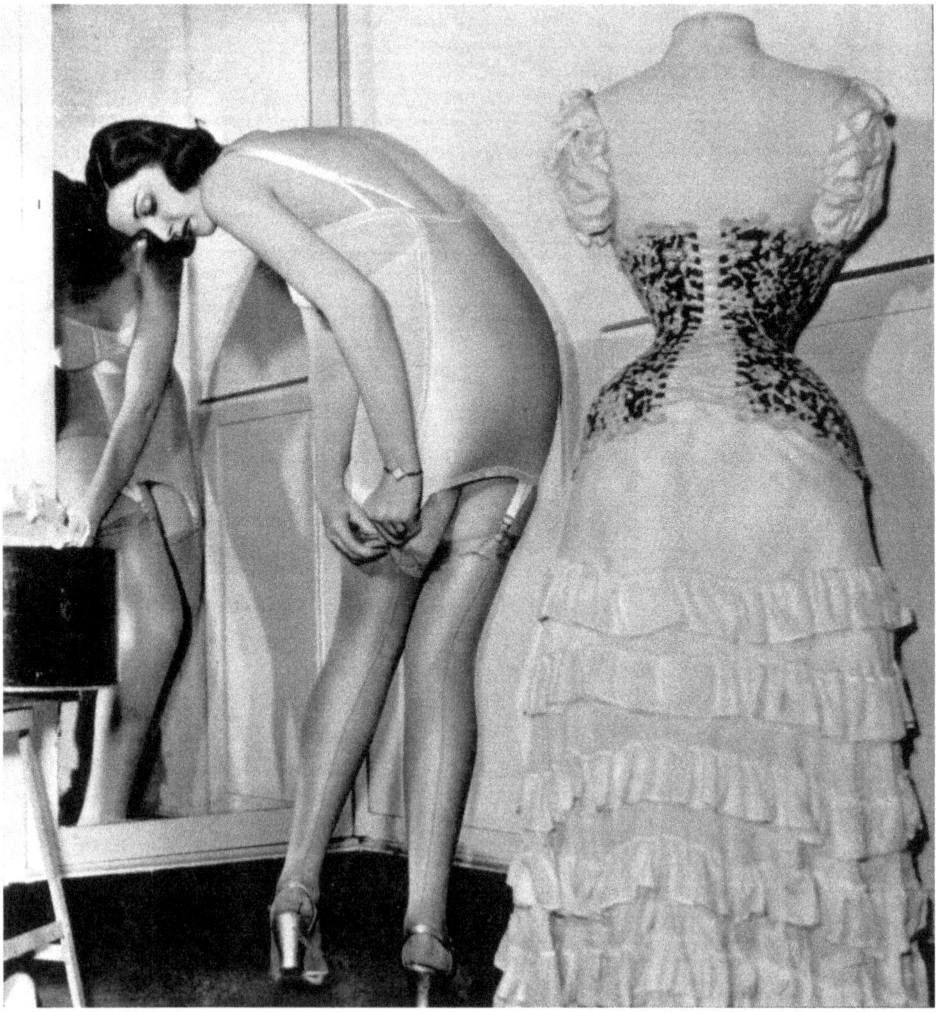

Figure 10 'Setting the Styles for the Modern Corset-Making Industry'. From 'The History of the Corset', *Picture Post*, 1 October 1938, p. 15. Kurt Hutton/Getty Images (2636893).

The other factor to emerge in this *Picture Post* article was that the silhouettes defined by these restrictive garments over the centuries could express particular meanings about the social role of the wearer. British fashion historian James Laver's historical review explored the idea that a metaphorical relationship existed between the deliberate restrictions of women's dress and their similarly restricted social context, raising the important idea that clothes carried specific cultural meanings.[22] If, for example, the wider hip line of Victorian dress implied the desire and capacity for childbirth, did the more slender hip currently fashionable have a connection with the falling birth rate in Britain?[23] Laver left the reader to consider this concluding thought.

In March 1940 and with Britain nearing the end of the Phoney War,[24] *Picture Post* returned to the subject of corsets. In a feature entitled 'War-Time Corsets' the magazine previewed the latest designs for both practical 'control without restriction' and traditional glamour shaping.[25] The article quoted the War Office requirement for women entering the armed or auxiliary forces to be 'corseted and corseted correctly' and showed photographs of designs for service women by foundation-wear manufacturer Frederick R. Berlei. All boning had been eliminated to allow for freedom of movement, with the necessary support and shaping coming from careful cut and choice of materials.[26]

In the intimate surroundings of a West End salon, fashion experts were seen absorbing the finer points of corset construction and styling. These practical garments were 'mostly two-piece affairs, girdle and brassiere ... to give a slight waist, uplifted bust and controlled torso'. There was a special pantee-girdle to be worn under trousers for girls in the Auxiliary Fire Service and driving ambulances, so protecting the latter against 'the danger of those spreading hips that may come after long hours of sitting.'[27]

In contrast, and for off-duty evening occasions, a taffeta, boned 'Gone with the Wind' corset was revealed, modelled on one worn by Vivienne Leigh in the eponymous film.[28] Needing a 'friend or husband' to tie up the back-lacing, Berlei here re-produced a garment from a period reflecting, ostensibly, a more traditional notion of femininity and one that would also capture something of the romance and passion associated with the film. Designed to be worn with a 'long, sweeping and off-the-shoulder' evening dress, the writer reflected that the Gone With The Wind corset was 'clearly a luxury, to be worn only on those occasions when it is permissible these days to go out dressed up for an evening'.[29]

The increasing numbers of women now wearing uniform of one sort or another had certainly had an effect on the fashion market for more glamorous full-length evening clothes, as noted in the Introduction.[30] By the winter of 1939 it had become inappropriate to wear such styles in the company of uniformed men or women and long or elaborate evening wear was also impractical under wartime conditions of black-out or possible air-raids. This type of clothing had become fashion's 'first casualty of war'.[31] Berlei's demure, if still alluring, white silk-laced garment recalled something of Mainbocher's pink satin corset photographed by Horst in 1939,[32] and retained, if in more modest form, a sex appeal and seductive power that might have been found wanting amid serge uniforms and service underwear.

Picture Post also carried advertising for foundation wear. On 10 December 1938, for example, an advertisement for three long-line corsets from corset manufacturer Ambrose Wilson appeared. This showed an '"All-In-One" Corselette' at 8s. 11d., featuring a 'wonderful underbelt with concealed busk that takes good care of slack abdominal muscles'; the '"Nu-Slim" Corselette' at 14s. 11d., considered 'revolutionary' and made in 'perforated, fleece-line rubber [and] rich Floral Broche to produce the very latest idea in slimming'; and the 'Full Figure Corset' at 8s. 11d. for the larger woman looking to 'control the heavy, bulky figure' and '"middle-age" spread'.[33]

The following March, Ambrose Wilson advertised two waist-length corsets. The first, the 'Matroform', priced 12s. 11d., was designed 'to make the matron look as attractive in figure as her daughter'. It featured an 'uplifting under-belt ... concealed beneath a front busk and full back-lacing' that allowed 'every adjustment'. The second, the 'Diaform', at 10s. 11d., again for the fuller figure, had an 'uplift Underbelt, clever boning, back lacing and special diaphragm strap' all of which controlled the '"waistline fat" which makes you look years older'.[34] The corset industry thus offered the figure-conscious a range of readymade

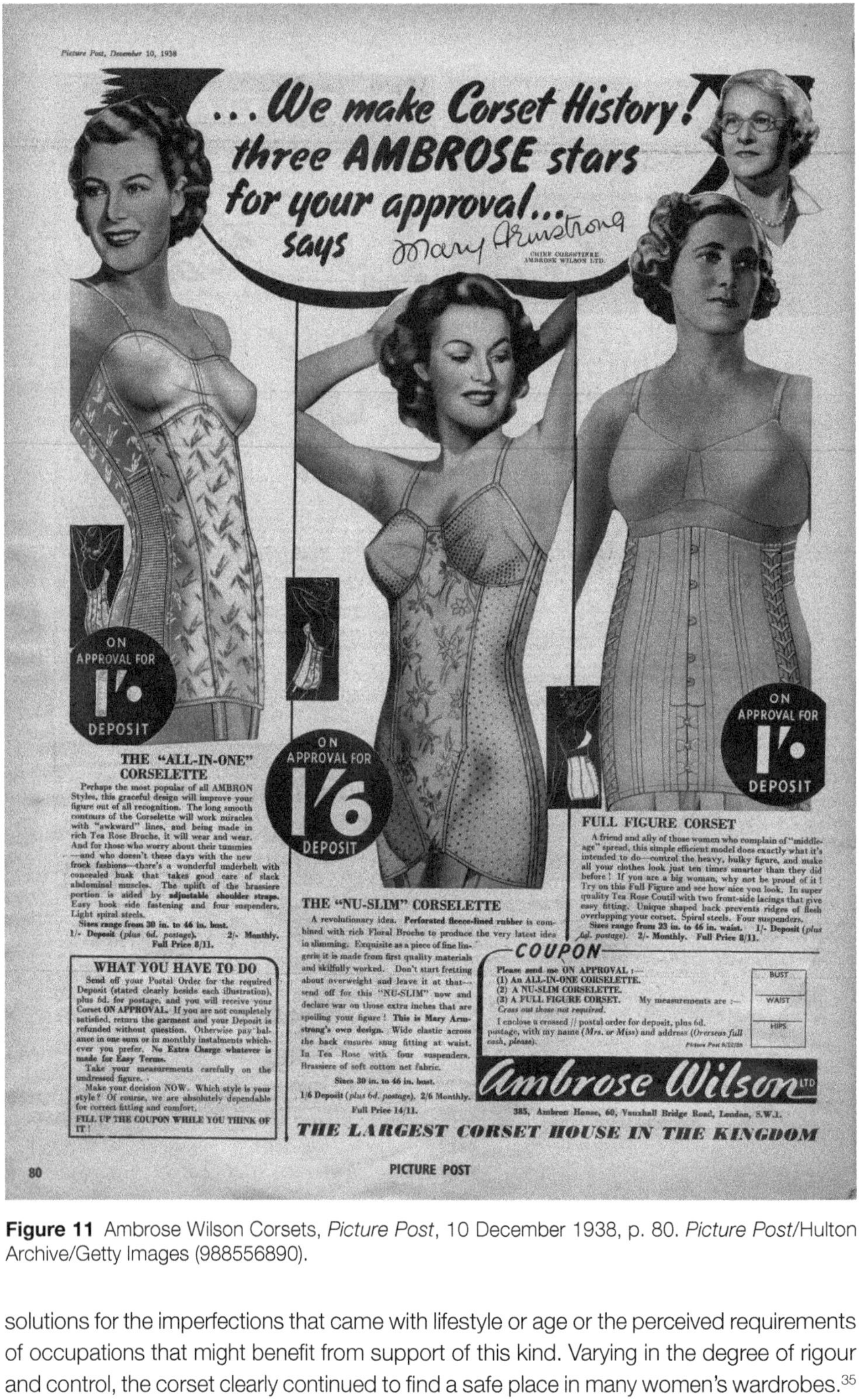

Figure 11 Ambrose Wilson Corsets, *Picture Post*, 10 December 1938, p. 80. *Picture Post*/Hulton Archive/Getty Images (988556890).

solutions for the imperfections that came with lifestyle or age or the perceived requirements of occupations that might benefit from support of this kind. Varying in the degree of rigour and control, the corset clearly continued to find a safe place in many women's wardrobes.[35]

While exercise and diet were the obvious choices for women wanting to lose weight, there were a number of branded over-the-counter tablets and topical creams now available claiming to aid weight loss. *Picture Post* carried advertisements for products such as Marmola, Dermina, Vitamox and Silf,[36] all of which, in one way or another, spoke confidently of their ability to help women regain slimmer figures. Sceptical though we may be about both the science and the effectiveness of such remedies, they reflect the existence of a niche self-help market for those struggling with weight issues.

Beauty treatments

Other solutions for improving nature's shortfalls in the desire to follow beauty's blueprint were to be found among the various treatments and procedures currently available at the beauty salon. *Picture Post* undertook several visits to explore the world of commercial beauty beginning in February 1939 with a report on the 'refresher courses'[37] for beauty guru Helena Rubenstein's field consultants. The photo-story by Tim Gidal depicted various stages of an 'advanced beauty culture' course that included exercise and massage techniques, skin analyses and treatments, and use of specialized equipment to tone and enhance the face and figure.

Opening a window on to what would have been for many a closed world, *Picture Post* revealed the level of sophistication at which the beauty industry now operated and

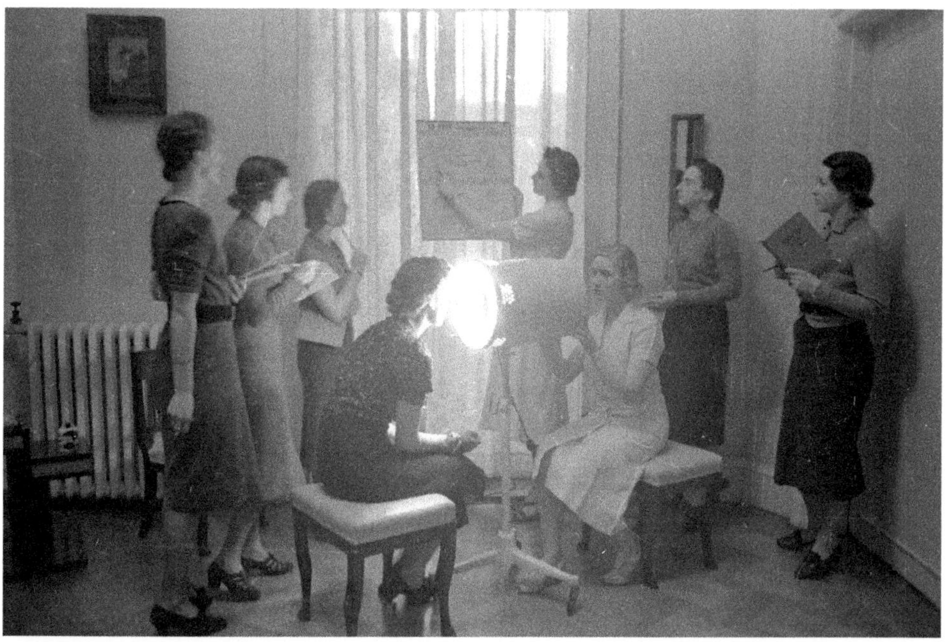

Figure 12 'She Looks into a Dermascope ... Before a beauty expert gets to work, she must know all about the face she has to work on. Her client sits before the dermascope. Inside is a system of lenses and lighting that will show up every blemish and wrinkle'. 'The School of Beauty', *Picture Post*, 11 February 1939, p. 30. Tim Gidal/*Picture Post*/Getty Images (3396174).

a sense of the professionalization inferred through its apparently specialized practices and its white-coated operators. Here women were trained to hold age temporarily at bay and to offer clients with the money and time a younger-looking, healthier version of themselves.

The following May *Picture Post* entered the beauty salon again, this time following a client through a variety of novel beauty treatments to explore 'What Women Do For Beauty'.[38] Quite a lot it seemed, as the photographer captured a client undergoing a variety of skin and body-toning treatments involving masks, oils, mud, a sun-bath[39] and a final reducing massage. All this was to be 'endured' in the name of beauty and the hope of achieving a 'younger and prettier' self.[40]

The beauty parlour[41] represented the glamorous apex of a highly successful beauty industry that was worth in the region of '£26 or £27 million a year'.[42] A good skin was seen as a key component of the beautiful woman. If expensive salon treatments were not an option, there were plenty of skincare products available on the high street that aimed to do the job at home.

Brands such as Pears, Ponds and Knights Castile regularly advertised in *Picture Post* establishing distinctive and familiar formulas that encouraged brand recognition and customer loyalty. Knight's Castile for example created a comic-strip 'soap'-opera featuring the everyday life of actress Norma Knight who always had time for her Knight's Castile beauty-soap routine,[43] while Pears used testimonials from beauty editors to endorse their 'tone-up before make-up' regime.[44] 'Beautiful Grandmothers' could try Crème Tokalon to 'look younger every morning',[45] and Potter and Moore's Powder Cream cared for the 'underskin' and contrived to make you 'lovely today, yes, but lovelier tomorrow!'[46]

Attractiveness and charm would increasingly become associated with personal freshness as the enforced togetherness of service life or nights in air-raid shelters brought people into a new proximity. The merits of simple hygiene practices to ensure this were reflected in advertisements for soaps like Vinolia and Lifebuoy.[47] In terms of the use of make-up *Picture Post* reported that there had been a significant rise during the inter-war years in the number of women wearing face powder, rouge and lipstick.[48] Stories included little specific information on the topic but readers could see for themselves through the photographs the careful delineation of eyebrow and lip that characterized, particularly in a black-and-white image, the face of high fashion at the time. The role of skin and hair preparations and make-up as part of the beauty blueprint would continue to retain currency even as wartime manufacturing limitations eventually caused diminishing high street supplies.[49]

Hair styling

The last component of the beauty blueprint concerned hair. A good introduction to the subject was provided by *Picture Post* reporter Antonia White who visited the Hair and Beauty Fair at Olympia in October 1938.[50] Various hair products, services, demonstrations and lectures were on offer alongside of the many stands for cosmetics and perfumery that were also included as 'most hairdressers run a beauty parlour as a profitable side-line'.[51]

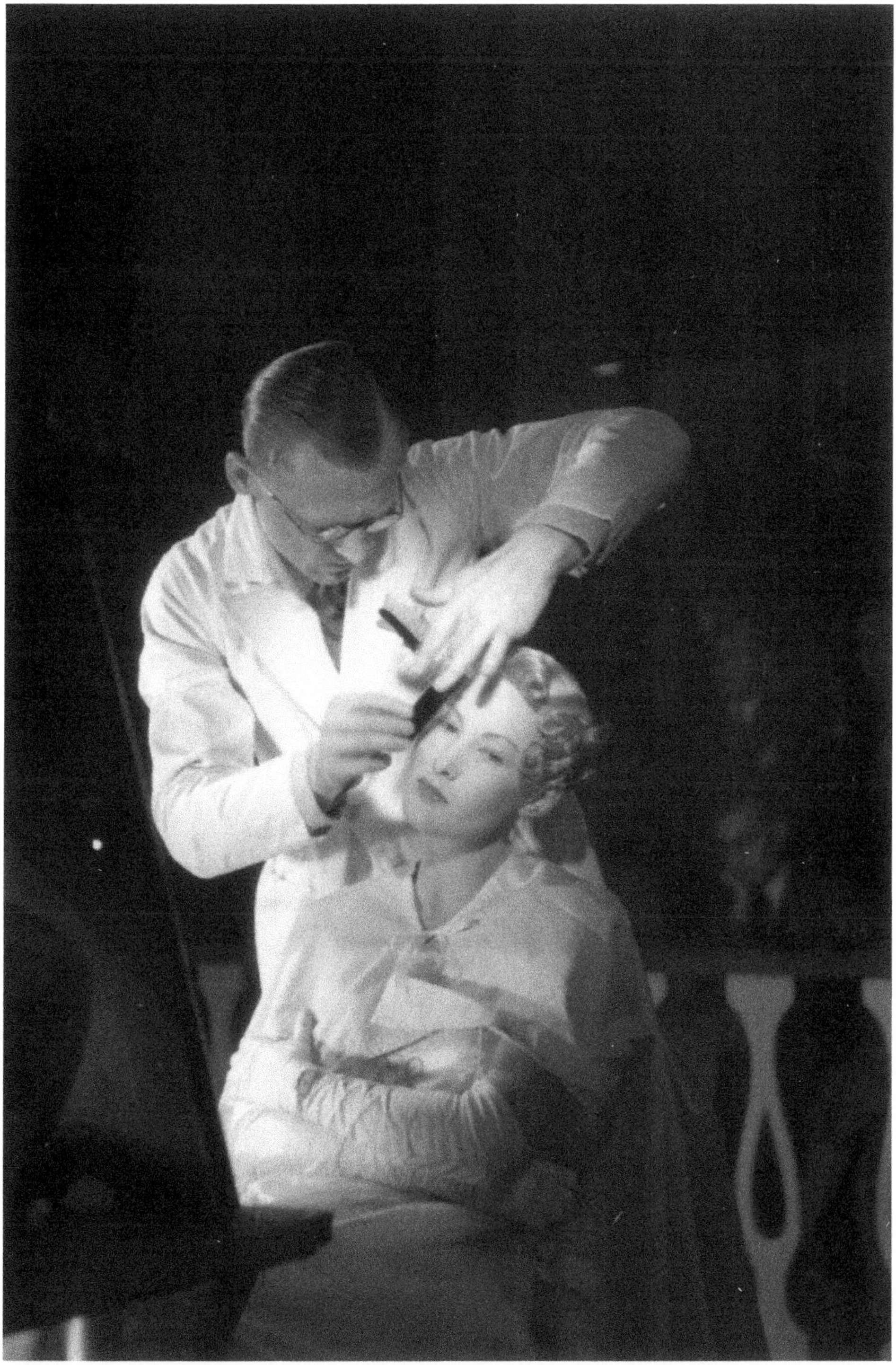

Figure 13 'Experts from all over the country competed anxiously for worth-while prizes at the Hair and Beauty Fair.' From 'Trouble about Hair', *Picture Post*, 8 October 1938, p. 55. Kurt Hutton/*Picture Post*/Getty Images (3169188).

Different forms of permanent waving were on show and given that 'seventy-five percent of women who can afford it have a "perm" about every six months', the desire to achieve fashionably wavy hair was certainly proving strong and worth the cost.[52] While there were images reflecting a popular trend from Paris to wear hair dressed upwards,[53] Kurt Hutton's photo-sequence was much more interested in revealing the tools of the hair dressing trade and its styling procedures.

Two aspects of the exhibition stood out for White. The first was the 'amazing variety of modern beautifying devices' now available across the hair and cosmetic spectrum, from the 'Robot-like perming machines to the convincing artificial eyelashes you can have grafted on to your own'. The second and perhaps most revealing was the 'often pathetic excitement with which women grasp at any straw which may help them look a little younger or more beautiful'.[54] White noted that over half the visitors to the Fair were 'elderly',[55] leaving readers to infer that the lure and appreciation of beauty culture was not merely the preserve of the young. In a curious and yet characteristically *Picture Post* way the photo-sequence depicting scenes at the Hair and beauty Fair is brought to an end with an image of two cleaning ladies scrubbing the floors of a makeshift salon at the end of another day. After all the art and artifice on display at the Fair this picture seems to prompt a moment's reflection that real life was not always beautiful and glamour was for many a strictly part-time phenomenon.

The *Picture Post* make-over

This theme is returned to in the article entitled 'Charlady into Glamour Girl' which appeared in June 1939. Long before the idea of the 'make-over' had become the stuff of popular media, *Picture Post* in its own Pygmalion-style story[56] revealed the remarkable transformative power of the twin arts of make-up and hairdressing as practised by two top professionals.

After a feature on charladies that had appeared the previous February,[57] Ern Westmore, a Hollywood make-up expert, wagered that he could turn a charlady into a 'glamour girl'. *Picture Post* sent photographer Felix Man to record the result.[58] Most readers would not, arguably, have been the least bit surprised to see that with the combined skills of a top Hollywood make-up artist and a champion hairstylist, charlady Mrs Nichols emerged at the end of three and a half hours looking more sophisticated than she had started out.

At a cost of £3 15s. 6d. – well over a week's wages for many working-class women – the twelve photographs reflected something of the Hollywood experience that most women might only dream about.[59] At the end of Mrs Nichol's make-over morning, she expressed the view that the artists had been very clever and that she was very pleased to see the results. Preparing to return home she 'wiped off' however 'all the artistically applied make-up, took down the elaborate coiffeur, destroyed the glamourous balance of form and colour'[60] and in so doing re-instated her natural self, her own identity as she saw it. If the beautification process had little relevance to the lifestyle it was meant to enhance it was just a painted mask without any real value.

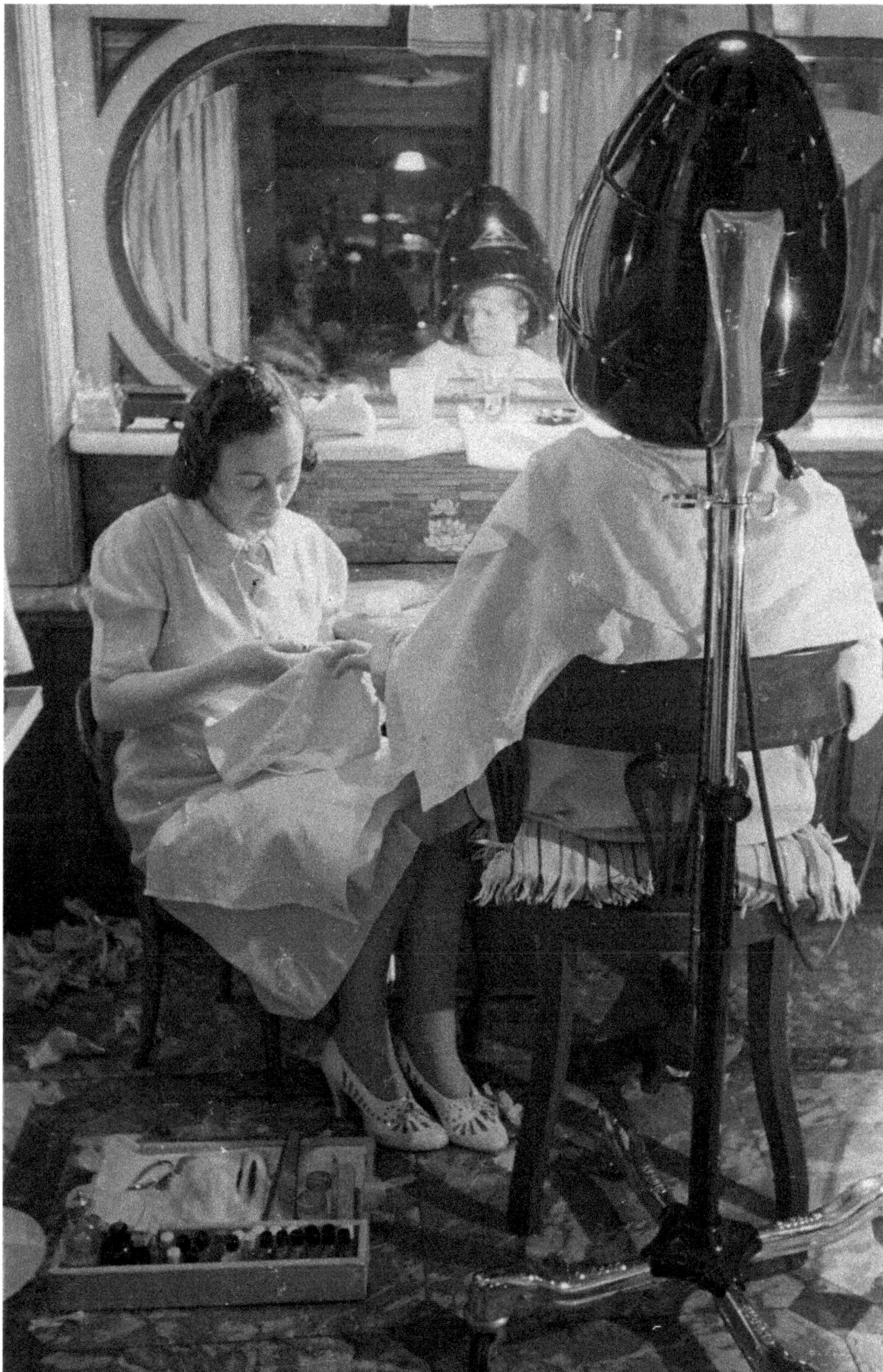

Figure 14 'Her Hands are Manicured; While her hair is drying in that imposing helmet, Mrs Nichols is given a manicure. Normal cost – with an elegant varnish for her nails – would be another 3s'. From 'Charlady into Glamour Girl', *Picture Post*, 17 June 1939, p. 53. Felix Man/*Picture Post*/Getty Images (3419126).

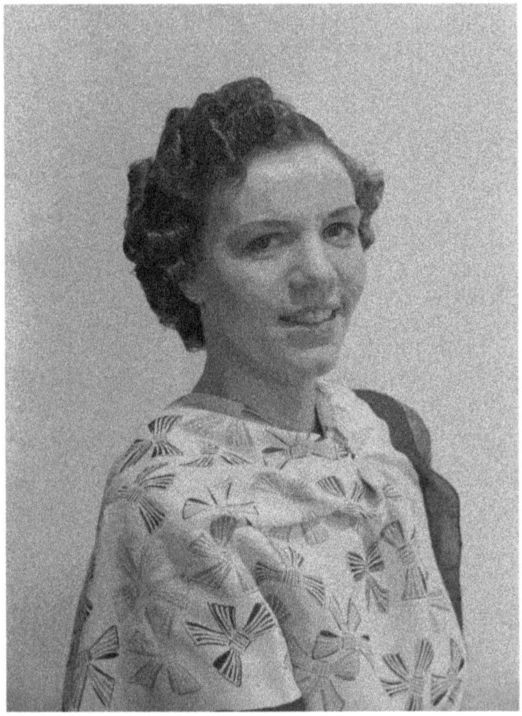

Figure 15a 'And This is the Result: The Transformed Charlady Sees Herself in the Glass.' Both images 'Charlady into Glamour Girl', *Picture Post*, 17 June 1939, p. 55. Felix Man/*Picture Post*/ Hulton Archive/Getty Images (984851300 and inset 984851360).

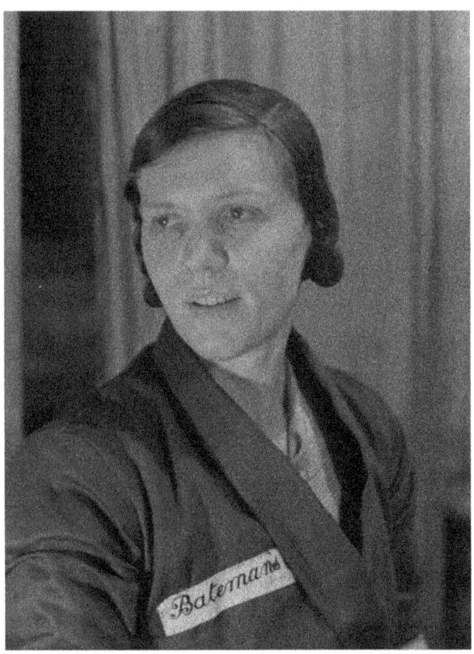

Figure 15b 'But Before Long She will go Back to her Ordinary Face'.

Conclusion

The beauty blueprint, therefore, came in various forms, each deriving meaning and value from the culture where it had been conceived and in which it subsequently operated. The unadorned, natural face of Mrs Nichols that appeared in the before-shots[61] was the face her husband liked, the face he knew, and we are not to suppose that this face didn't possess its own attractiveness. Beauty might have a blueprint based on a slender figure and the charm of a well-groomed appearance, but it allowed for many adaptations and modifications on this generic theme. From cabaret chic to charlady simplicity, stage glitterati to alfresco model, statuesque elegance to sublime energy, *Picture Post* reflected the many forms and faces from which beauty could be fashioned.

2 FASHION STORIES FROM EVERYDAY LIFE

Introduction

This chapter brings together a selection of stories drawn from *Picture Post's* first year and a half of publication from October 1938 to the spring of 1940. They reveal something of the range of fashionable clothing available – from popular seasonal and leisure styles to more established wardrobe classics – and the advent of specific types of uniform for women joining one of the civilian services now operating.[1] Each provides interesting and sometimes intriguing individual clothing or fashion cameos, specific to times, places and people. Together they build a fuller understanding of the fashions and dress practices current across various demographics in the transition to war.

The Queen as a fashion figurehead and the House of Hartnell

In November 1938, *Picture Post* visited couturier Norman Hartnell for an article entitled 'The Queen's Dressmaker'.[2] The photo-sequence showed Hartnell at work in his studio and included two photographs of evening wear designs-in-progress for his 'Most Distinguished Client', the Queen.[3] Readers were told that the Queen's recent state visit to Paris had inspired a new fashion there for 'Highland style, dresses and coats in Scottish tartans', a 'Scottish vogue … to honour the Scottish Queen'.[4] Hartnell's royal 'picture dresses', influenced by those depicted in the work of the nineteenth-century painter Franz Winterhalter, had been much admired by Parisian couturiers,[5] and Hartnell's 'challenge to France' was considered to be a 'serious one'.[6] This was no doubt considerably assisted by his role as royal dressmaker, and autumn fashions that year continued to reflect interest in historical styles.

The two designs photographed and captioned as 'Models for the Queen to Wear' revealed formal, full-length gowns with slender silhouettes. Opulently conceived, one in a pale sparkling fabric with a small train, the other in a darker material consonant with its fur trimmed collar and lower skirt, both had sumptuous fur accessories in the shape of a coat, muffler and stole. Here were examples of the highest of high fashion.

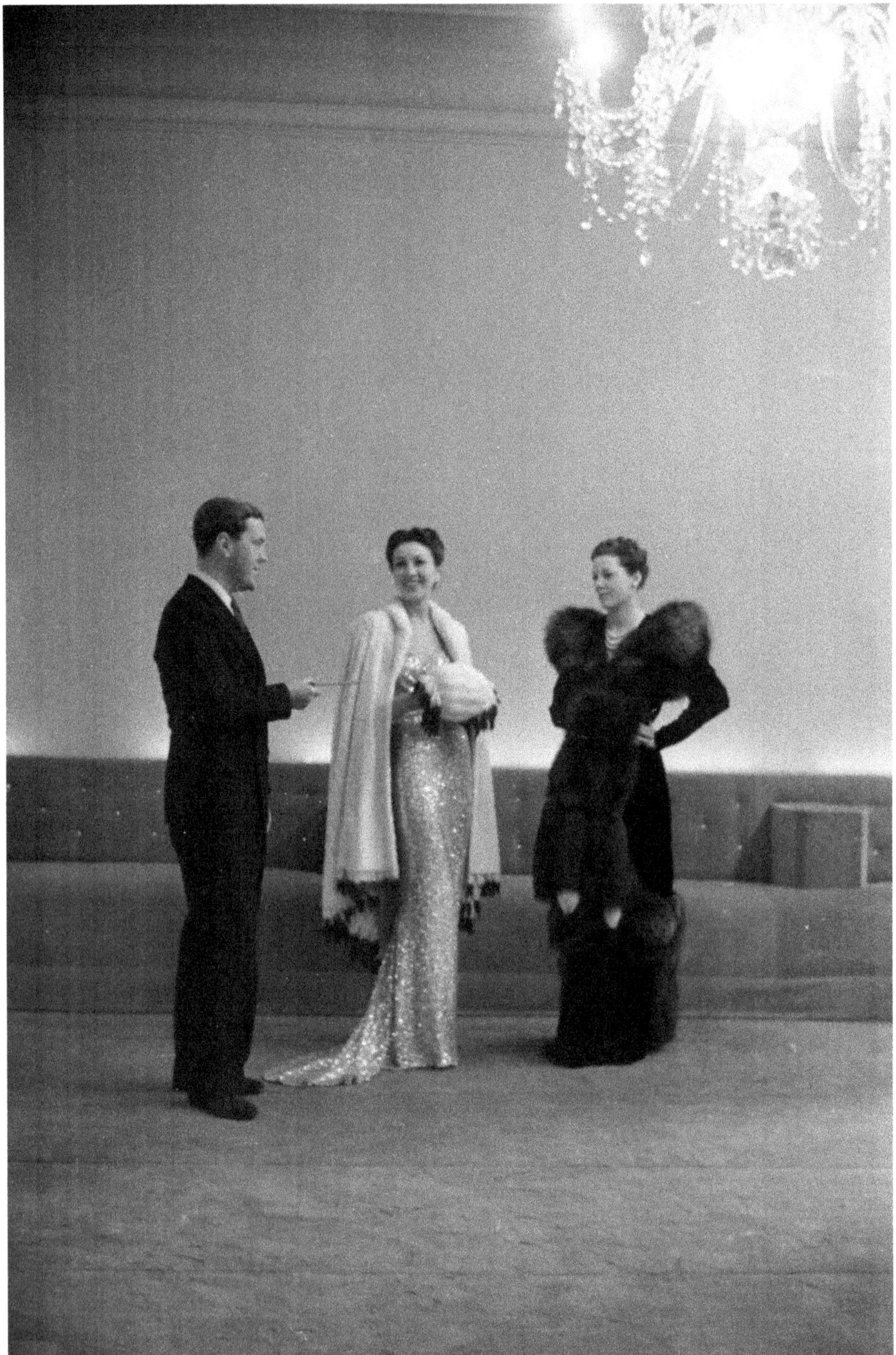

Figure 16 'Models for the Queen: Before being sent to Buckingham Palace, everything the Queen will wear is inspected by Norman Hartnell. Sometimes, even at this moment, he will change the material for a coat or dress'. From 'The Queen's Dressmaker', *Picture Post*, 19 November 1938, p. 27. Kurt Hutton/*Picture Post*/Getty Images (3367142).

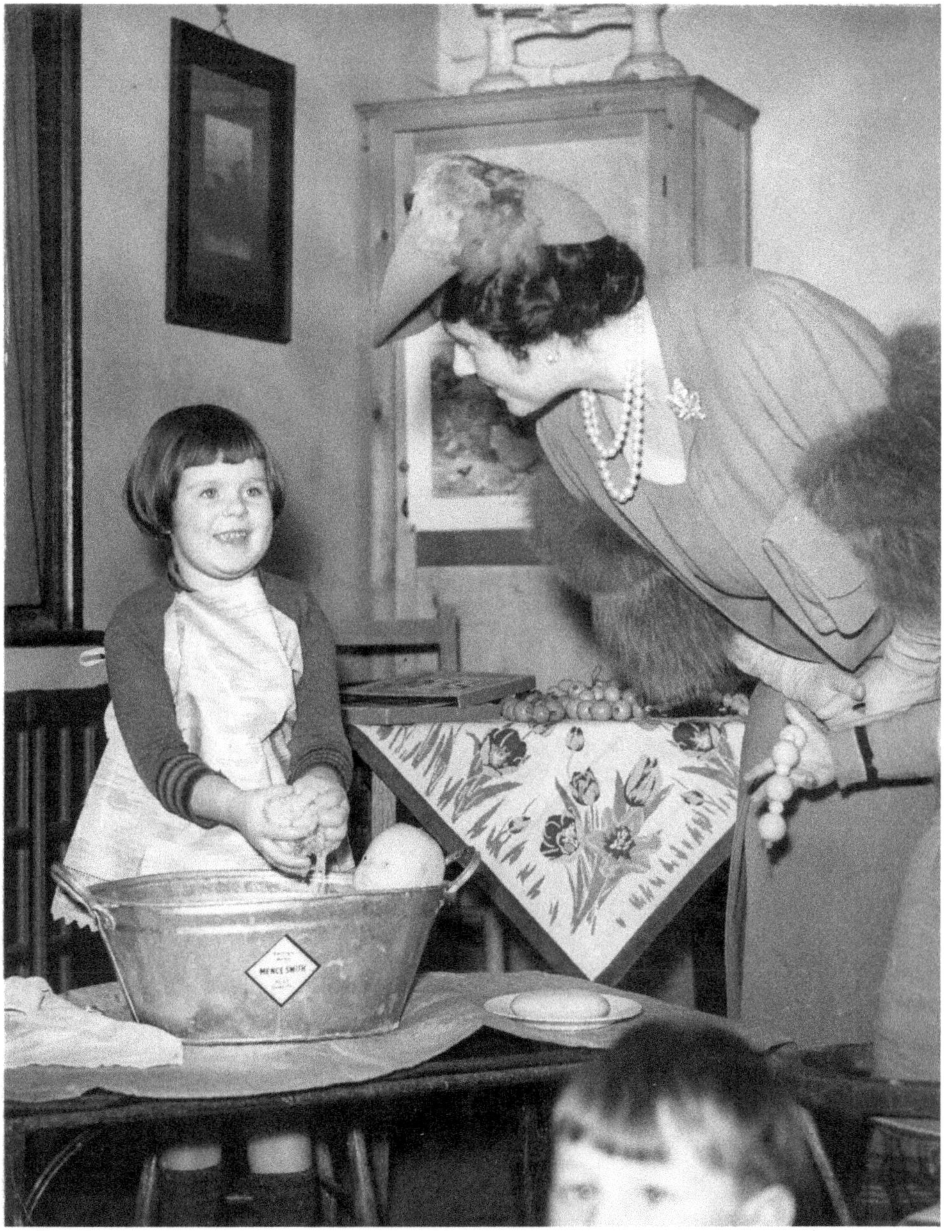

Figure 17 'The Queen with the Little Girl: The Queen visiting an evacuation school', *Picture Post*, 25 November 1939, p. 40. Keystone/Hulton Royal Collection/Getty Images (3336171).

The final picture in the story showed the Queen wearing a Hartnell three-quarter-length black velvet coat with Persian lamb trimming on both coat and halo hat, the modest leg-of-mutton sleeve design again reflecting the currency of historical detail.

Readers were informed that Hartnell 'had the task of creating everything the Queen wears, from head to foot: hair ornaments, hats, dresses, coats, furs, shoes, stockings, gloves and handbags',[7] as well as providing around 'fifty complete outfits every season for the Queen'.[8] This conveyed something of the royal consumption of clothing and accessories in the course of duty, offering interesting comparison with other wardrobes across the social spectrum.

Described as 'pre-eminently a British designer', *Picture Post* reported that after visiting New York, Hartnell had praised the Americans for 'make-up, stockings and accessories' but felt they could not 'touch the English woman for a certain "softness"'. While Americans were '"snappy" in their dress' they were 'neither "soft" nor "subtle"' and *Picture Post* concluded that 'Norman Hartnell should know'.[9]

A photograph taken of the Queen visiting an evacuation school a year later captures this sense of softly tailored fit. Wearing a dress and jacket with fur bolero and brimless peaked hat, the Queen is seen talking informally to a little girl evacuee.[10] A double string of beads, small leaf brooch and soft clutch handbag accessorized the Queen's unfussy outfit, and her quiet sense of style represented a classic elegance achieved through excellence in design and fabric. Another photograph taken of the Queen on a visit to Scotland in March 1940 also captured this soft elegance in a gently tailored coat with puffed sleeves and narrow draped lapels, worn with a small-crowned hat with decorated floral disc and a double string of pearls.[11] The Queen would continue to act as a fashion figurehead throughout the war, her classic, royal chic indelibly associated with keeping up morale and carrying on.

Other British couturiers featured in *Picture Post*

Other British couture houses covered by *Picture Post* during this time also reflected evening opulence and an interest in history. The House of Motley,[12] begun by three art students with an interest in theatre costume, had recently taken to designing off-stage clothing which *Picture Post* described as 'often dramatic, but ... not theatrical'.[13] The photographs, illustrations rather than a story in themselves, showed seven images of evening wear styles and two larger pictures of the audience at a Motley show. The rather bare surroundings of the Motley catwalk might have accounted for the audience wearing a good deal of fur in coats, collars and hats but revealed at the same time that the use of fur in one way or another was a customary feature of contemporary fashion.[14]

Front and back images of Motley's 'Dove Dress' showed a gathered and draped off-the-shoulder bodice fitting to the hip line and a full-length sash falling from behind. Described as having 'classical simplicity', this Grecian-style dress reflected another aspect of historically inspired design. Readers were reminded that Motley had launched the crinoline the previous season and a white satin and black lace full-length evening dress tied at the waist was considered to have 'all the charm of the crinoline ... without its discomfort'. This dress showed a generously full skirt falling in folds from a black bow at the back waist reflecting a muted version of Victorian and Edwardian style elements. Opulence was also revealed in a tailored evening jacket 'in the style of an Indian prince' and made out of 'bright pink wool embroidered with spangles and imitation jewels'. Here were colourful, statement clothes reflecting the signature drama of Motley and the exuberance of couture evening wear six months before war.

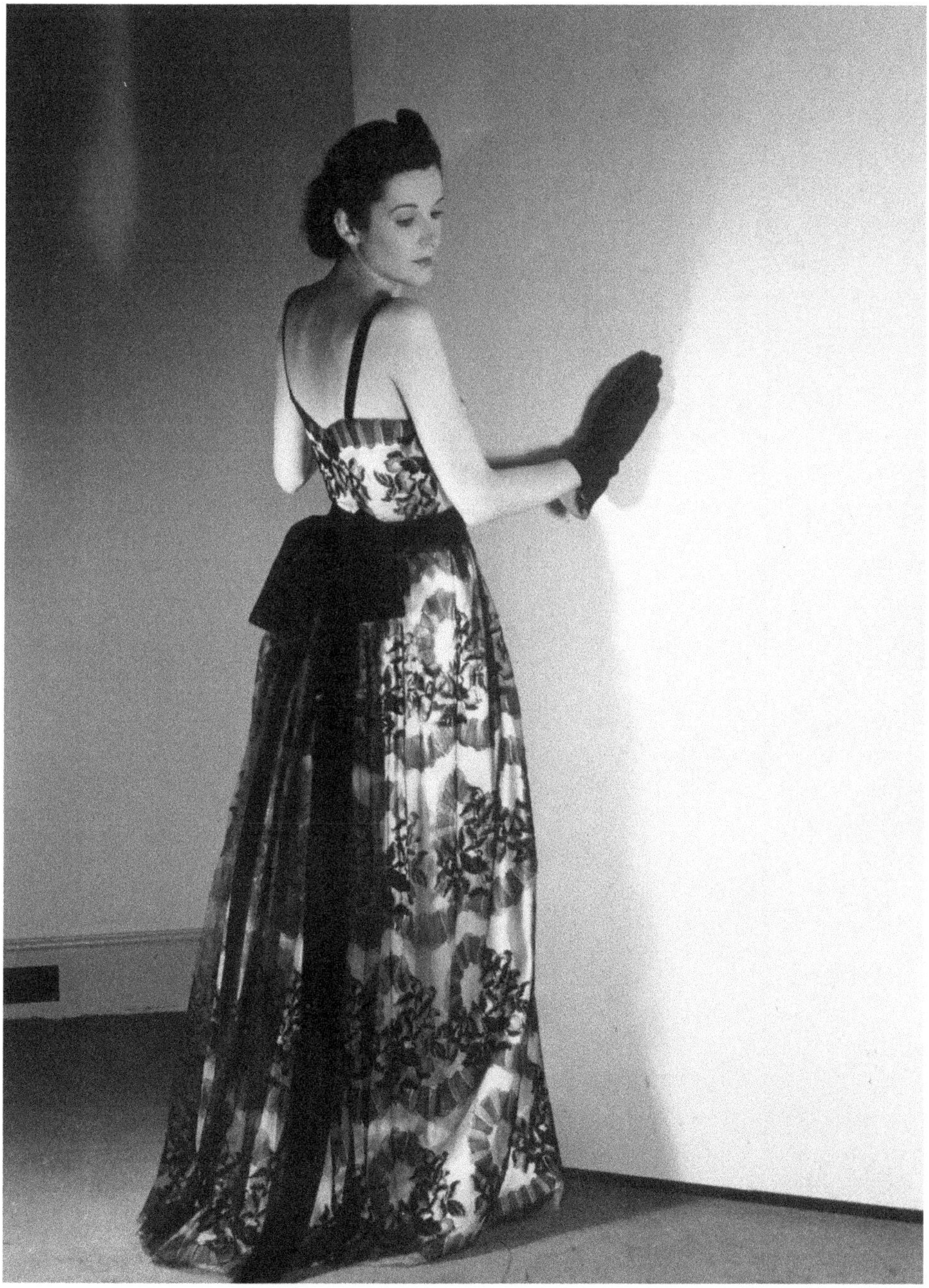

Figure 18 'The House that Launched the Crinoline Adopts the Full Flowing Skirt: This lovely evening frock of white satin has an overdress of shadowy black lace' From 'Design for Spring Time', *Picture Post*, 25 March 1939, p. 38. Horace Eliascheff/*Picture Post*/Getty Images (3374667).

In November 1939, almost three months into Britain's phoney war, *Picture Post* ran an article about 'The First War-time Travelling Fashion Parade' in a fashion feature entitled 'Fashion Show on Wheels'.[15] Responding to the fact that many 'smart women'[16] had left London after war was declared, couturier Digby Moreton, the Elizabeth Arden Beauty Salon, milliner Aage Thaarup and furrier Louis Woolf had created a travelling fashion show comprising the latest trends for clients now living in the country. The *Picture Post* photo-report captured four Bond Street mannequins taking the train to Bristol and then preparing for a runway show. The images concentrated more on the behind-the-scenes organization of the show than the actual fashions on offer but revealed in the process the importance that now attached to maintaining fashion sales as Britain moved into a state of war.

There had been a noticeable downturn in consumer spending on clothing after war had been declared. This had already begun to cause redundancies in the dress trade and the travelling show had been one step taken to proactively reverse this trend.[17] Readers were told that the show had been put on in order to fulfil the Queen's wish that the 'Bond Street Houses ... should go on with their businesses and keep the unemployment figures down'.[18] In an effort to do just that, thirty-six suits were shown, 'costing, on the average, 18 guineas each', along with the contents of 'ten hat boxes' and furs worth four thousand pounds.[19] The article did not relate how many of the 150 guests at the Bath Hotel were persuaded to buy.

A story from the Paris couture

The workings of a Parisian fashion house and the job of *making* rather than *designing* clothes was the theme for Antonia's White's fashion feature called 'Backstage at a Paris Fashion Show'.[20] This intriguing behind-the-scenes photo-story explored working life in the couture house of Paquin and introduced readers to the various employees on whose individual skills and experience much of the successful operation of the house depended. The fact that an exclusive couture, serving an affluent and socially privileged clientele, rested a good deal on the efforts of ordinary working people arguably went some way to dispelling its remote and esoteric image. It was, after all, just a business like any other which produced goods that some could afford and others couldn't.

Readers were informed about workers' wages, from apprentices earning ten shillings a week and assistants at twenty-five shillings,[21] to junior and senior hands at thirty-five and forty-five shillings, respectively – each band reflecting a level of experience, skill and craftsmanship. In contrast the 'thousands a year of monsieur or madame, the creative genius of the establishment',[22] and the generally better paid front-of-house staff including sales women, show-mannequins and house models, left the reader in little doubt that, despite the high price tag of the product, those employed to sew and finish remained on relatively lower incomes – even where they offered specialist abilities or knowledge.[23]

Jobs, however, appeared to offer a level of advancement and security and the backstage hands photographed were clearly excited by the prospect of another show and working hard towards its success. White concluded that backstage had revealed a mixture of 'factory, office, studio, secret service and theatre',[24] her human interest approach to the story arguably rendering the concept of the couture itself more approachable.

Styles from history

The crinoline

Design elements borrowed from costume history have already been referred to as part of the contemporary design lexicon, and *Picture Post* captured this trend in several of its fashion stories. The front cover for 5 November 1938, for example, captioned 'The Crinoline Comes Back', presented a glamorous image of a fashion model lying amid the skirt fabric of a sumptuous white silk harlequin-quilted gown, featuring a white cummerbund waist and softly quilted bodice and collar. This was followed up inside the magazine with a series of photographs revealing what the modern whalebone-hooped petticoat of 1938 looked like and showing examples of opulent full-skirted evening gowns for which they had been reinvented.

While the modern crinoline was more pliable than its Victorian counterpart, and could be easily removed, the style remained costly and cumbersome. The writer acknowledged that 'until the last six months, the return of the crinoline seemed about as probable as the return of the ice-age' but accounted for its new-found popularity as a result either of recent films and plays featuring Queen Victoria[25] or because of theories regarding the cyclical nature of fashion that required bell shape to follow tube.[26] Whatever the reason for this resurgence of design interest in crinolines and the occasional bustle,[27] the styles that resulted showed intricate and ornate design features and lavish use of fabric. Here again, as in Victorian times, the wealth and privilege of the wearer was on display.

Millinery uses history

Milliners too were deriving their design inspiration from several eras, some a good deal earlier than the Victorian period. In January 1939, for example, in an article titled 'Monk to Mannequin',[28] a growing fashion interest in hoods was traced back to the mediaeval cloister, while in 'The Wimple Returns',[29] the following month, the mediaeval wimple style that had come across from America was captioned as 'The Latest Thing in 1325: The Latest Thing Today'.[30] This reinterpretation of fourteenth-century style combined a length of fabric that could be draped in a number of different ways, with a small hat, varying in design from straw brimmed and pill box to welsh peasant. Readers were advised that wimples were seen to best advantage on women with the same willowy, lean figures as the original 'Gothic wimple-wearers' and that the style should only be worn to accompany 'slick, town clothes' as they 'just won't go with low heeled shoes, bulky fur coats, tailored coats and skirts'.[31]

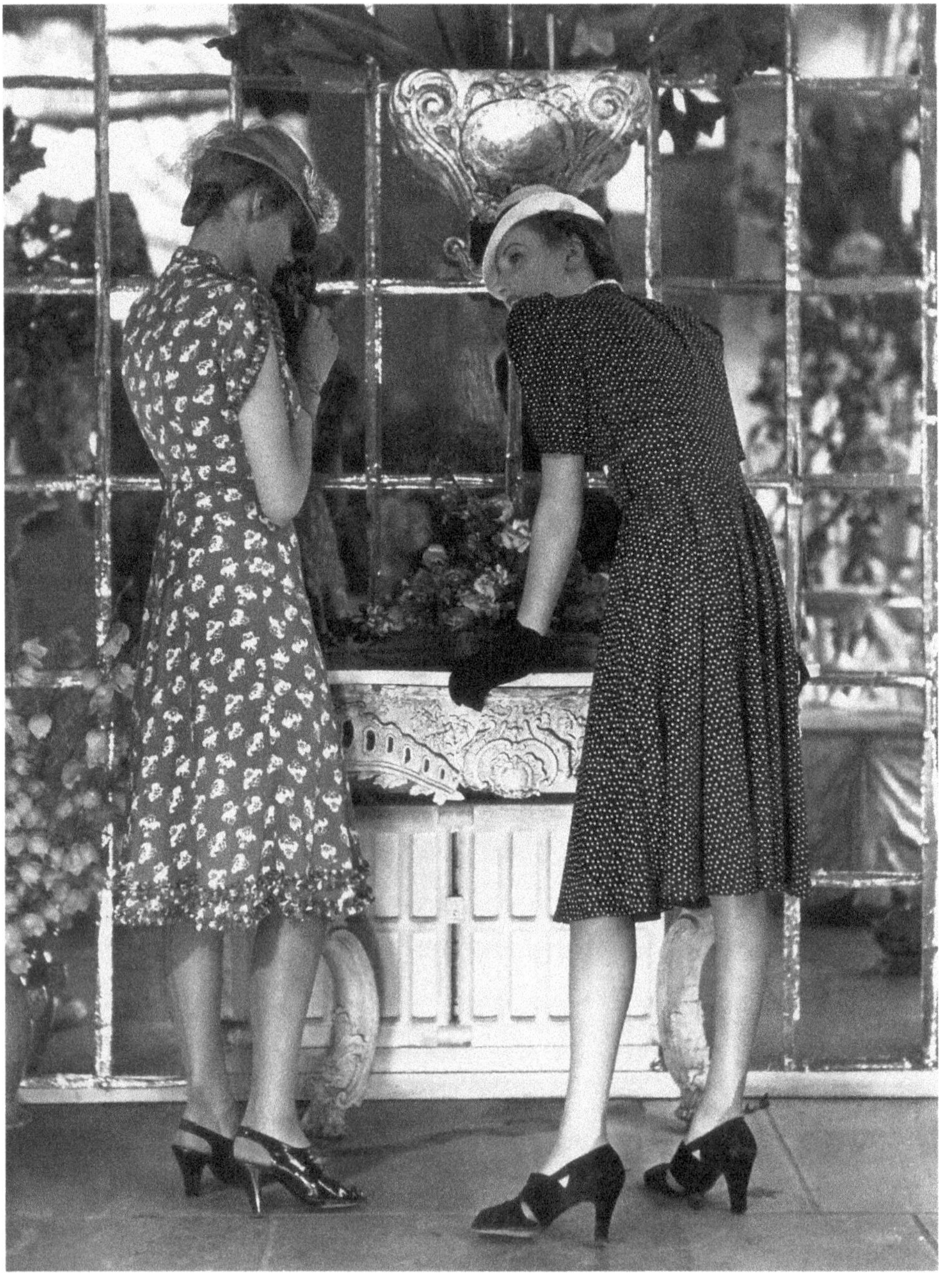

Figure 19 'Flower-Time Fashions. On the left, a printed floral crepe-de-chine in pale blue and white, with a cross-over bodice. The mushroom hat is in soft firefly blue. On the right a chic summer dress with white polka dots, and a high crowned sugar loaf hat from Paris. You can buy these dresses for 5 ½ guineas.' 'The Last Straws of Summer', *Picture Post*, 1 July 1939, p. 62. *Picture Post*/Hulton Archive/Getty Images (3060103).

A week later *Picture Post* informed readers that it took 'One Hundred and Thirty Five Feet of Veil to Make One Hat'[32] in an article introducing the latest vogue for Edwardian veiling that was now making fashion news. By April millinery was exploiting fin-de-siècle fashions for 'feathers, ribbons and flowers'. This prompted *Picture Post* to place photographs of Victorian styles side by side with modern interpretations, clearly reflecting that grandmother's hat had, indeed, come back and that 'fancy dress fashions have gone to our heads as well as everywhere else'.[33]

In 'The Last Straws of Summer'[34] *Picture Post* reported that the continuing trend for Victorian and Edwardian elements of design could be explained by a 'renewed respect for Grandmama – her clothes and her way of life',[35] which had provoked a rejection of the 'hard hectic fashions of the nineteen twenties'.[36] It was suggested that today's women, 'tired of wars and alarms and crises, seek a refuge even in their dress' with softer and more 'soothing' clothing surfacing as a result.[37] The article featured a range of millinery styles from straw boaters adorned with bows, flowers or feathers, to hats swathed and tied by veiling – all reflecting a clear interest in historic reference.

Photographs also revealed the current variegated fashions for daywear. These included a striped summer dress with puffed sleeves, Edwardian style, neatly fastened at the neck with a small bow; a classic two-piece suit in Irish Frieze,[38] representative of Britain's long-established reputation for quality country tailoring[39]; and two summer dresses featuring softly gathered skirts falling to just below the knee.

Each foreshadowed, in ways that could not have been known at the time, the simplicity and elegance that lay at the heart of British war style to come.

Many styles from many periods

Fashions in general continued to reflect this mix of many styles from many periods.[40] On 15 April *Picture Post* carried an article entitled 'Fashion Goes Wild' which explored the idea that there was no longer a particular line or silhouette being followed in the latest seasonal fashions.[41] Antonia White doubted whether there had 'ever been so many different fashions to choose from' and speculated on the reasons why this might be so: 'Perhaps it's because we're all so unsettled in our minds that we can't decide on one definite line. Perhaps fashion is protesting against totalitarian states with their uniform shirts and uniform ideas.'[42] In the wake of February's air-raid shelter deliveries for city homes vulnerable to bombing and April's plans for the evacuation of 2.5 million children in the event of war, it was not surprising that there was uncertainty about the future. For Britain, looking to the past – particularly a Victorian past when she was at the height of her industrial and colonial strength – was understandable, possibly reassuring.

In March the Territorial Army had announced plans to double their numbers,[43] and a month later the government revealed their intention to conscript men of twenty. Meanwhile the women's services had begun to muster. The Auxiliary Territorial Service had been inaugurated in September 1938,[44] the Women's Royal Naval Service in March 1939 and the Women's Auxiliary Air Force would come into operation in July 1939.[45] Although women in uniform would not be seen in any numbers until after war had been declared the coming September, there does seem to have been a desire, however consciously felt, to enjoy fashion in all its variety. White commented that the Paris collections had been 'like a series of fancy dress parades' and that fashion had 'run mad'.[46]

The various outfits *Picture Post* had captured to reflect this collage of costumes, from ingénue summer skirts of pleated georgette to panniered black satin evening wear, all had one thing in common. They were reminders of styles and times when a traditional sense of femininity prevailed, both in terms of the feminine silhouette referenced and the established relationship between the sexes the historical provenance might suggest. Whether fashion was retreating into the safety of the past or defying the uneasiness of the present, it offered a chance to dress up, and the variety available suggested it was possible to 'get away with almost anything'.[47] This would prove to be a final fling.

When the King and Queen returned in late June from a goodwill tour of Canada and the United States,[48] Britain's first conscripted men were being enrolled, and by July the situation in the free Baltic port of Danzig,[49] important gateway to the sea for Poland through the Polish Corridor, was deteriorating under increasing threat from Nazi aggression. The agreement signed in April between Britain and France to come to Poland's aid in the event of hostilities across her borders made the worsening situation there deeply unsettling. In Britain daily life now carried on in the shadow of these growing anxieties.

Clothing for occasions, recreations and new occupations

Such were the design themes and styles that created the fashion signature of the later 1930s. The stories that now follow not only reference elements of these contemporary fashions but also reveal the ways in which clothes were acquired and worn as occasion, recreation or new occupation demanded.

Dressing up for a wedding

While a wedding certainly presented an opportunity for dressing up, it was also the event most likely to cause expenditure on clothes and accessories, irrespective of income. *Picture Post* discovered just how much money, time and energy went into the affair if 'A Mayfair Girl Gets Married'.[50] There are perhaps few articles that reveal quite as much as this one about both the capacity to spend enjoyed by the seriously wealthy, and the protocols of consumption and acquisition associated with the society marriage. Phrases such as the 'maelstrom of shopping' and the decorating of a 'fashionable church ... almost like a theatre' for the 'wedding pageant'[51] may discreetly infer ambivalence towards endorsing the bride's social position in these ways, as might the article's concluding remark that, in other circles, a whole wedding could be bought 'for the price of a Bond Street bouquet or a few hundred wedding invitations'.[52]

Readers were reminded that 'by tradition' brides began married life with everything new.[53] For the Mayfair bride this required buying all 'town clothes, country clothes, evening frocks, furs, and lingerie'[54] which together with her wedding dress might create a trousseau costing between 'four or five hundred pounds', exclusive of really expensive fur coats and jewellery.[55] Her parents would also furnish her with new household textiles and linens and a new set of luggage. All the wedding paraphernalia, from invitations and church decorations to the wedding reception and wedding cake, incurred further expense so that ultimately cheques might have been written for well over a thousand pounds. This sum was also exclusive of the '"important" wedding present – a car, a pearl necklace, a mink coat, or even a house'.[56]

The photo-story moved from the choice of wedding gown, through the acquisition of furs and jewels, to the receiving of wedding presents. Throughout the sequence there was little in the facial expressions of mother or daughter to express the joy of the occasion. Rather the camera captured their reserved concentration on the matters in hand. It was only in the last of the pre-ceremony images that the bride-to-be is finally seen smiling in conversation with a bridesmaid. The rituals of expenditure and display involved in delivering a wedding commensurate with a bride's perceived status were clearly to be taken seriously. *Picture Post* offered readers who did not live like this a view of other people who did and left them to decide for themselves whether they were in sympathy with what they saw or not. Here also was a social culture manifesting a level of retail materialism that the restrictions of wartime living would soon render difficult or impossible.[57]

Clothes for holidays – beach wear

Picture Post generally took an interest in seasonal fashion, and one particular facet of this, investigated several times during the last summer before war, was beach wear. In February 1939 Antonia White reported on a pirate theme for beach clothing emerging from Paris, not very convincingly reflected in the four accompanying photographs. These featured brief brassiere tops, loose and fitting shorts, and a pair of wide-legged trousers with a mildly nautical tailored jacket.[58] The designs had been created out of new fine-weave woollen fabrics and appeared in heady colour mixtures such as striped verdigris and salmon-pink, and 'bold plaid checks in rust-red and bright azure blue'.[59]

The vogue for two-piece beach outfits revealed here was endorsed by a short article in July on the Fete de l'Eau in Paris which featured two more trunks-and-brassiere ensembles and a one-piece swimsuit in satin, all suggesting that beach wear had certainly moved on a good deal from the 'hard-wearing cotton, dyed navy blue, with a high neck-line and button shoulder-straps ... [worn] shamefacedly in your hurried trip from bathing hut to sea'.[60] Here at least history had been displaced.

April's article on 'Playsuits for Summer'[61] provided six photographs each showing quite different contemporary beach styles ranging from a softly feminine hooded beach coat and two-piece bathing ensemble to a more masculine tailored shirt and slacks outfit accompanied by a Mexican straw hat. Also on offer was a colourful, if perhaps busy ensemble of patchwork shorts and red and white check blouse, short or long skirts with matching blouses, and wide three-quarter-length 'slacks'. Choice, as in other fashion arenas, was broad. Apart from swimsuits which were 'scantier than ever', beach clothing in general, the writer believed, had moved away from 'bare-backed sun-bathing fashion' as a 'rich coppery tan doesn't go with this year's romantic, ultra-feminine fashions'. Instead 'smart women' were seeking 'Victorian lily and rose complexions' that complimented their 'Victorian and Edwardian clothes . . . pink veils and swishing skirts and embroidered petticoats by day and crinolines by night'.[62]

Clothes for a holiday camp

Holiday clothing also featured indirectly in August 1939, when *Picture Post* introduced readers to the relatively new pleasures in store at a holiday camp.[63] Felix Man's photo-story recorded the leisure activities and entertainments on offer in the 'modern, open-air, free and easy surroundings' of Butlin's, Skegness, which provided a holiday 'at a cost low enough for almost all'.[64] Writer Tom Wintringham reported that there was 'more to see and do . . . than can be achieved anywhere else by three-quarters or more of Britain's holidaymakers'.[65]

During the summer of 1939, sixty-five thousand people had visited this Butlin's camp, which could cater for four thousand residents at a time.[66] The private chalet-style accommodation and on-site entertainments, including a wide range of organized sports and all-weather activities, were offered for an all-inclusive price of '3 ½ (2 ½ off season) guineas' per adult, with no worry about unforeseen extras.[67] The photo-story captured the vitality and variety which characterized life at the camp and, in the process, the types of clothing chosen by holidaymakers for the day's activities. The range of garments and styles depicted might reasonably be supposed to represent something of what could be bought on the high street, or made at home, at price-points consonant, in general, with a week or fortnight's stay at Butlin's.[68]

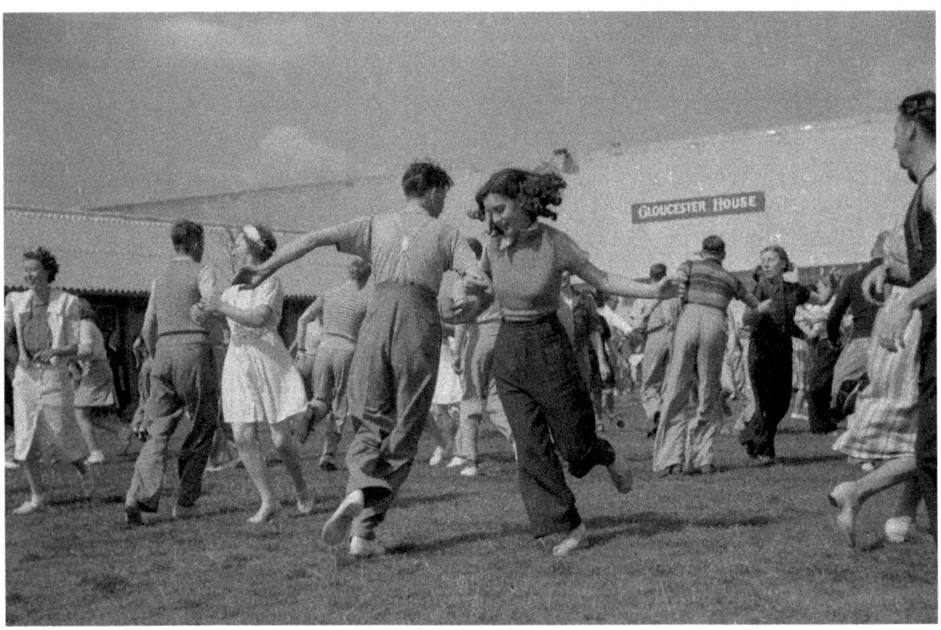

Figure 20 'Dancing on the Greens' from 'Holiday Camp', *Picture Post*, 5 August 1939, p. 45. Felix Man/*Picture Post*/Getty Images (3419054).

Holiday style in the play clothes[69] and beach-wear categories was particularly well illustrated here. Photographs revealed loose shorts and matching blouses, short, button-through play dresses, wide-legged trousers pleated to the waist, one-piece ruched swimming costumes and two-piece brassiere-and-trunks ensembles. The number of women wearing trousers and shorts for casual wear here confirms that, among younger women at least, trousers had begun to make their way into the everyday wardrobe.[70] It is also interesting to note in these images the readiness of women to wear the above-the-knee play-suit length for summer sports. Popular take-up of fashionable accessories such as white-rimmed sunglasses, practical canvas pumps and summer strap and ankle-tie sandals also suggested that fun fashions for summer were not just the preserve of the prosperous.

Fashions for cycling

Alongside of seasonal holiday clothing an ever-expanding interest in outdoor sports and pursuits had produced some interesting additions to existing leisure clothing. Cycling was one such activity that had established its own clothing protocols, examples of which were well illustrated in two *Picture Post* stories.

In 'A Day Awheel', Felix Man accompanied a group of cyclists from the Dulwich Paragon Cycling Club across the Sussex countryside introducing readers to what was now a very popular hobby.[71] Over one hundred thousand cyclists were enjoying the wider countryside on weekend escapes that offered a healthy outdoor alternative to working lives spent in 'offices, shops and factories'.[72] The hobby was cheap. A bicycle could be bought on an instalment plan and membership of one of the cycling organizations provided free advice on eating places along the route and the prices charged.[73]

Felix Man's photo-story provided a good deal of information on the clothes required. These were inexpensive and consisted of leather pump-style shoes, often with laces or a tongue detail; ankle or knee-length socks – the latter shown here in a range of spotted, plaid and plain patterns; shorts[74] (for summer cycling) and open-necked shirts. Shorts and shirts both cost around five shillings and outer wear such as a 'white or blue cotton dust-jacket ... or an elastic-waisted "golf" jacket with zipp fastener' both cost around seven shillings and sixpence. The British weather could be accommodated with a 'lightweight oiled-silk cape, leggings and sou'wester' which were the most expensive items that together cost fifteen shillings.[75]

Here was adventure on a budget with all the added benefits of healthy outdoor activity. Exercise had certainly become both fun, fashionable and affordable. From keeping fit with the Women's League for Health and Beauty to hiking and biking supported by cycling clubs and the Youth Hostels Association,[76] there is little doubt that the foundations of a new-found and extending interest in fitness were laid down during the 1930s. This in its turn was inspiring new priorities for self-presentation and the beauty blueprint that increasingly favoured a fresh-faced, outdoor naturalness and healthy vitality that derived from physical and mental well-being. The growing need to optimize the health of the nation under war conditions would only capitalize on these developments.

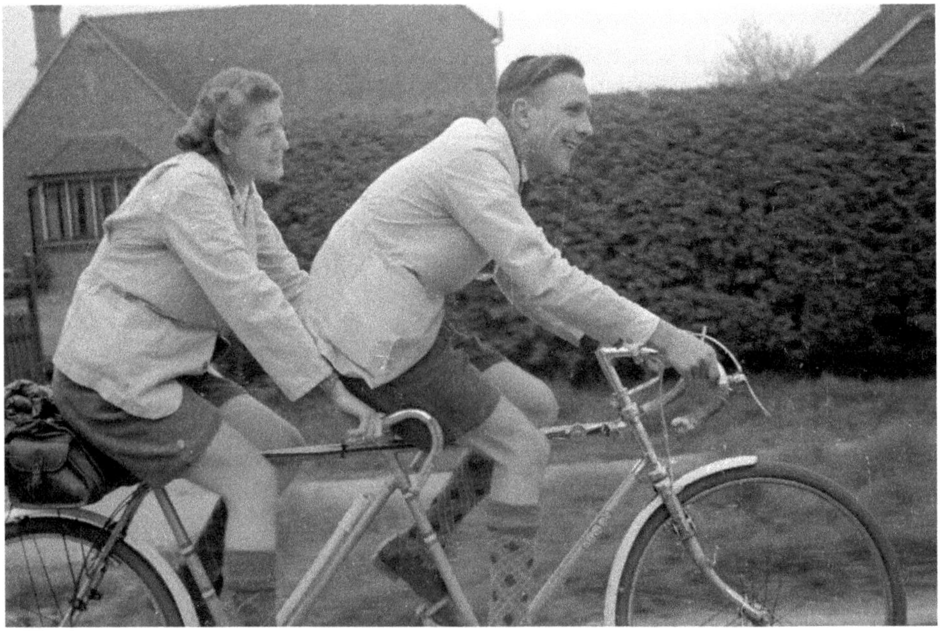

Figure 21 'Comrades of the Road: A Tandem' from 'A Day Awheel', *Picture Post*, 10 June 1939, p. 19. Felix Man/*Picture Post*/Getty Images (3400474).

The subject of cycling was returned to early in 1940 as the bike became more popular in the context of wartime petrol rationing.[77] *Picture Post* reported on the 'new cycling clothes – and the clothes to wear beneath them' that had arrived for women as a result.[78] London designers, it appeared, had recognized the impact cycling was making and had devised a series of new fashions that built on the established cycling club conventions of shorts or trousers and jackets.[79] The new styles featured well-cut trousers, breeches and matching jackets with accessorizing hoods, hats and footwear.

The photographs followed a young woman cyclist getting ready for an outing. For wearing under cycling breeches there was a woollen vest and shorts ensemble – 'a feminine version of men's underclothes'[80] – and long woollen ribbed stockings with elasticated tops that reached to the top of the shorts leaving no chilly gaps. Under long trousers there were ankle-length close-fitting jersey pants. Outerwear showed a tweed two-piece of breeches and jacket from the International Wool Secretariat, and a Jaeger trouser suit in wool and camel hair with trouser turn-ups[81] and a jacket featuring knitted sleeves and back. Trousers were wide and jackets buttoned either to a round neck or in the Norfolk style with it's 'short lapels and capacious pockets'.[82]

The final photograph of the cycling suit in action – complete with hood, trousers tucked into wool socks, flat suede shoes and over-the-shoulder satchel bag – produced a wintry mix of past and present as the warm ski resort style of the 'St Moritz holidaymaker' now also contained a 'hint of the Finnish soldier' in the warm winter hood.[83] If these clothes appeared less conventionally feminine the writer's last anecdote restored an arguably more traditional perspective. A young, smartly dressed woman cyclist had recently entered the Ritz. Readers were told that she was 'unconcerned' because:

> She was as chic as anyone else, with her tailored dress of grey-striped, light-weight wool, the divided skirt cut so that it fell in symmetry with the stripes, indistinguishable from an ordinary skirt. Her little black-velvet boater was securely held against the wind by elastic. Her coiffeur was perfect beneath her invisible hair net.

Here were neat, established lines upholding a feminine style status quo and revealing that there could be two sides to 'Petrol-Ration Fashions'.[84]

The need for recreational styles that were easy-wear and functional had continued to promote trousers for women. While they had featured pre-war in summer casual collections, as we have seen, and less often as working clothes, trousers had remained peripheral elements of most female wardrobes, particularly in the face of the ultra-feminine designs that immediately preceded hostilities. With the advent of war this situation began to change. There was little doubt as to the practical benefits women now derived by wearing trousers. While they would not displace traditional female wardrobe staples their adoption played a part in the process of undermining gendered preconceptions about clothing. *Picture Post* readers would later be asked whether they thought women should wear trousers in an article written by Anne Scott-James – herself pictured wearing trousers – and photographed by Bert Hardy.[85]

Uniforms

A number of new roles were emerging for women in the immediate pre-war and early wartime period that also required suitable forms of clothing, including trousers, and that in general placed emphasis on the utilitarian and serviceable elements of dress at the expense of more feminine design. For women in civilian life these types of dress tended to be for part-time training and auxiliary service roles, and they added to, rather than in any way replaced, existing clothing.

In October 1938 for example, *Picture Post* visited the Romford Flying Club at Chigwell to find out about the recently formed National Women's Air Reserve.[86] Begun as a drive to get new members, the Reserve had proved so popular that a nationwide scheme had been started under the auspices of Gabrielle Patterson, pilot and the first woman air instructor in Britain. The uniform for the three hundred women currently in training at Romford comprised white overalls and blue scarves, beret and badge and could be bought for 'well under a pound'.[87] The beret sat to the right side of the head, while the overalls were belted at the waist, had large front pockets, small lapels and buttoned left to the neck where the blue scarf was worn like a cravat. Photographs revealed no standardization as yet for shoes although the recruits appeared to have stuck to practical flats. This uniform, described as 'business-like',[88] was neat and simple, with no obvious feminization reflecting, as with a good deal of uniform, an identification with a role and function to which gender necessarily remained subordinate.

In a similar vein civil defence uniforms also often comprised of overalls or two-piece jacket and trouser battledress such as those worn by civilian women ambulance drivers and Air Raid Precaution wardens, one sixth of whom were women.[89] A full-time service that provided no formal skirt as part of the uniform, *only* different types of trouser, was the

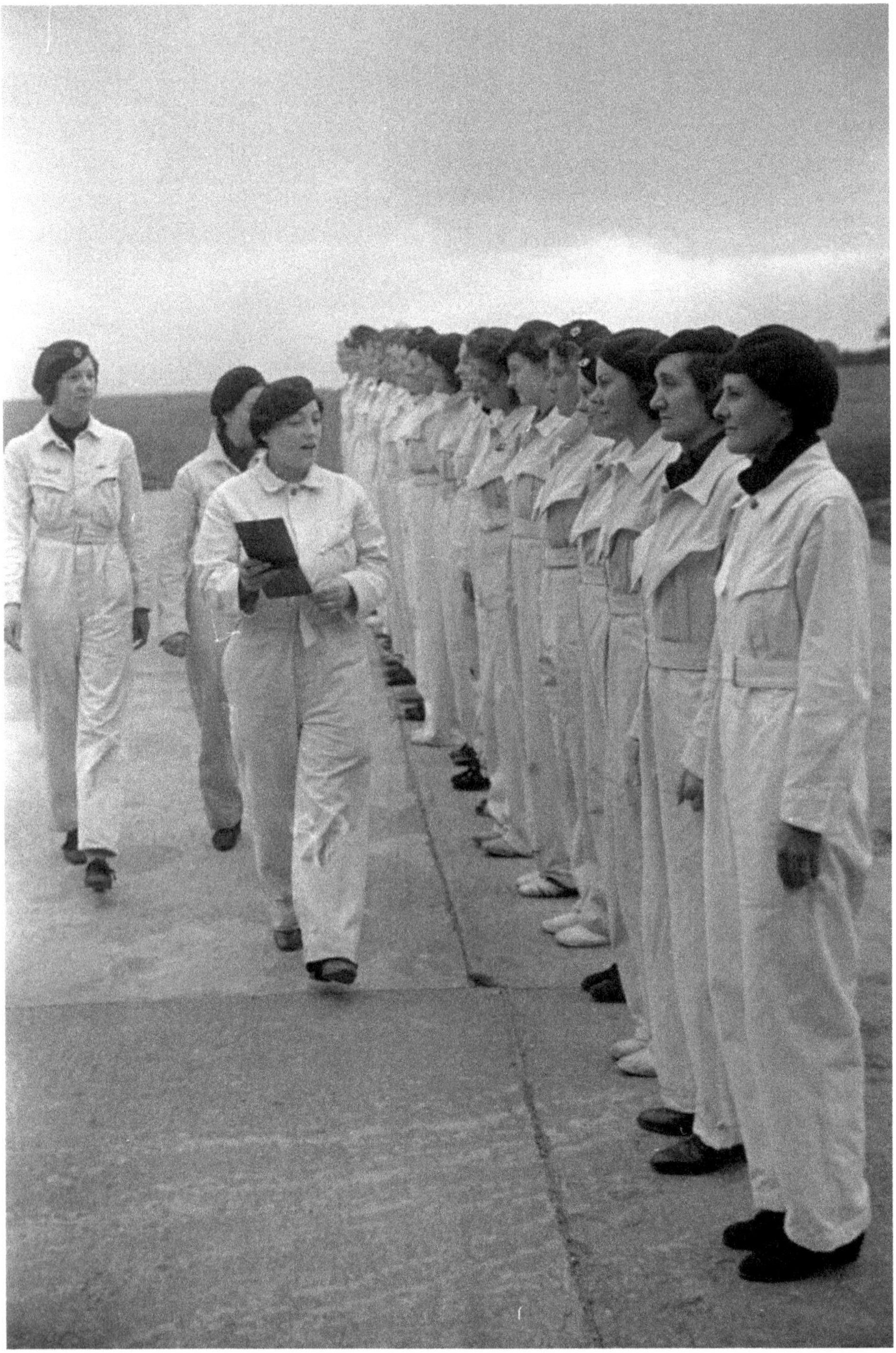

Figure 22 'Start of the Day: Sunday Morning Roll-Call ... Two stars on the tunic mark the flight leader'. From 'Girl Pilots', *Picture Post*, 22 October 1938, p. 48. Kurt Hutton/*Picture Post*/Getty Images (3368309).

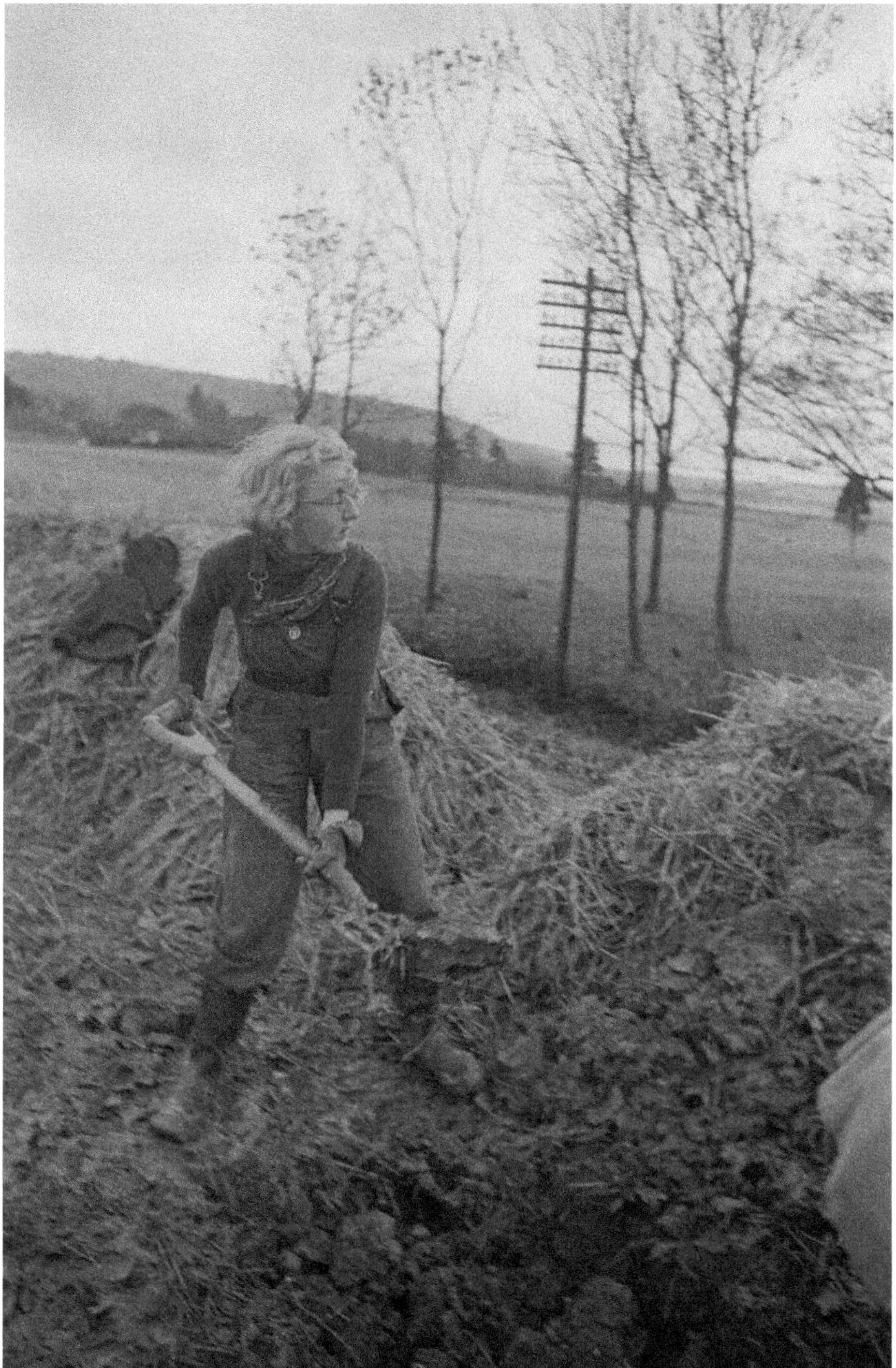

Figure 23 'Horticulture: Earthing a Potato Clamp'. 'This was the Women's Land Army', *Picture Post*, January 1940, p. 34. Haywood Magee/Picture Post/Hulton Archive/Getty Images (984851262).

Women's Land Army. These are well illustrated in an article called 'This was the Women's Land Army' which appeared in *Picture Post* on 13 January 1940.

Photographer Haywood Magee captured the different types of work for which Land Army women were being prepared while writer Douglas MacDonald Hastings reviewed the recruitment, training and take-up of women into the service by this time.[90] The article provided vivid images of life on the land and the functional, fit-for-purpose clothing that was now the everyday uniform of Land Army farm workers. Here were outfits of bib-and-brace dungarees, rubber boots and ribbed woollen jumpers, jodhpurs, jackets and headscarves, field overcoats, overalls and milking coats and hats.[91] Entirely practical, warm when needed and providing easy movement, these clothes established again the priority of functionality over a more traditional notion of femininity.

Conclusion

This chapter has investigated the various clothing practices and protocols that were current as Britain entered the last year of peace and the first few months of war. Fashion experienced a final exuberant flowering. Day and evening clothes referenced any number of styles from the past as well as soft contemporary tailoring. There were fun fashions for holidays and practical leisure and sports ensembles for days off and days out. As Britain transitioned from peace to war between 1938 and 1940 and the Auxiliary and Civil Defence forces became established, uniform of one sort or another also became a more commonplace wardrobe item.

The established conventions of feminine clothing that resided primarily in variants of the dress or skirt now increasingly accepted incursions by masculine elements to create practical, unfussy outfits as required. The traditional contours of femininity and feminine beauty would, however, continue to retain currency through a simpler less-adorned aesthetic and a healthy vitality consonant with the developing circumstances of wartime living. From fashion's final fling to fashion as a fighting force, *Picture Post* was there to capture the shifts and variations in dress protocols, practical living and the beauty blueprint.

3
PICTURE POST SHOWS LIFE ON LESS

Introduction

The previous chapter has explored seasonal styles and the types of clothing available that could be acquired – by those with the means to do so – to be fashionable, to have fun or to reflect new training or service work. Working to the same time frame, October 1938 to spring 1940, this chapter focuses on how dress functions as a component of the material culture of communities, which, to varying degrees, had to live life on less. *Picture Post* visited, for example, working-class communities in Whitechapel, Lambeth, Peckham, Stepney and Shoreditch, each of which revealed discrete levels of social hardship and economic struggle as a result of factors such as low pay, unemployment, ill-health or poor housing. Photojournalism provided a compelling medium through which the material culture of working-class lives could be both witnessed and more widely recognized, if not necessarily fully understood. Information on dress practice arises therefore indirectly from these stories as one of a number of elements of the broader material culture of home and community that represented how people from different working-class neighbourhoods lived and worked.

In exploring the nature and extent of disadvantage as it was reflected across a number of locations, it becomes clearer how the descent into poverty happened and to what effect. Clothing was just one of several commodities in the cost-of-living index that had to come out of a household budget covering rent, food, heating and lighting. On this basis the pursuit of enough and adequate clothing could be a struggle and garment choice was more often the outcome of an equation between price and need rather than fashion. The stories are, therefore, as much about the people, places and problems that together conditioned *how clothes were acquired and worn* as they are about the clothes themselves.

Living on less in Whitechapel and Lambeth

Picture Post's photo-stories from Whitechapel[1] and Lambeth[2] arguably did *not* reflect the acute poverty that existed elsewhere – either in London or further afield – yet both were clearly very poor. Whitechapel was described as 'London's Ghetto', with its mean streets and lanes, while Lambeth Walk exhibited 'severe poverty'.[3] Despite this both areas displayed an individual spirit and character acquired from the mix of peoples, work and leisure interests that together forged distinctive identities. Both photo-stories were taken by Humphrey Spender, with East End author William Cameron providing the text for 'Whitechapel' and local resident Ada Barber for 'Life in the Lambeth Walk'. Humphrey Spender's gift for social documentary, combined with the local knowledge and understanding of each author, provided an authentic and vivid picture of life in these two London neighbourhoods. Both economically stretched, they nevertheless manifested a specific and diverse social culture and sense of community.

Perhaps one of the most surprising things to emerge from Spender's photographs of Whitechapel was that despite the unprepossessing brick housing and tenements pictured and images of the 'mean and narrow streets',[4] Whitechapel residents appeared well turned out. Here were men of all ages largely wearing formal two- or three-piece suits, both for work and leisure. Collars and ties and waistcoats were popular, and outfits were often completed with bowler hats, trilbies or flat caps – the latter in use both with formal and informal dress. Attention was clearly paid to personal appearance and presentation. The same was true for women. Housework might be undertaken in aprons or housecoats,[5] but Spender captured other images: classic suits for shopping, a smart Sunday coat and hat, satin tops and silver shoes for dancing on a Saturday night and the coordinated coats, skirts and white high-heeled shoes worn by two young women pictured sitting outside on a warm day.

This ability to appear well dressed provides an interesting contrast with the environment in which the wearers moved. Cameron believed that 'the meanest street in Whitechapel

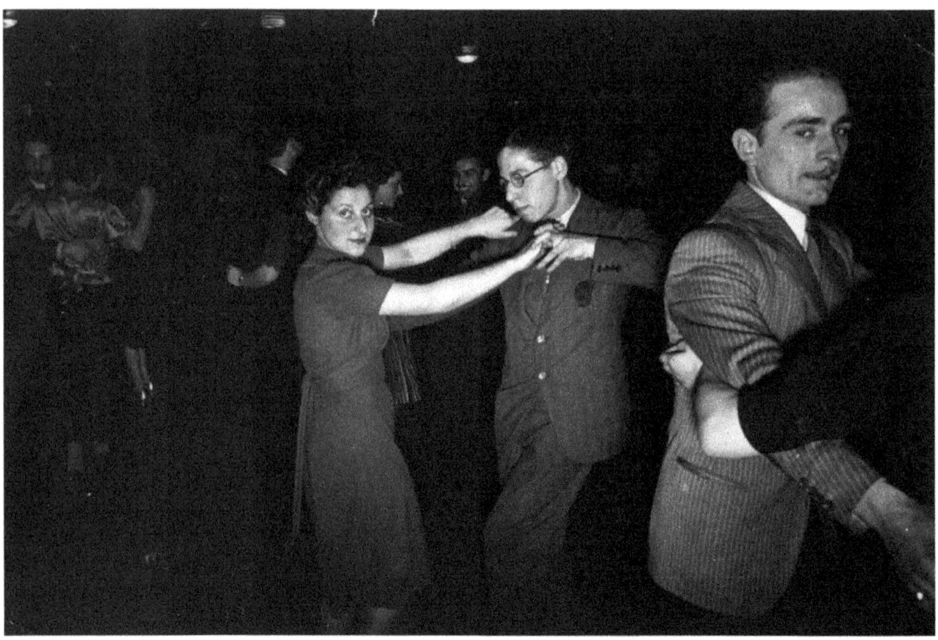

Figure 24 'Saturday Evening in a Dance Hall', from 'Whitechapel', *Picture Post*, 15 October 1938, p. 28. Humphrey Spender/*Picture Post*/Getty Images (3292364).

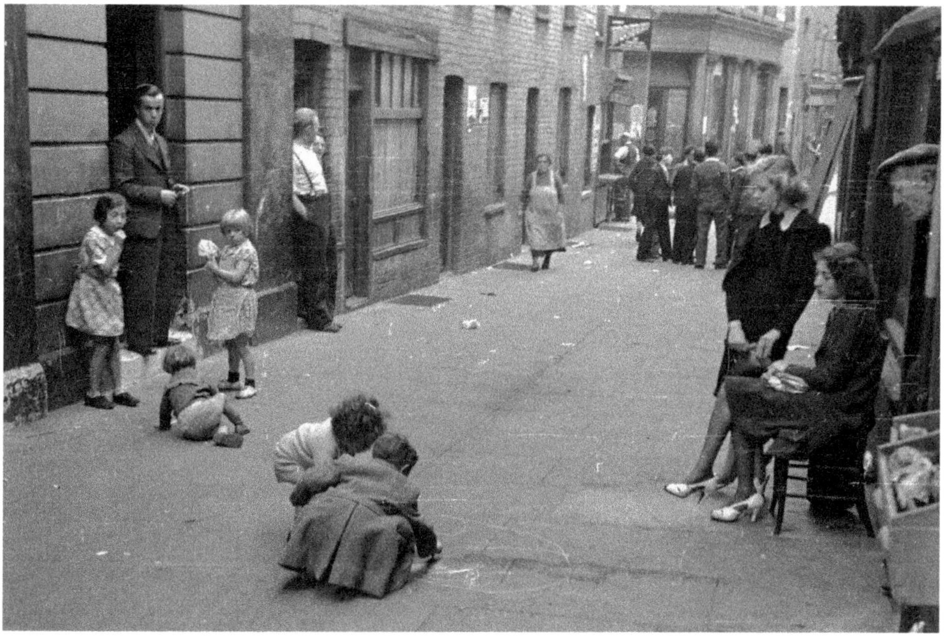

Figure 25 'Street Scene in Whitechapel', 'Whitechapel', *Picture Post*, 15 October 1938, p. 25. Humphrey Spender/*Picture Post*/Getty Images (3367644).

has a positive quality that you will find nowhere else in London. The East End is not ashamed. Its people are not crushed'.[6] Some sense of this 'positive quality' is surely reflected in the way clothes had been used to communicate a smartness and sense of style that signalled Whitechapel people resisting being defined by the 'ghetto' they called home.

Clothing as an aspect of the material culture of Whitechapel featured in several different ways. Some people made their living from tailoring, the 'schneiderman's ... game', learning to cope with its seasonal nature and the need to 'pull in your belt' as plentiful work gave way to none.[7] Spender's photographs of a fabric trader and a doorstep clothing shop provided a visual counterpart for Cameron's contention that 'nearly every house is a shop, and wrinkled old women bring out their goods from the front parlour and display them on the railings and steps'.[8] Shopping itself was 'not like shopping in the West End or the suburbs' but carried out by 'bargaining, done mainly on the pavement'.[9] Spender even captured four older men bartering a second-hand jacket 'by private treaty', a reminder that 'everything has a value in Whitechapel. You may think your coat worn-out, but someone will get life out of it'.[10] The making, selling and buying of clothing was clearly an everyday part of community life in Whitechapel. Doorstep shops and the informal haggling and negotiation that lay at the heart of the shopping process may also infer that in one way or another clothing might be acquired, no matter how little could be spent. The generally well-turned-out residents of Whitechapel seemed to bear testimony to this.

A similar story emerged from Lambeth. The leading image of a well-dressed elderly woman out on the Lambeth Walk set the tone for the feature. Wearing a coat with a generous fur-stole collar and decorated pillbox hat, she reflected a standard of formal dressing for leaving the house that was maintained by almost all the other women photographed, young or old, at leisure, in the pub or out shopping around the market stalls. Fur-collared coats were plentiful and the range of hats, from toques, Bretons and pillboxes to cloches, an ornate Tam O'Shanter and a woman's fedora, was particularly remarkable. Very few women were pictured hat-less.

While Lambeth was a poor area it maintained a 'racy and vigorous life of its own'[11] and certainly the photographs reflected a clear premium placed on dressing well despite life's difficulties. Spender's image of the row of dreary, brick-built terraced houses, unrelieved by grass or trees, bore witness to a poverty of circumstance considerably at variance with the generally smart and often stylish appearance of the Lambeth residents pictured. Yet the cheap meals provided by the hot-pie and stewed eel saloons, and the cramped, dingy backyard where the washing had to be hung, told a different story of straightened means and restricted living. Out of these circumstances appearing well-turned-out might well have been something of a victory against the grim surroundings and hardships of the everyday.

Life in Whitechapel or the Lambeth Walk might be trying but neither Spender nor Cameron and Barber portrayed these communities as either destitute or living in intolerable conditions. The 'almost aggressive vitality of life'[12] Cameron witnessed in Whitechapel spoke for a hardy capacity to withstand life's limitations, while an ability to keep up appearances reflected something of the human dignity that resided in the right clothing.

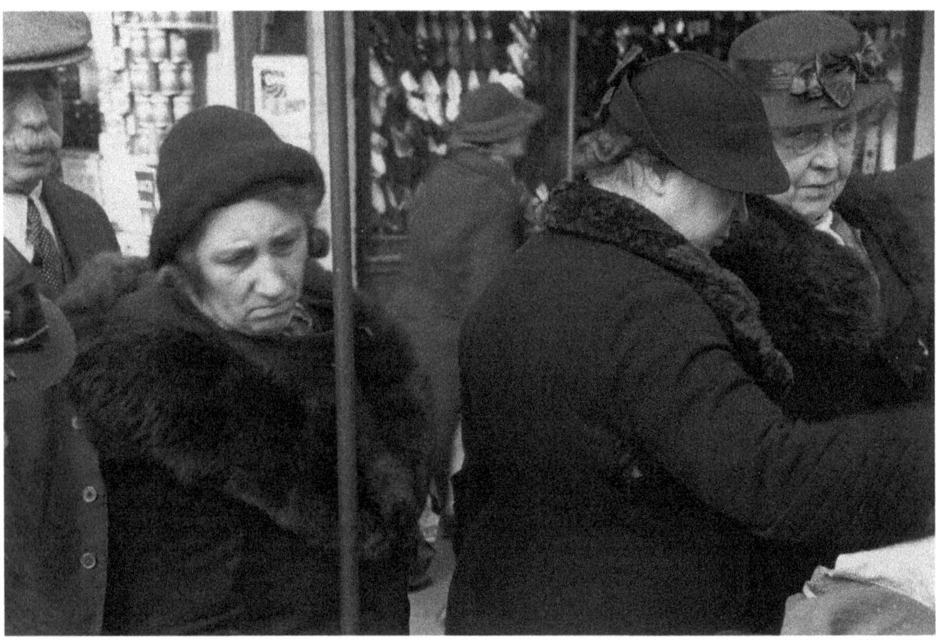

Figure 26 'Expressions In the Street Market: Dubious'. From 'Life in the Lambeth Walk', *Picture Post*, 31 December 1938, p. 52. Humphrey Spender/*Picture Post*/Getty Images (3438149).

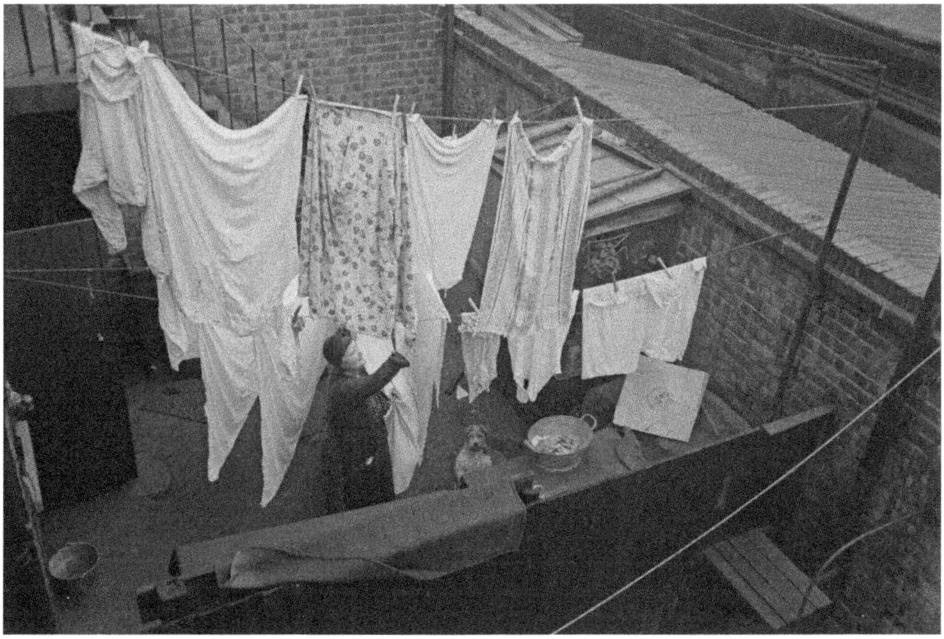

Figure 27 'Washing-day in the Backyards. "Especially if you've a big family it's hard to do the wash properly. We could all do with a bit more room"'. 'Life in the Lambeth Walk', *Picture Post*, 31 December 1938, p. 50. Humphrey Spender/*Picture Post*/Hulton Archive/Getty Images (984851280).

This was not so for some other areas Cameron knew of – those he described as having 'crumpled up under the pressure of poverty. Sometimes a whole street seems to be lying as if crushed, and even their shabby windows have a way of looking at you with shame and humiliation. Streets are like people, and some of them can't stand being poor'.[13] Home to some of the poorer and poorest communities in Britain, these streets and houses were evidence of a deprivation wherein everyday life was a remorseless struggle to survive on the slimmest of means.

Living on even less

Picture Post confronted the reality of this type of life on less in two ways.

- In the first instance it introduced readers to what it was like to live with the consequences of *long-term unemployment* by recording the day of an unemployed man from Peckham who had been out of work for three years.[14]
- In a second story it investigated the iniquitous and unhealthy living conditions prevailing in Stepney that had given rise to a 'recently discovered' form of social resistance – *the rent strike*.[15]

Images depicting the material culture of families and local communities provided disturbing evidence of the harsh reality of poverty, from bleak and cheerless local surroundings to the distressing deprivation of domestic life. In both cases either clothing or elements of the domestic interior contributed graphic and evocative parts of the photo-story.

Unemployment: The Smith family

During the Christmas holidays of 1938–1939, Kurt Hutton and Sydney Jacobson followed unemployed spray enamel worker Alf Smith on a typical day as he collected his unemployment pay and looked for work. A major cause of poverty at this time, unemployment affected over one and three-quarter million people in Britain.[16] With a wife and four children under ten – none born since he became unemployed – a good deal about the Smiths' life on the dole emerged.[17] They lived off unemployment assistance of 47s. 6d. a week from which they paid 14s. 6d. rent, 1s. 8d. insurance and 6s. for heating and lighting. The biggest expense after these essentials was food at 22s. a week which bought a relatively poor diet featuring bread and potatoes, a little meat and fish and 'very occasionally fresh fruit or greens'.[18] With what was left, 6s. was paid to clothing clubs after which the benefit had not only run out but on average the family had accrued a small but regular debt 'of about 4s'.[19]

Home was a damp tenement in Peckham which Jacobson described as offering a ground-floor bedroom and a basement living room with small kitchen where much of the space was taken up by a stove and sink. The basement had little natural light as half the living room window was below ground level and Hutton's photograph of this sash window – lowered against the area railings – offered a disturbing image of bars imprisoning the family, an apt metaphor for the fearful trap of unemployment.

Outside, the family had an 'unspeakably grim' backyard and there was no mention of any bathroom or toilet facilities. Jacobson praised Mrs Smith for her 'hard work' and 'scrupulous cleanliness' maintaining the tenement despite its deficiencies and sparse resources – resources further alluded to in the austere domestic interior where the Smiths were photographed eating.[20] This picture also captured the neat haircuts of both Alf Smith and his sons Peter and John. A letter that appeared in the 11 February issue of *Picture Post* talked of 'cheap haircuts' and 'baths' among other benefits for the unemployed.[21] Whether or not the Smith family had taken advantage of these some premium had clearly been placed on being as well turned out as might be possible.

Hutton's photographs revealed the twin trials of the unemployed life – the dreary round of claiming benefit while looking for work, and the domestic strain of providing a warm home, adequate food and clothing amid an unwholesome and depressing environment that afforded few, if any, of the material comforts associated with home life.

As Hutton and Jacobson's visit had coincided with Alf's weekly pay day, several of the photographs depicted the Smiths shopping. If Alf Smith felt as tired and worn as his baggy jacket and trousers looked, Mrs Smith and the children at least appeared relatively well turned out for a cold January day – the children in winter coats, wearing hats or caps and two of them with big scarves. Mrs Smith wore a neat toque trimmed with a small run of flowers, while oldest daughter Frances wore a cloche with a turned-back brim.

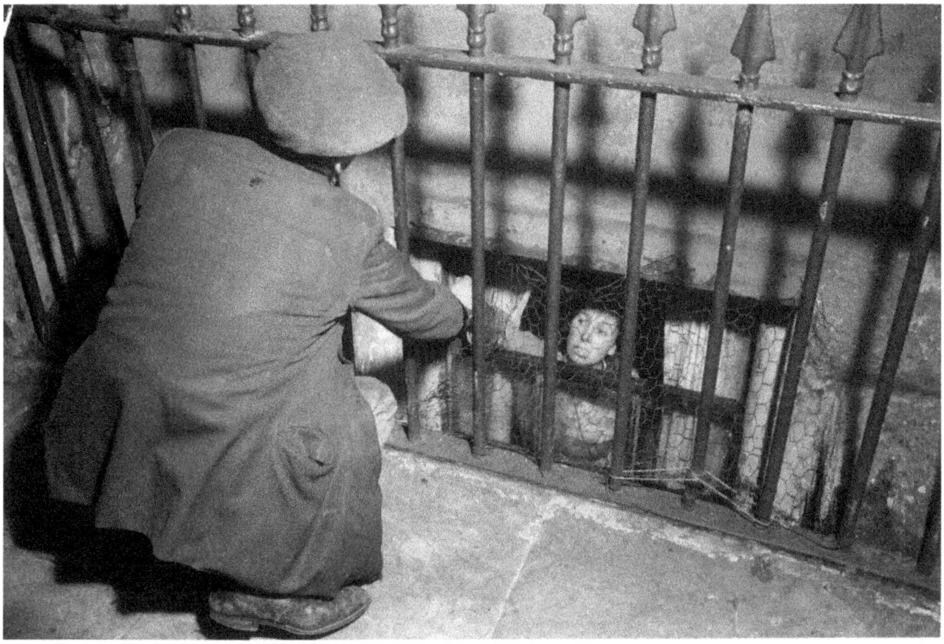

Figure 28 'After a Whole Day Looking for a Job, Alfred Smith Comes Home'. *Picture Post*, 21 January 1939, p. 18. Kurt Hutton/*Picture Post*/Getty Images (3367375).

These pictures can't reveal either the quality or durability of the clothing worn. They reflected, nevertheless, a family doing what it could, in terms of warm and sufficient clothing for winter, particularly given three out of the four children were not in good health. Mrs Smith was photographed browsing a market stall for 'cheap oddments – a pair of stockings for Frances, some shoes for Peter, a scarf for Edna'.[22] A winter blanket for the children's bed was found to be too expensive to buy in a shop rendering the cheaper street stalls the more affordable option.

In terms of buying clothing, readers were also informed that Mrs Smith paid an amount of money each week to 'clothing clubs'.[23] There is no further information given, but clubs of this sort were much used to buy goods in weekly instalments. Some of the older-established and local varieties genuinely endeavoured to help poorer families buy clothing on a very limited budget. Others simply exploited the poor by selling low-quality goods at inflated prices that included commercial operating premiums. This was an iniquitous system that sold badly made garments that would not last to those who most needed durability and longevity out of their few, necessary purchases.[24]

With regard to the use of such clubs, *Picture Post* carried a letter a couple of weeks later from a reader who 'as a working man's wife' said she would not 'dare spend 6s a week on clothing clubs, rather two' although she does not say how many children she had to clothe.[25] The clear inference was that 6s was too much on such a limited budget. Yet Jacobson had reported that Mrs Smith was a 'good "manager"' buying 'carefully in the cheapest market' and making very limited resources 'go a long way'.[26] Readers were left to speculate on whether spending nearly a quarter of the remaining weekly income

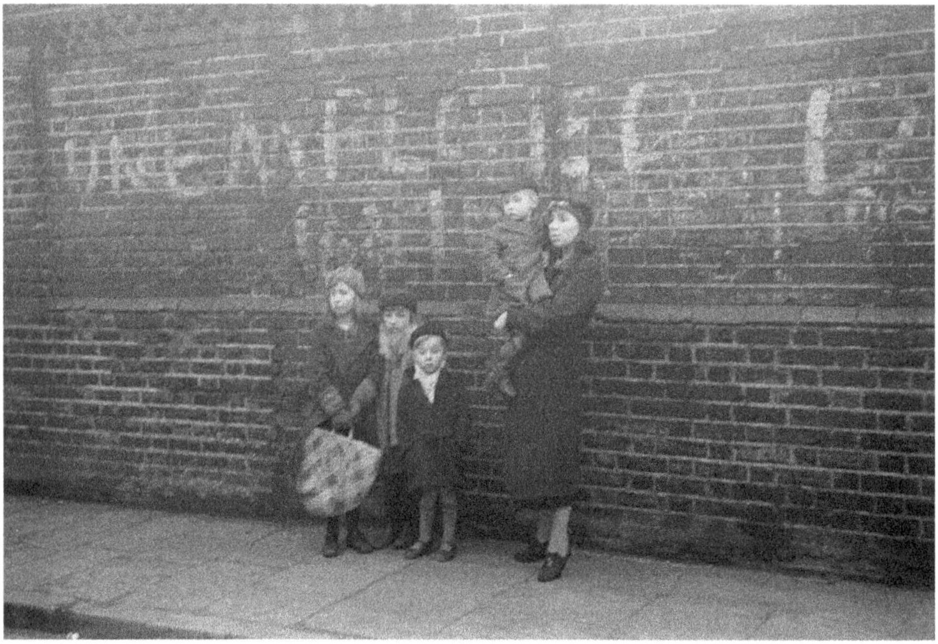

Figure 29 'Outside: Wife and Children Wait'. Alfred Smith's wife and children wait for him to pick up his unemployment benefit before going shopping. 'All last week's money was spent two days ago'. 'Unemployed', *Picture Post*, 21 January 1939, p. 13. Kurt Hutton/*Picture Post*/Hulton Archive/Getty Images (984851994).

in this manner had been less a matter of choice than of necessity. Some clothing needs had, perhaps, to be met for health and well-being, no matter how limited the budget, and met from whatever sources were offered despite incurring hardship.

The Smiths were reported as saying they could 'only live by getting into debt'. When something was needed – shoes or blankets were mentioned – readers were informed the family went without other things such as 'cutting down on food, or heat or light'.[27] This suggested that, in general, short-term going-without was preferable to increasing longer-term debt. Such were the necessities of life with which the unemployed and their families had to juggle and the constant struggle of living on less.

Only the low visibility of such genuine need, and a failure to confront the difficulties inherent in living on such slender means, could account for the poverty and privation of some children evacuated from slum areas in the autumn of 1939.[28] This was graphically revealed in the inadequate, poor-quality clothing with which some children arrived in the reception areas, associated with having had too little for too long. The existence of such poverty was both shocking and disturbing. While the Smiths did not *seem* to reflect this level of deprivation, their struggle to buy the things they needed at a price they could afford might well have made acquiring the clothing and toilet items stipulated for evacuees a real stretch – if it was even possible at all.

Fortunately circumstances changed for the Smith family. By the 11 February issue of *Picture Post*, Alf Smith was writing to thank readers for all their encouragement and to let them know that, as a result of the *Picture Post* article, he now had a job![29] Another result of the story had been readers offering help for the unemployed through charitable giving.[30] Reader K. W. believed the state needed to 'make a realistic attempt to deal with . . . the causes of unemployment' and expressed the view that 'charity is a balm for the conscience of those who refuse to recognise the misery that does exist'.[31]

While charity was clearly not the answer to the plight of unemployment, it was the basis for a good deal of philanthropic giving. By 25 February Joan Marsham for the Personal Services League[32] was thanking readers for the 'gifts of clothing for both women and children'. She went on to say that the League had 'needed all the garments we could get hold of during this very cold winter, for there has been a great deal of suffering among the people of the Depressed Areas, and it has been our most earnest wish to relieve as much of this distress as we possibly could'. A London address was given where readers could send their parcels of clothing direct.[33] Urgent need would continue to be ameliorated by charitable giving later in the year as the difficulties of some evacuating children emerged and as government response to the problem was slow and inefficient.[34] These schemes set important contemporary precedents for the donation of clothing so that by the onset of blitz conditions in September 1940, a good deal of sophisticated, civilian-based, infrastructure existed for the receiving and distributing of gifted clothing and domestic textiles.[35]

On 11 March *Picture Post* returned to Peckham to see how Alf Smith and his family were getting on now that Alf was back in work. After the original article had appeared, the family had received gifts of:

> money, food, cigarettes, clothes. Someone gave them a new suitcase filled with clothes for Smith. Mrs Smith got dresses, a fine overcoat with fur collar, shoes and handbag. A whole cupboard full of clothes, scarves and shoes came for the children; so did chocolates and toys.[36]

The description of the generosity of readers and their desire to help was, and remains, moving. Gift clothing not only allowed more of the family budget to go on food, but it also represented the provision of warmth and well-being for the care-worn and weary. Another job offer, entailing a move to the Cornish countryside, now held out the prospect of a healthier outdoor life for the Smiths' ailing children and an escape from the damp and confinement of slum living. Possibly the 'most significant aspect' of the story, the writer suggested in closing, was the 'number of people who wrote that, until they saw the article, they did not realise what Unemployment really meant'. The article finished: 'For twenty years unemployment has been a major problem in this country. One man has been rescued. But there are today over 2,000,000 others out of work.'[37] It would take a world war to remedy this situation.

The rent-strike

The second way of revealing what life was like living on less saw *Picture Post* investigating the rise of the 'rent-strike' and the living conditions in certain slum areas of London which had given rise to this new social phenomenon. 'Enough of All This!'[38] contained two stories running simultaneously. The photographic sequence focused on how living in such conditions had impacted on the children. The text meanwhile informed readers about what the residents had decided to do to reduce their rents and obtain the necessary, and often long overdue, repairs and renovations that would improve their quality of life. The material culture revealed within this photo-story – the type and quality of local buildings, details of domestic interiors, elements of domestic life – conveyed with shocking clarity the unhealthy and detrimental environment in which people had been forced to live.

For readers whose homes were not like this, the images of undecorated, comfortless rooms, sometimes without any natural light, and of walls 'so damp they are continually dripping', might well have been appalling.[39] The opening two pictures of children growing up in conditions of harrowing poverty remain shocking: a little girl sitting on the floor in a dark and dismal room, bare walls awaiting redecoration, playing with a cat; a little boy, carrying a small child, standing in a bleak and neglected tenement entrance with damp walls. A dank, forbidding place.

The full-page photograph of the Shoreditch backyards that followed was dire. Here in the dirty and rat-infested spaces between the grim outhouses, some of the children played and clean washing was hung out to dry. Everywhere appeared enclosed, dark, airless. Tenants were forced not only to live in these abhorrent and unhygienic conditions but to pay such high rents for them that too little money was left to feed families adequately.

The photo-story continued by showing a crowd of local children queuing outside the Hoxton Market Mission for dinner, which 'for many' was 'their one square meal of the day'.[40] The children looked suitably dressed in jumpers and coats for the still cool temperatures of early spring and neatly turned out. Readers, however, now knew the environments from which they came and something of the struggle it may well have been to keep a warm, wholesome home and provide fresh clothing. The children might not have appeared unhealthy, but did appearance belie reality? One photograph captured a large placard slung between two tenement windows bearing the slogan: 'Cleaner houses Heal their Children',[41] arguably inferring the harm that could emanate from less wholesome conditions. Poverty of circumstance, exploitation and ill health comprised a spiral of deprivation which simply had to be ended.

The text explained how local residents had joined together in rent-strikes against the unfair and unwarranted rental agreements they had been forced to enter into. The results had been outstanding. Initial success in getting landlords to agree to both rebates and repairs had brought a growing number of tenants into a new League, which now continued to fight for reasonable rents and 'a civilised standard of accommodation'. Not only had tenants more money for food in their pockets. To further their access to a healthier way of life, the League had organized 'a series of lectures by professors of hygiene'[42] who would, no doubt, have underscored the necessary relationship between environment and health.

The photo-story revealed the distressing reality of tenement living and a form of poverty that had been overlooked by both local and central government. The camera cannot tell us how healthy, well fed or suitably dressed the families of Stepney and other East End locations might really have been. We can infer from the words on the placard, and from the images taken both inside and outside of homes, that keeping up domestic standards and maintaining well-being had been an arduous and relentless task. This story proved the existence of a type of poverty and social injustice that exploited already poor and vulnerable families, limiting their access to better diet and tolerable, fit-for-purpose living conditions and the quality of life commensurate with both.

Evacuation and the confrontation with poverty

On 16 September 1939, in *Picture Post's* 'How the War Began' feature, which took up most of the issue, the mass evacuation of children from London was caught on camera. Photographs showed school children, with their suitcases, bags, gas masks and name labels round their necks, leaving for unknown destinations in long orderly lines. The exodus had started on Friday 1 September, and by the following Monday, the day after war between Britain and Germany had been officially declared, six hundred thousand vulnerable adults and children of all ages had arrived at reception areas.[43]

Little in the photographs of these children in *Picture Post* could have alerted readers to the outcry that followed. Those evacuated from some of the poorest areas of Britain took with them the only clothes they possessed and the only way of life they knew. Sometimes both were in stark contrast to the living conditions and standards of behaviour of their new host families. Much has subsequently been said of this confrontation between classes and lifestyles, and it was not something for which there had been any preparation, either by central government or the education authorities organizing the evacuation scheme. *Picture Post* with characteristic even-handedness published letters from both the happy and the unhappy, hosts and evacuees, providing something of an overview of the problems that had arisen.[44]

Some slum children from Liverpool had arrived with inadequate clothing which their hosts had felt duty bound to supplement for them, while others from the city appeared to be unfamiliar with basic hygiene – soiling floors, bedclothes and beds. After the first night 'dozens of beds had to be burnt'.[45] Some London evacuees had brought lice to their new homes and also ruined mattresses. The abrupt encounter between different backgrounds and behaviours caused by evacuation placed a good deal of strain on the good will necessary for the scheme to work. The extraordinary gulf that divided the haves and have-nots was now laid bare.

Picture Post also published a letter from a schoolboy who had been 'involved' in an evacuation of 'clean [London] children ... to dirty homes' without 'sanitation ... light [or] water ... one lavatory between two cottages' and large rats in the yard.[46] Either way the collision of two worlds was both shocking and disturbing. One reader saw the impoverished evacuees as victims of 'capitalist greed', another fourteen-and-a-half-year-old evacuee wrote tellingly of her sympathies for slum children placed in middle-class homes where they 'must feel as if they do not belong'. She suggested this was an opportunity not for grumbling but to 'teach the children how to be clean, self-respecting citizens' as a 'service to both the country and the children themselves'.[47]

Conclusion – lessons from the dispossessed

The problems raised by evacuation only confirmed the hideous inequalities that existed within British society. Alf Smith had described the unemployed as 'the forgotten people with nothing to look forward to but years of scraping along on the dole'.[48] They, together with others on the lowest of incomes, had to contend with the frustration and distress of everyday life amid cheerless and discouraging conditions that offered little in the way of material comfort or hope for the future. The rent-strike alone reflected that citizen voices could be heard and count. *Picture Post* was there to see and tell.

If Britain was to fight as a unified nation, all its citizens had to have equal access to life's necessities and more in return. A new spirit of fair shares had to be enshrined in social policy to reflect the equality of the wartime struggle.

Over two and a half years later *Picture Post* began a new series considering how Britain was 'being shaped by the war' and the effect it might be having on the British people. The first contributor to the series was writer and broadcaster J. B. Priestley. In an article entitled 'Britain's Silent Revolution', he recalled the 'fantastically gross and really sinful inequalities' of pre-war life, when there had existed a 'vast army of unemployed, ill-nourished and hopeless masses who felt that a curse lay heavy on their whole generation'.[49] For the many previously dispossessed and deprived, war, with a great and sad irony, had brought paid work and a better, more secure standard of living. Priestley expressed the view that war had saved Britain from the threat of social 'decay' and now more than ever was the time to reject the old social order that had led to such unfairness and 'go forward to something much better or to something even worse. But there is no return'. War had required people to 'think and act differently' as new priorities for living presented themselves. Out of war Britain now had a 'great chance to fashion a really healthy society'.[50]

4
BRITAIN AND THE FIRST FASHIONS OF WAR

Introduction

As Britain acclimatized to the condition of being at war, more and more women began to take up paid employment beyond the home in the new war industries or civilian home-front services. Each of these occupations had their own appropriate forms of dress and the population became increasingly used to seeing women in overalls, work trousers or other forms of uniform. These were not fashions in the usual sense of the word, but reflected the new currency of practical hardwearing attire right for the job in hand. Trousers increasingly became part of this alternative working wardrobe, not without some concern expressed by those who felt the established conventions of female clothing were being undermined. Women were also now joining the armed services in greater numbers, and until early 1940 service dress had to be worn even on home leave.[1] There was, as a result, a much higher visibility of uniform of one sort or another intermingling with the everyday working and domestic clothing of the general population.

Picture Post photographed some of the ways women were now being employed within the new war-related industries or community services, further publicizing both the growing need to employ women as the country mobilized for war and the ever-widening lexicon of occupational dress that was helping to fashion a developing war aesthetic. The first section of this chapter, therefore, investigates how *Picture Post* stories reflected some of the new employment challenges and the extent to which forms of dress and self-presentation accommodated themselves to these and to the new surroundings women were now entering. The second section of the chapter will explore *Picture Post*'s coverage of the changing face and fortunes of fashion during the earlier years of the war and how fashion retained its relevance despite the various factors that now began to operate against it.

Wartime workwear for women

ARP warden attire

The 4 November 1939 edition of *Picture Post* ran a double-page photo-feature on Valerie Hudson who, at just seventeen, was a fully trained ARP warden.[2] With the magazine's predictable interest in glamour, the focus of the story was the dual role performed by Valerie, who attended to ARP duties when not employed by the Windmill Theatre as a showgirl. While the photographs of Windmill performers in a bizarre range of revealing costumes might have suggested that normal life continued unabated, the first two images of Valerie as a warden reflected the new normal. They were particularly interesting as they illustrated both her take on fit-for-purpose clothing and something of the way the idea of uniform was being taken up at the time.

The government had agreed in July 1939 to supply a free uniform for ARP workers but this did not materialize until the autumn when 'Macintosh-type overall coats for women … in dark "bluette" denim' were eventually produced.[3] In the meanwhile Valerie's combination of ribbed sleeveless pullover, short puff-sleeved blouse with pointed shirt collar, jodhpurs and dark boots provided a practical clothing solution to a relatively new problem – a suitable outfit for war work of this type. These clothes, together with the siren suit readers were told Valerie owned,[4] were worn, arguably, as practical substitutes for the official uniform to come. Valerie's short sleeves meant no ARP armband was visible, the tin helmet had no visible letter-mark[5] and Valerie appeared not to be wearing an ARP badge,[6] so the only official regalia that did exist are not on display.[7] Despite this, and with stirrup pump and bucket in tow, Valerie looked the part as her civilian ensemble imitated the idea of uniform. This smart, chic image was war-ready and efficient, a metaphor in many ways for the attitude with which women so often faced up to new wartime roles and responsibilities.

Women in engineering

March 1941 found *Picture Post* photographing some of the women attending engineering training courses at the Paddington Technical Institute to accompany an article on 'Women in War', written by M. P. Ellen Wilkinson.[8] From 'every class and calling', young and older, novices or experienced, trainees were obtaining the skills necessary to take over industry roles vacated by men leaving for military service. Dressed in rather shapeless overalls,[9] with notched or shawl collars, the dress code was first and foremost functional. Hats were of the simple turban, knotted scarf or beret type, or, as in the final image of munition workers, a cap with the crown pleated into a flat head-band.

Overalls of one sort or another had already become standard protective clothing for women working in almost any engineering or factory production role. They covered the personal clothing beneath, disguising rather than displacing the more conventional contours of women's dress.

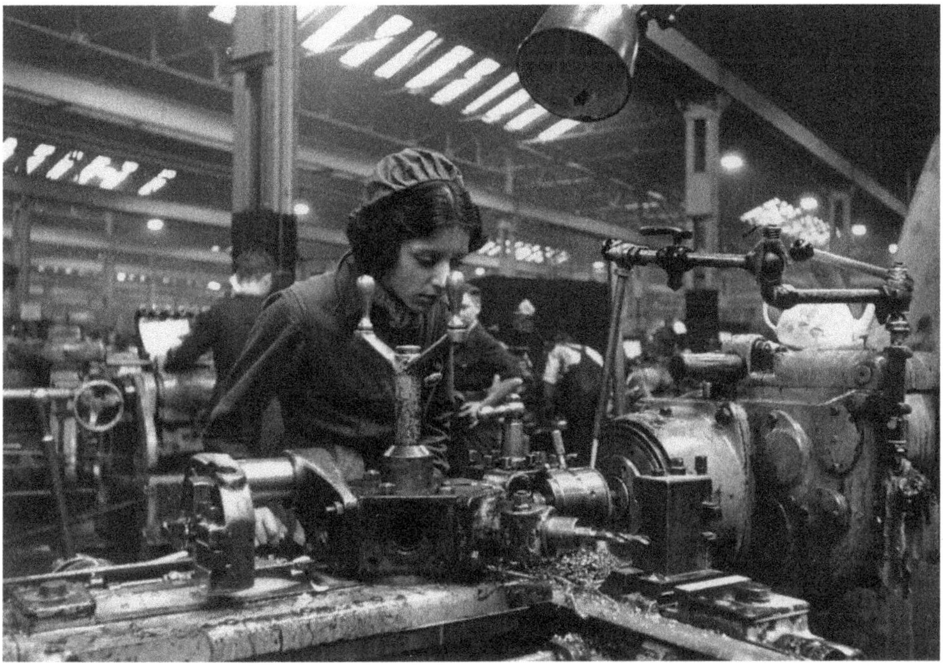

Figure 30 'The Girl Who Has Taken Her Place in the War Machine', 'They Make The Guns We Need', *Picture Post*, 5 July 1941, p. 24. Bert Hardy/*Picture Post*/Getty Images (3134054)[10].

The overall, along with trousers, the boiler suit and dungarees all contributed to the fashioning of an alternative female identity, one now doing 'a real man's job'[11] whether working a milling machine or helping build a new plane. While these images are almost taken for granted today they remain significant as a visual record of how many women – from all classes and backgrounds – took on blue-collar employment, often in tandem with existing home and family responsibilities.

'I conduct a "Midland Red"'

In the winter of 1941, as part of a series on 'Women at War', women's editor Anne Scott-James had a go at being a bus conductress on a 'Midland Red'.[12] A *Picture Post* photographer recorded her first full day. The set of pictures were designed to demystify the experience of becoming a transport worker and encourage urgently needed new recruits into the field. After reporting to the bus depot, Scott-James received her uniform which she described as:

> Well-cut and warm. It consists of a navy blue tunic with good square shoulders, a slim, well-cut navy blue skirt with red stripe at each side, white shirt and collar, tie, cap and overcoat. It's a self-respecting outfit, avoids such unflattering faults as narrow shoulders and a baggy skirt. It is issued free, but you have to give up coupons for it[13].

If precious coupons had to be expended, at least wearing uniform helped to conserve off-duty clothing. Some of the photographs suggested that trousers were also available as part of the working ensemble and practical, flat shoes were worn as there were 'plenty of athletics'.[14] Longer hair was drawn away from the face and worn rolled up around the cap or pulled back to the nape of the neck, presumably to keep looking groomed despite all the running 'from deck to deck'.[15] Presenting a smart appearance to the public was clearly an important component of this energetic work, alongside of being 'a dab at figures, juggling and back chat'.[16]

These three examples of civilian war-work offer only a small, if representative, sample of the range of employment now absorbing women's labour. While the increasing variety of occupational dress reflected these many new roles, it also provided a constant visual reinforcement of women's extending capabilities.

Changing dress codes for wartime living

The fashion industry had its own adjustments to make so that seasonal collections reflected trends and lines relevant to the changing social and economic circumstances of war. Evening styles as we have seen were some of the first to be affected, both by the anti-social and dangerous conditions of blackout, and the growing incidence of uniform which rendered much evening attire over-dressy. The industry now had to consider which fashion sectors could continue to prosper irrespective of conflict and which would need to evolve, in one way or another, in response to hostile and volatile times.

'The First War Fashion', according to a *Picture Post* photographer out on the street in September 1939, was a small white skull-cap decorated with the 'flags of friendly nations and neutrals'.[17] Worn by a young woman in London here was a small symbol of alliance and union in a fragmenting world. In other images from the same article entitled 'The Changed Face of London',[18] people were seen carrying their gas masks, while a shop advertised gas mask cases for sale to replace the official issue of cardboard box and string.[19] While hardly a fashion in itself the fashion industry did start selling more attractive and durable cases in an attempt to create a stylish accessory out of an unprepossessing necessity.[20]

Outerwear 1940

In an article entitled 'February Fashions',[21] *Picture Post* covered a new-season range of outerwear that celebrated the collaboration between fashion and science. This had produced fully waterproofed clothing that was both practical and pretty. The oil silk raincoat featured offered wide sleeves and a storm collar on a wrap-around belted coat, accessorized by a turban-cum-scarf rain hood – both fully waterproof. A Dorothy bag in the same material and pair of shiny ankle boots completed the outfit. The caption commented on the combination of modern with historical elements – grandmother's bootees and mother's bag – signalling that fashion's pre-war interest in the past had

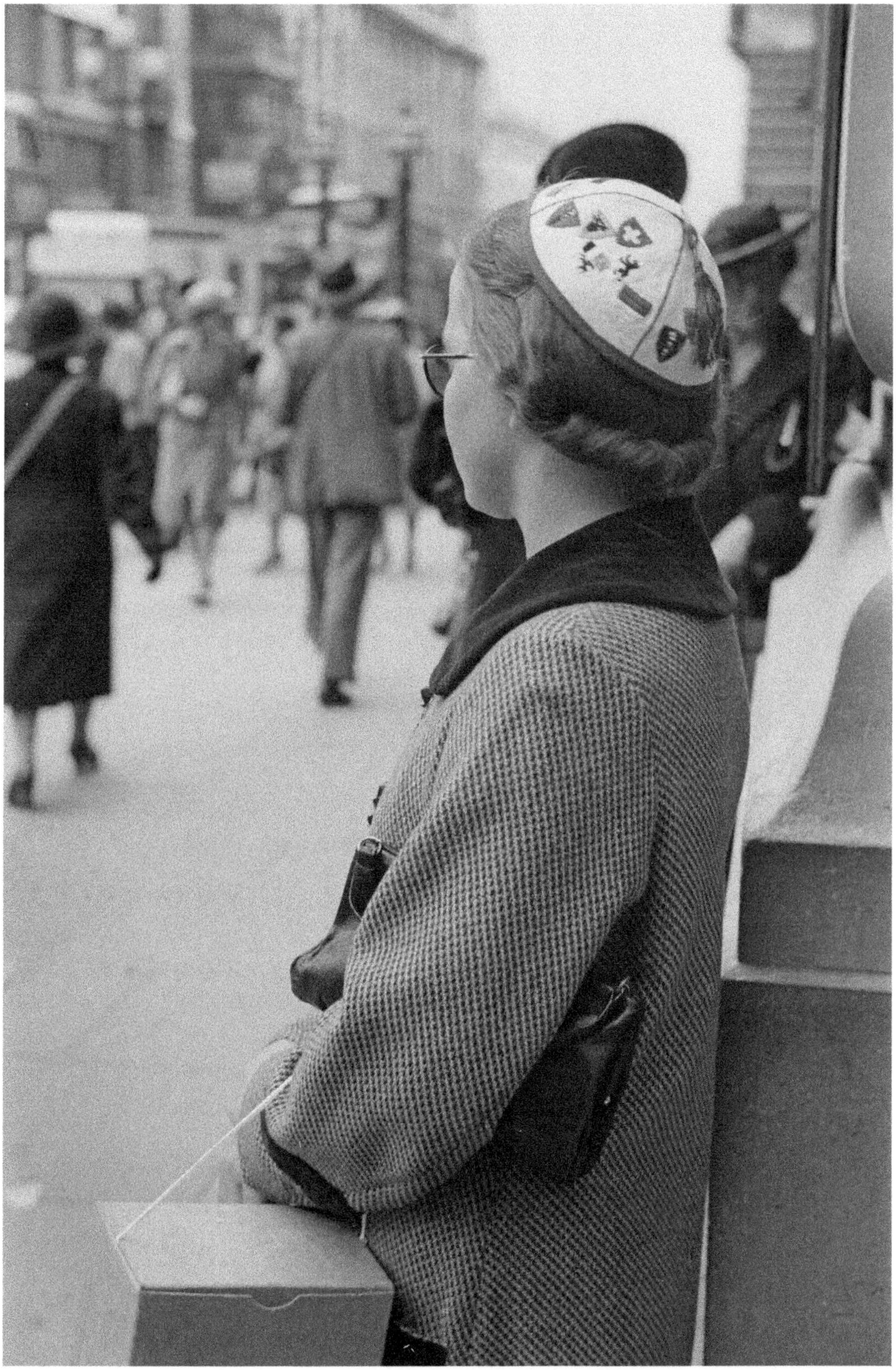

Figure 31 'The First War Fashion. Flags of friendly nations and neutrals on a white skull-cap'. 'Diary of the War: No. 4, The Second Week, The Changed Face of London', *Picture Post*, 30 September 1939, p. 27. Tim Gidal/*Picture Post*/Hulton Archive/Getty Images (984851272).

not abated. Light and easy to wear, as it seemed was the waterproof cape pictured and stored in a large-crowned bucket-hat, the new waterproofs were practical and efficient. A two-piece jerkin and skirt in a shiny waterproofed fabric, considered to be the 'very latest in fashions for wear in deceitful weather', was easy to put on and take off as each piece fastened with a zip,[22] while a Scottish plaid-lined rain-proof coat with large buttons, rolled button-down collar and large cowl hood, offered a warm, protective solution to the worst of weather. Also depicted was a military-style great coat with concealed front fastenings that featured large flap pockets to hold 'more than it's comfortable to carry'.[23]

Fashion had clearly taken practicality and suitability to heart yet retained a fashion-forward element through innovative fabrics or design features. The new styles also promoted 'sensible well-cut boots' that were easy to walk in and 'husky shoes with tough crepe rubber soles, often more than half an inch thick, through which no damp can possibly penetrate … (The lower the heel the higher the fashion value)'.[24] Comfortable, easy movement was now becoming fashionable in a 'world of changing values' and the fashionable woman, the narrative believed, was 'prepared for any reasonable change, she's gay and she's unchangeably pretty'.[25]

May 1940 saw Winston Churchill taking over as prime minister shortly before the fall of Holland and then Belgium to Blitzkrieg.[26] The evacuation of British troupes from the beaches of Dunkirk from late May to early June[27] preceded the final defeat of France, leaving Britain at her most vulnerable to Nazi invasion. At this point Britain began to construct a comprehensive series of coastal and field defences around beaches and inland approach routes, while the recently formed force of Local Defence Volunteers watched for signs of invasion across the country.[28]

Beach wear

The days of taking beach holidays were about to be strictly numbered. *Picture Post*'s article in mid-May 1940 on the new swimsuit fashions poignantly preserves some of the optimism of the last days of the phoney war before Dunkirk, the Battle of Britain and the blitz.[29] The writer acknowledged that the war had made holidaying in the south of France impossible, thereby limiting the range of beach wear available, but new styles had emerged, nevertheless, to lift the spirits of the shopper seeking 'the sea and the open air'.[30] As there was less wool available to the home market[31] other fabrics were now being used instead, such as satin lastex, 'ever so slightly controlling just where you need it',[32] satin, cotton and rayon with prices ranging from 30s. to 35s. for satins down to 10s. to 20s. for the cheaper materials.

Styles ranged from one-piece swimsuits in lively prints to two-piece brassiere-and-shorts outfits, one of which, in fringed towelling, was chosen as the magazine's front cover. Waists were cinched and accentuated by matching skirts and shorts of one sort or another such as a floral two-piece in wool stockinette by Windsor Water Woollies. A play suit consisting of a split skirt and buttoned bodice that could be worn over swimwear was suggested as an easy way to move away from the beach, and printed cotton versions of these were available at prices between 12s. 11d. and 25s.

By September 1940, however, in an article entitled 'Something We Rather Missed This Summer'[33] *Picture Post* was bemoaning the fact that swimsuits had tended to stay in the shops. The preparations for summer, advocated back in May, had lost relevance as women were increasingly 'wearing uniform or working long hours in factories'. Meanwhile the beaches had been 'festooned with wire, wire with spikes on it'.[34]

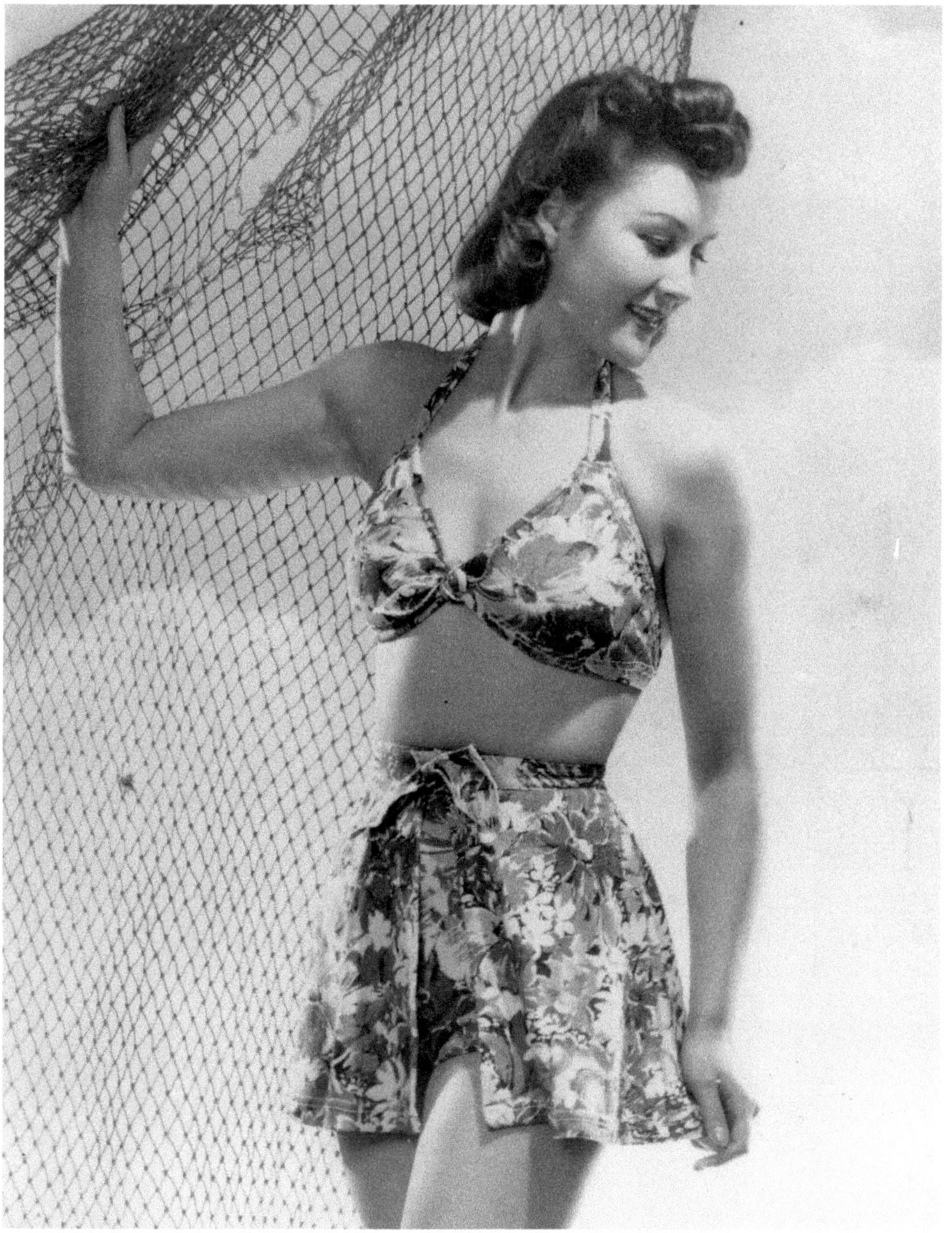

Figure 32 'Floral Two-piece: This gaily coloured model in wool stockinette is by Windsor Water Woollies. The little apron skirt is detachable'. From 'The New Swim-Suits Arrive', *Picture Post*, 18 May 1940, p. 28. *Picture Post*/Getty Images (3397127).

Journalistic interest in swimwear persisted, however, despite the adverse wartime conditions. By January 1941, in an article entitled 'Ideas For Next Summer: they Come from the South Seas',[35] a Hawaiian collection of floral and patterned beachwear featuring brassiere-and-shorts swimsuits, playsuits, sarongs and tropical evening wear, was hailed as a real 'fillip' for life on the home front. The 'liveliest and prettiest fashions' for the beach, these outfits were modelled by Californians 'always quick on the uptake', and the text suggested that 'what Californians wear in January, England will seize on when its own swimming season comes along'.[36] While swimming was more likely to be in swimming pools than in the sea in Britain, the text remained hopeful that these new styles would become a part of the coming summer's offering.

The tone was resolutely upbeat given the blitz conditions Britain was enduring – perhaps because of them. The writer offered a picture of summer sun-bathing in 'vivid playsuits with very short, very full skirts' worn with 'necklaces of flowers or shells' and later dancing in 'Hawaiian frocks or pyjamas' in bold tropical prints.[37] A surprise was in store for British shoppers, however, as summer got under way. With escalating clothes prices and the need to harbour textile resources the government introduced clothes rationing on 1 June 1941. This did not initially stop hopeful holidaymakers buying the swimming outfits they might want, but it put a break on the capacity to acquire clothing in general and, in due course, limited the types of clothing it was possible to buy.[38]

Stockings

In October 1940, the government had taken the decision to withdraw silk from civilian production. Only stockings made from other materials would now be manufactured and these tended to have neither the quality nor kudos of silk.[39] By March of the following year *Picture Post*'s 'Practical Living' section was providing information on what type of stockings could be purchased in place of silk.[40] Woman's Editor Anne Scott-James started out by describing the ban as 'a big shock for all of us' and 'sensational news', establishing something of the importance of silk stockings to the fashion world of the time.

New weaves of rayon, lisle and wool were to save the day. These were the results of developing textile technologies that could now produce, for example, a 'rayon . . . as dull as silk . . . fully fashioned . . . woven exactly like silk' and with a final surface 'indistinguishable from silk'.[41] There was 'a little difference in the feeling', however, and rayon was not as supple as silk, although it could be bought in attractive variants, such as rayon crepe and mesh weaves.[42] Lisle stockings also came in a finer mesh weave suitable for smarter town wear, while 'ribbed lisle stockings stride about the country – frankly chunky, like the new country shoes'.[43] Wool stockings were being produced in bright colours and a lace variety and Scott-James also suggested 'knee-length wool socks – a fashion stolen from the American college girl' for young women.[44]

She went on to warn readers that supply would now be the difficulty as government restrictions meant possibly only half as many stockings being manufactured compared to last year. Regular washing 'every day or every two days' in lukewarm water using good-quality soap flakes was recommended, as was pegging by the heels and toes when drying.[45] Rayon became fragile when wet and was to be handled carefully. Ladders in general were to be dealt with inexpensively using the services of professional menders on-hand in store repairing departments.[46]

Shopping on the high street – daywear

The price of clothing had been rising steadily since the outbreak of war.[47] In a double-page photo-story from March 1941 entitled 'Shopping for Spring',[48] a young woman shopper was seen buying items for the spring and summer season ahead. Anne Scott-James described the particular fashion philosophy that underpinned the shopper's garment choices, and reflected on its relevance to the specific wartime circumstances of diminishing supplies and higher costs. Shopper Thelma Gordon had made a list of her existing clothing and what she felt she needed. She had then bought 'no more than the necessities' so avoiding the wasted expense of 'buying oddments she doesn't want'. She also bought the items she was after all together so that colours and styles could be successfully matched. This reduced the likelihood of buying a 'failure'.[49] Planning a wardrobe in this way would soon be crucial to successfully managing the coupon allocations that came with clothes rationing – now only two months away.[50]

Thelma was first photographed in a knee-length, gored plaid skirt, neatly fitted jacket, dark court shoes and a soft brimmed hat, also dark and plain. This outfit[51] was typical of the softly tailored look of the early war years and clearly sustained the pre-war fashion for traditional British styling and its familiar forms of femininity.

Thelma was next seen selecting pieces that could do duty for different wartime occasions and seasons with not a trouser or overall in sight.

Her first choice at department store Bourne and Hollingsworth,[52] was a two-piece navy sailor suit of skirt and blouse. This had a detachable white pique sailor collar and white sailor's knot detail above a small concealed breast pocket. While the fabric wasn't mentioned, the outfit was considered practical for doing duty with a jacket for spring and then on its own in summer. The dark colour was hard wearing and Thelma believed it made her look 'incredibly slim'.[53] Teamed later with a navy sailor hat with white trim, the look was simple yet crisp and cost 73s. 6d. (£3. 13. 6d.) for the suit and 18s. 11d. for the hat.[54]

Her choice of jacket for daywear was a tailored, hip-length style in baize green wool with puffed sleeves, discreet breast and hip pockets and three series of three buttons to close. Chosen to coordinate with skirts, dresses and trousers, this was a flexible fashion piece that would remain a classic component of the wartime wardrobe. The white pointed collar of the sailor blouse worn outside the jacket suggested a collarless or small-collared design that would facilitate other collar and scarf choices to create a range of looks simply and cheaply. A natural straw hat at 10s. 11d. and ghillie sports shoes completed purchases for daywear. The ghillies, costing 45s. (£2. 5s.), were chosen by Thelma for their sensible square heels and two colours,[55] while her boyfriend saw them as practical and comfortable.

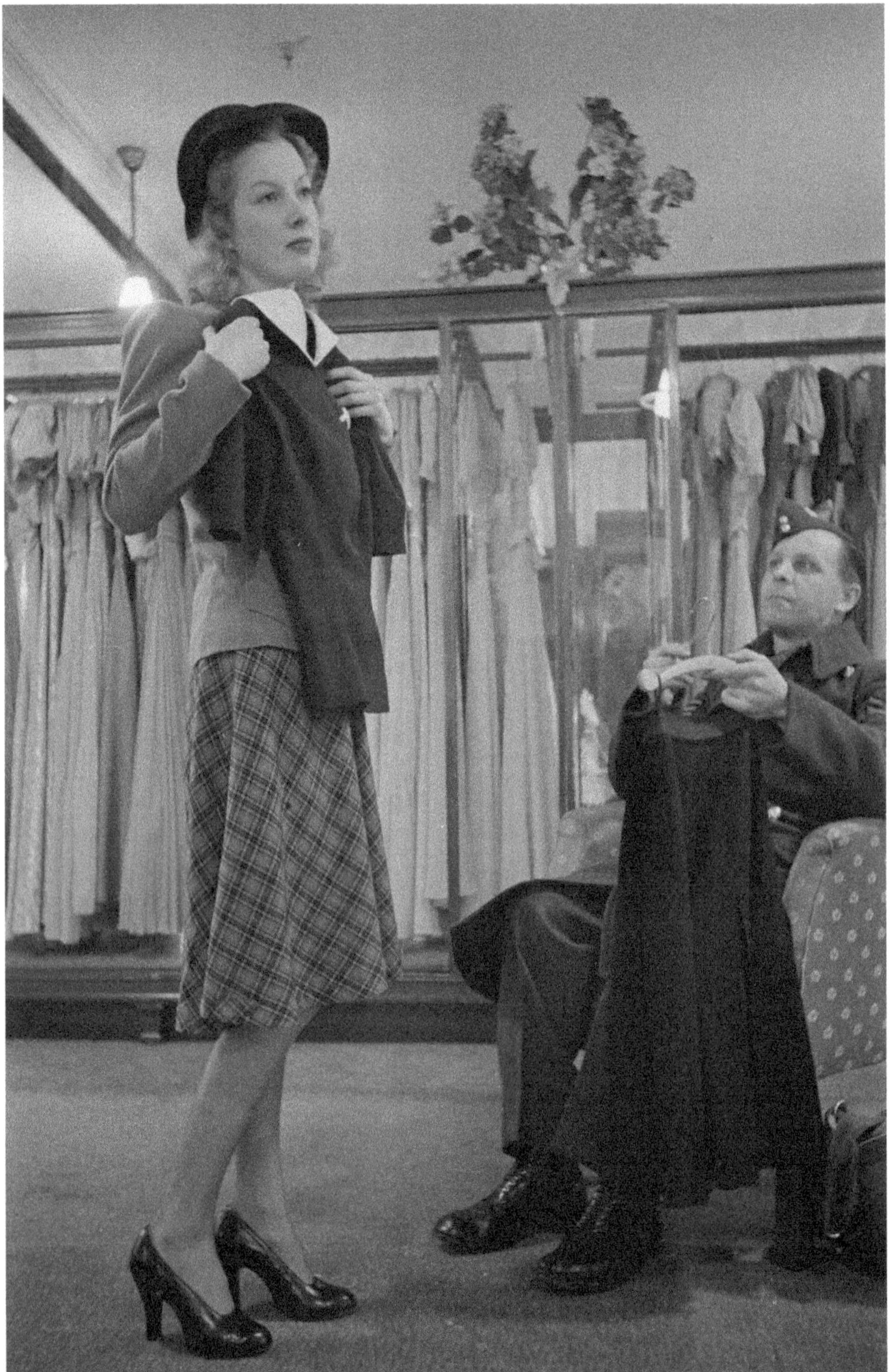

Figure 33 'The Shopping Trip', 'Shopping for Spring', *Picture Post*, 29 March 1941, p. 30. Bert Hardy/*Picture Post*/Hulton Archive/Getty Images (988545718).

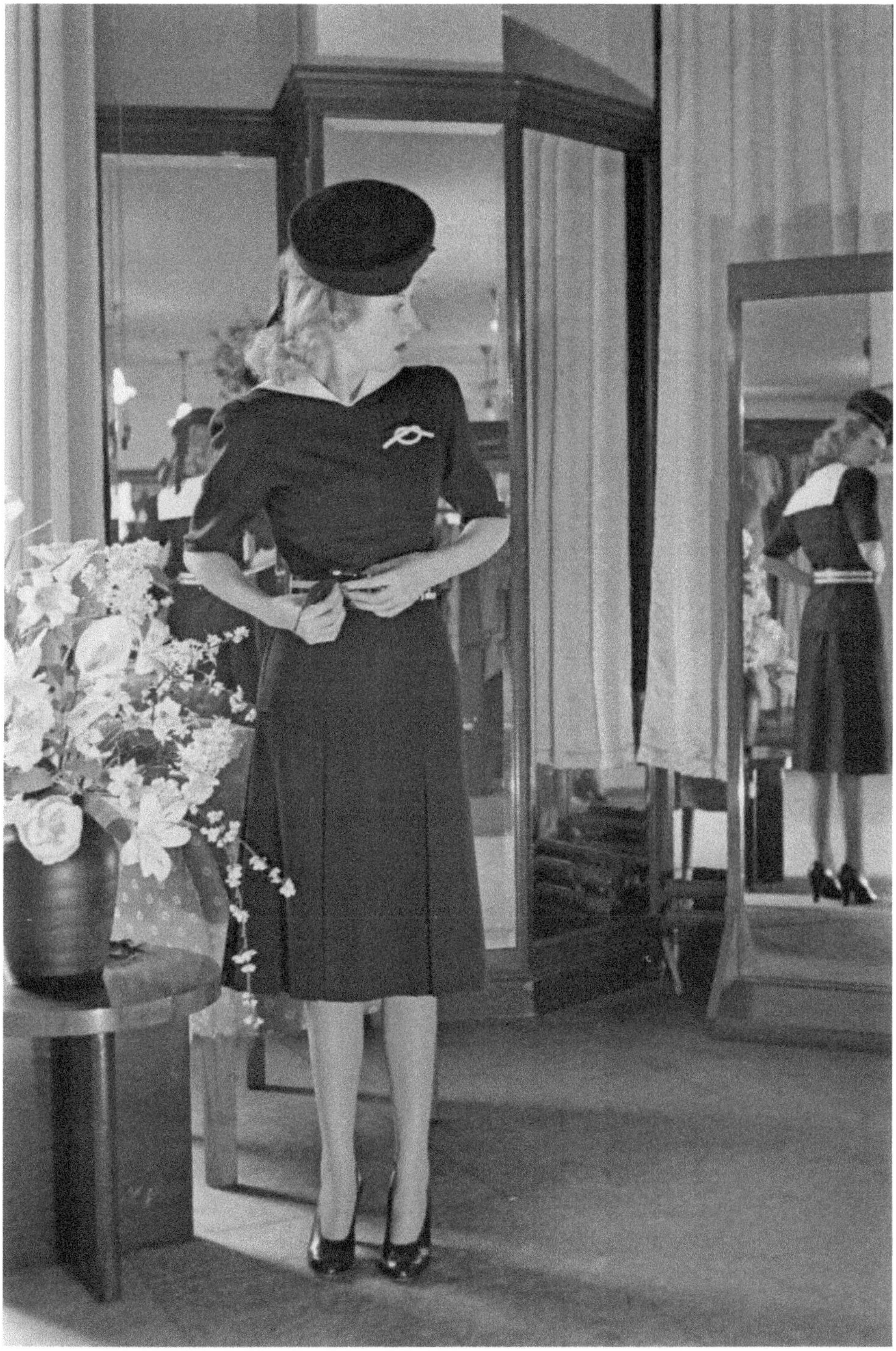

Figure 34 'The Sailor Suit', 'Shopping for Spring', *Picture Post*, 29 March 1941, p. 30. Bert Hardy/*Picture Post*/Hulton Archive/Getty Images (988546104).

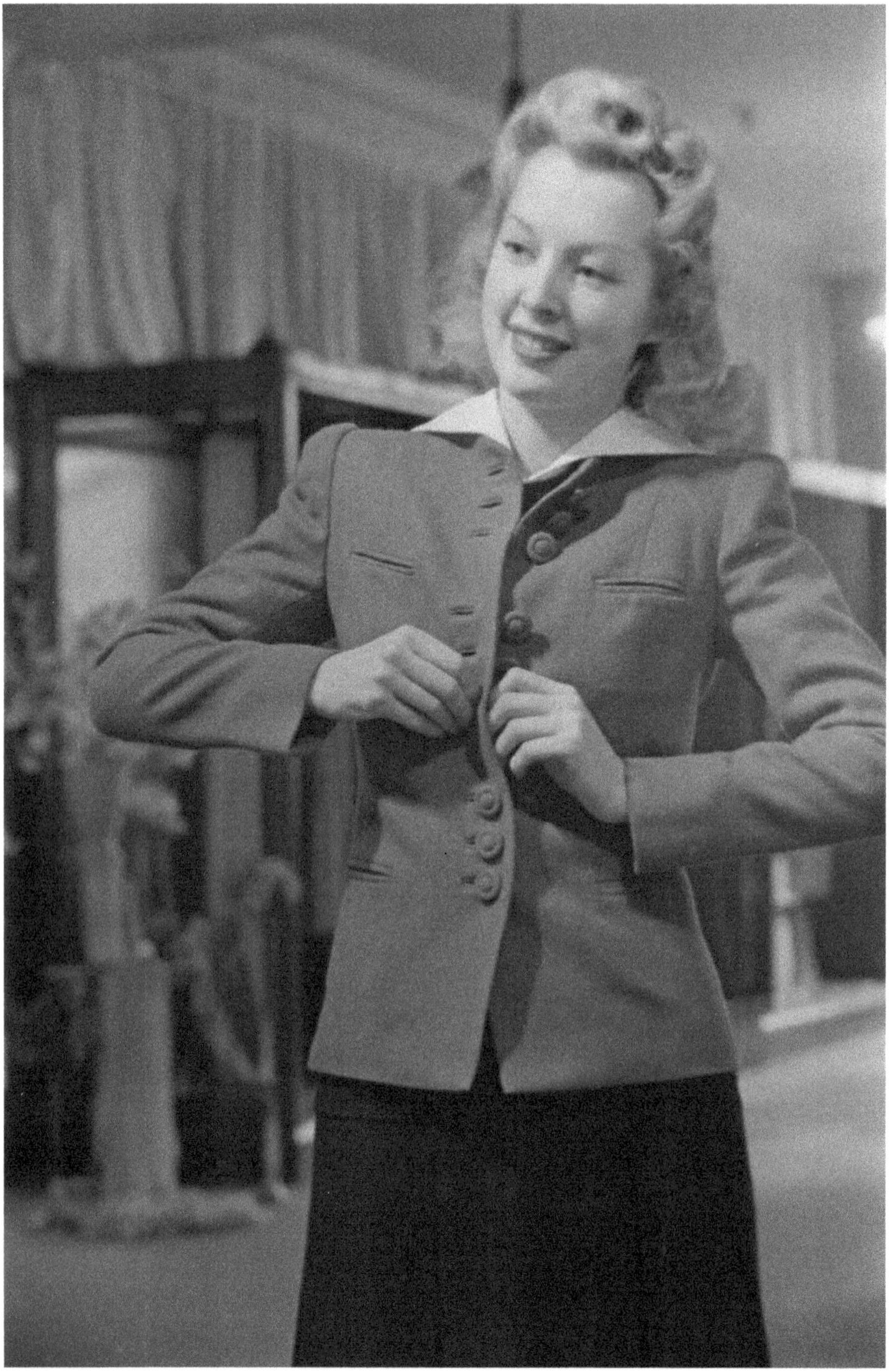

Figure 35 'The Jacket', 'Shopping for Spring', *Picture Post*, 29 March 1941, p. 31. Bert Hardy/*Picture Post*/Hulton Archive/Getty Images (988545730).

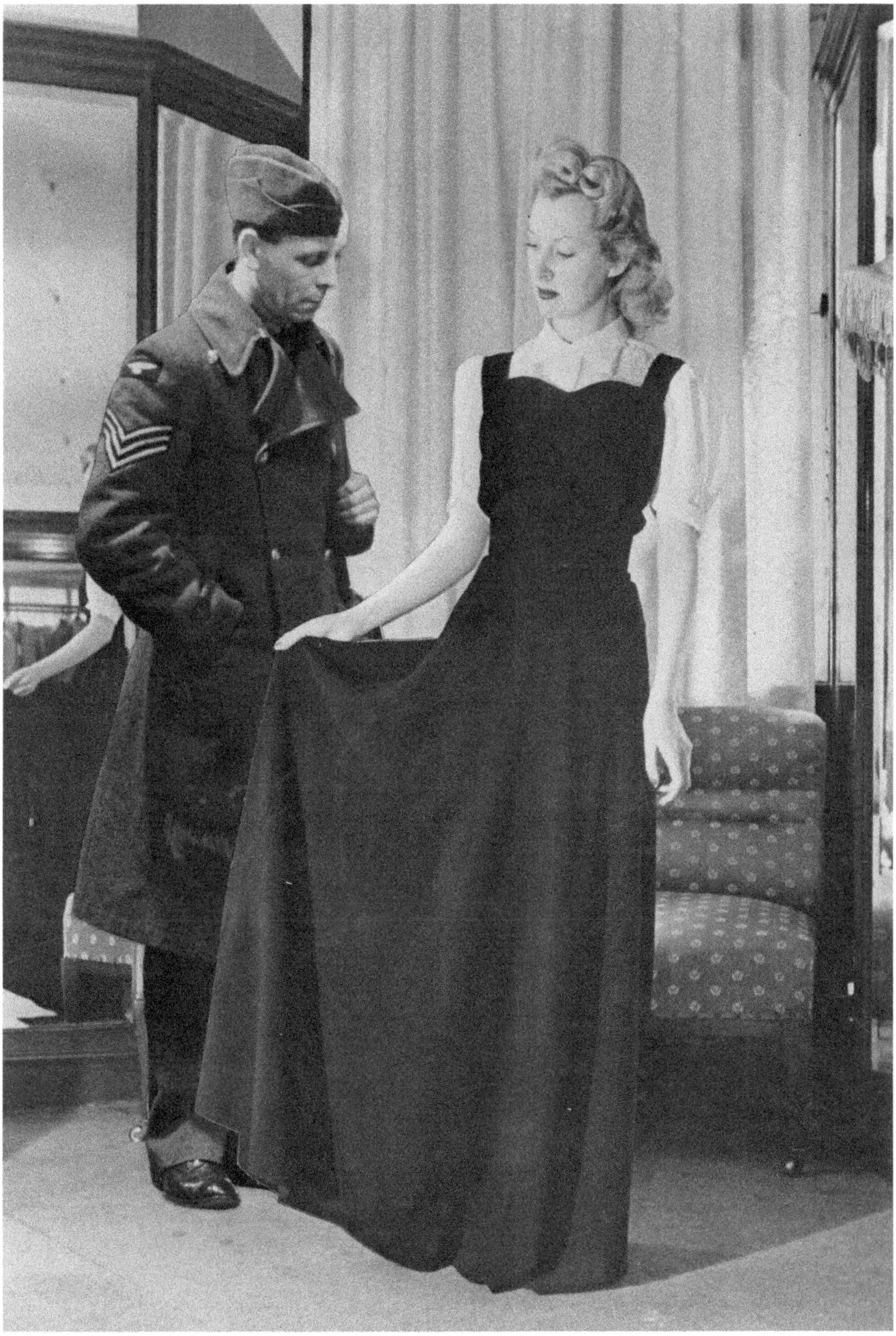

Figure 36 'The Dinner Frock', 'Shopping for Spring', *Picture Post*, 29 March 1941, p. 31. Bert Hardy/*Picture Post*/Hulton Archive/Getty Images (988545684).

Shopping on the high street – evening wear

Thelma Gordon's final purchase was the only one for evening wear. The number of occasions requiring evening wear had noticeably diminished as war progressed.[56] The need for ease of movement and warmth in the event of air raids or walking in the blackout had brought about a vogue for both less opulent and shorter garments. Thelma had, nevertheless, opted for a long black wool pinafore dress although in a stylishly simple design. The bodice had wide straps and a scalloped neckline and was loosely drawn into the waistband, from which the skirt fell with some fullness to the floor. Reflecting an unadorned type of formal clothing that was still being worn 'in the evening at home or to the Air Force dance',[57] this garment could be dressed up or down depending on what it was worn with, from a woollen jumper to a georgette blouse. Given that planning was a prime principle behind Thelma's purchases, buying such a dress at a cost of 4 ½ guineas (£4. 14s. 6d.), appeared to indicate that there were still occasions in her own life for which the style remained suitable and that she had not bought a rather expensive white elephant.[58]

Evening wear it seemed was never entirely supplanted by cocktail length but gave way to plainer more practical fabrics and simpler shapes. Extravagance was now démodé and would soon become impossible given the limitations that would shortly be placed on fabric and labour under clothing control. The demise of opulence, no matter how temporarily, effectively removed one of the clearest visual indicators of wealth and privilege. In tandem with the increasingly common practice of wearing a uniform of one sort or another, dress now emphasized class difference rather less, a phenomenon which would be continued through the fabric and style limitations that followed on from clothes rationing.[59]

Night wear

If glamorous evening wear had had its day for the duration, there was some evidence that the bedroom continued to provide an outlet for soigne full-length dressing. In an article entitled 'Here Are Two New Ways of Going to Bed',[60] *Picture Post* reported on two very different approaches to dressing for night-time.

In a three-page photo-story, one set of images illustrated a collection of sheer, diaphanous, pale-coloured outfits made in fabrics such as lace, satin or chiffon. While some of the night-gowns were see-through, readers were told that 'even this transparent type . . . has its own form of modesty, for these, too, cover you well'.[61] In soft greens, pinks, peaches and white, sometimes with lace or ribbon decoration in accent colours, necklines were generally high and shoulders and arms largely covered. There was, apparently, 'nothing cute about these night-gowns. They are essentially languorous, and have to be worn gracefully'.[62] As they also weren't very warm 'brief jackets or long negligees to match, tying at the waist with ribbons' were available, whether or not effective.[63] Feminine allure, it appeared, could still flourish.

The other set of images showed all-in-one sleep suits or two-piece pyjamas. These were clearly designed for complete coverage and warmth and highly practical for cold and often disturbed nights. In marked contrast to the neighbouring images, feminine fun informed the bright wool envelope night suits replete with feet or pixie hoods and the gaily patterned pyjamas. More evidence of the developing vogue for practicality over glamour these amusing pieces brought an ingénue charm into the bedroom. The warmth and comfort of childhood styles and motifs arguably provided an interesting counterbalance to the very real and adult world of night raids. When the bedroom was a damp and chilly garden shelter[64] there was no competition as to the most suitable of the two styles on offer.

Public dress codes

Spending time in an Anderson shelter might well have encouraged a pragmatic approach to dress choice that prioritized sensible, snug clothing appropriate to the conditions. Meanwhile in the larger communal shelters or underground stations, that pragmatism also had to take cognizance of the very much more public experience shelterers encountered. When *Picture Post* visited a London shelter in October 1940[65] the resulting images captured not only the sense of making the best of things, as people slept against bare walls and in concrete corridors, but also the degree to which shelterers, all in their normal outdoor clothes, had made few if any concessions to the inconveniences or difficulties of shelter life. Here an elderly couple slept sitting up wrapped in blankets but still wearing their hats, one decorated with flowers; there a young woman in a smart coat and court shoes continued to apply her make-up. The enforced intimacy of the public shelter was arguably held at bay by maintaining the formal dress codes of the shelterers' public as opposed to private lives.

In March 1941 *Picture Post* made another foray into the communal shelter[66] and found the same adherence to normal day clothing just as strong, from the collar and ties of the young men in a discussion group and the handy-man in his three-piece suit and cap, to the dresses and neat hairstyles of the ladies in the underground sewing bee.

Conclusion

The two sections of this chapter, working clothing and the continuation or cessation of seasonal fashions, have provided examples from *Picture Post* of some of the shifts in dress codes and fashionable dressing witnessed during the earlier years of the war. The higher visibility of work-specific dress or uniform for women across all social classes bore testimony to the expanding range of duties women were now taking on. The widespread adoption of workwear more generally associated with men, such as factory overalls or boiler suits, simply reflected that women had the same need for practical clothing as the men they were now replacing. As the second section of the chapter revealed, fashion

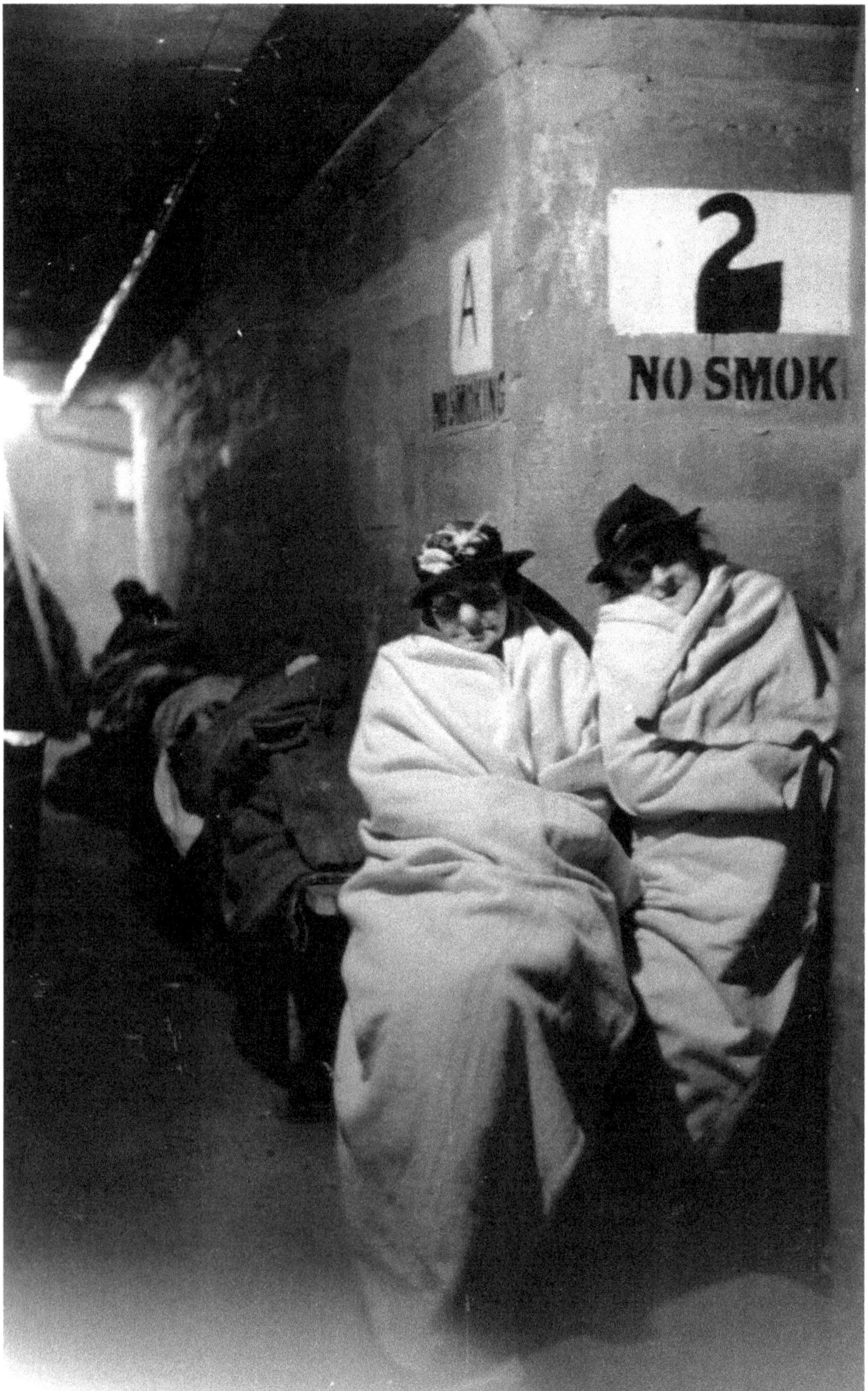

Figure 37 'Here One Must Sleep Sitting Up', from 'Shelter Life', *Picture Post*, 26 October 1940, p. 9. Zoltan Glass/Getty Images (2636758).

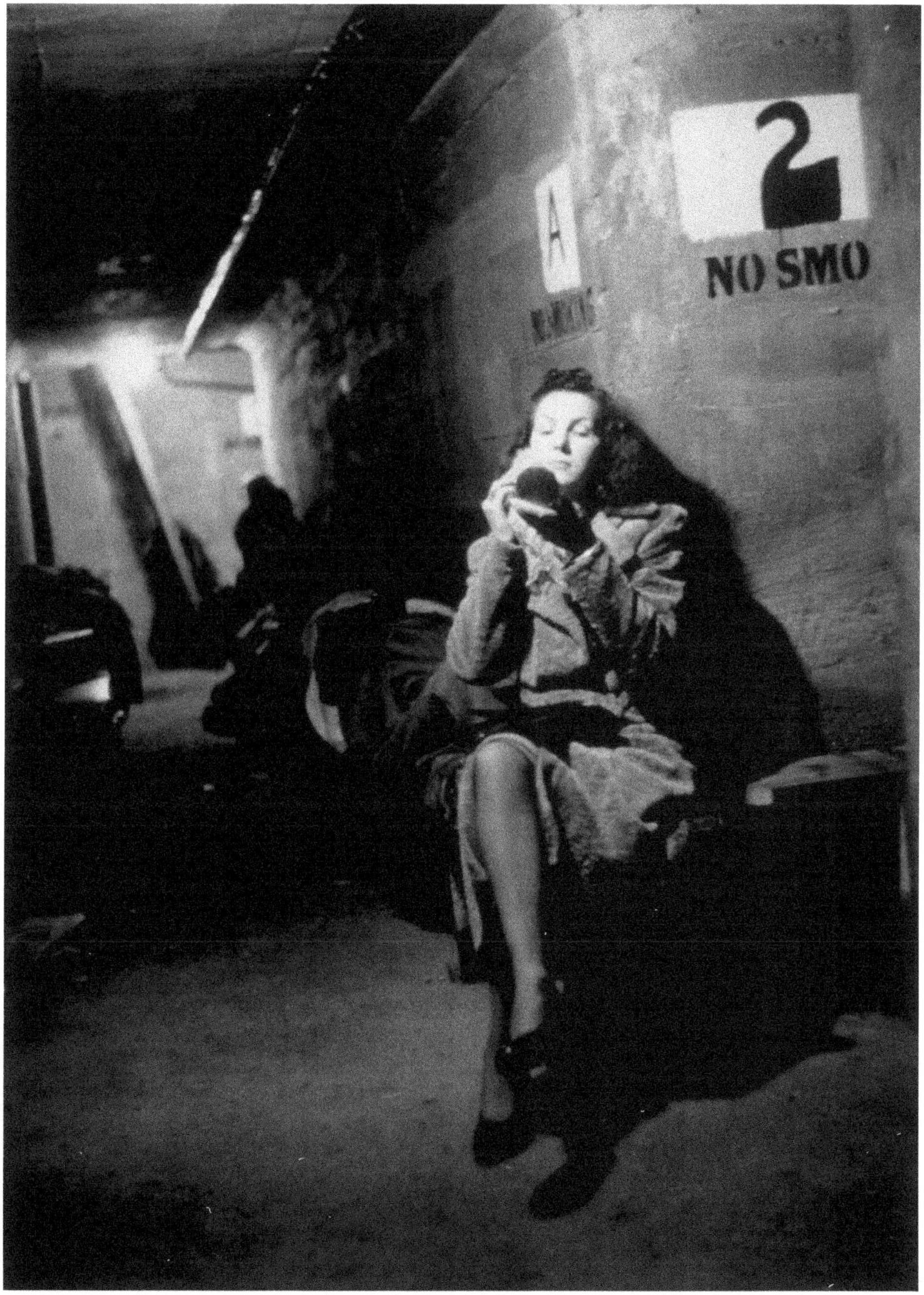

Figure 38 'Here All One's Life Is Public. Privacy, so highly cherished by Britons, is gone. Family life at evening has vanished. Here nothing is intimate. One talks, eats, sleeps, lives, with a hundred, a thousand, others'. From 'Shelter life', *Picture Post*, 26 October 1940, p. 9. Zoltan Glass/Getty Images (2659776).

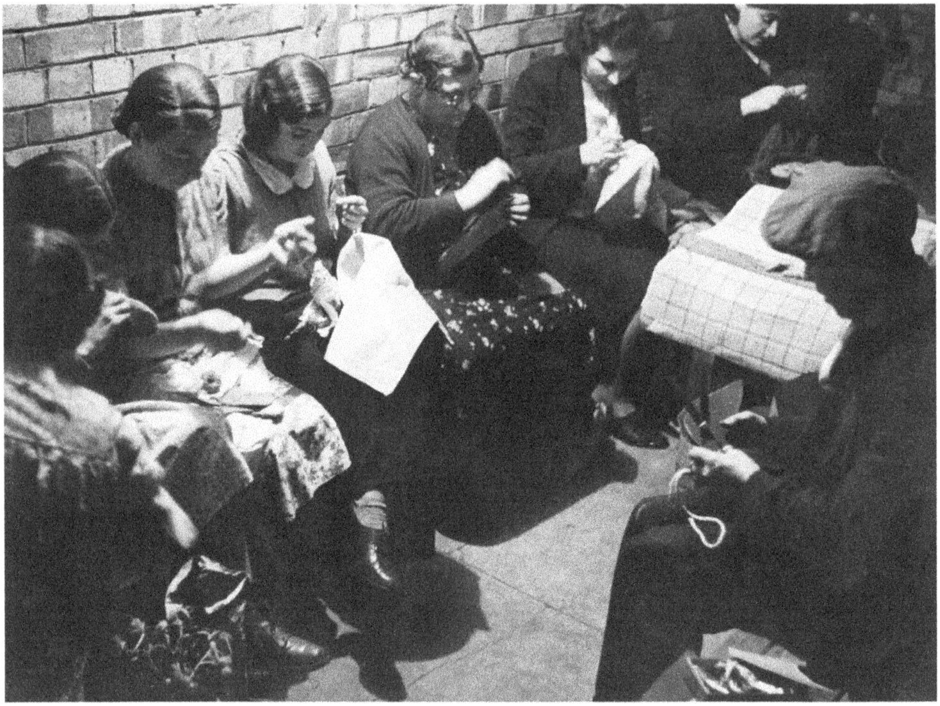

Figure 39 'The Underground Sewing Bee: Unheeding the bombs, the shelterers are busy. Some make slippers. Some make dresses. Some make patchwork quilts. One ambitious girl is hand-hooking a wool rug'. From 'Down in the Shelter There Is Life', *Picture Post*, 29 March 1941, p. 16. Bert Hardy/*Picture Post*/Hulton Archive/Getty Images (89729042).

itself was far from moribund under these circumstances. Innovation whether in design or fabric was ongoing, now with a distinctively practical edge, while emerging trends had continued to offer fresh perspectives across the fashion spectrum from flexible daywear to the bedroom. The tailored pieces and soft separates of pre-war fashions retained currency because they continued to offer a smart and practical chic suited to the new conditions. Crucially, there was little that was completely new in the fashion lexicon. Overt opulence was out; sensible, smart, unfussy fashion was in.

5
PRACTICAL LIVING WITH *PICTURE POST*

Introduction

In the context of dangerous times and diminishing supplies, *Picture Post*'s first Woman's Editor, Anne Scott-James, started a new 'Practical Living' feature in February 1941, a little over five months after the onset of the blitz.[1] Hoping to provide practical help on a wide variety of topics relating to domestic life under the deteriorating conditions of war, she intended to run stories on 'Fashion, beauty, decoration, sewing and knitting,

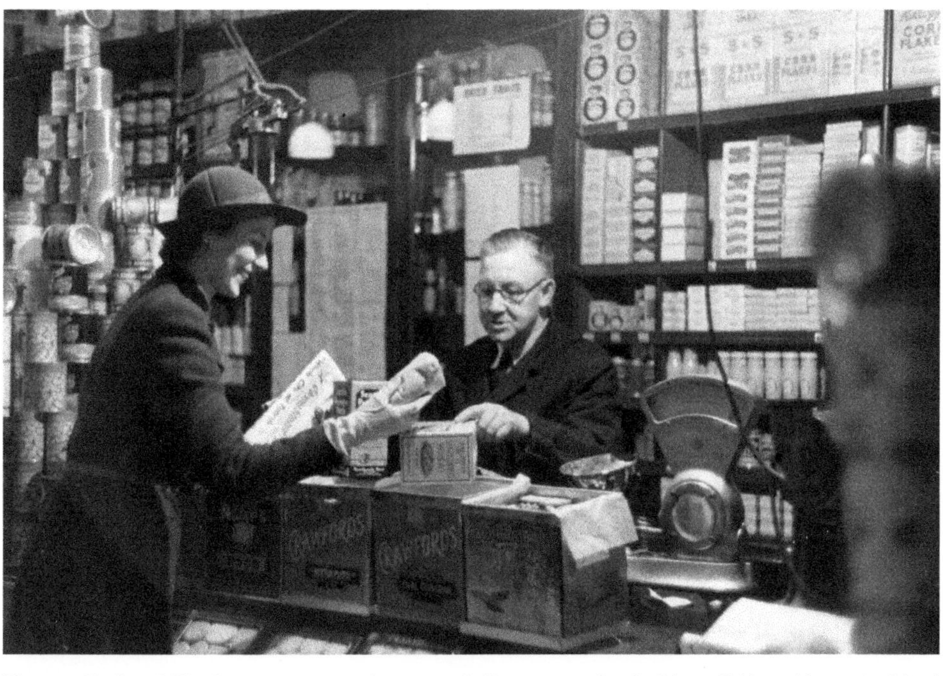

Figure 40 'Lord Woolton recommends oatmeal. Do grocers back this up? Yes, this one, picked at random, says it's delicious with honey or milk.' 'We Appoint a Woman's Editor', *Picture Post*, 8 February 1941, p. 33. *Picture Post*/Hulton Archive/Getty Images (3321763).

cooking, gardening, ideas for comfort, economy, warmth and pleasure'. Her aim was to help women make the best use of the 'simple clothes, cosmetics, food and amenities' now available, through corralling the 'top ideas and tips and news' into a weekly guide on 'everything practical'.[2]

Her first article included a stylish portrait image of herself with neatly waved hair, necklace and earrings, befitting the former assistant editor of fashion magazine *Vogue*. Further photographs captured Scott-James visiting a beauty salon, fashion house, grocery store and a housewife's home, all as part of her research for reports to readers. Her philosophy was clear. Women had much to do and keeping up morale through attention to such things as appearance, or the provision of a comfortable home, would not always be easy. Her job was to support women in maintaining standards, 'to look as pretty and live as comfortably as you possibly can' rather than see ugliness and discomfort as 'necessary evils of war'.[3] This would take ingenuity and 'in the long run, ideas count for far more than money'.[4]

Advice about cosmetics

In March, in an article called 'Make Up and Cut Down', Scott-James explored the various ways of making cosmetics go further now that fewer products were being produced.[5] With the same theme of keeping standards up in mind, Scott-James encouraged readers to continue using cosmetics, rather than offering 'a pale shiny face to the world (not much of a spirit-raiser in wartime)'; avoid potentially harmful 'home-brewed beauty aids'[6]; buy only products they were sure would work rather than have 'failures . . . languish[ing] on the bathroom shelf'. Where possible make-up was to be applied in more economical ways – a small lip brush for example created definition using less lipstick – and perfumes should always be sprayed on rather than 'splashing them about'. Hair, 'a sort of barometer of morale', had to be 'well-cut and well-set',[7] regularly washed and brushed often to remove dust and keep the scalp healthy. While much of this information was really little more than practical good sense, the advice served as a useful reminder of the need for thrift and economy while confirming that traditional beauty protocols could and should be continued.

Clothes rationing

On 1 June 1941 the Government introduced clothes rationing. Clothes would still be purchased for money in the same way as before, but coupons now had to be surrendered for every article bought, limiting the amount of clothing each individual could have. All garments, knitting wools and most fabrics were given a coupon value dependent on the fabric type and the amount of it used in a garment. The Board of Trade, under whose auspices clothes rationing fell, had calculated the average yearly clothing needs of the population and would now make sure enough civilian clothing was manufactured to honour this ration. While there would only be minor fluctuations in coupon values across

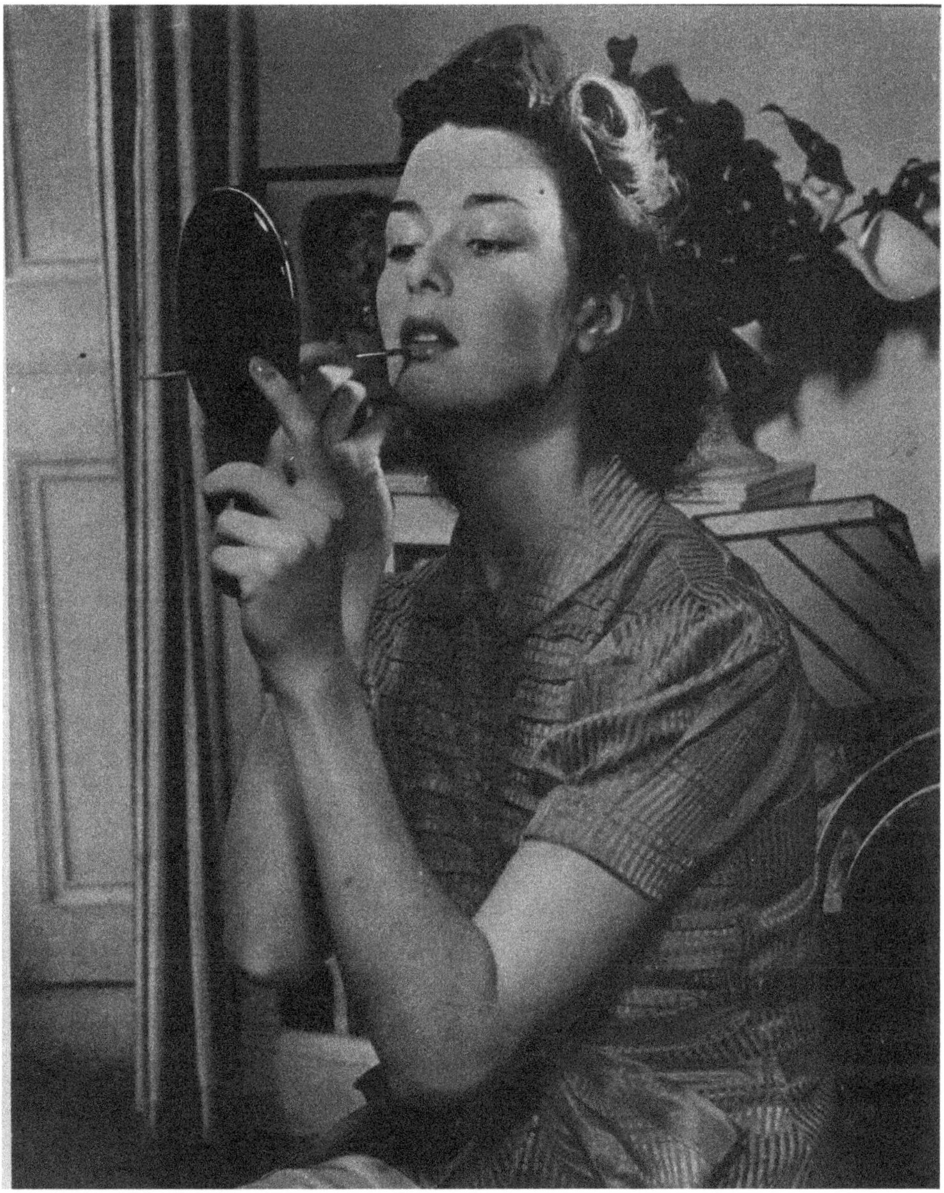

Figure 41 'A Brush Saves Lipstick. You will use less lipstick – if you paint it on! The clear-cut line makes your mouth look just as definite with less actual colour. Any small paint-brush does the trick'. 'Make Up and Cut Down', *Picture Post*, 15 March 1941, p. 32. IPC Magazines/*Picture Post*/Hulton Archive/Getty Images (591229579).

the remainder of the war, up-pointing or down-pointing items in line with scarcity or glut, the number of coupons would, however, decrease over the same period as materials and labour were absorbed by the demands of war.[8]

A reduced range of off-duty, civilian clothing was the result of this process, while the austerity design measures that followed-on from rationing in the spring and summer of

1942 saw the fashion industry providing increasingly more restrained design ideas in all clothing categories. Anne Scott-James confronted the new complexities inherent in shopping for rationed textiles and clothing and offered advice on how to plan for and acquire a well-balanced, flexible and still stylish wardrobe. From the summer of 1941 until the spring of 1946[9] coupons would effectively curtail the acquisition of clothing. Achieving the maximum benefit from a diminishing coupon allocation meant thinking ahead and taking a realistic review of wardrobe needs for both work and leisure and the changing seasons that affected both.

On 7 June, less than a week after clothes rationing was announced, 'Practical Living' ran a three-page photo-story on casual summer styles entitled 'Fashions for the Farm'.[10] Put together in all probability just before or around, the same time as the new clothing controls appeared, the collection continued to reflect contemporary interest in fresh, feminine fashion with a practical edge. Comprising dresses, skirts and blouses and a range of matching shorts and dungarees for women and children, designs revealed a distinctly bucolic rather than essentially realistic attitude towards farm life. Nothing was said about coupons.[11] Photographs showed cotton garments in a range of playful, pretty and more functional styles that offered variations on the seasonal theme. Unbeknown to readers this would be the last summer that commercial clothing would be able to offer a wider flared skirt, generous collar or plentiful use of buttons as seen in some of the clothes here. The following year's austerity regulations would effectively restrict these features.

The short-sleeved shirt-style bodice and generous skirt of the dress pictured above the article title was captioned as 'the perfect frock in which to milk a cow, drive a pig, go to market – or simply lie in the sun'.[12] This established something of the fantasy-farm-fashion that was to come, particularly in the context of Land Army and Timber Corps uniforms that were truly purpose-built for serious work on the land. Slim waists were emphasized, and poke bonnets and sun hats in straw were the fashionable accessories. Cotton print dresses captioned 'Goosegirl' and 'Milkmaid' continued this fantasy-feel for farming life, showing an 'apron frock' with matching pixie hood and a laced-bodice and dirndl dress respectively, while the 'Farmer's Wife' and 'Jack-and-Jill Dress' suggested cotton could also work for more formal designs with a less immediately country feel. The 'long, wired skirt!' and fichu collar of the former and multiple buttoned bodice and pleated poke bonnet of the latter revealed something of a rear-guard action by designers to maintain a more sophisticated element to summer fashions, possibly as a counterweight to the dungarees and shorts outfits also shown.[13] While cotton was now rationed Anne Scott-James reassured readers that fashions like these could still be bought and that dying existing pale cotton garments with 'plain, brilliant colour'[14] would give them a contemporary lift.

By 21 June writers and readers had had three weeks to acclimatize to the facts of clothes rationing. 'Practical Living' now tackled 'How to Run Your Dress Allowance',[15] confronting the reality of the limitations and restrictions implicit in the coupon system. The key idea was the need to plan ahead. Anne Scott-James suggested considering which garments readers might really need over the next six months, so through autumn into winter, always bearing in mind that *'you can't buy more than one major item in a year'*.[16] Sixty-six coupons was not that many annually[17] and a key skill to acquire would be that of 'stretching' the ration or making the coupons go as far as possible.[18]

Readers were advised to buy garments only when absolutely necessary, or invest in low coupon accessories such as collars[19] that would add variety to basic wardrobe pieces. For those able to make clothing at home, simple economic designs that saved on fabric[20] were recommended, such as 'narrow skirts, single-breasted fastenings, collarless necklines and short sleeves'. For those that had them, a redundant evening dress or cruise wear item could be remodelled into something more practical. This could be done at home or with the help of one of the professional alteration services 'now being started all over the country'.[21]

Perhaps the most compelling part of the article was the clever way in which one dark dress, with narrow bracelet sleeves and a bodice made 'to fasten down the front', formed the basis of six quite different outfits using a selection of collars, hats and hairstyles. Three of the photographs simply added collars to the dress – from the neat simplicity of the 'Eton Boy' to the more staid and traditional lace shawl collar or broderie Anglaise bib – while the other three required the bodice to be opened up into a 'V' shape allowing a fichu, Pierrot ruffle or cricket-shirt collar to be tucked neatly into place.[22] Appropriate hats, from a trim pill box for the office or 'felt sombrero' for a more tailored town outfit to the 'almost fluffy' look of the 'skull-cap with the flowers and veil' for an evening ocassion,[23] worked in tandem with the collars to add character to the six outfits. Long hair dressed in a variety of ways further embellished the final look. The ability to turn a practical idea into a smart, contemporary outfit with little cost or coupon outlay would now be at least one of the starting points for future fashion.

On 5 July 'Practical Living' returned to rationed fashion with a story on 'Clothes for a Coupon Summer'.[24] Key ideas were to buy practical clothes that would wash well and give service beyond the summer as 'your coupons won't allow you to pack things away for nine months of the year'.[25] Pinafores were considered a 'charming American fashion' offering 'genuine all-the-year-round'[26] flexibility as they could be worn with summer blouses or winter knits, while a waistcoat could provide another layer throughout the year. The ankle length dungarees pictured reflected that trousers continued to play a part in the fashion lexicon, here suitably feminized through the use of bright floral and checked fabrics. Cotton summer dresses were good value as they washed well and could be worn with jumpers and coats later in the year, while the divided cycling skirt featured was no doubt a sound idea in principle, if rather impractical in the pale fabric shown.

'Fancy sandals' were 'definitely a luxury'. Readers were advised to buy either durable 'classic leather sandals' that would 'wear for ever' or 'medium weight sports shoes' that were able, presumably, to give service beyond the summer.[27] The article also acclimatized readers to the idea of the coupon values of various garments. Prices shown reflected that shopping in one of the medium to higher-end department stores, such as John Lewis, Fenwick's or Bourne and Hollingsworth, might provide good-quality clothing but at a significantly higher cost than the chain stores.[28]

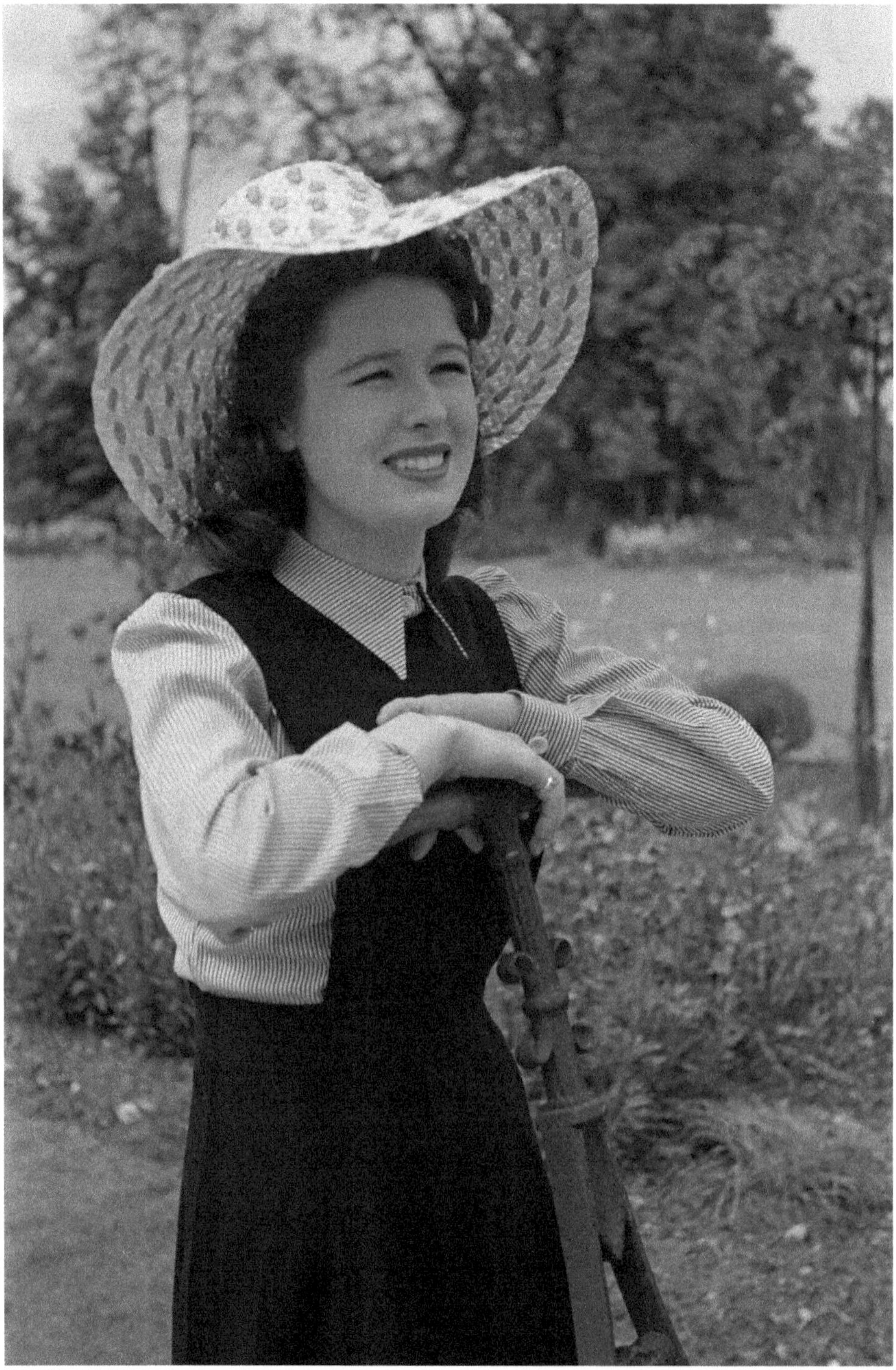

Figure 42 'The Pinnie Dress: A pinafore dress, a striped, stiff-collared blouse. From Fenwick. The frock is navy wool, 69s. 6d. 8 coupons'. 'Clothes for a Coupon Summer'. *Picture Post*, 5 July 1941, p. 26. Zoltan Glass/*Picture Post*/Hulton Archive/Getty Images (481627067).

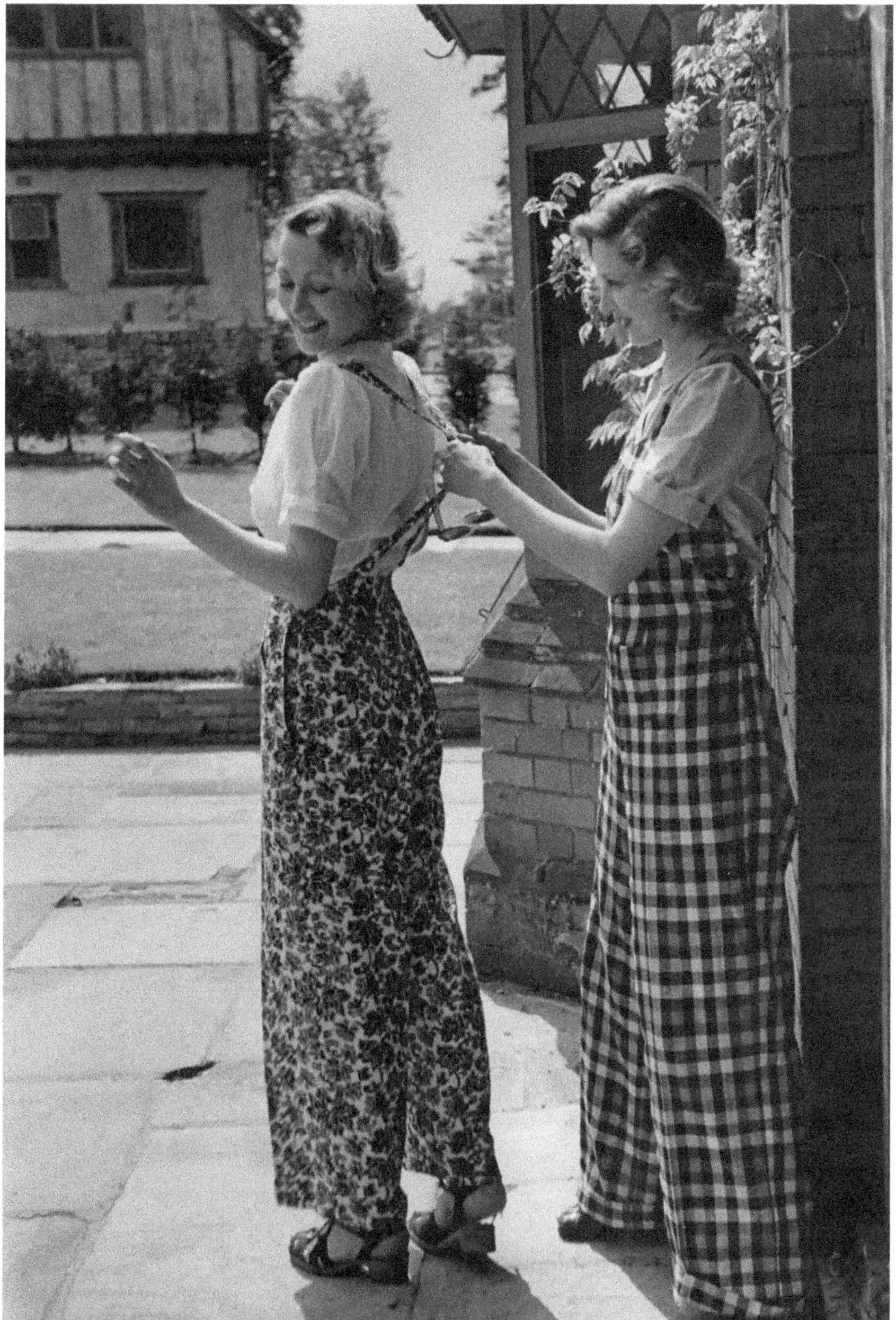

Figure 43 'Rainbow Trousers. Newest trousers show all colours of the rainbow. The floral dungarees cost 19s. 11d., check linen pair 55s. 9d., John Lewis. 6 Coupons'. 'Clothes for a Coupon Summer', *Picture Post*, 5 July 1941, p. 26. Zoltan Glass/*Picture Post*/Hulton Archive/Getty Images (481627025).

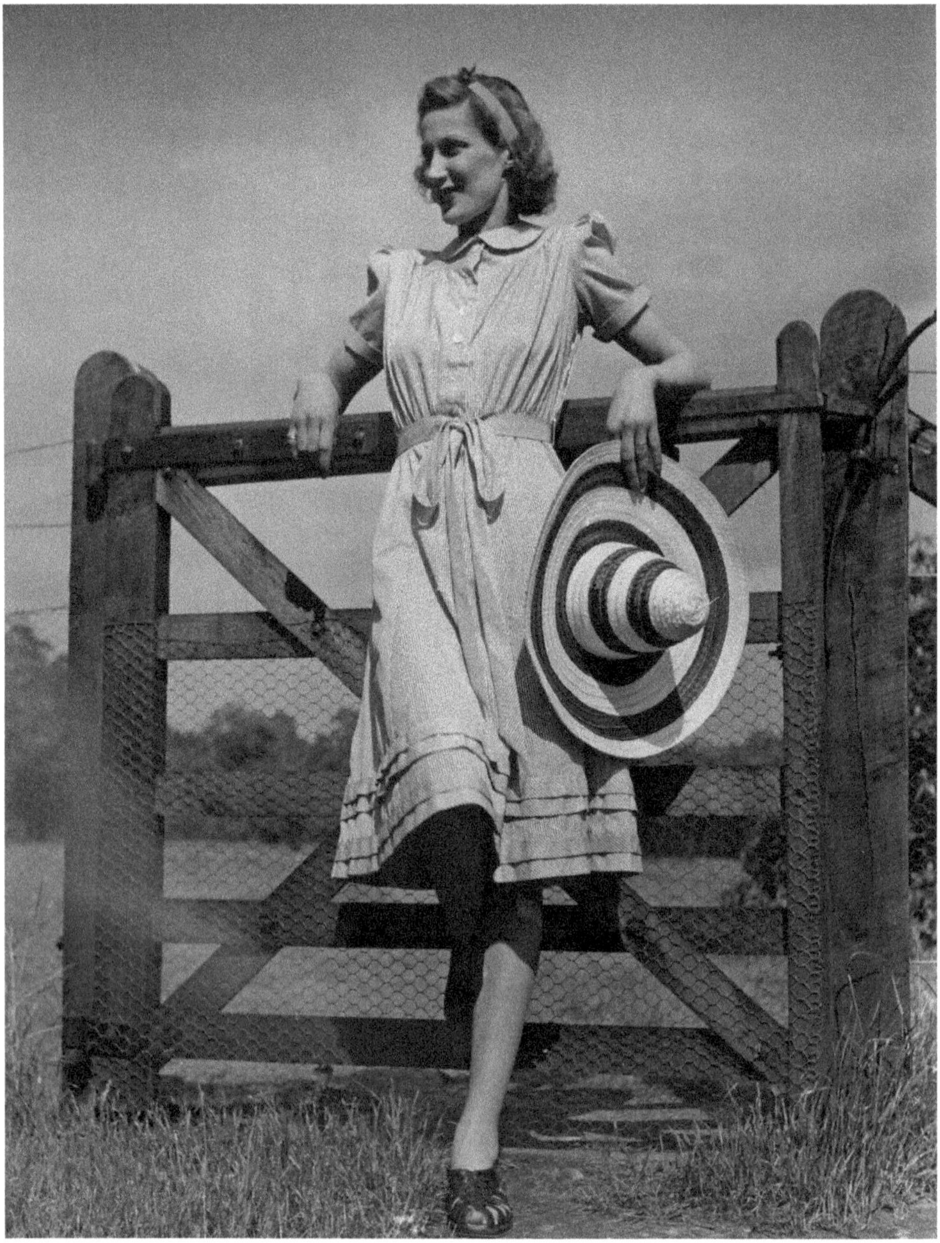

Figure 44 'Alice-in-Wonderland. Glamorous in a striped cotton "Alice" frock with stiff collar, full skirt. 4 guineas, 7 coupons. Bourne & Hollingsworth.' 'Clothes for a Coupon Summer', *Picture Post*, 5 July 1941, p. 27. Zoltan Glass/*Picture Post*/Hulton Archive/Getty Images (481626983).

Anne Scott-James asks, 'Should women wear trousers?'

Five months after clothes rationing had been established Anne Scott-James asked *Picture Post* readers what they thought about women wearing trousers. A two-page photo-story by Bert Hardy revealed that women were taking to trousers for many on- and off-duty occupations and that choices now ranged from baggy slacks and boiler suits to softly tailored jacket and trouser combinations. Scott-James expressed the view that it was 'obviously' right for women to adopt these practical styles.[29] What was more important to know, however, was 'when, where and how' they should be worn.

Trousers were to take over when skirts became unsuitable. 'You can't fight an incendiary with confidence in clothes that flutter, or even sleep decently in a shelter in a skirt.' Scott-James listed a range of situations, both official and domestic, where trousers were now right and a 'natural' alternative, the consistent theme being practicality. In her opinion, however, there were certain provisos in terms of the when and how. For the when, there was 'no need to keep [trousers] on after working hours' and although 'slacks around the street may save stocking coupons ... they certainly don't improve the look of the town'. This suggested a somewhat ambivalent attitude. Trousers, it seemed, were necessary incomers to the female wardrobe but not fully accepted as feminine fashion.[30]

As to the how, Scott-James recommended teeming trousers with 'sensible (but not too-masculine) accessories'. These included 'flat shoes, tailored shirts and jerseys, [and] good long jackets ... at least as long as a man's'. She cautioned against 'close-cropped hair [and] ... a high shirt with a tie', both of which were 'overdoing the thing'.[31] Anything approaching a too masculine feel, it seemed, went beyond the invisible boundaries of style.

One of the most interesting aspects of this photo-story was the fact that Scott-James had herself taken part in it. Wearing a pin-stripe suit, trousers with turn-ups, a white shirt and short tie, she is seen perched on a bar stool with a cigarette and a bottle of beer chatting to a barmaid. With hair brushed away from her face to look short, here was the more masculine image she had warned women to avoid. Of all the photographs making up the story this one stands out as different because it has a sharp, androgynous edge emphasized, no doubt deliberately, by Scott-James's masculine body language. For someone who represented in many ways a classic sense of feminine style such an image could show how unreliable appearances could be when considering the idea of gender.

Several of the other photographs revealed women wearing trousers tempered in one way or another by more feminine styling – either smart little sweaters, softly tailored jackets or simply softer hairstyles. The collection together was designed to provide an overview on some of the trouser styles currently visible on the streets and, perhaps, question the degree to which changing dress codes were broadening perceptions about the nature of femininity. The largest picture certainly focused on the connection between gender identity and clothing. In this lead image Burt Hardy had photographed a man and woman arm in arm about the town – the man in a kilt, the woman in a boiler suit.

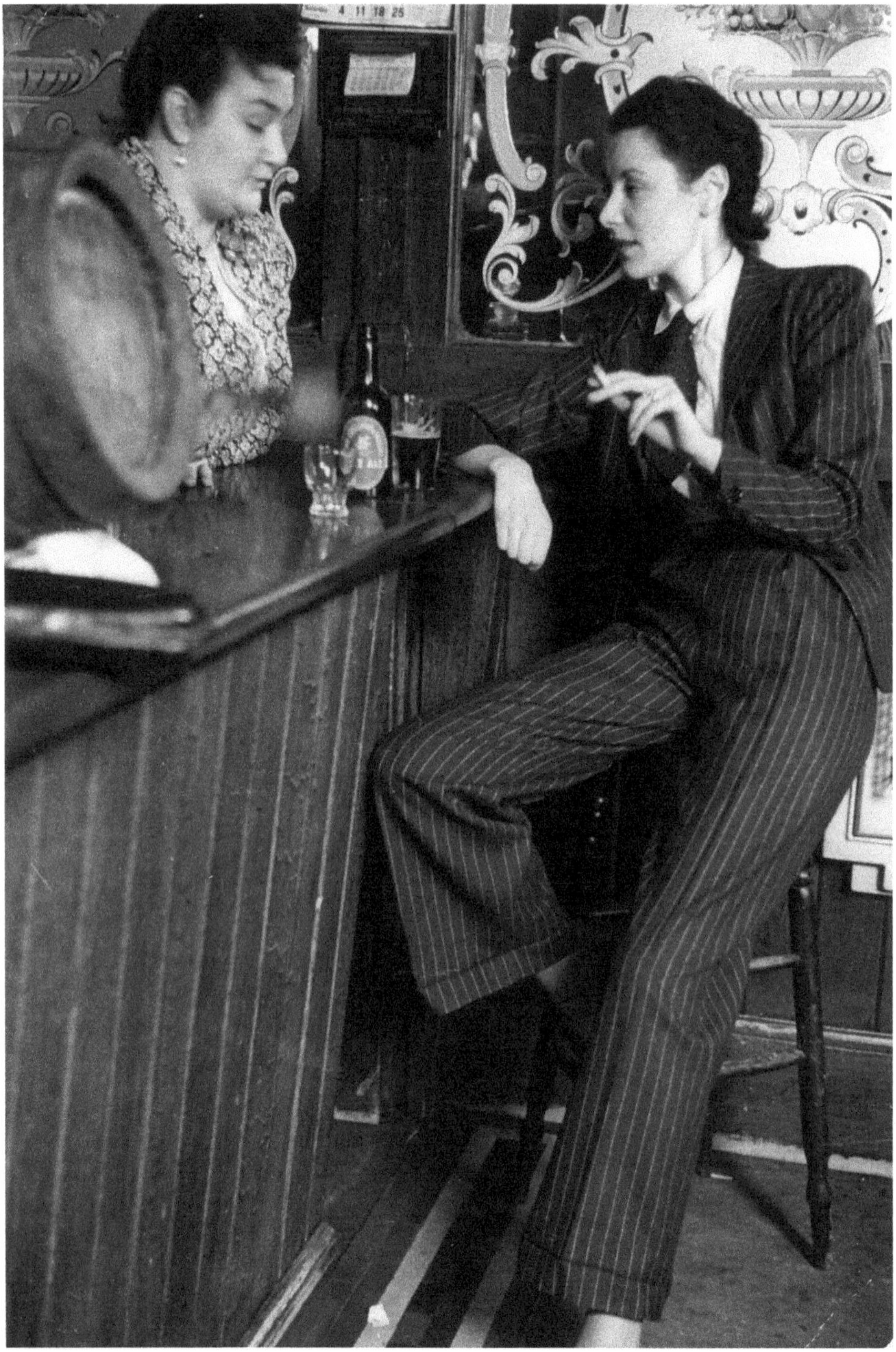

Figure 45 'Should Women Wear Trousers?' 1 November 1941, p. 22. Burt Hardy/*Picture Post*/ Getty Images (3071551) (The image above, available from the Getty Collection, is not the one published in *Picture Post* but is almost identical. The barmaid's position has shifted slightly in the original which is currently untraceable.)

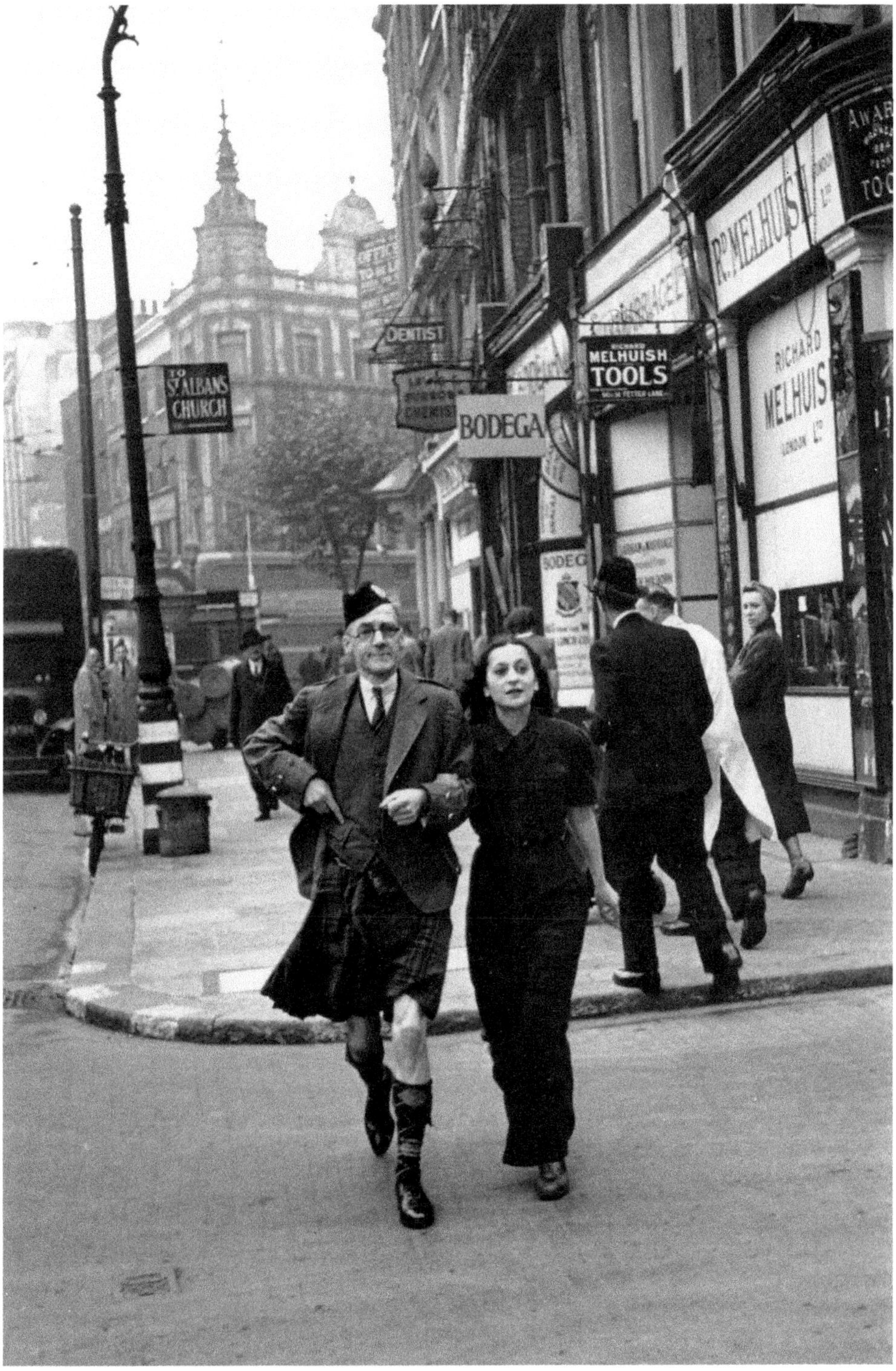

Figure 46 'Our photographer went out to snap women in trousers. He got this couple first shot'. From 'Should Women Wear Trousers?' *Picture Post*, 1 November 1941, p. 22. Burt Hardy/*Picture Post*/Getty Images (2637107).

The Utility scheme and Austerity

While rationing guaranteed fair shares of the civilian clothing available, it was also necessary to ensure that the clothing on which precious coupons were to be expended was both durable, fit for purpose and affordable. The Board of Trade now established new quality and price controls, therefore, on both textiles and clothing manufacture to the end that no one would find themselves either unable to afford essential wardrobe commodities or giving up coupons and paying for a garment that would not stand up to reasonable wear.

Utility clothing

The scheme responsible for delivering fabric and clothing to government specification was known as Utility.[32] In March 1942, *Picture Post* photographed rising star Deborah Kerr[33] in some of the latest Utility outfits which far from being in any way standardized or Government issue were, according to Anne Scott-James, 'excellent'.[34] Calling Utility a 'fashion revolution' she went on to tell readers that almost all clothing, except women's dressing gowns and shoes, were now available under the scheme, in good colours with subtle shades and in a 'considerable variety of designs'. Women used to buying more expensive clothes might find the fabrics offered not quite so good but were told that 'the best firms are offsetting this necessary lowering of standards by putting good cut, finish and colour schemes into their Utility models'.[35]

Dresses were no longer as generously cut but still showed flared or pleated skirts. Coats came in both 'square boxy' and the 'fitted, belted type', while suits could be either in 'soft, lightweight' or in 'tailored country' designs.[36] The styles worn by Deborah Kerr included a 'typical Utility dress' in pale blue wool with a short-sleeved, double-breasted bodice and box pleating in the skirt.[37]

A simple wraparound Utility coat in ice blue wool was pleated into the back waist, had a tie belt and, when viewed from the front, was seen to have generously cut lapels and shoulder-padded bell sleeves.

The suits featured neatly tailored jackets and skirts and the ensembles generally captured the graceful, simpler designs that were becoming the signature style of wartime dressing. The fashions featured had all been selected from more expensive independent retailers such as Dereta and Jaeger and some reached the 'typical maximum prices' stipulated under the scheme which was 62s. 10d. for a dress, 95s. 1d. for a coat (making Dereta's coat a little cheaper at 83s. 11d.) and 97s. 4d for a suit, the price of the Jaeger raspberry tweed suit pictured.[38] That the Utility scheme was providing clothing across *all* the buying demographics was, perhaps, reflected in the fact, shared with readers, that 'the full price list takes up some sixty-five pages of a Government Order'.[39]

The Utility scheme did not account for all production of cloth and clothing however,[40] and Scott-James raised her concern that the 'gulf between the mass trade and the luxury trade is prodigiously wide'. She spoke of 'elaborate day dresses ... containing six, eight, ten yards of fabric. Evening gowns ... laboriously embroidered by hand sell[ing] for fifty guineas or so. Fashion shows are organised, at which women sit for hours watching furs

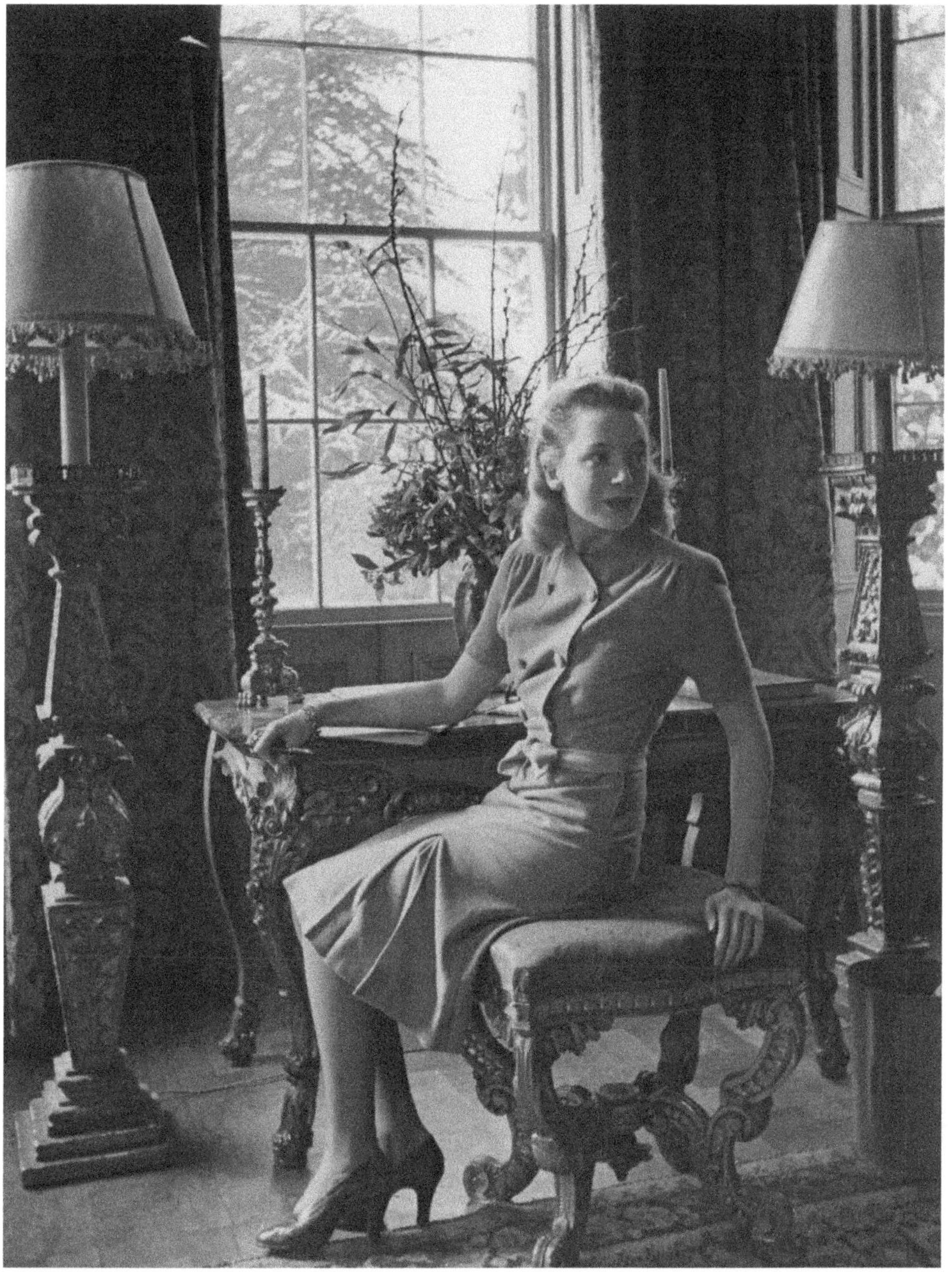

Figure 47 'Dresses: Here is a typical Utility Dress. Of pale blue light woollen, it has a double-breasted bodice and pleats in the skirt. A Spectator Model, 62s. 10d. Everything about it is top-flight, except the price.' 'Deborah Kerr Shows Off The New Utility Clothes For Women', *Picture Post*, 28 March 1942, p. 18. Felix Man/*Picture Post*/Hulton Archive/Getty Images (984851376).

and high fashion gowns parade past – often the same women, afternoon after afternoon'.[41] This seemed inappropriate in the face of war news: 'While the fall of Singapore and the Hong Kong atrocities fill the headlines, the luxury fashion trade flourishes.'[42]

Why not apply the design restrictions universally? Her closing remark was combative: 'If Mayfair hasn't the necessary skill to cut a good dress from three or four yards of material with five or six buttons, it must learn – or go under.'[43] By this stage in the scheme the restrictions on design and embellishment, known in due course as the austerity regulations, had not yet been introduced.[44] When they were and alongside of the dwindling supply of luxury fabrics, there was little choice for the couture end of the fashion industry but to adjust their working practices accordingly.[45]

In May, in an article entitled 'American Fashions for Summer',[46] Anne Scott-James began by recollecting that before the war England had begun to import 'large quantities of gay, cheap fashions from the U.S.A.', including well-cut, washable summer dresses or 'tub-frocks'. These were no longer available under war conditions but *Picture Post* had commissioned a London store to create 'a set of practical summer clothes copying American styles, American colour schemes, and American sizes. Here they are'.[47] The outfits were all photographed in outdoor locations, arguably in deference to the fact that 'Americans have always understood the art of dressing for open-air activities – probably because they have better weather than we do, and take outdoor life as a matter of course'.[48] Fashions featured included a pair of dungarees – showing a trouser line drawn

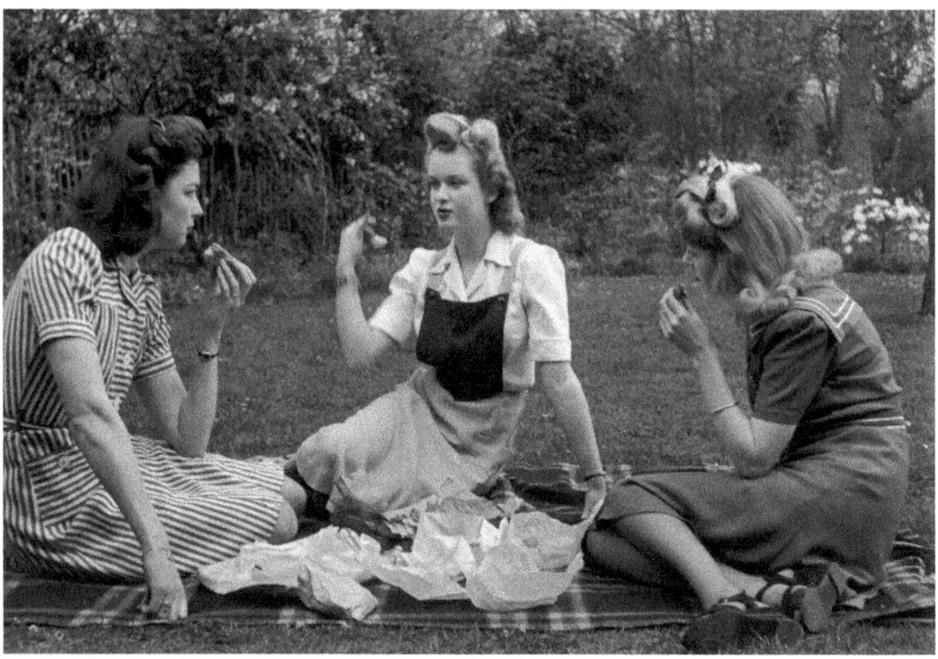

Figure 48 'Coloured Cotton Wash Frocks Are Practical for a Wartime Summer: … The navy blue and white striped Utility shirt dress costs 36s 6d. The saxe blue frock with navy bib and white sports shirt costs 45s 11d. complete.' The 'American Sailor Frock' in blue cotton with white trim was priced at two guineas. From 'American Fashions For Summer', *Picture Post*, 16 May 1942, p. 22. Kurt Hutton/Getty Images (2696647).

in to the ankle with a cuff – a boiler suit, American-style shirt-waist button-through dresses and the practical pinafore. A removable apron front on the dungarees allowed for easy laundering of that part of the garment most likely to catch the dirt, while the boiler suit had white spotted revers which detached for washing. Knee-length dresses, all in bright, fresh colourways, had 'skirts shorter than they've been for years'[49] either cut straight or in dirndl style. Only one dress was officially Utility, being made in Utility fabric, although the other outfits were considered comparable with Utility in terms of 'cost and value'.[50]

That the rest of the collection was not Utility would seem to confirm that there was still a residual amount of non-Utility fabric available for the civilian market and that, at this time, transition to full Utility production had not yet been achieved. The photographs revealed, however, a relatively utilitarian set of styles which in many ways pre-empted the leaner, paired back design ethos of the Austerity-Utility clothing to come.

Austerity clothing

By August 1942 the austerity measures were beginning to be noticeable. In an article entitled 'Austerity Clothes for the Fourth Year of the War',[51] Anne Scott-James looked at some examples of the 'first season of Austerity clothes'[52] and compared them with fashions from before the war. This revealed the scale of the changes that had occurred. In all cases the wartime garments featured, from a wedding outfit and evening dresses to a town suit and day-time party dress, reflected an economy of fabric and a simplicity of cut-and-make considerably at odds with the more opulently conceived pre-war clothing.

Designers across the price spectrum were now focused on making the best use of the limited fabrics and decorative elements allowed under the austerity measures. Creating well-cut, simpler styles in all clothing categories, garments were practical yet also pretty and chic. Readers were given some idea of the various new rules affecting clothing design and reminded that although there might still be 'plenty of pleated skirts in the shops, frilled blouses, lace-trimmed coats', these would be superseded in due course by those made under the new controls. While it took time for Board of Trade regulations to become effective through the process of design and manufacture, 'all clothes that are being made to-day are "Austerity"'.[53]

One photo-comparison showed the differences that now existed between a pre-war town suit and the Austerity version. The first featured a flared skirt, curvaceously tailored jacket with fur shawl collar and matching fur cuffs. This was clearly a more opulent use of material and luxury trimmings than the simpler, less adorned, wartime suit pictured alongside it. Here the longer line jacket with modest notched lapels and hip pockets continued to create a softly tailored look but without the accented waist or ostentatious finishing.[54] The simpler lines not only required less fabric and trim but needed less labour and time to produce, both important factors as the textile industry was streamlined in favour of other forms of war production such as munitions.[55] A similar sense of simplicity and paired-back chic invested the just-below-the-knee-length Austerity 'At Home Dress' when compared to the pre-war long dress with tiered skirt which was now, of course, 'forbidden'.[56]

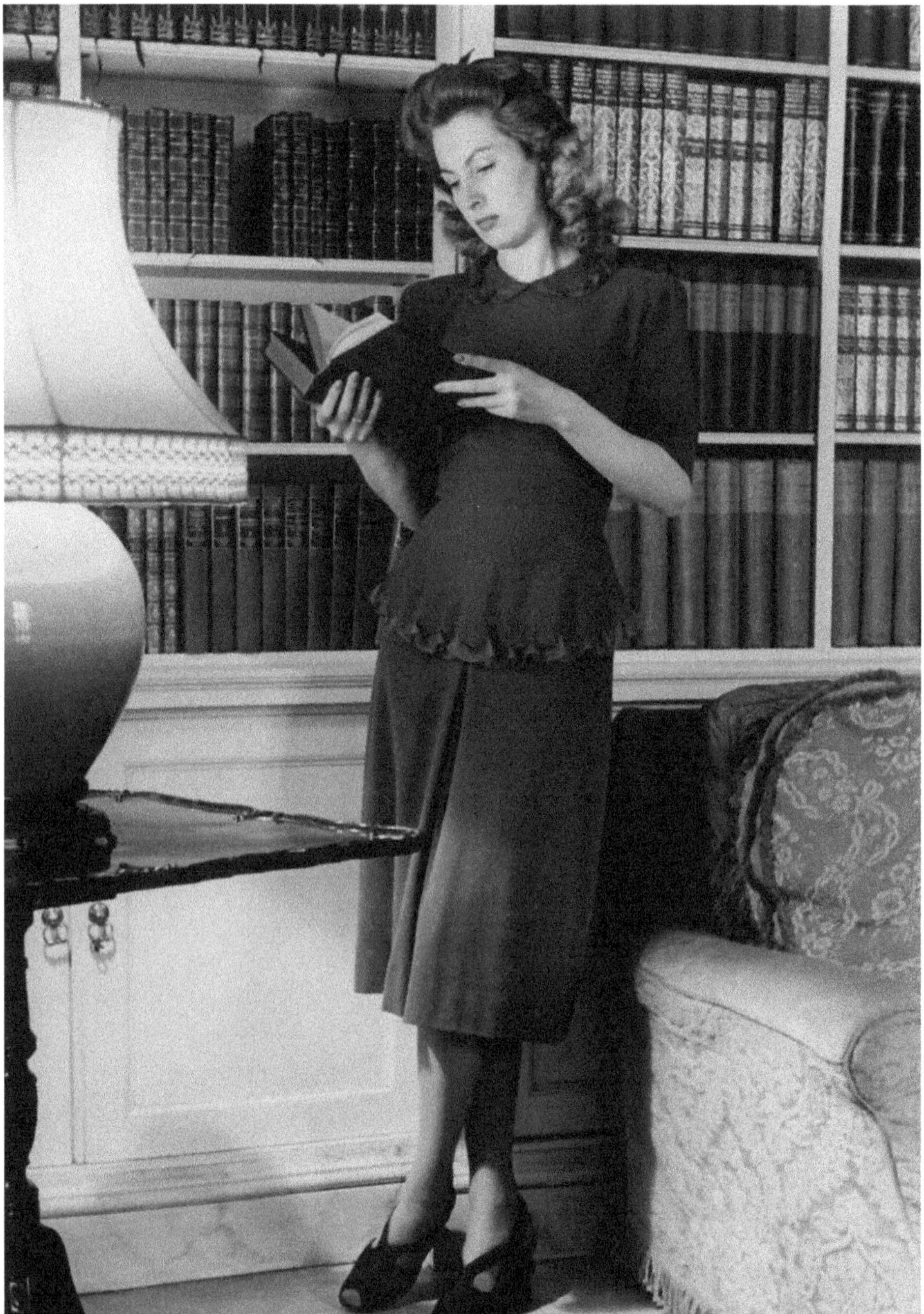

Figure 49 'At Home Dress. Today, we wear the same short simple dress for afternoons and evenings. From Rose & Blairman.' 'Austerity Clothes for the Fourth Year of the War'. *Picture Post*, 29 August 1942, p. 22. Felix Man/*Picture Post*/Hulton Archive/Getty Images (180262940).

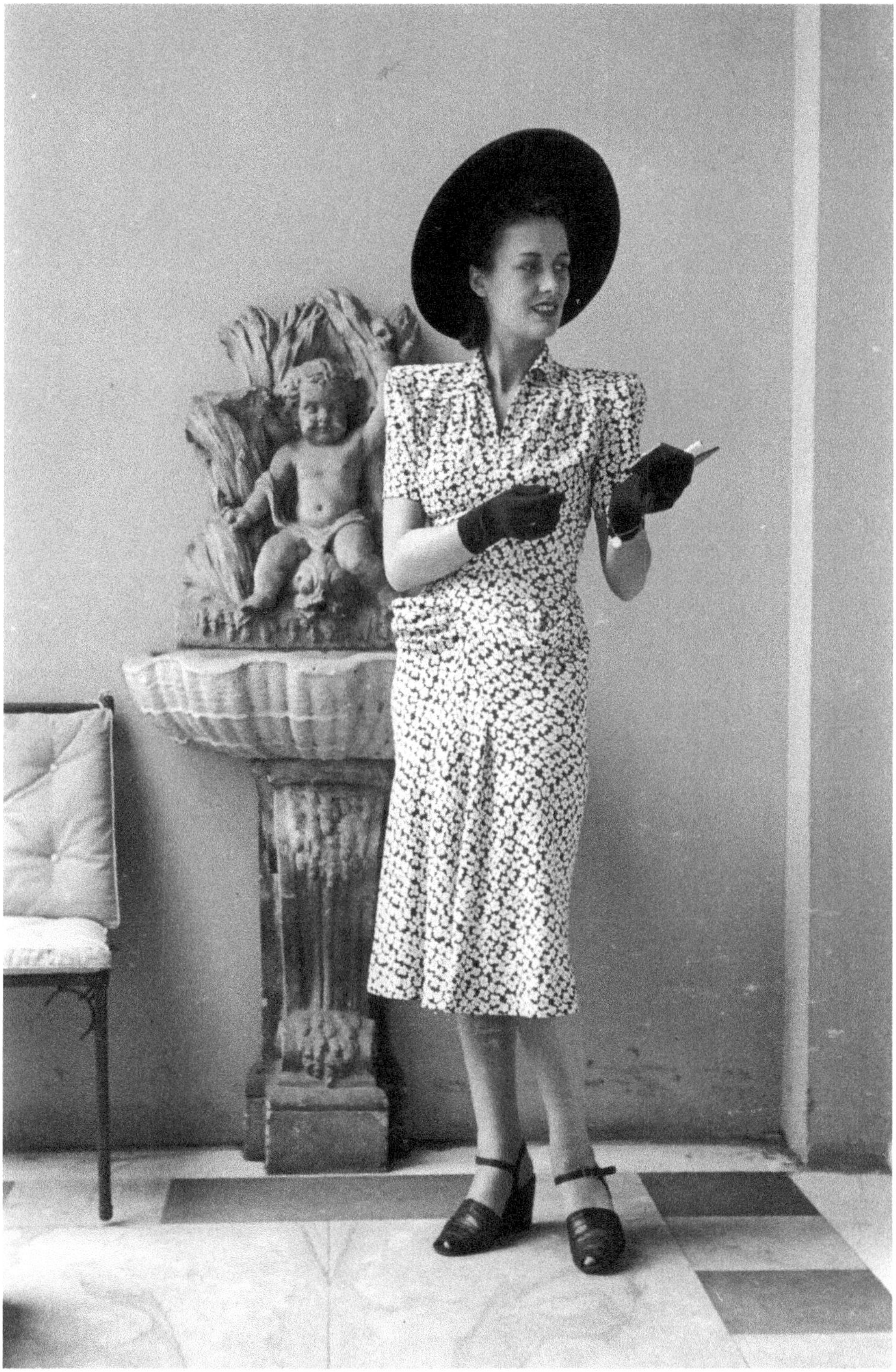

Figure 50 'Daytime Parties. Formal parties don't exist. A short print frock (from Rhavis) is the dressiest kind made.' 'Austerity Clothes for the Fourth Year of the War', *Picture Post*, 29 August 1942, p. 23. Felix Man/*Picture Post*/Getty Images (2696616).

Scott-James had again gone for relatively up-market examples of Utility wear from independent high street retailers like Rhavis and Spectator Sports and from couturier Digby Morton. These clothes, in her opinion, were 'typical examples of the best Austerity' where fabrics and trimmings had been used 'with real taste and skill'.[57] Couturiers and fashion brands were both clearly embracing the limitations imposed on them by Austerity to produce quiet, clean-lined versions of classic designs while also meeting the need for durable, practical pieces that would serve for a variety of occasions.

How wartime style continued under austerity

Summer fashions for 1943 showed little major change to the simpler, understated silhouettes emerging from the design constraints. In an article entitled 'Fashions for Summer: All Under £3', Anne Scott-James confronted the fact that 'in a war like this, fashion stands still. Neither time, nor labour, nor inspiration can be spared for the creation of new fashion season after season'.[58] The minor alterations that did affect established lines and silhouettes tended to increase practicality, such as the 'new version of the summer shirt-dress'. This now consisted of a 'separate shirt and skirt which looks like a one piece'.[59] The benefit of this was that for only one extra coupon buyers gained an additional shirt that could be used with other existing garments. In a similar vein sweaters were becoming increasingly plain and uncomplicated, whether low fastening or buttoning to the neck, with 'one simple jersey . . . do[ing] the work of several' by the addition of little accessories. Modest changes such as wearing rolled-up sleeves 'the way American girls are doing' made the sweater 'workmanlike'.[60] Blouses had mostly consolidated around a shirt-style design with 'tailored collars and sleeves' such as one in a striped strawberry pink fabric captioned 'The Prettiest Shirt of the Summer'.[61] The 'new loose lines and long, full sleeves' of the Cricketer's Shirt revealed, perhaps surprisingly, that it was possible to create some generosity of line within the design restrictions.[62]

The most pervasive styles were the shirt-dress, available in a range of colours and prints, the knitted sweater or twin set, the versatile box jacket that was easy to wear with trousers, uncomplicated skirts or dresses, the latter often button-through, and the softly tailored two-piece suit.[63] Photographs captured some of the variety offered by quality department stores such as John Lewis, Fenwick, Bourne and Hollingsworth, and Selfridge's where prices were at the medium to higher end of Utility manufacture.[64] Dresses ranged from 45s. 6d. to 53s. 7d., blouses 17s. 11d. to 23s. 4d., and the twin set shown added up to 43s. 7d. Femininity was to the fore in the popular long wavy hairstyles of the models that could be brushed into a top knot, bun or set in rolls around the head. Anne Scott-James expressed the view that 'classic clothes fit the mood today; all the best designers are making them' and that it was up to readers to 'pick basic styles, and make them look different'.[65]

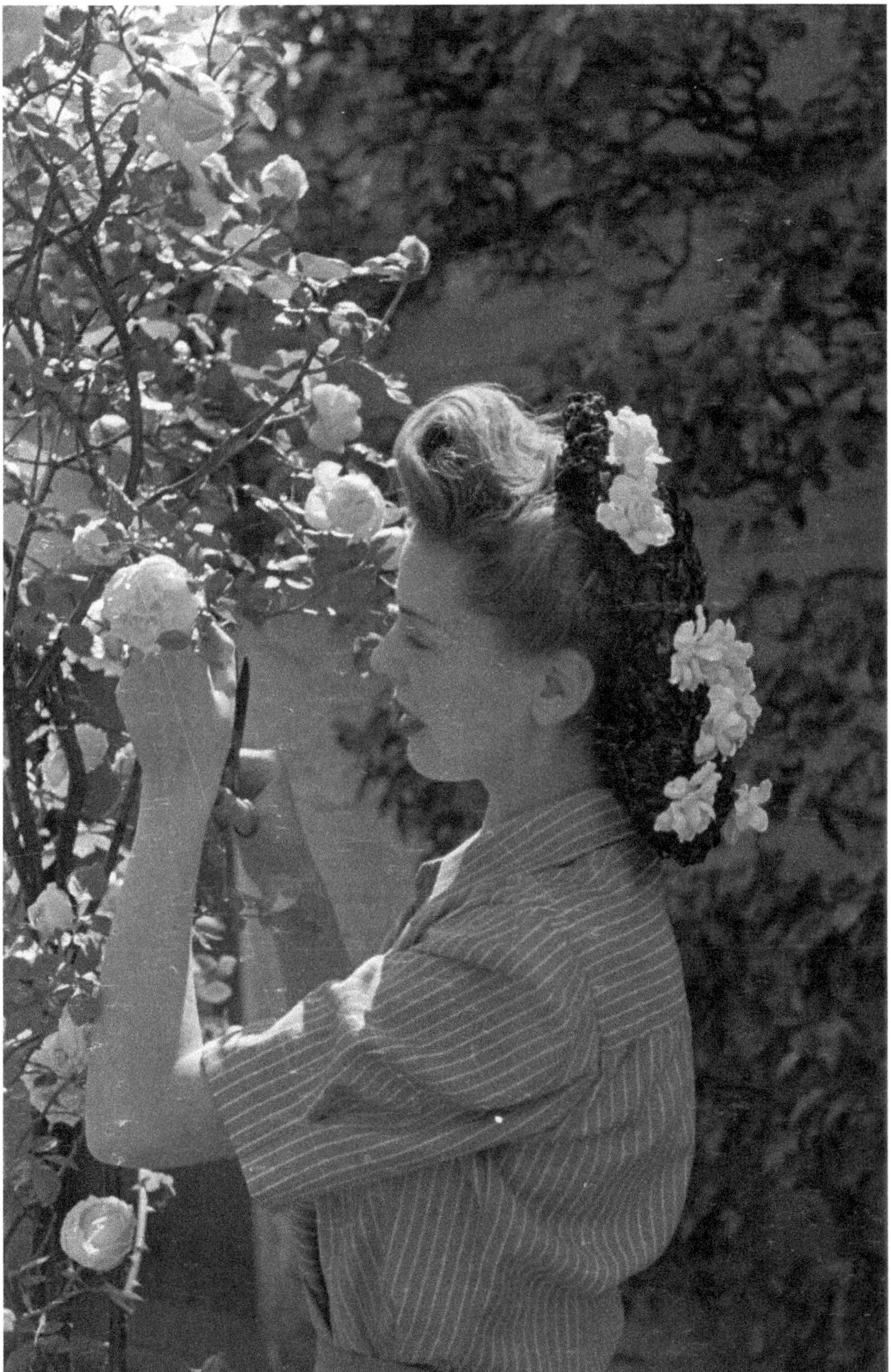

Figure 51 'The Prettiest Shirt of the Summer: It's striped strawberry pink; 17s. 11d. The snood is a gay extravagance. Bourne and Hollingsworth.' From 'Fashions for Summer: All Under £3'. *Picture Post*, 19 June 1943, p. 24. Kurt Hutton/*Picture Post*/Getty Images (3379565).

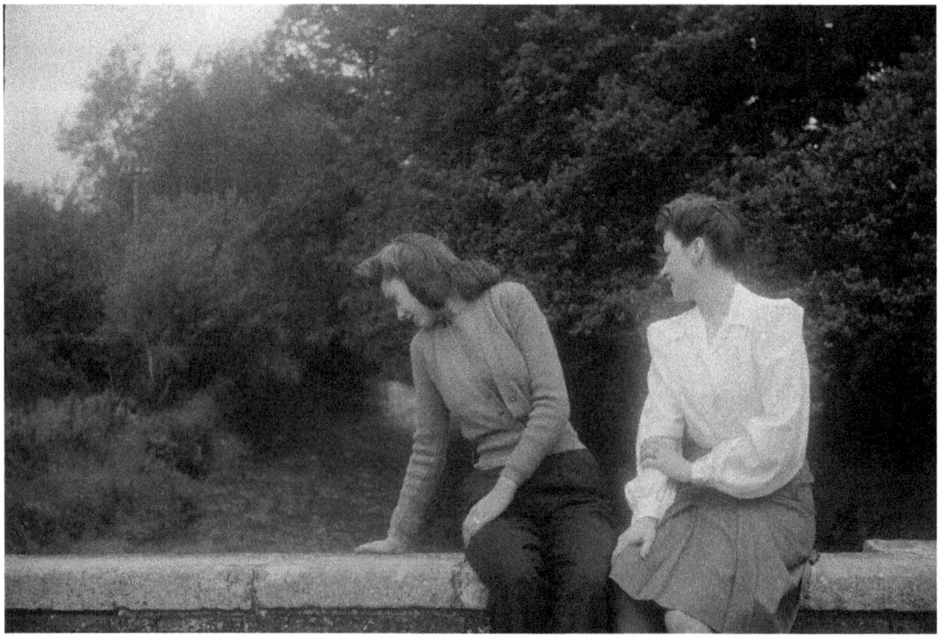

Figure 52 'Classic Sweaters and a Cricketer's Shirt: This twin set is in a green brushed rayon that looks like wool; 20s. 11d. for the jersey, 22s. 8d. for the cardigan. The brown cotton slacks cost 24s. 4d., take only 5 coupons. The white blouse has new loose lines and long, full sleeves; 21s. 5d. All from Selfridge's.' From 'Fashions For Summer: All Under £3', *Picture Post*, 19 June 1943, p. 25. Kurt Hutton/*Picture Post*/Getty Images (3378955).

Some fashion news from America

Two fashion bulletins from America delivered some interesting and less predictable fashion and beauty news during the autumn and winter of 1943. The first one entitled 'So That's What They Mean by a Leg Bar'[66] reported on the Elizabeth Arden leg bar in New York. This was offering 'good-as-new feet and good-as-the-real-thing stockings' in the comfort of an attractive salon employing trained pedicurists.[67] While the text proceeded to consider why tired feet and legs were so much more current and what could be done about this in Britain, the photographs illustrated the treatments on offer in this American salon. Here 'beauty and utility' combined to rehabilitate legs and feet and provide a leg make-up creating the illusion of stockings. Well-dressed New York clients were seen receiving the application of a liquid foundation 'film' as part of a pampering beauty parlour experience, revealing that American women, too, were affected by a shortage of stockings.[68]

In December 1943 a further style bulletin from the United States introduced *Picture Post* readers to 'A Crazy New Fashion' for knitted 'one-piece woollies'.[69] Worn by American college girls these knitted tights-and-tops combinations were called 'leotards' and provided 'the warmest fashion in years'. Made of jersey or wool and in jazzy stripes as well as plain colours, these outfits certainly created a quite new departure for fashion. Teemed with laced-up espadrilles – a summer shoe with a winter outfit – the figure-revealing style was 'soften[ed]' by the addition of a 'skirt or wrap-around tunic'. The text expressed the view that 'American college girls are notorious chasers after novelty, and with their neat figures and fresh good looks they can wear some absurd things and get away with them'.[70]

The writer suggested these styles were unlikely to be seen in Britain. Not only were the close fitting garments 'not too flattering to your legs and figure', there was just too little wool to make them under the current restrictions. One caption reported that while the college girls featured could look like 'dancers or racing cyclists', they could also resemble 'frogs or gnomes', an equivocal response that somewhat compromised the attraction of the garment's snug protection against the 'sharp cold of the American winter'.[71]

What *Picture Post* readers might not have known was that the top left-hand photograph of the article had formed the front cover of American *Life* magazine back in September 1943.[72] Captioned simply 'Leotards' it showcased the work of American designer Claire McCardell, who had promoted the use of wool jersey since the early thirties. Yohannan and Nolf in their book on McCardell report that the designs were first called 'funny tights' by *Life* and that although they generated 'media attention for their forward-looking originality they later proved too expensive to produce for the designer's mid-market clientele'.[73] Whatever the final fate of this fashion it certainly provided *Picture Post* readers with a view less ordinary and a momentary glimpse of what would prove to be a part of fashion's future.

In February 1944, when a new batch of clothing coupons out of the year's allocation was released to the public, Anne Scott-James expressed the view that 'most of us have extremely few clothes left. Even women with lavish pre-war wardrobes find that the old materials are worn poor and thin. You can't afford a single failure'.[74] This risk was lessened by a good deal of the available clothing reflecting the familiar, safe, classic fashion lines of wartime. These continued to comprise simple dresses, tailored suits and slim-line coats replete with practical front pockets. The 'fitted swagger' was new for 1944, falling open at the front but tailored into the waist at the back, superseding the old and more generous 'balloon' swagger shape.[75] Distinctive decorative hand-stitching also surfaced as new, while the range of colours mentioned – pistachio, scarlet, green and red plaid, golden stripe and sky blue – arguably went some way to ameliorating largely predictable, if still stylish, silhouettes.[76]

Scott-James now suggested buying 'a formal frock' with 'a little more to it', such as a 'draped neck or a moulded waistline'. These need cost no more in terms of 'coupons or cash' apparently and would achieve a 'well-dressed' look at a time when it was 'only too easy to look underdressed' because of shoe and accessory shortages and the very high prices of hats. Hats had not been rationed, but much of the materials from which they were made were either scarce or themselves rationed. Scott-James expressed the view that 'no amount of excuses from either the hat trade or officialdom will convince us that the price of hats is anything but exploitation' – a state of affairs no doubt accounting for the popularity of the 'schoolgirl beret' that could be bought for around ten shillings.[77]

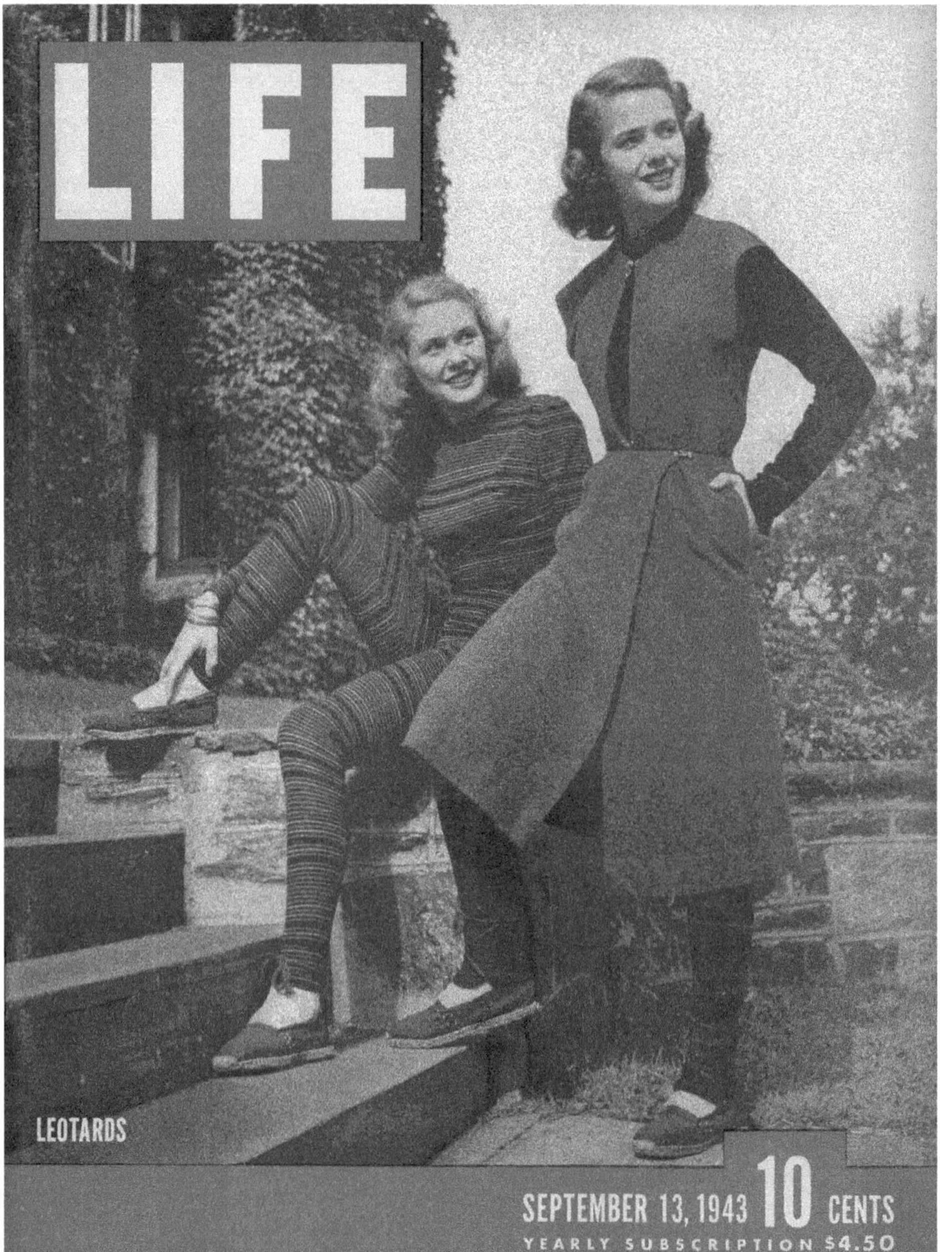

Figure 53 *Life* Magazine Cover, 13 September 1943. Nina Leen/The *Life* Premium Collection/Getty Images (160544470).

Conclusion

The high street continued to offer a controlled amount of Utility fashion alongside of haberdashery items such as ribbon[78] and lace net which could be purchased without coupons. *Picture Post* also carried official notices from the Ministry of Information such as 'What do I do ... with Clothing Coupons marked "X"?'[79] and 'What do I do ... to use my clothing coupons wisely?'[80] These were designed to keep the public aware of the constraints of rationing and help them identify their wardrobe needs before letting go of irreplaceable coupons. Advice on caring for clothing provided by the Board of Trade in notices such as 'Do you care for clothes?'[81] and 'How they grow!'[82] also offered practical suggestions for maintaining clothing and making running repairs.

The Board of Trade Notices above ended with a reminder to the public that 'once your coupons are gone they're gone'. The giving up of precious coupons remained a 'responsible business'.[83] 'Practical Living', and other fashion features, offered readers overviews and opinions on the nature of fashion, any options available and the changing priorities for dress. As rationing, Utility and Austerity brought about unprecedented changes to the manufacture and retailing of clothing *Picture Post* reflected how fashion was being kept alive, not by distinctive seasonal shifts in fabric or line, but by subtle changes in the details of design, cut and making-up and the imaginative application of available accessories.

6
PICTURE POST REPORTS ON WARTIME CLOTHING INITIATIVES

Introduction

This chapter focuses on articles from *Picture Post* that reported on new ways of providing additional clothing and textile goods for services such as hospitals and refuge centres. It explores the growth of voluntary making before clothes rationing, the importance of gift donations of clothing and associated material comforts and the new initiatives that arose to cope with both the ongoing domestic hardships of war and the stringencies caused by clothing control. The efficient recycling of textiles lay at the heart of much of this provision, alongside of unknown amounts of home-made items generated both by individuals, groups and larger organizations.

From the Blitz onwards Britain endured the continual threat of aerial bombardment until March 1945.[1] There was, in consequence, an ongoing need for additional clothing and domestic textiles as home front victims began to remake their lives. *Picture Post* investigated various voluntary organizations that had formed to create, or in other ways acquire, and distribute these commodities and reported on the type of help they offered. In the process the magazine brought to greater public notice how these groups were assisting both the essential services and those struggling to cope with the difficulties of day-to-day living as a result of such things as bombing, too little money or, after rationing, coupon shortage. From knitting circles to clothing exchanges, organizations arose to meet the challenges of potential need and *Picture Post* was there to celebrate the insight, ingenuity and industry they revealed.

Early schemes to provide additional clothing

Government intervention: Clothing for disadvantaged evacuees

Following the first mass evacuation scheme which ran from 1 to 4 September 1939, the inadequate clothing of children from deprived neighbourhoods[2] had revealed how impoverished the living conditions of some of the poorest communities in Britain were. This had triggered the first scheme to collect and distribute essential clothing. Facilitated by a government grant, children from these areas, whose poverty of circumstance could be ameliorated in no other way, became the first beneficiaries of this new departure in social welfare.[3] Evacuation had triggered a necessary intervention by government to provide clothing commensurate with warmth and good health. This was an important first step.[4]

The Women's Voluntary Service and the 'Children's Hotel'

During the summer of 1940, as the threat from German forces escalated, further waves of evacuation took place and clothing deficiencies were again met by the government clothing scheme.[5] For children too young to be evacuated with schools, or who could not, for whatever reason, be accompanied by their mothers, a new system had been inaugurated by the Women's Voluntary Services (henceforth WVS[6]) in London. *Picture Post* went along to the 'Children's Hotel' at Cromwell House, Highgate Hill, to investigate.[7]

The Hotel welcomed children for a two-night respite stay in order to prepare them for evacuation to reception areas. Three-year-old Dennis, whose father was dead and whose mother was about to have an operation, was one guest, as was four-year-old Reginald. His day nursery had closed down and with a soldier father missing since May and a mother wanting to work, he had been successfully selected for evacuation through the Hotel.

The children largely came from poorer homes or overcrowded areas. Being able to roam in a garden with lawns, trees and flowers was quite new for youngsters used to 'only streets and back-yards', and having a bath alone might also have been unusual.[8] Young guests were given medical check-ups, good food and two nights in their own 'tiny bed', which had a bright patchwork quilt and a 'flowered linen bag' on the bedpost containing their clothes.[9] When it was time to leave they were given, if necessary, 'a suitcase full of new clothes', provided by the WVS, who had been the fortunate recipient of money for equipment and clothing from both the American Red Cross and 'numerous British organisations'.[10]

The full list of clothing each child was to take comprised a good supply of underwear and nightwear, at least one change of outerwear, shoes and Wellingtons, and a coat and gloves. This list was included in the article and represented, arguably, what was considered a sufficient supply of clothes consonant with a small child's well-being.[11]

Towards the end of the article, a photograph appeared of five of the children sitting on the Hotel steps waiting for their bus to the country. Each reflected in their small face different expressions, from happy smile to more forlorn resignation. Whatever their thoughts about what lay ahead, the Hotel was sending them off well cared for and physically fit: 'Healthy, clean and equipped with new clothes'.[12] The Children's Hotel, one of two that now operated in the London area,[13] worked to provide a secure start for their young guests which was, in every sense, a world away from the inauspicious beginnings endured by too many young disadvantaged evacuees in the past.

Local and national organizations providing clothes and textiles

Several types of voluntary groups existed early on in the war to meet the specific needs of either children, members of the armed or auxiliary forces or home-front institutions and services. The WVS, for example, would play an important role in various initiatives to acquire and disperse clothing and textiles. From helping with evacuees in a number of ways to setting up refuge centres for bomb victims, the service needed ready access to textile-based commodities of one sort or another to function adequately.

Other groups and organizations were newer and had arisen in response to a specific wartime need. *Picture Post* began to introduce readers to a selection of these and the type of contribution they were making to the war effort. Such organizations set about addressing the realistic, practical needs of communities at war in their own ways, either by augmenting official or civilian clothing supplies or helping to distribute commodities to the right people in the most effective way. *Picture Post* recognized the contribution of both smaller, independent and informal work parties and those organizations that combined the output of many groups to create more sophisticated logistical operations. Together such sources contrived to supply whatever the vicissitudes of war demanded, from surgical dressings to summer dresses.

Happy knitters and the Mayfair Sewing Bee

In February 1940, still during the Phony War, *Picture Post* paid a visit to the Women's Work Guild of Keswick, a knitting circle with four hundred members who met regularly at the Keswick Hotel.[14] The Keswick knitters had made it their business to trace local people now serving away from home and send a personalized parcel to each one. This contained a pullover, scarf, hat, mittens and socks and also included soap and a towel, cigarettes, a book, toffees and a pot of the local rum butter. The name of the knitter or a little note was included. Since 5 October 1939, when the group had started up, they had sent over three hundred parcels out containing two thousand five hundred garments. The desire and ability of home front women to band together in these numbers and create such a wealth of handcrafted goods was worthy of remark. The article finished by suggesting that the knitters of Keswick could well provide 'a pattern for thousands of willing knitters all over the country'.[15]

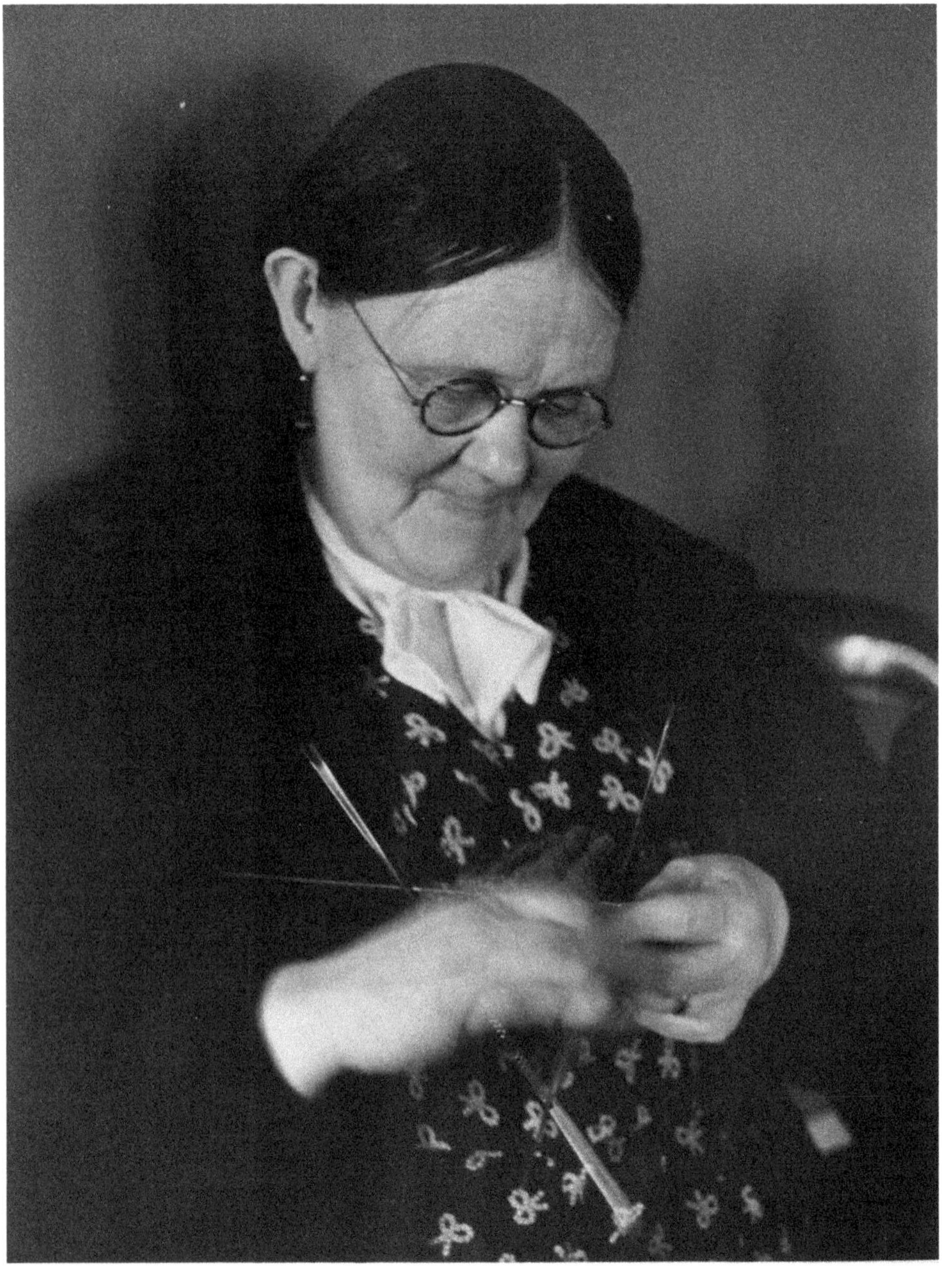

Figure 54 'Retired Farmer's Wife ... she learned to knit when hand-made Keswick knitwear was famous throughout Britain.' From 'The Happy Knitters', *Picture Post*, 17 February 1940, p. 29. Gerti Deutsch/*Picture Post*/Getty Images (3422625).

The following week journalist Antonia White contributed an article on a similar theme. The Keswick knitters, while hardly a small group, were local and community based. The Central Hospital Supply Service Committee (CHSSC) operated on a quite different scale.

Comprising numerous groups of women across Britain who had volunteered to knit or sew items required by the health services, it combined the talents of the Red Cross, WVS and the Order of St John.[16] An organization of quite considerable size, therefore, it had twelve regional divisions spanning the country, each of which could have many smaller groups under its control.

One such group was 'Mayfair's Own Sewing-Bee'[17] whose membership consisted entirely of the wives and daughters of foreign diplomats from neutral countries. 'Socialite Mrs Ronald Greville' opened her Mayfair drawing room for the Bee whose home representative was Lady Halifax, the wife of Britain's Foreign Secretary. Members arrived every Wednesday afternoon to help provide the supplies required by the CHSSC.[18] The twenty or so women worked on materials they had paid for themselves[19] and used 'official patterns approved by the Red Cross' for hospital comforts such as 'mittens, socks, scarves, pyjamas and dressing gowns'.[20] Members worked in white nursing-style headdresses and white overalls, as befitted a hospital working party, and although they happened to be seated in a Mayfair drawing room on Regency chairs, the work they did as part of the CHSSC was being reproduced 'every day of the week from Tooting to Aberdeen'.[21]

The London and Greater London region of this organization was the responsibility of Lady Gordon Finlayson. The scale of her work and the level of administration required soon became apparent. She ran 'fifteen clearing houses, 365 work-parties and 12,000 individual workers'.[22] Material for the work parties was cut out by professional pattern cutters in clearing houses before being sent out to local groups to be made up. Leftover fabric was saved to make patchwork bedspreads or knitted squares for blankets.

The needs of hospitals had to be matched by the output of work parties so that a matron did not 'receive a hundred operation stockings when she wants a hundred open-back shirts'. This process was facilitated by a comprehensive filing system that recorded the particular contributions of each affiliate. White finished by observing that 'devoted women, from ambassadors' wives to tweenies, are busy making everything the wounded will need'.[23] This was not only a remarkable story about the capacity of women to mobilize so effectively so early on in the war. It also reflected the sophisticated logistics that had arisen to create hospital supplies in readiness to meet demand whenever it might occur.

The WVS support the bombed-out

When the blitz began early in September 1940, the need intensified for an infrastructure of community refuges and support centres to provide local help for people whose homes had been damaged or destroyed. Some residents fell victim to the threat of time bombs and waited anxiously to hear if their homes could be saved. Others suffered the trauma and devastation of losing everything. Both needed to know what to do next.

A *Picture Post* article entitled 'Bombed-Out', published just over a month after the start of the blitz,[24] reported that 'delay and muddle' had already become associated with the process of helping bomb victims. The problem of the homeless, *Picture Post* revealed, was 'a vast and terrible one … for which there has been appallingly little preparation'.[25] Retaking control over lives torn apart by bomb devastation involved a laborious and time-consuming round of visits to billeting officers, rehoming centres and offices dispensing things such as food coupons, money or, after June 1941, clothing coupons. For those waiting to hear if their homes could be saved from time bombs, and whose lives were, therefore, on hold, there was neither access to billets nor official strategies for seeking help.

Some areas had fared better than others depending on the degree of voluntary support available. Photographer Bert Hardy went down to Stepney where a support unit that catered for time bombers was being run by members of the WVS. Here there was also canteen support from other volunteers, recruited by the London County Council, including 'nuns, Salvation Army lasses and socialite slummers'.[26] Here he met up with Caroline Wright, a local Stepney resident and her seven-month-old son, Harry. Caroline, 'in her bedroom slippers, with her baby son and her cardboard suitcase in her hand',[27] had just emerged from a night in a public shelter to find access to her home denied. With no public information on display as to what she should do or where she should go, she was fortunate to find a police sergeant who knew of a local centre that helped the 'temporarily homeless'.[28]

This had been set up 'in the basement of the People's Palace in the Mile End Road'.[29] Once there, Caroline and her son were reassured by a WVS member that they would be looked after for as long as it took to resolve the time bomb problem. Having left home hurriedly, Caroline had only one woolly dress for Harry in her suitcase. The WVS were able to find something for him, however, from their own clothing supplies, and a photograph

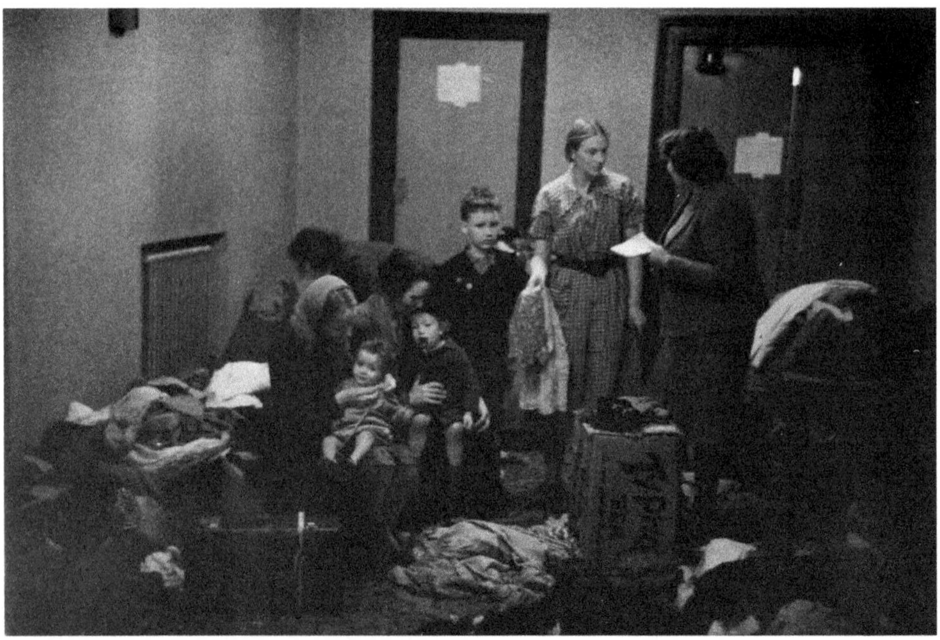

Figure 55 'New Clothes for Homeless Children: "I'd left home in such a hurry, I had only one woolly dress for baby Harry. But W.V.S. ladies were on the spot with a change of clothes"'. From 'Bombed-Out', *Picture Post*, 12 October 1940, p. 10. Bert Hardy/*Picture Post*/Hulton Archive/Getty Images (95887707).

showed other mothers and children also receiving gift clothing from a WVS member – presiding beside an upturned packing case.[30]

Here again it was the local group of a voluntary service that had mobilized to provide support and encouragement to the victims of war and to make up for shortfalls in national policy and decision-making.[31] *Picture Post* also took the opportunity to inform readers about two Ministry of Health Circulars that appeared to be little known about. These declared councils could requisition unused homes immediately and that the government would pay for accommodating people in flats and houses.[32]

Picture Post's own knitting fund

One last story that appeared before clothes rationing was inaugurated, concerning the making and distributing of gift clothing, featured an initiative taken by *Picture Post's* own Anne Scott-James. By March 1941 her Practical Living section had begun its own knitting drive for the sailors of Harwich.[33] Scott-James informed readers that the need for knitted comforts was 'now very great' and that what the sailors aboard the minesweepers and trawlers wanted most were 'gloves, sweaters and sea-boot stockings. The men can't have too many of them'. The seamen's wish list also included, among other knitted items, caps 'in positively gaudy colours with pom-poms on top' and patchwork blankets. For off-duty hours, readers were asked to send books, games, hussifs[34] and 'particularly jigsaws'.

Scott-James suggested that if readers knitted with friends and bought the same wool, they would need less as leftover yarn could be used up between them. The seamen were known personally to Mrs Stewart – the local overseer of the comforts store in Harwich – and knitters were encouraged to append their names, addresses and a note on their garments as the men 'love to know who sent things, and to write and thank you'.[35] Such communication between knitter and recipient allowed serving men and women to see that they were thought about and cared for even by people they didn't know, while the scheme as a whole offered a particular direction for home knitters without other service connections.

Other organizations offering help with clothing

In June 1941, after the advent of clothes rationing, clothing as a commodity became strictly controlled. Certain safeguards were put in place by government to address specific problems arising from rationing. Additional coupons were provided for expectant mothers, growing children, and, in due course, working people whose jobs were especially hard on clothing.[36] Victims of bombing who lost everything were entitled to a set of replacement coupons.[37] Coupon assistance was also available through direct application to the Board of Trade who could dispense additional coupons to those whose needs were considered great enough.[38] For others struggling to live within the ration, for whatever reason, the options for finding further clothing were limited.

Second-hand goods could be obtained coupon-free but only if they were sold at or below fixed prices stipulated by the Board of Trade.[39] Gift clothing and clothing from an organization such as the WVS now also became subject to coupon surrender. From the number of coupons handed back in total, the Board of Trade could calculate how clothing and textiles were being consumed.[40] The public were exhorted to get the maximum amount of use from their existing clothing in order to help the nation at large to harbour its resources.

Picture Post offered information on two ways in which families struggling to cope might find additional help. One avenue was discovered as a response to a story run in September 1941. In 'The Life of an Airman's Wife',[41] Anne Scott-James explored the difficulties air force wife Mrs Bicknell experienced feeding and clothing six children on her sergeant husband's pay. Left with an invidious choice between providing proper meals or adequate clothing but not both, this was 'not a case of immediate want, but of worry and difficulty amounting to serious hardship'.[42]

Accounts showed that all the weekly income of £3 11s. 6d. was swallowed up by rent, fuel and lighting, and food. Scott-James remarked that Mrs Bicknell's was 'a pretty typical case ... The wives of serving men already suffer more mental strain than any other class in the community. It is all the more unfair that they should be the worst financial sufferers in this war'. In her view the families of serving men should be 'free from this anxiety'.[43]

The photo-story was by Kurt Hutton and ran for three pages. The first two explored different elements of Mrs Bicknell's life as a housewife, while the last page followed the family to the heath for a Sunday outing. The theme of clothing was given some importance. The first and largest image showed Mrs Bicknell mending her son's trousers with the caption 'Brian Comes in for Running Repairs: All Part of the Day's Work'. Readers were told that Brian came in 'twice a day with torn pants or shirt or with holes in his socks .... he'll need new trousers soon'.[44] Two other images reflected on the labour involved in laundering for seven people, one showing Mrs Bicknell ironing on the kitchen table with washing airing on a line behind her, while the other showed two of the children helping to operate a large mangle outside. Another image captured Mrs Bicknell doing her weekly budget with a caption that confirmed there was 'no surplus for clothes'.[45]

The Airman's wife was clearly looking after her family's clothing in exactly the way the public would be continually asked to do in the years ahead. But 'the children wear through shoes and pants and jerseys at a terrifying rate', and once garments became too worn to be mended, there were no funds to replace them. No mention was made of coupons. The problem was a wage just too low to support the family despite receiving a seven shillings hardship allowance.[46]

A month later in the Readers' Letters section of *Picture Post*, there were some useful responses to this dilemma. The chairman of the Soldiers', Sailors' and Airmen's Families Association (SSAFA) wrote offering help with clothing and reported that 'over the last seven months', the organization had 'distributed 337,194 garments' and were receiving 'most wonderful consignments of clothes from our colonies and from America'.[47] Service wives in need of help were asked to contact SSAFA at their Central Clothing Depot in Cadogan Square, London.

Another avenue of help was suggested by the Honourable Secretary of the Citizen's Advice Bureau (CAB) who explained that the bureau had been 'successful on various occasions in getting the hardship allowance raised where circumstances appear to justify it'. 'Airmen's Wives – and Others' were invited to visit their nearest CAB to see what could be done.[48]

Help, it would seem, was available just not well publicized enough. Photo-stories like these provided visual narratives about real people undergoing real hardship yet carrying on with extraordinary tenacity. They celebrated this strength, while emphasizing the very pressing problems that had arisen from war conditions. In providing an opportunity for charitable and self-help organizations to introduce their services, *Picture Post* was also, arguably, reflecting that information on topics like this was not as accessible or widespread as it needed to be.

Clothing exchanges

In October 1943 *Picture Post* was revealing a new way to cope with clothing shortages that could operate within the restrictions imposed by rationing. With all purchases being controlled by the number of coupons required, the need for replacement clothing by families with growing children could often no longer be met. While children received both the statutory number of coupons and an official coupon supplement according to their age, insufficient coupons could still be a problem.[49] In response the WVS had set up an organization where people could find necessary clothing without surrendering coupons. In an article entitled 'This Is a Clothes Exchange',[50] Kurt Hutton and Anne Scott-James explored the origins of the scheme and how it operated.

Emerging from a headmaster's request for the WVS to 'arrange an exchange of clothes among his pupils',[51] the principle of handing on outgrown but not outworn clothing was established. Donated clothing had to be 'perfectly clean and in good condition' or it was not accepted. Any children's clothing, boots and shoes that no longer fitted could be taken to the clothing exchange, which opened one afternoon a week. Here they would be valued at a certain number of points. Parents could then obtain clothing items in return 'up to the same number of points'[52] without money or coupons being involved.

The photo-story showed children of all ages busy trying on clothing with the help of WVS assistants in working overalls. The atmosphere was clearly relaxed and informal and the range of goods considerable. Only one photograph presented a different and contrasting picture. This was of a mother, sitting quietly with her young daughter, deliberating on the points she would need for the clothes she wanted. Maintaining family wardrobes was a serious matter and required careful thought. The image was, perhaps, a reminder that finding clothing to exchange and making sure that it was in the right condition were not always easy tasks.

Mothers had 'welcomed the Exchanges with open arms'. They not only provided a valuable source of quality items for all ages of children but might also offer occasional 'rarities, like jodhpurs, ballet shoes, or Wellington boots'.[53] This initiative not only helped families alleviate the difficulty of providing sufficient and appropriate clothing for growing children. It also helped maintain the viability of the yearly clothes ration as it opened up alternative opportunities for obtaining clothing from the supply *already in existence*. This mechanism of quality recycling was of increasing value, arguably, as individual coupon

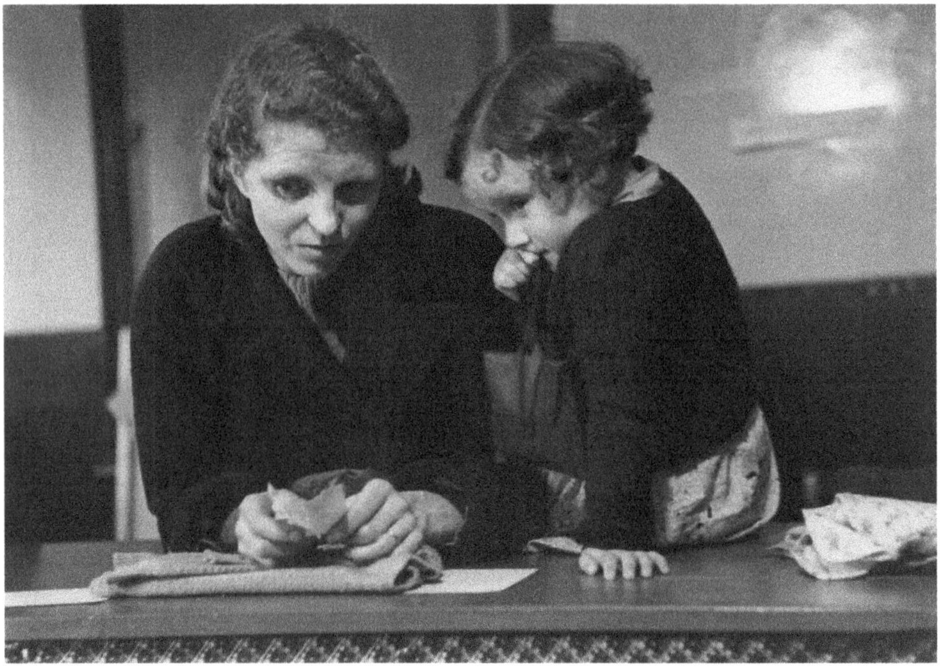

Figure 56 '"Only Eight Coupons Left. Oh, Mother, What a Problem!" Oh dear, it's worse than arithmetic. We've eight coupons left. They want six for the jersey – we could manage that – but ten for the lovely coat. Let's go home, Mummy, and turn out my cupboard. We could swap one of my nightgowns – I don't need them a bit.' From 'This Is a Clothes Exchange', *Picture Post*, 2 October 1943, p.25. Kurt Hutton/*Picture Post*/Hulton Archive/Getty Images (959577586).

allocations fell over the duration of the war and beyond. Having access to such a rich repository of clothing, based solely on the capacity to donate, may also have been an added incentive to *look after* existing clothing as it now became the means of addressing future wardrobe needs. Clothing had become a form of currency.

Provision of material comforts

By 1945 *Picture Post* was reporting on 'The Store Where Everything Is Free'.[54] Once again this was an initiative undertaken by the WVS who had requisitioned certain London warehouses to receive supplies of household items. These were for use by local people who had been bombed out. The previous year had seen the capital sustain an almost continuous barrage of aerial attack, ending with the destruction wrought by the V1 and V2 rockets which had been 'among the worst assaults of the entire war'.[55]

The WVS had seen how 'very hard it had been for men and women without much money to make their homes comfortable again'.[56] In response they had developed a scheme whereby counties far less affected by bombing than London and the South were asked to donate household goods they could do without. These were sent to one or more districts that had sustained heavy bombardment. Articles were valued in

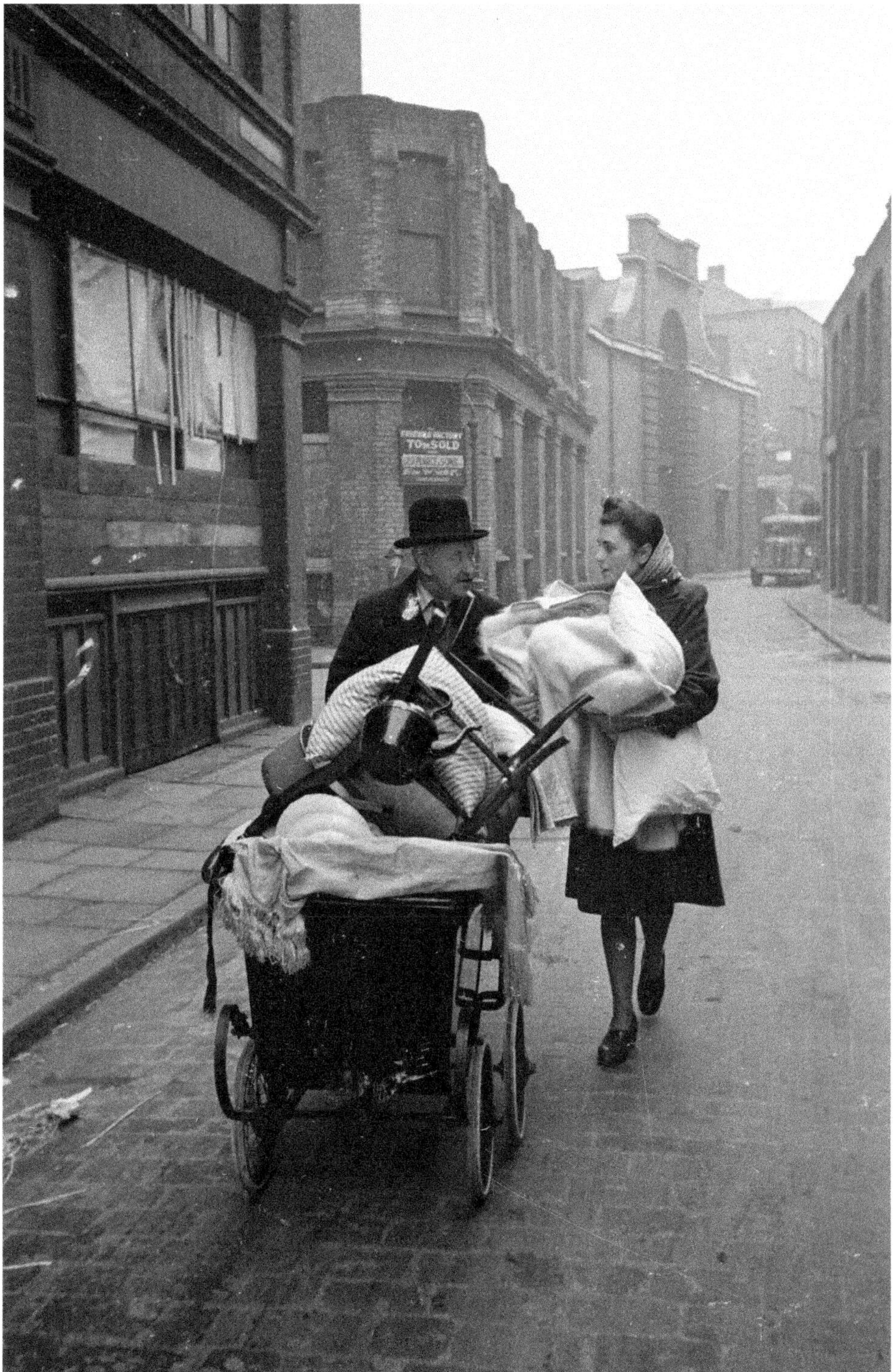

Figure 57 'The Mayor of Shoreditch Lends a Hand', from 'The Store Where Everything Is Free', *Picture Post*, 3 March 1945, p. 25. Haywood Magee/*Picture Post*/Getty Images (33950295).

points – for example a chair at fifteen points, a blanket at fifteen points, cups and saucers at five points – while victims of bombing received points according to their need. A family who had lost everything received fifty points and a further thirty points per family member.

Photographs showed all manner of household goods available from chairs and mangles to pitchers, cradles and soft furnishings. One photograph showed a shelf full of eiderdowns or quilts, while another showed a shopper clutching fabric goods and a pillow while wheeling a pram full of more soft furnishings or bedding. Sheets were clearly at a premium as only one was allowed per family.

The destructive capacity of the V bombs was responsible for 'over 30,000 civilian casualties and left hundreds of thousands homeless'.[57] This meant that as the war neared its close, there was still a significant number of people experiencing serious hardship and needing prompt, practical help. The free shopping scheme endeavoured to provide the things they needed to get going again and was another example of the redistribution of existing goods to get the maximum value out of commodities already in circulation.

Conclusion

During the rationing year 1944–1945, the British clothing ration was again reduced. The reasons for this were connected to the increasing demand, on a much concentrated textile and clothing industry, for commodities needed in response to wartime events such as demobilization and the provision of relief clothing for parts of Europe.[58] Even as the war drew to its close, therefore, self-help schemes rendered significant service to communities under duress. As the last phase of aerial hostilities continued to devastate lives and livelihoods, these schemes remained an integral part of the nation's capacity to cope with crisis.

Picture Post stories on the various groups and organizations that had arisen to meet the needs of discrete sectors of the wartime home front and armed services highlighted the capacity to both foresee and respond to the shifting requirements of a country at war. The contribution of the WVS and the many other women's groups across the country, both in terms of the services they offered and the supplies they garnered, organized and disbursed, remains incalculable, and the nation owed a tremendous debt of gratitude to them all.[59]

7
MAKING AND LOOKING AFTER CLOTHES

Introduction

This chapter looks at *Picture Post* stories that addressed how individuals could manage and maintain their own wardrobes. After the implementation of clothes rationing, acquiring clothes on the high street clearly became more difficult. Coupons limited the amount of new clothing it was possible to buy, and restrictions on the manufacture of commercial clothing also limited stock for sale. The ordinary man and woman in the street were encouraged to think about how they could get the best use out of the clothes they had, rather than buying new. New fabrics for home-made garments also required coupon expenditure and so with very few exceptions only what was already in the wardrobe was restriction free. Some level of home-crafting skill was now generally required to remake or refresh tired or worn-out clothes, along with the prescience to judge which projects were doable and which would only end in disappointment and waste.

Thrift became a defining element of wartime domestic life. *Picture Post* reflected this in three distinct ways: It featured articles on various aspects of making clothes at home; it was a vehicle for official government announcements from the Board of Trade, Ministry of Information and Ministry of Supply on the need for thrift at both an individual and community level; it carried advertising that in its own way sought to promote careful housekeeping.

The limitations placed on supplies of civilian clothing to the high street, and the steadily rising price of clothing during the year prior to clothes rationing and controls,[1] had already begun to rekindle interest in home-made items. For those who had generally relied on buying their clothing,[2] the skills for making at home would either need some brushing up or had to be learnt from scratch.

Picture Post explores home sewing

In the spring of 1941, Anne Scott-James presented *Picture Post* readers with two opportunities to try their hand at fashion projects – one for a spring hat, the other a 'model outfit'. Both of these were about *making new* clothes, at this stage in the war, and were responses to higher clothing prices and the difficulty, according to Anne Scott-James, of finding 'good clothes' elsewhere.[3] They were also both presented as quite manageable for the amateur home-sewer. The tone was unselfconsciously middle class and assumed a shared world of dressmakers, well-stocked haberdashery drawers and the wherewithal to buy six yards of expensive Viyella fabric for a summer suit.

The first exercise was a collaboration with couture milliner Aage Thaarup to provide readers with a small-brimmed felt hat with pleated crown to freshen up a spring wardrobe.[4] Taking only two hours to complete and at a cost of 'under two shillings', Scott-James presented the project as 'attractive, easy, economical'. While she did not refer to the escalating price of clothing directly the thrifty nature of this little hat was clear.[5]

Thaarup was apparently well aware of the 'snags of home hat-making' and so had provided a design without 'complicated modelling' or the need for 'expert fingers'.[6] The amateur, it seemed, could achieve complete success. The double-page spread featured two large photographs of the finished hat accessorized with either flowers and veiling or a draped scarf. Running across the bottom of both pages was a photographic step-by-step guide. Only basic cutting, pressing and sewing skills appeared to be needed – 'not very difficult, you'll agree'[7] – and the design used under half a yard of felt at 4s. 6d. a yard. Scott-James blithely suggested that the finishing touches would probably cost 'nothing since you're sure to have flowers or veiling stowed away in a drawer, or a scarf you can spare'.[8]

With similar up-beat and encouraging rhetoric, Scott-James introduced readers to a rather more challenging set of projects the following May. A 'whole model wardrobe' could now be created through investing in 'the PICTURE POST Pattern'.[9] This sewing enterprise assumed, to a much greater extent than the hat project, an ability to handle relatively sophisticated dressmaking schemes. The quality and quantity of fabric used would certainly have provided the 'good clothes' that were currently 'hard to come by' although there was no expectation, necessarily, for readers to choose higher-end fabrics.

Picture Post, in association with professional designer-dressmaker Phienka, had contrived to create a 'special pattern' not in paper but in muslin. Known to 'smart Parisian dressmakers' as a toile, this fabric pattern had several advantages over paper. Most importantly, and justifying the hefty five shilling price tag, the various pieces on offer fitted together to create a range of garments comprising 'a suit, a silk summer dress, a long-sleeved town frock, and a nightgown ... four patterns in one!' Home dressmakers could try out the styles in the toile fabric avoiding the 'risk of wasting good fabric on a dress that doesn't fit or doesn't suit you'.[10]

The first of two pages of photographs showed the toile being tacked together and fitted, fabrics decided upon and finally the cutting out of the four outfits from the toile. The second page revealed a chic and sophisticated daywear collection together with a nightdress of the 'new tailored variety'.[11] These images also provided a record for posterity of the styles popular in Britain in early summer 1941, immediately prior to the introduction of clothing controls. This would be the last summer when styles using generous amounts of fabric and more complex patterns would be possible. As we have seen elsewhere the austerity restrictions that followed rationing – largely introduced by the summer of 1942 – would put pay to the liberal use of fabric in features such as sun-ray pleating and wide sash belts.[12]

In the meantime dressmaker Phienka was applauded for understanding the desire for 'practical as well as pretty' clothes for all body shapes, and for recognizing that patterns for 'amateur dressmakers must be extremely simple to cut and sew'.[13] The outfits shown, however, don't appear to be that simple. The striped Viyella suit, for example, consisted of a short-sleeved, hip length, front-buttoning jacket with contrasting linen shawl-collar and cuffs, worn over a circular pleated skirt.[14] The look was tailored, needed six yards of material and might, arguably, have been something of a challenge for the inexperienced dressmaker. The dress and nightgown, too, required more than rudimentary skills. Using five-and-a-half yards of 'Courtauld's Tested Quality rayon crepe', the summer frock had a softly tailored bodice with fitted three-quarter-length sleeves gathered into small shoulder puffs, a wide ornamental sash at the waist and a softly draping skirt. The nightdress required four yards of crepe or satin as it was full length, had a fitted blouse-style bodice with a tie belt at the waist and short puffed sleeves.

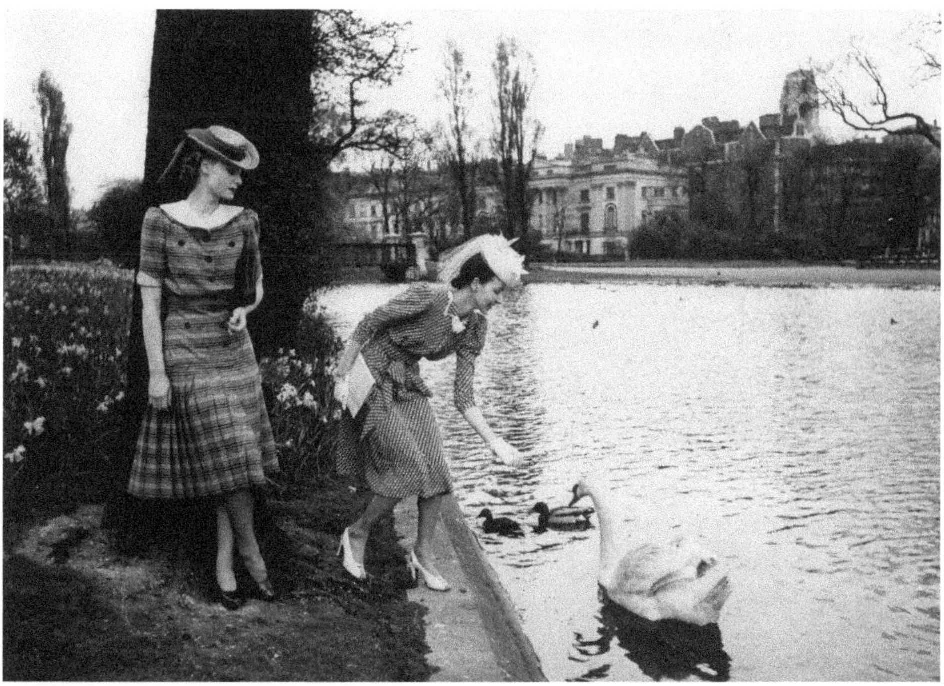

Figure 58 'And Here's What They Make ... First a Suit, Second, a Summer Frock.' The suit has 'gay stripes and swinging skirt ... pink pique revers and cuffs'. The 'summery print frock of red and white crepe' is 'as soft as the suit is tailored'. From 'Make Yourself a Model Outfit', *Picture Post*, 31 May 1941, p. 31. Felix Man/*Picture Post*/Getty Images (3375922).

Yet the extent to which readers could sew was not, it seemed, particularly at issue here. 'Practical Living' wanted to demonstrate that 'good clothes' that were now 'hard to buy'[15] could be made at home, a fact that would garner greater interest in the months and years ahead. The growth in make-do and mend classes in response to the strictures of clothes rationing bore witness, however, to a widespread lack of skill in making, alterations and mending that was yet to surface.

Altering clothes

On 26 July 1941, a little under two months after the implementation of clothes rationing, the need to manage wardrobes more carefully saw *Picture Post* putting forward suggestions for home-sewing projects based around re-using clothing or fabrics. In an article entitled 'Old Clothes Make News',[16] Anne Scott-James announced that alterations had become 'today's big fashion story'.

Once again the rhetoric implied, perhaps unconsciously, a shared experience of privilege. If altering clothes had once been the trade of 'the odd little dressmaker in a top-floor room', now the best designers were offering alterations so that this 'trade' had become 'an art' and fashionable.[17] With dressmaker Phienka once again, the wardrobe and linen cupboard of a supposedly 'typical young woman' were scrutinized for items that 'hadn't been worn for years'. These could now be turned into serviceable garments. The results of the remodelling were revealed in before and after photographs across two pages. Aware, perhaps, of the complexity of some of these ideas, Scott-James offered to supply details of 'sewing and repairing services ... [and] also details of typical dressmakers' charges if you would like any of your own dresses altered'.[18]

The clothing selected for re-use included a 'white satin dress' now 'quite useless', an 'Indian cloak' of a type that 'most women have ... tucked away',[19] a 'black cire dinner dress ... [with] a fishtail train'[20] and a black velveteen coat. The fact that 'most women' were, in reality, unlikely to have such bountiful wardrobes only served to underline that Scott-James appeared to assume her readership was relatively well-heeled, whether it was, in fact, or not. More readers, however, might have owned a cotton tufted candlewick bedspread, as pictured, although the decision to turn this into a coat, rather than a dressing gown, was perhaps rather surprising if eye-catching.[21]

The photo-story might have reflected the more privileged end of the recycling spectrum, but in the spirit of the times Scott-James showed what was possible *in principle*, if not necessarily in practice. Any domestic wardrobe was now to be regarded as an important resource. For sectors of the general public less well-endowed with clothing to start with, making the most of the clothing they already had would become, arguably, even more pressing. The 'Indian cloak into Day Dress' and velveteen coat into 'simple' two-piece suit[22] might both reflect a road less travelled by the chain-store shopper, but they did not undermine the new imperative of looking with fresh eyes on the possibilities lying in old clothes.

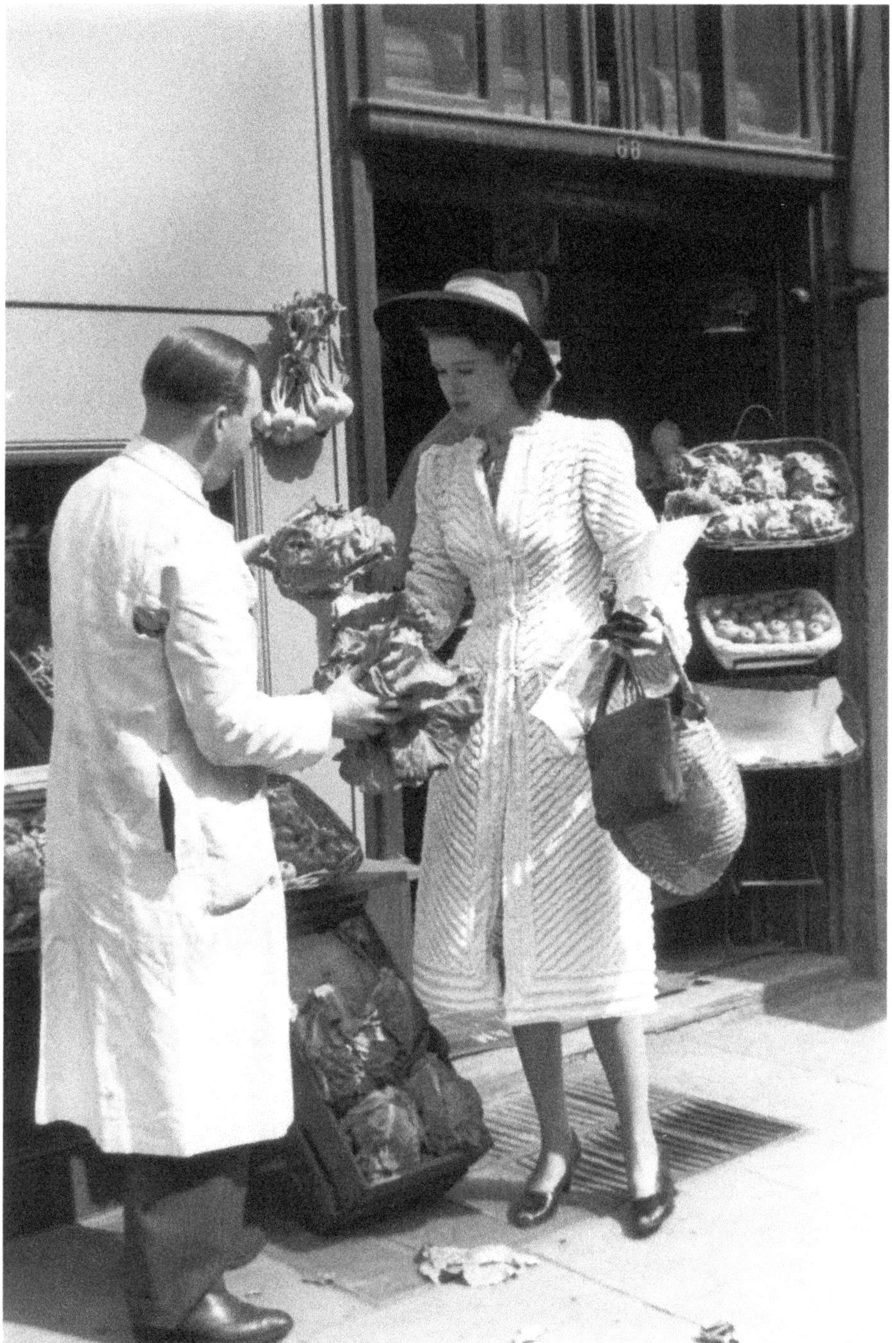

Figure 59 'The Bedspread She Sleeps Under at Night becomes the Coat She Wears in the day: Any bedspreads you don't use? Here's an idea for making a gay coat from a spread of white candlewick – that lovely washable tufted material. Cut from any paper pattern; but be sure to cut so that the borders run round the front and hem of your coat.' From 'Old Clothes Make News', *Picture Post*, 26 July 1941, p. 26. Zoltan Glass/*Picture Post*/Getty Images (2696570).

Patchwork

A form of home sewing with which more people, perhaps, would have been familiar was the art of patchwork. In August 1941 Anne Scott-James turned her attention to this traditional skill now making a fashion comeback.[23] Originating as a 'cottage fashion' and still practised by 'cottage people' – associating both the skill and its practitioners with historical roots in domestic crafting – patchwork was now moving beyond its established use for quilts and cushions into a new fashion arena. Photographs showed a Digby Morton short-sleeved blouse, a sleeveless home-made bolero, a pair of slippers and two Aage Thaarup sailor hats, all featuring patching or patchwork. 'Gay and gaudy' it used up oddments of material with great effectiveness, was relatively easy to do and saved on both coupons and cash.

Scott-James remarked on the current wartime trend to 'pick the neutral coat, the "safe" hat, the classic suit, that won't look laughable a couple of years from now'. She suggested that in this context patchwork, in all its colour and variety, added accent interest and a visual 'pick-me-up ... a heaven sent novelty that satisfies both eye and conscience'. Barely more than two months into clothes rationing, she described patchwork as a tonic for the 'ration-weary wardrobe', a remark that seemed to indicate the extent to which clothing was now either generally expressing the safe and sensible or had already become stuck in a rut rather than fashion forward.[24]

There were no strict protocols as to how to construct patchwork. The 'old Victorian' model was the more accurate and painstaking one. It required careful cutting out of identical geometric fabric shapes, usually in pale-coloured, quietly patterned cottons, that were then neatly sewn together. Conversely 'crazy patchwork' allowed almost any shapes, fabrics and patterns to be used. Stitching could be visible and in contrasting coloured threads.[25] Small individual patches could be sewn directly on to slippers,[26] hat crowns or suit revers, while larger pieces of patchwork making up fabric lengths could be used for whole garments. From simple patched pockets to couture pieces, patchwork created something out of almost nothing. While it might have been an exaggeration to think it made 'the smartest clothes in town',[27] patchwork, it seemed, was becoming acceptable chic and to an extent, therefore, fashionable. Readers were warned, however, that patchwork accessories should only be worn with clothes that were 'deadly plain, because patchwork has to be used with discretion – or you'll look like a Christmas tree'.[28]

Projects needing 'very little money, very few coupons'

By July 1942 the austerity regulations controlling the cut and make of all commercially produced clothing had been introduced.[29] These had the effect of producing simpler, unadorned clothing that became the hallmark of British fashion for the remainder of the war.[30] A new set of twenty clothing coupons had been issued the previous month to cover the period until October. This mechanism of batch-release was designed to spread coupon expenditure evenly across the year and so minimize the risk of consumers running out of coupons too soon. Despite this new allocation Anne Scott-James, perhaps reflecting on the much reduced capacity for buying new that twenty coupons represented, ran an article entitled 'Next to No Coupons'. This offered readers a range of knitting and sewing projects that could all be undertaken at home cheaply and with little coupon outlay.[31]

A complete pattern was included for making a sequined sweater and matching skull-cap, together needing seven ounces of wool and 'about 2,000 sequins'.[32] Readers were invited to write in to *Picture Post* enclosing an addressed envelope if they were interested in having patterns for any of the other fashion items photographed.[33] There were four knitting projects: a classic button-through ribbed cardigan, close fitting and with small puffed sleeves that helped to create the fashionable squared shoulder; a short-sleeved knitted jacket also with the square, military shoulder, flat collar and revers, described as 'easy-to-knit'[34]; an 'American Stocking Cap',[35] hard to see in detail but a cross between a winter bobble and a night cap, that could be made out of left over wool-ends; and the sequined jumper and skull-cap. Together these provided classic wardrobe staples alongside some fun hats and the photographs showed how the garments might be accessorized with blouses, summer scarves and, for the sequined sweater, a broad sash.

The sequined hat had been cleverly styled to fit perfectly inside the model's halo of rolled hair, while the knitted and knotted American pull-on hat had been teemed with a classic, velvet-collared, puffed-sleeve wool coat. This had considerably upped an informal little hat's game and suggested that more things were now right for fashion than might have previously been the case. The remaining projects featured a small beret and two tops, one a short-sleeved bolero jacket and the other a draped kimono blouse, both of which had been made from three-foot square scarves.[36] Hats had become 'fabulously expensive' to buy,[37] but the cotton beret pictured, trimmed with a cluster of little beads, could be crocheted at home in a day and was another idea for something quite plain that could be decorated with what was to hand.

Here was a range of garments, therefore, for both summer and winter, informal and more formal occasions, all of which could be made at home if the maker was reasonably adept at knitting or sewing. The kimono blouse and bolero also reflected again that there were more imaginative and unpredictable elements of dress being devised and accepted into the fashion lexicon, and these could add colour and originality to an outfit. The fact that Utility fabrics continued to be manufactured in any number of patterns and colourways also meant that although wardrobe basics might now reflect a range of similar, relatively classic styles, individuality could be achieved through the mixing and matching of colour shades and accent accessories.

Another way of achieving colour economically was the vogue for Fairisle knitting which absorbed any leftover wool-ends into its bright and lively designs. Hailed early in 1943 as 'the great fashion for saving coupons', Fairisle patterning was popular not only for sweaters but also 'gloves, knee-length socks trimmed with Fairisle, and lumber jackets', as featured in *Picture Post* in February of that year.[38]

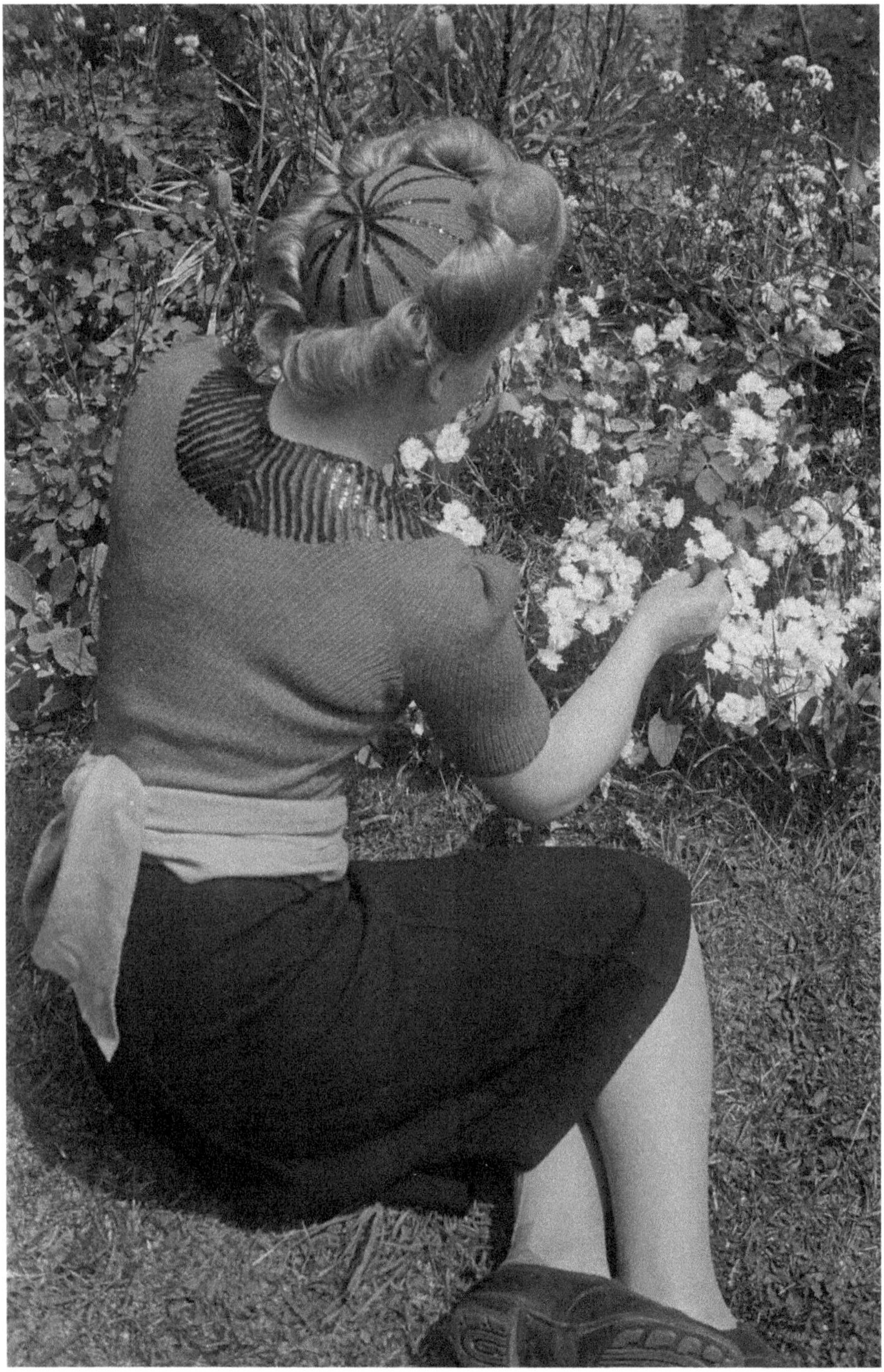

Figure 60 'The Jersey That's Good Enough for Evening. Good by day with a black suit, by night for a wartime party. This scarlet sweater, designed by Monna Steinbach, has a collar of sequins and a skull-cap to match.' 'Next to No Coupons', *Picture Post*, 11 July 1942, p. 19. Kurt Hutton/*Picture Post*/Hulton Archive/Getty Images (984851082).

A no-coupon craft option

By the summer of 1943 with clothes rationing becoming 'really tight, and ideas for coupon-free fashions ... more and more important', the availability 'nearly everywhere' of unrationed 'skins and skivers in bright colours' prompted *Picture Post* to provide some ideas on what sort of fashions they could be turned into.[39] Skivers of sheepskin formed the basis for most of the projects, while rabbit skin was suggested for extra warmth on the back of mittens. Patterns and basic instructions were provided for matching mother-and-son waistcoats, the mittens, a hat and a handbag.[40]

A diagram, explaining how to cut out and dart the waistcoat pieces, revealed that the sleeves were to be knitted. This would require five-and-a-half ounces of wool for both waistcoats, an amount assumed to come from supplies in the work-basket if the title of the article was to remain true. The darts on the child's waistcoat were not to be cut away, leaving room for growth. The photograph of the finished outfits showed both waistcoats closing to the neck – the mother's with decorative buttons – and both worn with serviceable, wide-legged trousers.

The shallow halo beret, accessorizing a smart button-through day dress, had achieved its shape by stiffening the pelt with buckram or canvas. Another diagram was included showing how to create the beret template from suitably sized plates and saucers. The only additional materials needed to complete this project were some little 'oddments of silk' for lining and petersham binding for the headband.[41]

This collection of home-made items was styled to look both chic and practical, encouraging would be home-crafters that it was all worth the effort. Stitching was to be done by hand and the simple home-made template for mittens of any size might well have attracted readers with very limited skills or confidence to have a go.

Looking after clothes

Any element of the wardrobe was now a precious personal commodity and needed to be appropriately looked after to keep its good looks and maintain its longevity. It was equally in the country's best interests that this was done, and the government promoted clothing care as another component of patriotic thrift. By the summer of 1942 the Board of Trade was regularly publishing advice to the public on how to look after clothes. This included how to launder different fabrics safely and the benefits of everyday attention such as brushing, hanging and ironing out creases after wear. Airing fabrics outside got rid of moth eggs, and undertaking running repairs prevented greater damage.[42]

Readers were encouraged to see the value of remnants for making small items such as gloves or for patching worn fabrics, and to get every possible use out of old towels and bedding.[43] Only once textiles were completely beyond any further domestic use could they be added to the 'rag-bag' for salvage collection. The Ministry of Information was keen to point out that rags could be 'made into garments and equipment for fighting men' and reminded readers in September 1942 that before the war 700,000 cwts of rags had been imported but that 'now these ships cannot be spared'.[44]

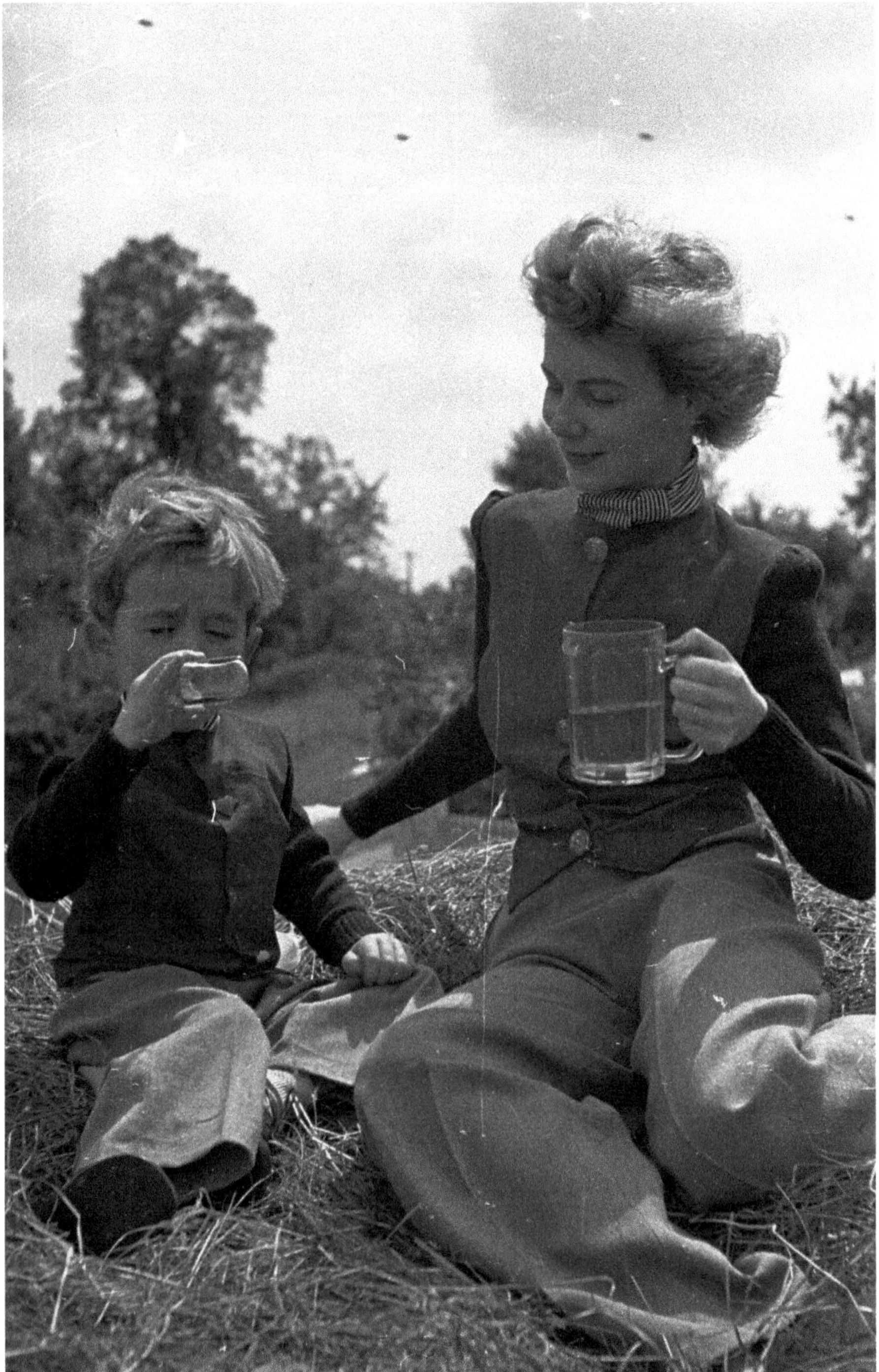

Figure 61 'Waistcoats from Skins: Two good-sized skins make delightful mother-and-son waistcoats; the sleeves are knitted.' From 'Clothes without Coupons', *Picture Post*, 28 August 1943, p. 24. Kurt Hutton/*Picture Post*/Getty Images (3383032).

In January 1943 *Picture Post* ran a rather different story on caring for clothing after visiting an army training camp under Eastern Command where new recruits were being taught to sew. Off-duty volunteers from the A.T.S were helping soldiers once a week to mend their own clothes, accruing obvious benefits to both soldiers on active service and uniform stocks.

Every recruit was issued with a hussif containing sewing essentials which up until now had been 'merely an object to be laid out for kit inspection'. Now Command had had the 'revolutionary idea' of teaching the men what to do with it.[45]

Readers were also encouraged to care for clothing through the advertising rhetoric adopted by soap flake manufacturers. Brands were keen to associate their products with efficient laundering methods that would keep clothing clean, bright and preserve its durability. *Rinso*, for example, advertised a no-boil method which did away with the more traditional reliance on boiling clothes to remove dirt. Instead a twenty-minute soak – later reduced to twelve – using Rinso dissolved in hot tap water, followed by washing and rinsing, would deliver clean clothes with a considerable saving of time and fuel.[46] *Rinso* customers were later advised they could use half their usual amount of water and two-thirds of the soap powder and still get the clothes clean, saving on soap coupons as well as fuel bills.[47] The method was considered gentler on fabrics: 'Me **boil** and **rub** clothes? Not likely! They're far too precious nowadays',[48] while the time-saving factor meant washing became less of a chore.[49]

Lux marketed its soap powder on the basis that it provided a low-temperature wash; 'No need to use hot water for wearables – blouses, cotton frocks and overalls, children's things ... undies.' Lux 'pure' flakes dissolved completely in lukewarm water – 'the safe temperature'[50] for all types of fabrics and coloureds – and its lather lifted dirt out without the need for harmful rubbing so conserving textiles.[51] By 1942 Lux had devised their 'Wartime Clothes Service' sponsored by 'The Lux Washability and Renovation Bureau'. Here Lux was directly associating itself with the nationwide campaign for mending and making-do by marketing their soap powder alongside a succession of remodelling schemes. These included ideas such as turning a summer dress into a Magyar blouse, or an old tennis dress into a waistcoat, beret, '"dickie" front' and 'pleated jabot'.[52]

In an advertisement carried in October 1943, half way through describing another Clothes Service renovation project to turn net curtains into French style brassieres, it emerged that there was, in fact, no more Lux available.[53] Readers were reminded, therefore, that when using other products careful rinsing was especially essential to avoid undissolved soap residue remaining on fabrics.

Meanwhile supplies of other household soap powders continued unabated. Persil, for example, traded on a reputation for gentle washing and extra whiteness, while Oxydol offered 'Make-do and Mend Washday Wisdom' and recommended its 'busy bubble lather' for extending the life of clothing, also through gentle laundering.[54]

Dunlop advised readers to prolong the life of their rubber-proofed coats by not drying them by a fire or in sunlight and avoiding contact with grease or oil which could dissolve the fabric. Cleaning was tricky as washing a rubber-proofed coat was 'not practical and should not be attempted'. Readers were also reminded that dry-cleaning a raincoat 'impair[ed] the rubberless proofing' requiring the garment to be reproofed 'at the same time'.[55] Keeping either type of coat away from heavy soiling was, arguably, the most prudent course.

Conclusion

With the advent of rationing almost everyone had to reconsider the clothes they had and to what extent they could afford – in coupon terms – anything new. *Picture Post* reflected these new ways of thinking about clothing as monitoring and maintaining personal wardrobes became a way of life affecting every home in Britain. Enterprises from patchwork slippers to pelt waistcoats revealed the broadening arena of fashion ideas now ceded by the controls. *Picture Post* articles saw domestic ingenuity and energy on the home front as a way of remaining well-turned out, fresh and fashionable in the face of rationing and restrictions, while photographs of knitted, patched or home-sewn garments or accessories became colourful and creative metaphors for the ability to carry on despite often dreary, difficult and dangerous times.

8
A FASHION FOR FITNESS

Introduction

No matter what sort of life individuals might be leading, in the armed or auxiliary services or on the home front, good health was promoted as being each person's responsibility. Eating properly, keeping fit and getting enough sleep were seen as fundamental to keeping pace with the arduous and often unpredictable conditions of wartime living. Good health fostered a positive attitude and the energy to cope, attributes that became increasingly significant as war hardships escalated. Several of the new wartime occupations for women clearly demanded physical resilience and stamina. Surviving on the home front, whether undertaking community work, running a home or both, also now required greater physical and emotional reserves given the strenuous and draining pressures of war. In these circumstances the capacity to carry on was celebrated.

Picture Post imagery from a variety of stories on both wartime work and off-duty activities confirmed that fitness was both recommended and de rigueur. Physical fitness also belied myths of feminine fragility that still retained currency at the outset of the war in some quarters – arguably with some justification. Women's capacity for hard physical work was, in many spheres, simply untried. As they entered into new roles in services such as the Women's Land Army or the Women's Auxiliary Airforce, their ability to shoulder the tasks and responsibilities they now encountered began to render older stereotypes about female inadequacy or vulnerability both misleading and mistaken. Women were now demonstrating a strength, energy and physical resilience considerably at odds with older preconceptions of female frailty.[1]

The first section of this chapter reviews stories from *Picture Post* that explored some of the new service roles for women demanding high levels of physical stamina. It also considers the extent to which these new lifestyles were supported from within the service structure. The second section investigates how *Picture Post* covered keeping fit on the home front and some of the opportunities available for leisure activities that promoted health, well-being and exercise of one sort or another. Together the sections reveal the connection between health, fitness and the now shifting perceptions of female potential.

Fitness for war work

Health and well-being were certainly essential components of many new wartime occupations now being taken on by women. Recruits to the Land Army had to demonstrate a physical capacity for agricultural work in order to disprove claims by some farmers that women would be 'of no practical use as farm labourers'.[2] Land Army members already employed on farms by early 1940 were putting in a forty-eight-hour week of 'hard manual labour' and working across the farming spectrum from dairy to arable, poultry to ploughing.[3] In a second *Picture Post* article on 'The Land Girl' in November 1941, *The Farmer's Weekly* writer Jane Morgan went to review how life was shaping up for some Land Army women working on a mixed farm in southern England.

She immediately confirmed that the life was certainly 'no rest cure' and that girls needed a 'strong physique' to cope with the 'hard outdoor life' that was on offer.[4] The two-page photo-story showed images of land girls in sweaters and dungarees getting on with tasks such as hoeing, potato sorting and gathering straw, among other typical farm jobs. It was Morgan's text, however, that established what it *felt* like to be a new recruit facing these physical challenges for the first time, challenges that the seasoned land girls caught on camera had, by now, overcome. Working alongside these experienced hands for a week, Morgan first encountered 'pulling beetroot' which '*looked* easy'. After a couple of hours keeping pace with the tractor lifting the crop, however, her back was breaking. The girls told her that 'the third day would be worst. It was. After that the muscles began to do the work intended for them'.[5]

Stamina appeared to develop along with the job, assisted by 'satisfying' billet food.[6] During her week on the farm, Morgan took on jobs such as forking up carrots and hoeing spring greens, interspersed with other aspects of market gardening, all of which involved various levels of physical and often repetitive work.

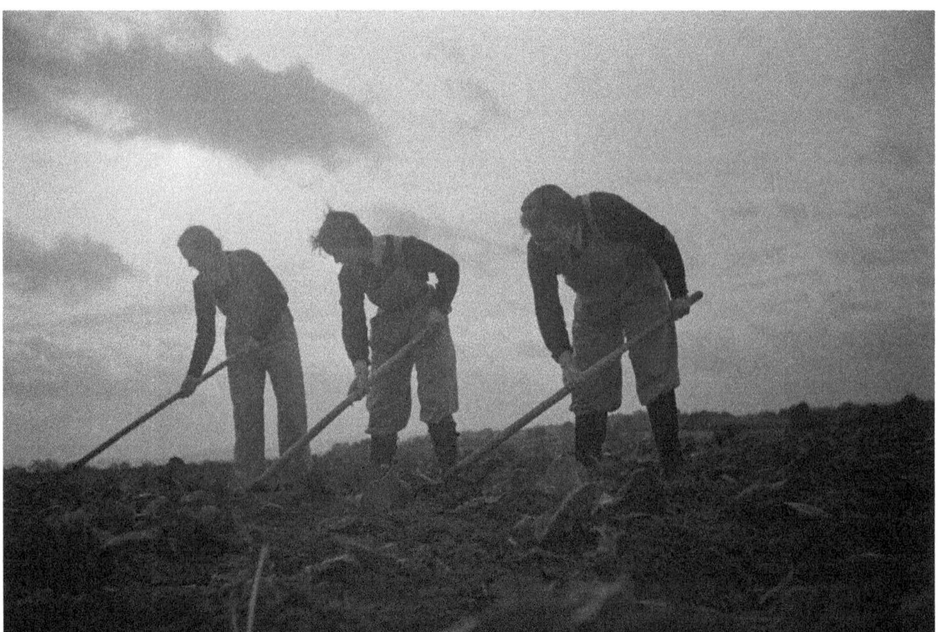

Figure 62 'A Good Spring Crop Needs Autumn Hoeing. Fields of spring greens must be hoed before the frosts. "Bend right down to it" is the farmer's advice', *Picture Post*, 29 November 1941, p. 19. Kurt Hutton/*Picture Post*/Hulton Archive/Getty Images (984851060).

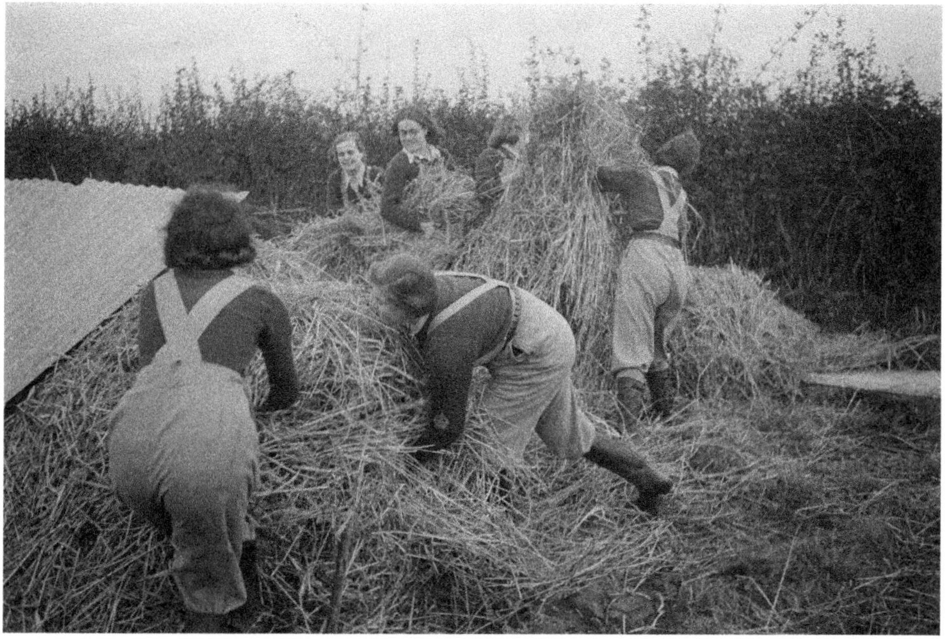

Figure 63 'Land Girls Gather Straw for the Cows', *Picture Post*, 29 November 1941, p. 19. Kurt Hutton/*Picture Post*/Hulton Archive/Getty Images (984851058).

On the evening Morgan left, two of the girls 'with none of my aching limbs' were heading off for a dance.[7] This life would clearly not suit everyone. Morgan told readers that at interview the potential recruit had a 'gloomy picture painted to her of what working on the land means'. Emphasizing the rigour and physical nature of this rural occupation was 'chiefly for the benefit of the girl who has dabbled in a little haymaking during the summer holiday and imagines she is a fully-fledged farmer'.[8] This was a tough life and needed tough people to do it.

In another of the *Picture Post* 'Women at War' series, Red Cross nurse Nerina Shute spent a week at the Westminster hospital. A photo-story by Kurt Hutton took readers inside the hospital and showed them the sort of work she was doing, while Shute herself reflected on the everyday challenges nursing offered.[9] She was keen to be realistic about what the profession really entailed and not to write 'flattering nonsense' that might attract women who were 'totally unsuitable'. She made it clear that 'to be a good Red Cross nurse you must also be a good charwoman and, what is more, a good-tempered charwoman'. As a Voluntary Aid Detachment nurse (or VAD), her job included cleaning the wards, the sluice room, the ward Sister's and surgeon's rooms as well as helping in the ward kitchen. Nursing life was 'full of dirty jobs' alongside of the role of caring for patients and assisting in theatre.[10]

In her opinion it was 'the hardest work' and also 'in certain ways the most heart-breaking profession, any woman can tackle'. Entailing 'nine and a half hours of hard physical labour' for junior nurses, and an hour or so more for senior nurses, there were long shifts, a strict hierarchy and rigorous discipline.[11] If, however, a woman had the 'stamina for a job like this', there was much happiness in providing compassionate service to others.[12] Shute wrote tellingly of the love many nurses had for their role despite its drawbacks and how nine out of ten of them felt 'the charm and inspiration behind all these hard Florence Nightingale traditions' which kept them going.[13]

At the end of Shute's first day, a nurse colleague expressed the view that nursing was 'a grand life – if you don't weaken'.[14] Recruits to this profession had to be 'prepared for a hard life' and would need physical and emotional strength to cope.[15]

Another story about nursing the following year opened up some of the challenges the profession could offer women as war fronts extended. In 'Our Nurses in Tobruk',[16] *Picture Post* reported on the Hadfield-Spears Hospital Unit which provided nurses for the war in the Western Desert. Attached to the Free French Forces, this unit was a mix of French, British and Australian nurses and Motor Transport (MT) drivers assisted by Senegalese orderlies. They were 'tough, fearless women who have seen front-line service in many parts of the world'.[17]

Commanding Officer, Lady Spears, ran this one hundred plus strong unit, the members of which lived 'like soldiers. They sleep in tents in the desert, eat in a mess-tent, wear regular battle-dress, consisting of khaki blouses, shirts, ties and trousers, topped with neat berets'.[18] Femininity of dress was clearly unsuitable on desert duty and only inside the hospital at Tobruk would the women change into a nursing uniform of dresses, white head veils and white shoes. This corps demonstrated a 'vigour and efficiency' that the writer believed was 'largely due to the hard work and strong character of Lady Spears herself', while photographs of the nurses – attending to casualties, standing outside the 'bomb-scarred hospital', relaxing off-duty still in battledress – revealed something of what life was like for these women as they encountered the dangers and isolation of desert life.[19]

This story revealed an ability to adapt to, and endure, ways of living and conditions of service that were both physically and mentally demanding. For readers of *Picture Post* who had followed the siege of Tobruk by General Rommel's forces for over seven months the preceding year, this location would have been well-known. The siege had ended in late November but exactly three months after this article was published Tobruk garrison would fall to the Axis on 21 June 1942. The context therefore in which these women were serving was, arguably, high risk and makes sense of *Picture Post*'s opening statement that this nursing unit was 'the real thing'.[20]

Picture Post's first report on the Auxiliary Territorial Service early in 1940 had related that only women in 'perfect health' were being recruited.[21] In a four-page follow-up photo-story[22] readers were taken inside an ATS training depot. Here they could see for themselves how the women recruits were absorbed into military life, from hutment living and fire drill to anti-aircraft training. Writer June Head 'tried the life herself' and reported back on a variety of topics, from the 'exciting business of being fitted for uniforms' to the cooking, cleaning and basic training experienced by all ATS recruits. The life at first seemed 'impossibly strenuous. But after a few days we get toughened'.[23]

The effect of the disciplined army routine, the 'regular hours – lights are put out at ten o'clock – plenty of fresh air and exercise, community living . . . learning to drill and parade', was to mould the women into a functioning military unit.[24] In the mixed anti-aircraft battery,

Head saw ATS girls now being drilled alongside male soldiers and becoming 'hardened to wind and weather' as they worked their instruments on the gun sites. Here were 'cool, precise, alert' women trained to be reliable and quick, performing work without which the gun sites could not operate.[25]

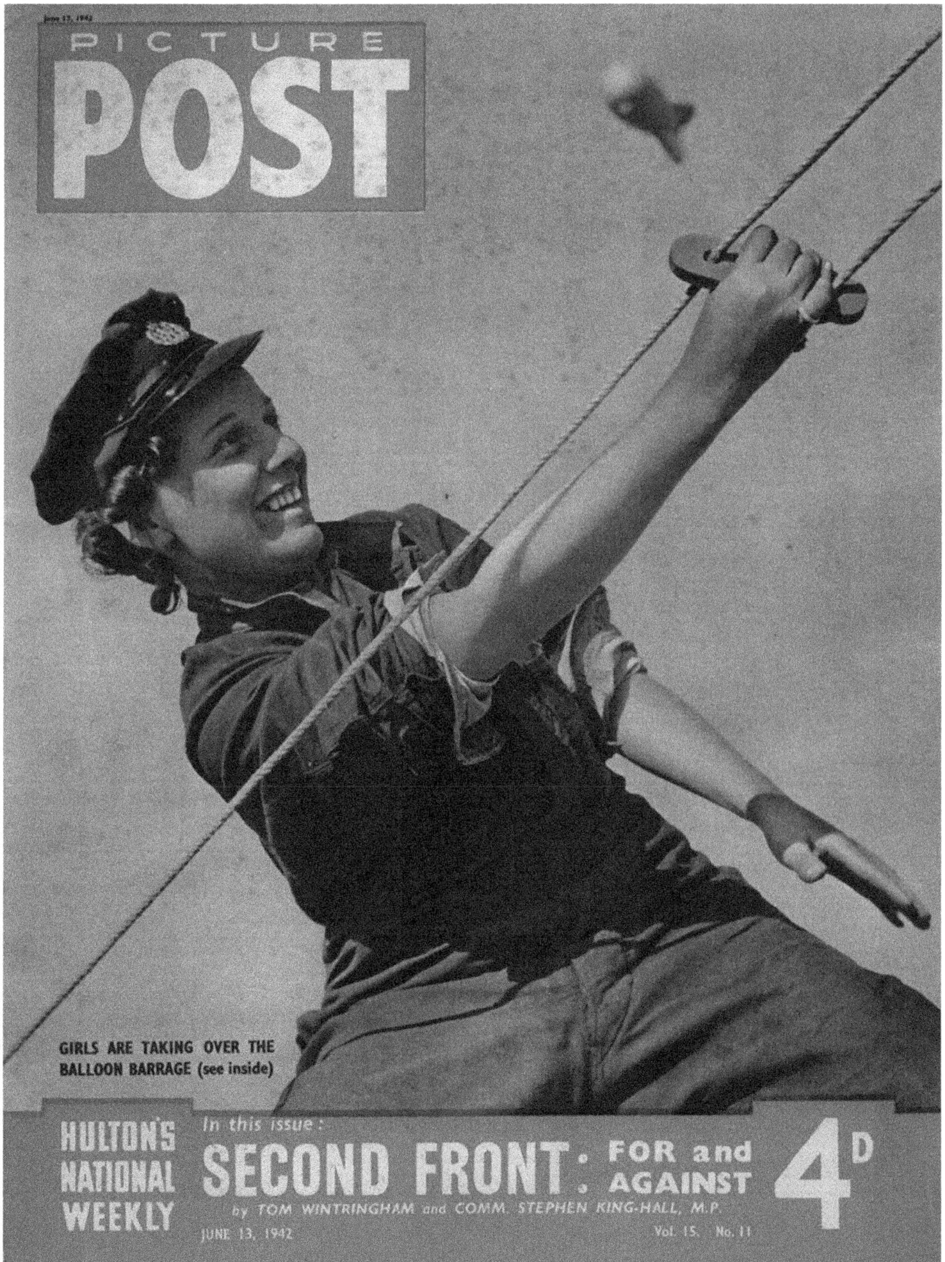

Figure 64 'Girls Are Taking Over The Balloon Barrage', *Picture Post*, 13 June 1942. IPC Magazines/*Picture Post*/Getty Images (3070472).

Physical strength and resilience were also essential attributes of members of the Women's Auxiliary Air Force, Balloon Operators unit. Volunteers for this service needed to be 'lithe, active and physically fit' and also 'cheerful and adaptable, and fond of outdoor life'. After the 'toughest training',[26] they carried out all jobs connected with handling the large blimps or barrage balloons, except moving the hydraulic cylinders used to fill them.

The photo-story is particularly successful at communicating the sheer size of the inflated barrage balloons and of the hangars in which they were stored. Something of the immensity of the task of handling such large and potentially unwieldly balloons emerges as a result, endorsed by the writer's comment that 'balloon handling in a gale is no fun; a balloon cable has been known to pick up a motor-car and put it in a tree'.[27] Despite the initial concern expressed by the 'high-ups'[28] that the job would be too physically demanding for women, the recruits had proved 'such a success that they are now no longer considered an experiment. They are a permanency', allowing 'more and more men [to be] released for other jobs'.[29]

There were two specific themes running through *Picture Post*'s coverage of women now entering the services. It was still a relatively new thing to see, in some cases completely new, and their stories had value because of this; the lifestyles of these women were not easy and demanded a level of commitment, resilience and vitality that could only be achieved by those suited to the type of work concerned. The women featured were inferred to be physically well and adaptable to the often challenging new working and living conditions they faced. The ability to knuckle down to the mundane and menial tasks that came as part of the training was another dimension to this adaptability and reflected something of the strength of character required to both engage with the new roles and successfully accommodate the new way of life. Here were women who were willing and able to serve and were proving themselves fighting fit.

Keeping fit

Physical fitness and mental balance were predicated upon a healthy lifestyle that combined the benefits of exercise, rest and nutritious food. With so many hardships to contend with on the home front, it was important for the public to keep in mind the benefits of healthy living and the various ways in which it could be achieved. *Picture Post* carried several stories featuring either exercise regimes of one sort or another that might encourage readers to take their own fitness in hand, or ways of relaxing that incorporated healthy living often in healthy places.

Advice on food and nutrition also appeared regularly through official notices from the Ministry of Food. This helped to make a broad range of information on diet more accessible for anyone preparing meals within the constraints brought about by food rationing. The Ministry also provided recipes that used more readily available commodities in dishes that would sustain some level of mealtime variety and interest. That it was each person's responsibility to eat as well as they might and keep as healthy and active as they could was axiomatic to wartime living.

Exercising at home

While physical training was an integral part of military service, there was no such built-in fitness regime for civilian living. Many women were now undertaking long hours in home-front services or juggling family life with part-time work. For those who continued to run the home full–time, there were all the new challenges of carrying on under wartime conditions. War changed everyday life and individuals had to confront the additional demands as best they could. Personal fitness on the home front remained a private responsibility that had to be effectively managed on top of everything else.

Picture Post's self-help articles on exercise regimes might have been relatively light-hearted and entertaining, but they were also an acknowledgement of this very real need to keep fit. Stories reflected that the type of exercise chosen had to find a place in already busy lives, need little or no equipment and be easily carried out at home. The upbeat and encouraging tone encouraged practical participation from the war weary and promoted the difference that exercise could make.

In August 1941 Anne Scott-James introduced *Picture Post* readers to 'Rag-Doll Exercises'. Illustrated with photographic sequences to help readers participate, this routine was based on the idea of exercising and relaxing alternately to boost flagging energy levels.[30] With typical Scott-James bonhomie she suggested to readers that relaxation is 'more than a matter of sitting down dog-tired with the evening paper and a drink, hoping you'll feel better after half an hour's collapse'.[31] The increased tensions of wartime living and long working days left many people tired 'long before they can get to bed'. The art of relaxing was something that had to be learnt to counter physical tiredness and the mental and emotional activity that 'throws your physical harmony out of balance'.[32]

The stretching and resting exercises depicted could be done in ten minutes after work, five if time was tight, with a final stretch-and-release lying down on the bed. At this point the mind was allowed to 'go blank' for 'ten minutes of nothingness',[33] after which the individual should feel recharged. With 'health officers ... welfare experts ... and the A.T.S.'[34] all recommending this type of exercise, readers could feel confident that they would benefit from having a go.

In June 1942, *Picture Post* covered another set of stretching movements devised by beauty guru Helena Rubenstein. In an article entitled 'Can You Do These New Summer Exercises?'[35] the focus this time was on stretching for toning and slimming. The routine used the various exercises 'to strengthen your muscles, work away any surplus fat and improve your circulation'. Gone were the days of 'massages ... mud baths ... fruit diets' – for those who had been able to indulge in them. Now 'no one has time for elaborate treatments or exercises'.[36]

Instead Rubinstein had put together a simple set of movements that were performed using her 'lithe-line'.[37] This consisted of a length of elastic looped at both ends for use by either hands or feet. Stretching the line between different areas of the body effectively targeted individual muscles. A number of exercises were described for toning waist, stomach and hips, with photographs showing how to achieve the correct positions. Readers were advised to start 'with two simple stretches and then work up to harder ones'.[38] A list of which exercises to do first was provided with simple instructions. Having a go would lead to feeling 'fresh and energetic' as well as trimming up the figure for summer.[39]

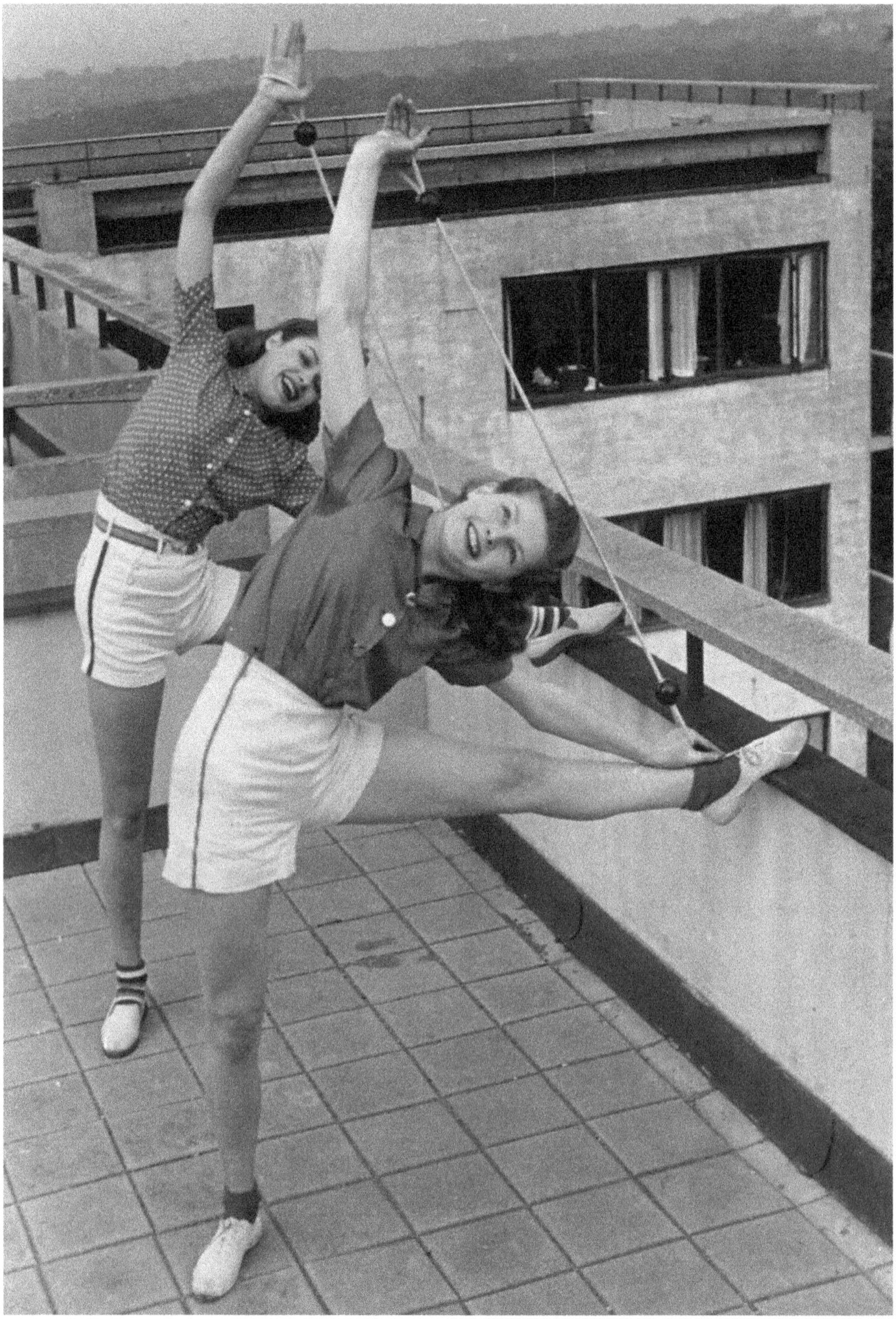

Figure 65 'The Sideways Bend: First to the left, then to the right, this exercise keeps the waist muscles supple'. From 'Can You Do These New Summer Exercises?' *Picture Post*, 20 June 1942, p. 22. Kurt Hutton/*Picture Post*/Getty Images (3134235).

Healthy leisure opportunities

Taking healthy breaks or holidays that could access plenty of outdoor activity and fresh air were also good ways of restoring energy levels, particularly for those whose daily lives were largely based inside. A holiday that could combine a healthy environment, exercise and rest was a world away from the quotidian pressures of wartime. *Picture Post* covered two such getaways.

The first, in September 1942, featured a 'Holiday Camp for War Workers' located on the Odney Estate in Cookham, Berkshire.[40] For 7s. 6d. for a weekend or 30s. a week, war workers could enjoy 'open-air life in the meadows beside the river, sleeping under canvas, eating in the open, swimming, playing games, cycling, walking – or perhaps just lazing in the sun'. No mention was made of the likely inclemency of the British weather, although there was a 'big marquee for games'. Photographs showed bell-tents for sleeping in, a field for sports and a quiet backwater of the River Thames where a camper was paddling. All the residents pictured were women, although the camp was not reported as segregated. Set up by a committee 'representing the Ministry of Labour, the Slough Social Centre, the Bucks Education Committee and the Central Council of Recreative Physical Training', the camp took a hundred residents and also provided three meals a day.

Menus were planned with guidance from the Ministry of Food and a typical day's meals revealed traditional fare, from breakfast porridge and lunch-time roasts, to

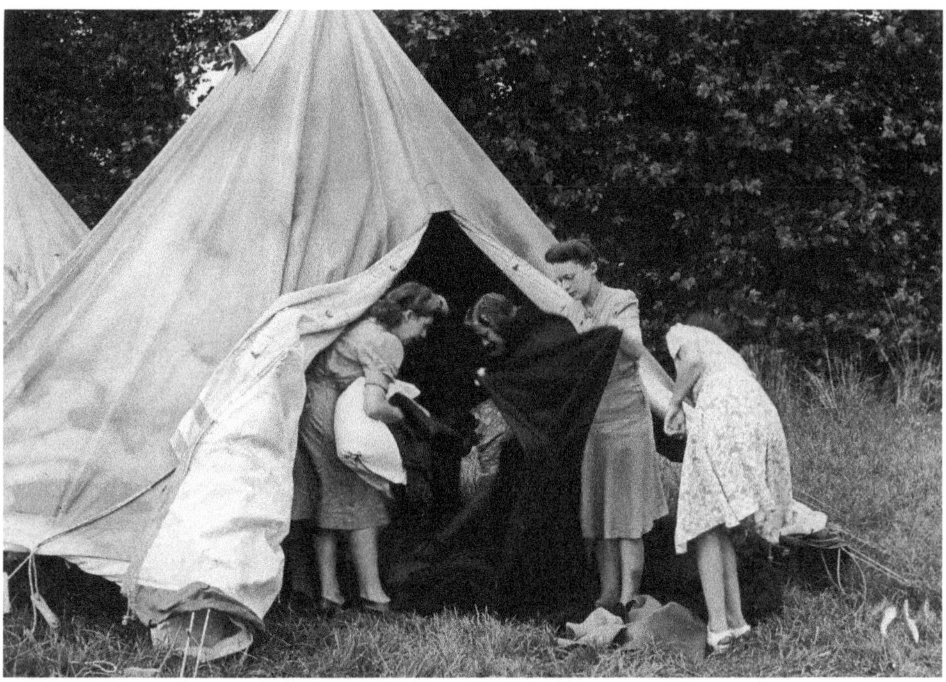

Figure 66 'They Sleep Under Canvas', from 'Holiday Camp for War Workers', *Picture Post*, 26 September 1942, p. 16. Bill Brandt/*Picture Post*/Getty Images (51195012).

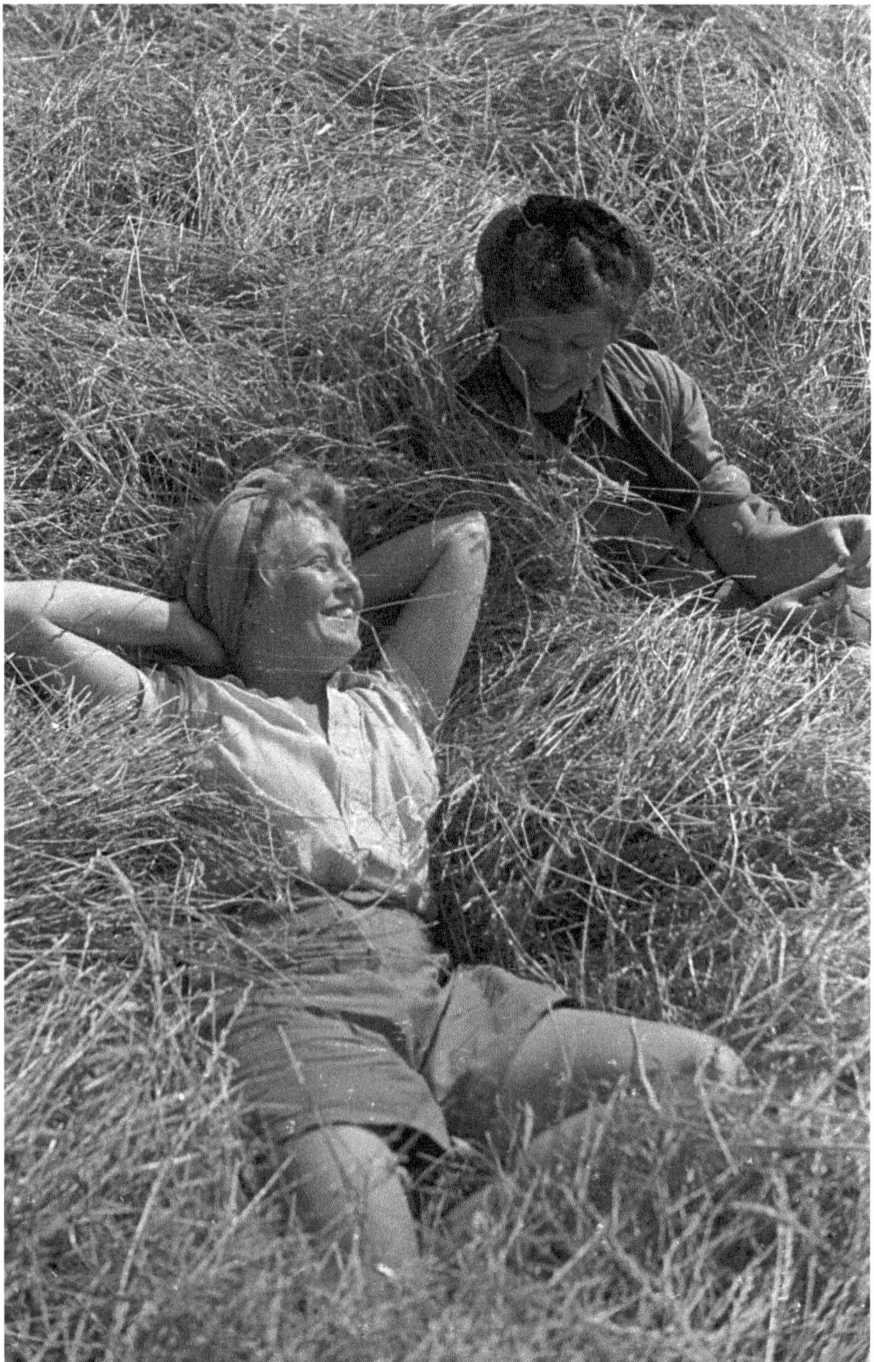

Figure 67 'Day's End in a Farming Camp: English Girl and French Girl Get Together .... [They] regularly spend spare time on the land. People who go once in a life-time are welcome, but less useful.' From 'Off-Duty in the Farming Camp', *Picture Post*, 17 July 1943, p. 22. Kurt Hutton/*Picture Post*/Getty Images (3378940).

cauliflower cheese at high tea. Much effort, it appeared, had been put into creating a healthy and happy environment around the several pleasures of sports, fitness and friendship. Here for at least 'one week in the year' a war worker could simply relax and recharge.[41] The tin mugs, bare wood tables and canvas tents might have offered simple living, but of much more importance was an affordable opportunity to rest, restore vitality and have fun.

In the summer of 1943, *Picture Post* investigated a break with a difference when it went 'Off-Duty in the Farming Camp'.[42] In order to bring in a harvest that would allow Britain to be '60 per cent self-supporting', townspeople from every walk of life were gathering as volunteers to work in farm camps.[43] The article reported that the number of helpers needed was high – sixty thousand just for the Home Counties. What was on offer, however, was a 'holiday that earns health'. Paying four shillings a day to live in camp, and working a minimum of four days, volunteers slept on straw palliases under canvas, washed under canvas and received a hearty main meal. Male workers received in return one shilling an hour, women workers ten pence, for turning to 'stooking and carting corn, picking and packing fruit, weeding, threshing, [and] potato lifting'.[44]

Photographs revealed the rewards of an off-duty break in the British countryside, with campers airing beds in the sunlight, relaxing in the long grass or the fields with friends and sharing communal meals. Here was hard work and healthy living side-by-side. As subtle propaganda for camp life, at a time when Britain was producing 'the biggest crop of food this island has ever grown', there was much that must have been persuasive. One 'representative group of workers',[45] assembled for lunch amid the mown fields of Chesfield Park and looking healthy and relaxed, also reflected the way war had brought people together. The picture of the German refugee, Canadian nurse, English shorthand-typist, French worker from Free French Headquarters and Army officer,[46] who were all helping to bring in the British harvest, illustrated something of the new and extended possibilities for friendship and unity that war had, ironically, facilitated.

Food for fitness and well-being

The foregoing stories all depicted ways of achieving a healthy life despite the toll of war work. If some of the fixes were limited in time, they at least offered useful pointers towards achieving a fit and balanced life. The other component central to the achievement of personal fitness was, of course, adequate and suitable food. While some home-front occupations offered a midday meal, or a suitable alternative for shift workers, most civilians wrestled daily with the twin difficulties of food rationing and food shortages in order to put meals on the table.[47]

The key to successful meal preparation, according to the Ministry of Food, was to 'Plan your meals the 4 group way'[48] and include something from each food group in every meal. The four groups – body building foods, energy foods and two categories of protective foods – reflected the inter-relationship between diet and health. This particular communication went on to include some representative examples of foods that fell within each group. Ministry of Food news and information notices of this kind, alongside of other initiatives such as the morning radio *Kitchen Front Talks*, publicized the importance of a balanced and nourishing diet and the varied ways this could be achieved with the foods available.

In similar vein 'Food Facts No. 10' from the Ministry of Food stated 'Here is *health* advice, *efficiency* advice and even *beauty* advice – all in one message from the Scientific Advisor to the Ministry of Food'. To keep the population fit during the winter just around the corner, a healthy diet was essential. Protective foods would help prevent illness and keep people functioning efficiently. On top of these benefits, 'resistance to strain and fatigue will be stronger – and incidentally, your complexion will be clearer.' Fruit and vegetables, wholemeal bread, dairy foods, eggs, oily fish and liver were all identified as 'Chief Protective Foods' and a recipe was printed for vegetable soup which provided a cheering hot drink 'at a time of shock or strain'.[49]

The accumulating hardships of living under war conditions meant that it became more important than ever that the public keep mentally and physically strong. Meals were not to be 'neglected' and foods such as 'bread and potatoes' were recommended for 'bodily warmth, and energy to cope with present difficulties'.[50] In terms of general health, protective foods like potatoes helped ward off illness and 'keep the digestive system in order', while carrots were 'splendid for the complexion' and assisted in preventing infection 'especially colds'.[51] 'Greens of all kinds' were 'Nature's Tonic Foods' containing vitamin C and iron which would 'tone and cheer you up, and . . . bring colour to your cheeks and lips'.[52] Dried produce such as beans, peas or lentils offered 'health protecting vitamins' while powdered egg gave all the body building nourishment and 'health protecting value' of the real thing.[53]

The health of expectant and nursing mothers and children was given special attention. A number of notices were produced promoting the types of food mothers and children should be having and the food supplements available for them. All pregnant women became entitled first to extra milk, then eggs and thereafter orange juice, cod-liver oil, vitamin D and vitamin A tablets. Children, dependent on age, became entitled to additional milk, orange juice, cod liver oil and 'vitamin products'.[54]

The National Milk Scheme, under which the additional milk outlined above was supplied, had been introduced in July 1940 and was 'an immediate success'.[55] The National Vitamins Scheme followed in December 1941 to offset any dietary inadequacies caused by 'lack of fruit, particularly oranges, and the shortage of butter and eggs'.[56] Titmuss remarked how both schemes, together with the provision of school meals, were introduced quickly and with remarkable political unanimity. Designed to benefit the whole population, welfare initiatives like these were of special value for poorer families who now gained access to important nutritional supplements and without 'social discrimination'.[57] This had the broader effect of ameliorating at least some of the nutritional inequalities that existed between social groups, particularly those affecting mothers and younger children.[58]

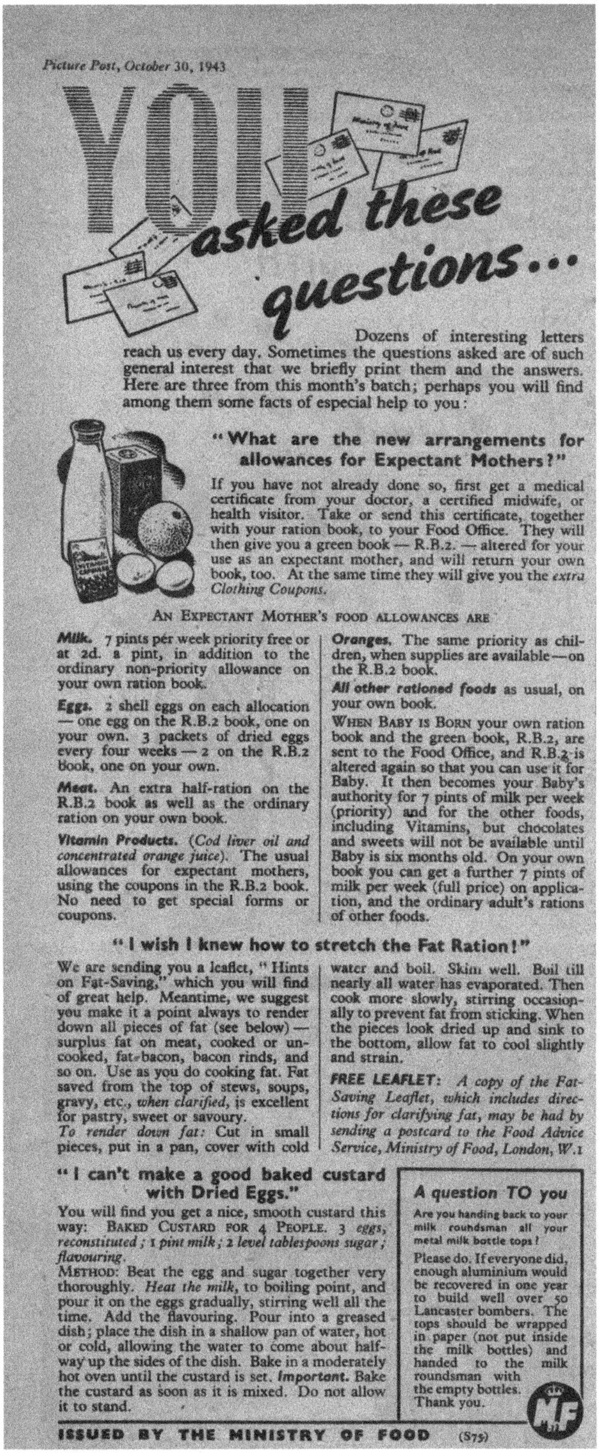
Picture Post, October 30, 1943

YOU *asked these questions...*

Dozens of interesting letters reach us every day. Sometimes the questions asked are of such general interest that we briefly print them and the answers. Here are three from this month's batch; perhaps you will find among them some facts of especial help to you:

"What are the new arrangements for allowances for Expectant Mothers?"

If you have not already done so, first get a medical certificate from your doctor, a certified midwife, or health visitor. Take or send this certificate, together with your ration book, to your Food Office. They will then give you a green book — R.B.2. — altered for your use as an expectant mother, and will return your own book, too. At the same time they will give you the *extra Clothing Coupons.*

AN EXPECTANT MOTHER'S FOOD ALLOWANCES ARE

Milk. 7 pints per week priority free or at 2d. a pint, in addition to the ordinary non-priority allowance on your own ration book.

Eggs. 2 shell eggs on each allocation — one egg on the R.B.2 book, one on your own. 3 packets of dried eggs every four weeks — 2 on the R.B.2 book, one on your own.

Meat. An extra half-ration on the R.B.2 book as well as the ordinary ration on your own book.

Vitamin Products. (*Cod liver oil and concentrated orange juice*). The usual allowances for expectant mothers, using the coupons in the R.B.2 book. No need to get special forms or coupons.

Oranges. The same priority as children, when supplies are available — on the R.B.2 book.

All other rationed foods as usual, on your own book.

WHEN BABY IS BORN your own ration book and the green book, R.B.2, are sent to the Food Office, and R.B.2 is altered again so that you can use it for Baby. It then becomes your Baby's authority for 7 pints of milk per week (priority) and for the other foods, including Vitamins, but chocolates and sweets will not be available until Baby is six months old. On your own book you can get a further 7 pints of milk per week (full price) on application, and the ordinary adult's rations of other foods.

"I wish I knew how to stretch the Fat Ration!"

We are sending you a leaflet, "Hints on Fat-Saving," which you will find of great help. Meantime, we suggest you make it a point always to render down all pieces of fat (see below) — surplus fat on meat, cooked or uncooked, fat bacon, bacon rinds, and so on. Use as you do cooking fat. Fat saved from the top of stews, soups, gravy, etc., *when clarified*, is excellent for pastry, sweet or savoury.

To render down fat: Cut in small pieces, put in a pan, cover with cold water and boil. Skim well. Boil till nearly all water has evaporated. Then cook more slowly, stirring occasionally to prevent fat from sticking. When the pieces look dried up and sink to the bottom, allow fat to cool slightly and strain.

FREE LEAFLET: *A copy of the Fat-Saving Leaflet, which includes directions for clarifying fat, may be had by sending a postcard to the Food Advice Service, Ministry of Food, London, W.1*

"I can't make a good baked custard with Dried Eggs."

You will find you get a nice, smooth custard this way: BAKED CUSTARD FOR 4 PEOPLE. 3 *eggs, reconstituted; 1 pint milk; 2 level tablespoons sugar; flavouring.*

METHOD: Beat the egg and sugar together very thoroughly. *Heat the milk*, to boiling point, and pour it on the eggs gradually, stirring well all the time. Add the flavouring. Pour into a greased dish; place the dish in a shallow pan of water, hot or cold, allowing the water to come about half-way up the sides of the dish. Bake in a moderately hot oven until the custard is set. ***Important.*** Bake the custard as soon as it is mixed. Do not allow it to stand.

A question TO you

Are you handing back to your milk roundsman all your metal milk bottle tops!

Please do. If everyone did, enough aluminium would be recovered in one year to build well over 50 Lancaster bombers. The tops should be wrapped in paper (not put inside the milk bottles) and handed to the milk roundsman with the empty bottles. Thank you.

ISSUED BY THE MINISTRY OF FOOD (S75)

Figure 68 'YOU asked these questions ... ', *Picture Post*, 30 October 1943, p. 4. *Picture Post*/ Hulton Archive/Getty Images (988556878).

Conclusion

Picture Post explored a number of the new lifestyles women were now experiencing and how health and fitness necessarily played a part in the successful commission of these roles. Those taking part in drills and PT were becoming ever fitter as a natural part of a service life, while those working on the land built up strength through hard physical labour under all weathers. The levels of fitness these women demonstrated were, in turn, supported by wholesome and substantial meals and a routine that regularized the balance between activity and rest.

For civilian women with less organized protocols for keeping strong and well, exercise, nutritious and appetizing food, combined with sufficient rest and relaxation offered the best countermeasures to war strain and war weariness. Fitness, like food, was a munition of war. Safeguarding health was both a political and a personal responsibility and lay at the heart of being able to keep cheerful and carry on.

9

EPILOGUE: *PICTURE POST* REPORTS ON FASHION NEWS FROM FRANCE

Introduction

After the Nazi occupation of France from June 1940, British contact with the French couture ceased.[1] *Picture Post* stories thereafter showed that British wartime style continued to reflect the mix of fashions that had been popular up to this point, some of which had been inspired by British ideas anyway. Alongside of these, at times, historically inclined dress styles and accessories, British tailored classics and country mix-and-match separates sustained their popularity, particularly as they offered the practical and durable pieces women wanted for wartime living. Clothes rationing was a manufacturing rather than a style watershed, although the reduced capacity to buy clothing did result in some interesting style ideas for the home wardrobe, as *Picture Post* readers would have been aware.

Stories about dress in Britain from the spring of 1942 generally reflected the appearance of Utility clothing, which would eventually provide almost all high street apparel, and the progress of the austerity restrictions that would control Utility style. Design consolidated around a relatively unadorned, pared-back line for suits, coats and dresses with a focus on neat tailoring, practical, hard-wearing fabrics and a continuing capacity to mix and match. *Picture Post* readers, as we have seen, were kept up-to-date with the minor changes in detail – rather than silhouette – that now came to represent fashion, and informed about the new fashion values inherent in home-made and making-do. This was the story of fashion in Britain for the remainder of the war.

That fashion had been taking a very different course in occupied France came as a surprise. *Picture Post* offered four articles on Paris fashion between 1943 and 1945, each providing slightly different viewpoints which charted the magazine's reaction to, and consideration of, what Paris designers had been doing and for whom. As stories on British fashion continued to reiterate the less-is-more philosophy shaped by clothing control, it was French fashion that was, if only very sporadically, making news. This final chapter looks at these four stories, not only as they revealed the contrasts between controlled British and

French couture wartime style, but also as they signalled new ways of thinking about fashion for the peace.

Picture Post receives a copy of the *Album de la Mode Figaro*

In the spring of 1943 *Picture Post* reported that a copy of the French magazine *Album de la Mode Figaro* had appeared in their office. It contained 120 pages 'packed with beautiful drawings of magnificent clothes'.[2] The article went on to report that the album 'showed a wealth and luxury which is the last thing one associates with Paris in war'. Staff pondered whether the edition was, perhaps, a propaganda exercise? Was such clothing really being made and worn despite the tragic conditions of occupation? Subsequent investigation revealed 'a strange story .... In Paris, incredibly, the fashionable life goes on'.[3] The elaborate and opulent outfits reproduced, together with some examples of design features and accessories, all revealed fashions 'as beautiful and luxurious as in pre-war days'.

Anne Scott-James reported that these clothes were being made right now and included 'evening dresses in dozens, draped, décolleté, embroidered, jewelled. There are pleated frocks, fur-trimmed coats, lace-trimmed blouses, none of which may be made in England, taking yards of material. There are tucked sleeves and embroidered pockets involving many hours of hand-work'.[4] Yet Paris was experiencing 'starvation and barefoot poverty'.[5] In addition there was also 'new jewellery and perfumes to match'[6] in contrast to the situation in Britain where jewellery and perfumery had both been extensively controlled under wartime Limitation and Prohibition Orders.[7] Here were some perplexing revelations about the 'Nazi New Order'.[8]

Clothes by France Obre, Jean Patou, Maggy Rouff and Robert Piguet were featured, each in their own way reflecting the ornate styling of an industry apparently undiminished by regulation or restraint. The small print accompanying the images described variously: a new dress line by Obre, characterized by fullness in the lower skirt and a decorative bow in moiré draped at the hip; a long tunic-style fitted jacket by Patou in multi-coloured brocade with asymmetric closure and tassel detail worn over a narrow crepe sheath; and two outfits by Maggy Rouff, one with a long line fitted and pin-tucked bodice embroidered above the waist with paillettes and worn over a gathered skirt, the other a dress and coat ensemble in padded taffeta lined with velvet and with an ostrich feather sleeve.

Some unascribed drawings showed a sumptuous fur coat replete with fur hood and muffler beside an ornate cut-away jacket with polonaise-style peplum and generous roll collar. Smaller inset drawings, similarly unascribed, focused on design details such as an embroidered pocket and an opulent fur hood. A black velvet 'Party Frock' by Robert Piguet was distinguished by its 'Velasquez skirt' and the 'glittering sequins' that decorated the low-cut bodice and pannier-style hip shaping.[9] Extravagant and audacious in design terms, these clothes were now setting the Nazi elite and its wealthy French collaborators apart from the rest of the French population.

The article went on to consider the lifestyle of these 2,000 or so collaborators who had turned their backs on the 'rags and squalor' witnessed in 'most of the pictures that come out of France' and were currently enjoying the 'doubtful blessing of Nazi patronage'. Possession of a *'carte de haute couture*' or buying permit entitled any 'recognized collaborator' to buy opulent clothing at the design houses without restriction. The 'theatres, dinners, cocktail and restaurant parties' that continued to operate under the Occupation provided the opportunity to dress up.[10]

Meanwhile, for the 'vast majority' of the French people 'too loyal to collaborate and too poor to buy in the Black Market . . . the Germans provide nothing'. There had been 'no attempt at rationing or a Utility scheme, for there is no bulk supply of fabric in France. The Germans have looted all the stocks and taken most of the workers'.[11]

This first article on the continuation of French couture fashion clearly separated out the 'small Franco-German set' still enjoying the good life from the 'humbler' citizens of France now enduring hardship and shortage. While remarking on the 'splendid isolation' of these few who chose to 'ignore the poverty and squalor of the rest of the people', Scott-James made no direct comment on the work of the couture houses other than to register some of the styles, the high prices and the extent of the labour invloved.[12] The Album de la Mode Figaro had revealed to Picture Post staff and readers alike a new and unexpected view of life under the Occupation.

Picture Post reports that 'Paris fashions are quick off the mark'

Well over a year later and only a little more than a month after the liberation of Paris,[13] *Picture Post* returned to the subject of Paris fashion.[14] This time the focus was on French fashion designers and the type of war they had fought. Six photographs showing anonymous daywear outfits – three captioned 'The Models in Reserve' – established the continuing difference between French and British fashion. None were directly referred to in the text.

Large and ornately decorated hats, in particular, were a feature of these photographs, alongside dresses made with generous skirts, and worn with higher-heeled and wedge-heeled shoes. All these reflected the styles on which couturiers had been working and the liberal resources at their disposal. Determined in the cause of fashion 'war or no war', here were models that suggested, according to the writer, that 'the Fashion Trade is ready for peace'. Yet the caption went on to remark that it was 'perhaps truer to say that the French fashion designers have always been ready for peace since they never knew war. There were always buyers for their models'. The fashion industry had carried on with its trade irrespective of the changed context and clientele. Designers knew, it was suggested, that 'though Frenchmen might die in the Maquis, the future of the fashion industry was secure'.

A final short paragraph added, 'Perhaps the Resistance Movement, when it has time, will be able to thank the dress designers – both those who stayed and those who

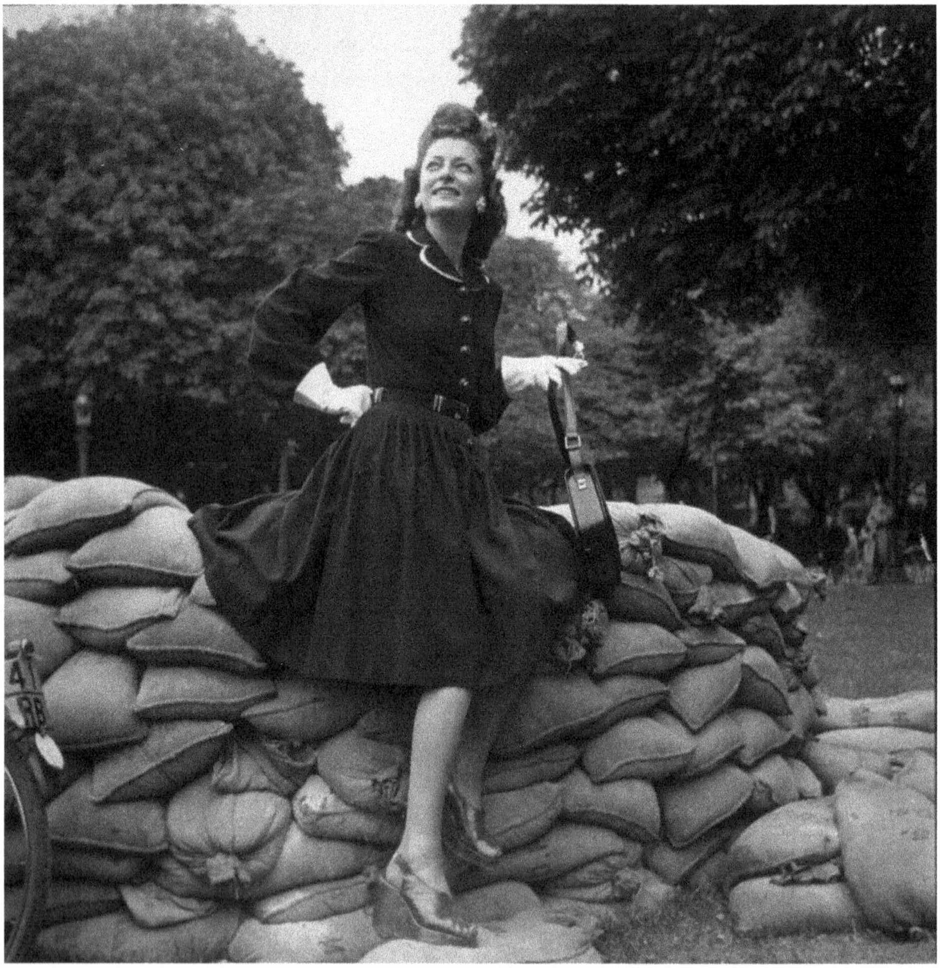

Figure 69 'The Incidental Background. The war has limited materials; but not for the smart coutourieres who make their models, war or no war.' 'Paris Fashion Are Quick Off the Mark', *Picture Post*, 7 October 1944, p. 19. Bob Landry/Getty Images (2661225).

fought so well in New York – for their contribution to France's liberation'.[15] Business as usual clearly struck the writer as controversial. Yet the irony would prove to be double-edged. The argument for keeping designer doors open is now a familiar one.[16] In doing so both the industry and the untold number of jobs and livelihoods it saved and supported were secured ready, indeed, for the peace and all that that would so soon bring.[17] In fighting for its survival the couture industry had been waging a very different type of war, arguably, from that being fought by the Maquis, a fact that would only become clear with the benefit of historic hindsight.

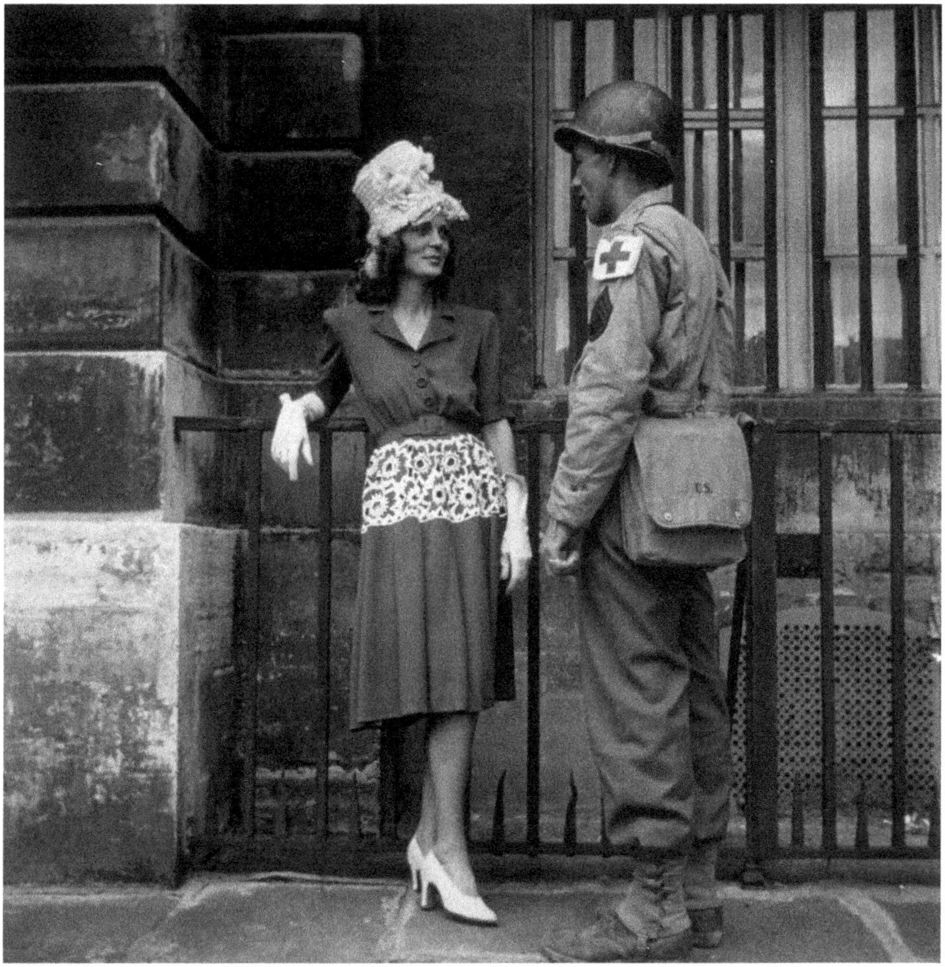

Figure 70 'The Fashion Trade is Ready for Peace: The Models in Reserve'. From 'Paris Fashions Are Quick Off the Mark, *Picture Post*, 7 October 1944, p. 19. Bob Landry/*Picture Post*/Getty Images (3315087).

Picture Post shows 'what a *Vogue* photographer sees in Paris'

If the last article had been about the fashion industry and its apparently single-minded determination to survive, this story now took a different approach altogether.[18] It seemed to piece together two different if connected narratives. The *Vogue* photographer had taken images of some of the new 'Liberation Modes'[19] now emerging from a selection of Paris fashion houses. These fashions appeared to show that designers were continuing to produce luxury garments. Images showed fur coats, hats and mufflers and softly tailored coats offering some generosity of cut. A chic fitted lace jacket with narrow waist and short peplum worn over a pencil skirt reflected a more ornate response to the familiar lines of allied wartime fashion. All were accessorized with statuesque statement hats, and satchel bags or mufflers. Luxury fashion might have 'helped to keep up morale and confound the occupying Germans' before the liberation, but it was clearly still being produced.[20] The liberation itself seemed to have had little effect on design. The second page of images focused on how hairdressing was now being carried out in a Paris where fuel shortages had created the need for a 'two-day hair do'.[21]

The text meanwhile reproduced material that had first appeared in the *Observer* newspaper on women who had been 'passive spectators of the Occupation'.[22] Fashion writer and ex-editor of British *Vogue* Alison Settle[23] explained that these women were not collaborators. They had taken the view that their duty was to carry on their lives 'as if the Germans were not there'. Settle stated that they were 'everywhere in Paris' wearing rich and exotic clothing, and that she had recently seen them herself at 'the most expensive dressmakers … ordering dresses which cost 50 guineas each' and at beauty parlours and hairstylists. It was Settle's contention that because there was no specific 'national work' to occupy these women, they saw nothing wrong in their 'idle and luxurious' lives.[24]

Settle does not answer the question she poses as to how such women could be brought 'into the orbit of the national necessity'. Her summary of contemporary feminist campaigns that followed revealed many issues to fight for, but no practical strategies for joining 'the patriotic body of women who will work and live for the renewed greatness of France'.[25] Settle never says that sumptuous clothing and time-consuming beauty protocols were unacceptable in themselves. Her remarks were not about the state of the couture or associated glamour industries, although the accompanying photographs were. Rather they were about women who might achieve a good deal more with their lives than remaining the profligate and passive clothes-horses they had become.

London: Can It Become A World Fashion Centre?'

When Alice Settle next wrote about French fashion in *Picture Post*, who was wearing it and why was no longer at issue. In a three-page article asking whether London could be a contender on the world fashion stage, a series of photographs compared the styles for particular types of clothing coming out of France and Britain.[26] In each case the clear divide remained between design largesse, generosity of fabric, or opulent ornamentation on the one hand and design simplicity, thrift-consciousness and unadorned chic on the other.

As Britain entered the final months of war, the Utility and austerity regulations still controlled the manufacture of all commercial clothing, and clothes rationing continued to limit civilian consumption.[27] A caption accompanying an image of a coat from the French house of Marcelle Alix stated that 'over-luxurious lines have been modified to meet British opinion'. Yet the coat – now with 'only half the material used last season'– still looked generously cut, both in the body and sleeves, when compared to British couturier Peter Russell's tailored trench pictured beneath.[28]

French couture clearly offered a considerable contrast to controlled British design. The key, Settle argued, to British designers standing any chance of competing in the international fashion stakes against either Paris or New York, was having access to sufficient textiles of the right type. Such supplies would facilitate the new designs needed to promote a British fashion industry. Both Paris and New York had 'plenty of fabrics' according to Settle. If war restrictions continued to make additional textiles hard to come by for British designers, then 'short lengths' of fabric for 'experimental purposes' ought to be made available at the very least. British couturiers could not at the moment create even the 25 models allowed for a seasonal show, as against the 160 models currently permitted in Paris. Unless the situation changed, Settle suggested, Britain would have no fashion exports once the war ended.[29]

The photographs did much of the work to reveal the quite different platforms on which fashion design was being realized in France and Britain. A glamorous French astrakhan

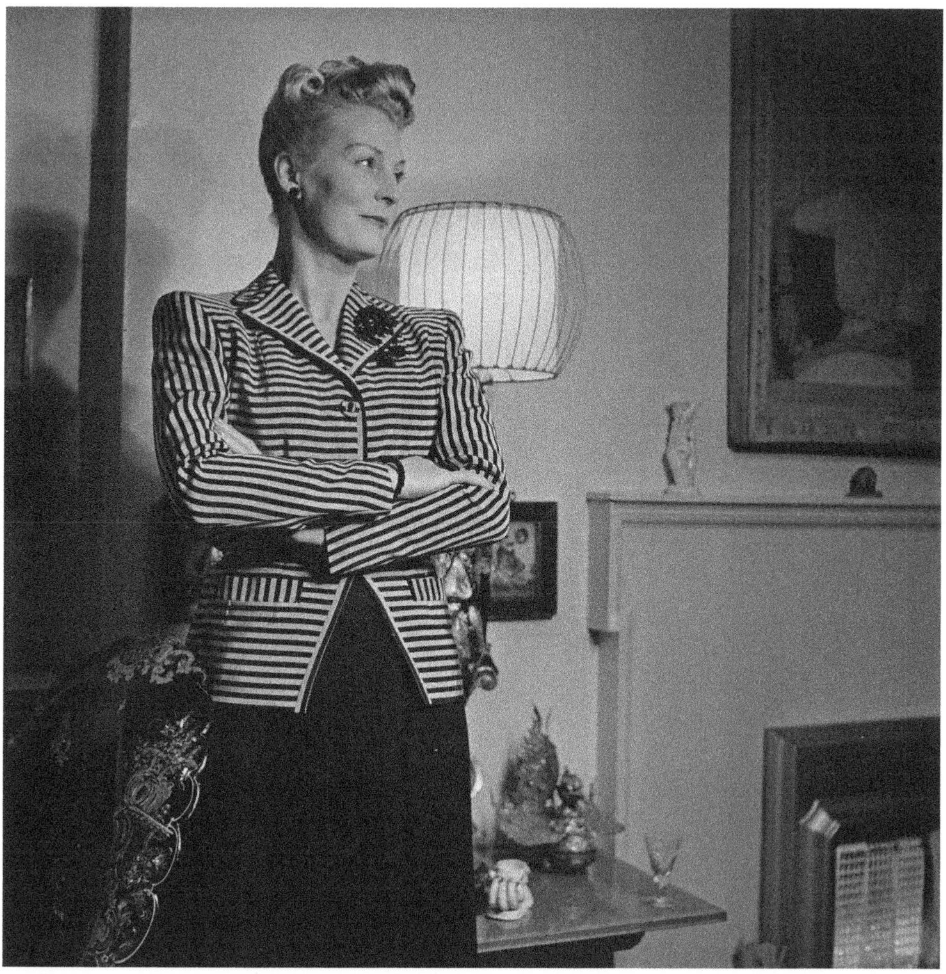

Figure 71 'London: A Digby Morton Suit, which shows the spirited designing still possible under austerity rules'. From 'London: Can It Become A World Fashion Centre?', *Picture Post*, 6 January 1945, p. 19. Felix Man/*Picture Post*/Hulton Archive/Getty Images (985846338).

jacket with generously raised shoulders and tabard style peplum with lace edging was contrasted to a short cut-away suit jacket with squared shoulder line and trim revers from Britain. A fuller-skirted evening dress with silk petticoat and leg-of-mutton style sleeves 'embroidered in jet and sequins'[30] was pictured above a narrow, fitted evening dress with squared neckline and three-quarter-length sleeves, whose ornamentation lay chiefly in the linear print of the fabric. Two further opulent, full-length evening outfits, one liberal in its use of velvet and silk, the other of satin, sat above smaller images of elegant, if restrained, evening wear, one dress featuring black net sleeves and bodice decoration, the other a central diamond motif around which fabric from the hip and bust line had been carefully gathered. While less-is-more home front fashion had been a necessary outcome of necessary limitations, continuing to impose creative constraints as the political landscape brightened might prove counter-productive. It seemed Britain might be just too slow off the mark by the end of hostilities to offer serious competition to either France or America despite its reputation for beautiful tailored clothing and its heritage of exceptional traditional fabrics.[31]

Conclusion

Picture Post captured something of both the controversy and the challenge that surfaced as French fashion began to come to public attention once again. That the French couture could have retained such opulence and grandeur, despite the privation and hardship by which it was surrounded, had been unforeseen and this news was, at the time it came to light, rather bewildering. In retrospect *Picture Post* can be seen to have registered and recorded the way in which the information was initially received, and some of the variable viewpoints on the clothes, their creators and purchasers that subsequently emerged. Here was the struggle, played out in real time, to come to terms with the sight of couture luxury amid an evolving context of mitigating factors and extenuating wartime circumstances. It was not the full history as it would later be understood. Perhaps, rather, the stories together revealed a way of life in Paris profoundly at variance with what had been imagined, and one where the ambiguities that surrounded the creation and acquisition of couture clothing brought into focus something of the moral maze of living under the Occupation.

CONCLUSION

In the Introduction I suggested that *Picture Post* provided a unique archive of dress, fashion and fashionability for the period leading up to and including the Second World War. Comprising stories and features that brought together material on both the social fabric of individual women's lives and communities and the cultural contexts which shaped them, I maintained that the magazine provided both a diverse and detailed source of information that invited further investigation. This was a view formed from my own experience of studying *Picture Post* as a researcher and from seeing photographs from the magazine chosen as illustrations for books and museum exhibitions. I believed there was room for a study of *Picture Post* in its own right that would pay tribute to the photo-journalism method it embraced and the capacities this revealed for extending cultural awareness of people, places and politics, particularly those rarely included elsewhere. I hope that this book has gone at least some way towards doing this.

The stories discussed here have tried to reflect the breadth of vision characteristic of *Picture Post* and the capacity of its photojournalism to capture dress practice in authentic and reliable narratives. Together these two components have provided the range and type of material necessary for exploring the relationship between lifestyle and dress caused by such defining factors as privilege or poverty, peace or war. I have tried to identify through my choice of stories and articles the various ways in which aspects of fashion and dress were covered within *Picture Post* from straightforward fashion reporting on trends and tendencies to photo-stories that went further in placing aspects of dress and material culture into the broader framework of lifestyle and period. Of special value to me in terms of seeing and reading photo-narratives are those stories which for one reason or another provided new perspectives on, and perceptions of, real life for women at this time and the degree of empathy with them, or with a sense of period, these could open up. *Picture Post* contains many such stories. My choices are certainly not the only ones.

The photo-journalism of *Picture Post* provides historical narratives that can be both vivid and, at times, almost visceral records of people, places and events. The photographers who worked for *Picture Post* – such as Kurt Hutton, Felix Man, Bert Hardy – established reputations for truthful, largely unstaged, photo-stories that created, week by week, a real-time visual history of a world moving towards and into war. With integrity, humanity and compassion, these photographers, along with their writing associates, provided readers with the chance to explore the ordinary and less ordinary topics that now emerged out of daily life, while also opening up new portals into the unknown physical and mental landscapes of war. This panoramic view across a period experiencing unprecedented emotional and cultural upheaval is a specific legacy of the *Picture Post* photo-story and one of lasting value for its appeal to both the intellect and the imagination.

Picture Post's campaigning voice

From the outset *Picture Post*'s desire to bring the everyday lives of ordinary people into public prominence, alongside of its determination to tread the road less travelled in terms of confronting social inequality and deprivation, began to forge a distinctive voice and recognizable style. Never aligned to a particular political party but rather pursuing its own editorial philosophy of social justice and social inclusivity, *Picture Post* quickly established its signature approach in the years before the war. During this time, as we have seen, it carried stories on the quality of life in some of the poorer and poorest communities, recording the existence of a hardship, depleted health and lack of opportunity for which there seemed little hope of political redress. Dress emerged here as one of several material culture barometers of want or distress.

As wartime industries absorbed the unemployed, and other new roles in service and civilian life also offered the chance of paid work, much of the economic distress of the immediate pre-war years was ameliorated. *Picture Post* continued, however, to champion the interests of the previously dispossessed so that there could be no return to such hardship in the post-war world. Anne Scott-James recalled *Picture Post* as being a 'visionary magazine' because it 'looked into the future as well as the present' and maintained its 'potent advocacy' for social reform.[1]

In January 1941, for example, *Picture Post* published 'A Plan for Britain'.[2] Planning for a better post-war life was described as 'an essential part of our war aims',[3] and the issue went on to promote principles such as full employment, a minimum wage, social insurance and a state medical service. In June of the following year, in a series called 'Britain's Silent Revolution', J. B. Priestley remarked that wartime employment and the system of rationing commodities for the good of everyone had already changed life for the better. British society now had to 'keep on changing ... to meet the new challenges of peace'.[4]

In the same series Jennie Lee considered to what extent women's current levels of employment could be sustained once the war was over. In an article called 'A New Life Opens Out for Women', Lee stated that women were now being encouraged into 'trades and professions wholly or partly barred to them in the peace years'.[5] Despite some advances by Trades Unions to create fairer working conditions, it was still common practice, however, for women not to hold equality with men in terms of pay or promotion. Similarly, although the war had created full employment, Lee suggested that if work became scarce again after the war, the 'family breadwinner' would claim 'the first right to whatever jobs are available'. As it was 'usually assumed that the breadwinner is a man', even though this was not always so, she expressed the view that only when everyone had job security would women achieve it.[6]

She too looked forward to a fairer society once peace came, where working for the common good would 'take precedence over the claims of specially pampered groups'.[7] A 'charter of emancipation for the modern women', in Lee's opinion, would include work and 'civilized' housing for all, equality of education, pay and conditions of service and some kind of state support for families.[8] For readers of *Picture Post*, and indeed for us as readers today, memories of the living conditions in Stepney for example, or of the deprivation caused by unemployment, made Lee's hopes for decent homes and happier, healthier domestic lives all too understandable.

The publication of the Beveridge Report into social welfare in November 1942 prompted *Picture Post* to produce an entire issue the following January dedicated to what the future of Britain could and should be to benefit the country and its people.[9] Strongly supportive of the Report's initiatives on social security and public welfare, *Picture Post* set about reviewing the changes within society and the lives of the British people that had occurred as a result of war and speculated on how a brighter and better future might be achieved. In the process the 'Five Giant Evils: Want, disease, ignorance, squalor, idleness' would need to be confronted.[10] Thus was *Picture Post*'s campaigning voice sustained across the war years, always endorsing a fairer and more equal society with a persuasive pragmatism, solicitude and compassion.[11]

Picture Post and wartime women

Picture Post's platform of humanitarian values and social inclusivity established early on the broad range of cultural material its readers might expect. From the drawing rooms of Mayfair to the kitchens of Lambeth, the magazine quickly developed stories on women across classes and communities, establishing a historic record of particular lifestyles and creating awareness of some of the specific social and economic factors that gave rise to them. Each had a dress code and practice that helped to further define a discrete cultural context, details of which emerged as a contingent part of the photo-story. In this way *Picture Post* built up a picture of the diversity of women's lifestyles at this time, while the visual narratives of dress, fashion and fashionability helped to define something of the quality of life – or lack of it – and standard of living each one represented.

The transition from peacetime to conflict clearly brought about noticeable shifts in these dress codes and practices as priorities for self-presentation and dress adjusted to the constraints and controls of war. *Picture Post* witnessed this process. It captured on camera the obvious changes as women joined the armed forces and dressed in uniform, or entered civilian war-industries and adopted practical work-wear. It also provided visual evidence of the more gradual re-alignment of everyday style as women sought out clothing pieces and outfits suitable for the hard work now attendant on running a home or providing voluntary service. Style and silhouette responded to the requirements of war while in turn becoming metaphors for the lifestyle changes women experienced as part of adjusting to, and accepting, life as it now had to be.

Whether facing the day-to-day difficulties of rationing on the home front, or working in unfamiliar jobs and places, perhaps even serving abroad, each new life had a material culture of clothing, accessories and surroundings that helped to tell a specific story. If the smart battledress of the women ferry pilots serving in the Air Transport Auxiliary[12] or the field uniforms worn by the WAAF balloon barrage handlers represented some of the newer occupations being undertaken by women – and of special interest because of this – the home-front styles worn in response to the everyday conditions of war often traced more subtle changes in dressing.

Featured in articles such as 'Clothes for a Coupon Summer' or 'Fashions for Summer: All Under £3', here were dress options for a world contending with the restrictions of

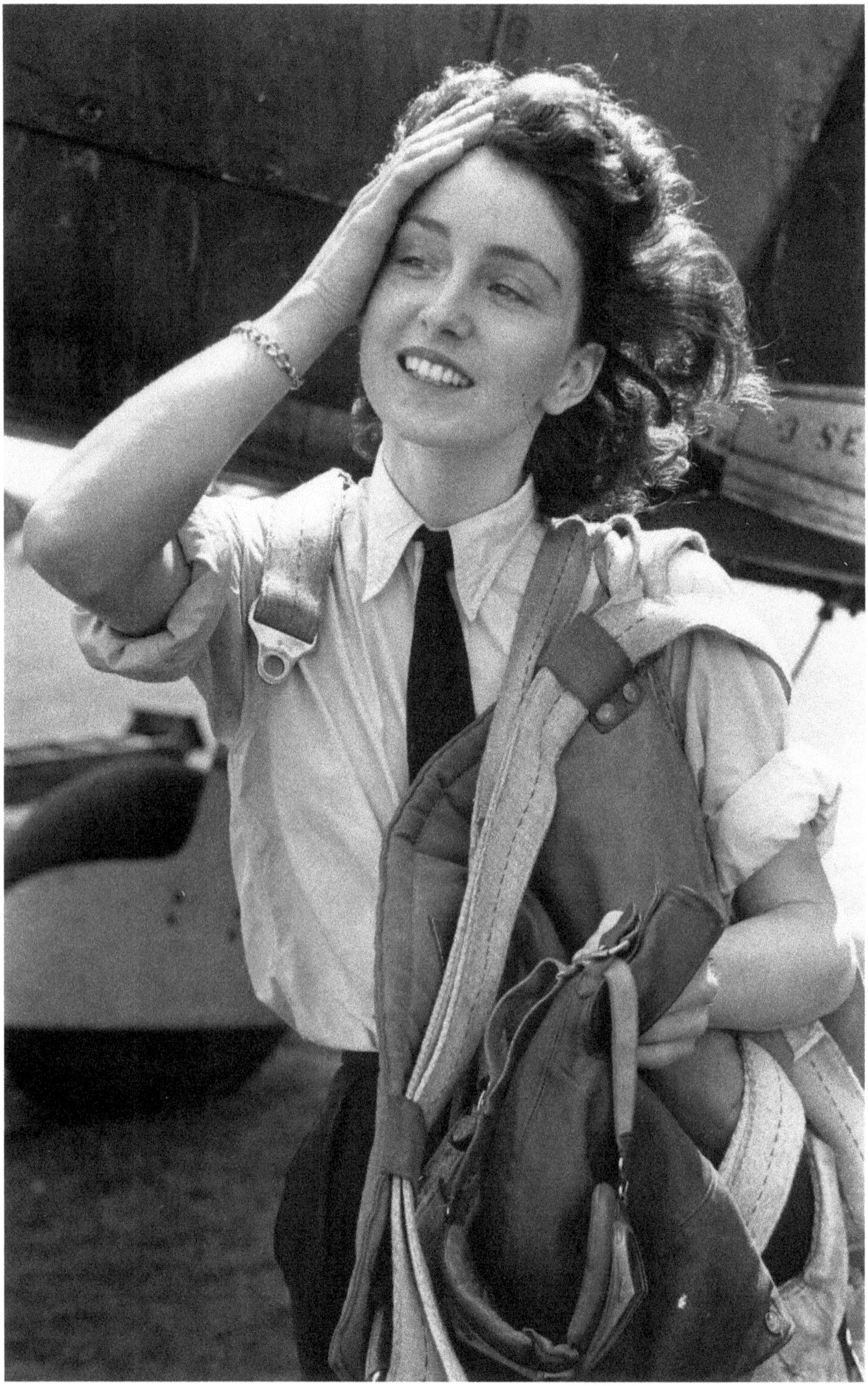

Figure 72 'The Story of the A.T.A.', *Picture Post*, 16 September 1944, front cover. Leonard McCombe/*Picture Post*/Getty Images (3069141).

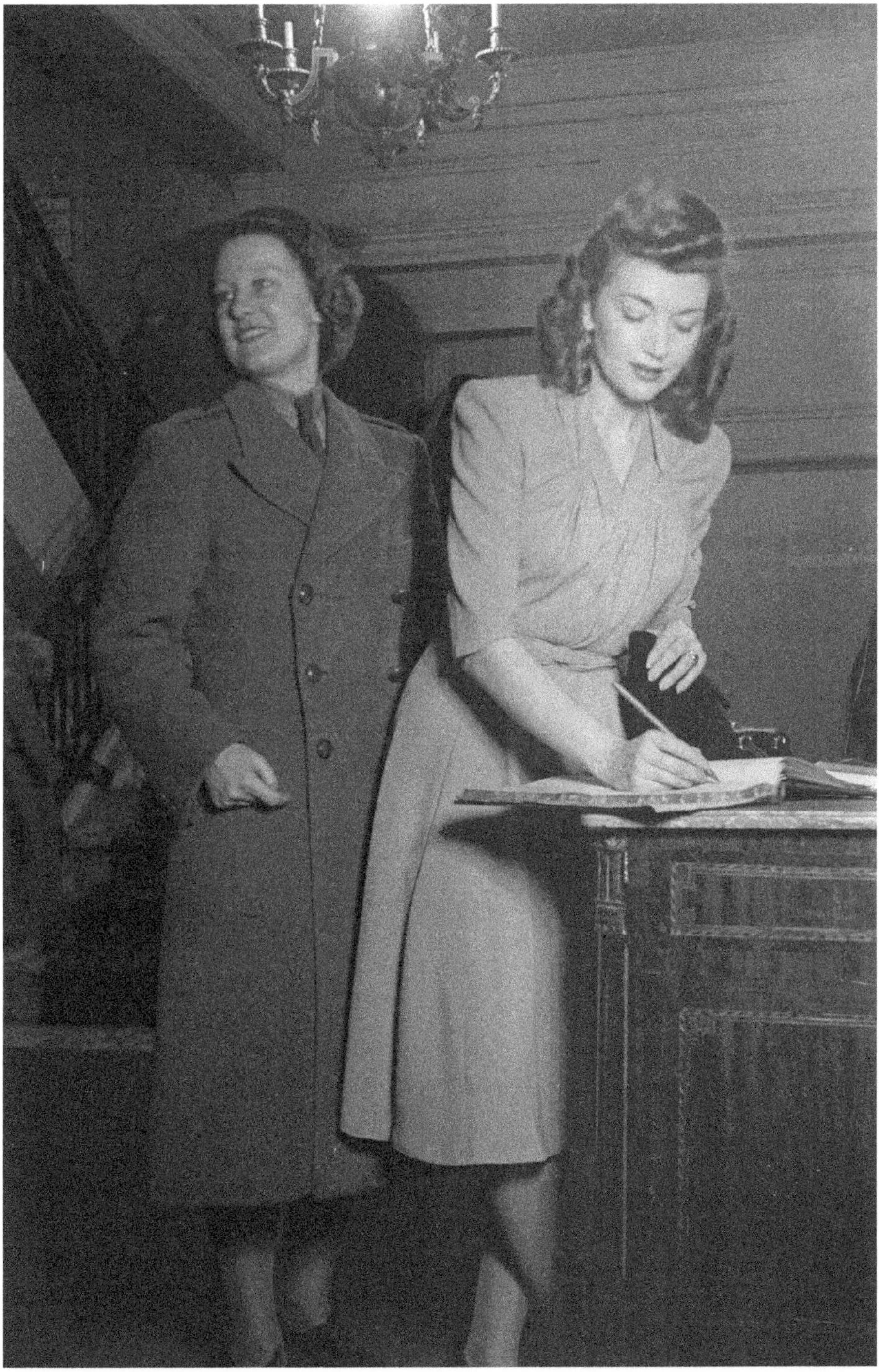

Figure 73 'The Dressier Dress. A pistachio crepe dress has a beautifully draped bodice. Rembrandt, from Waring & Gillow; £8 4s. 6d.; 7 coupons'. 'Some Clothes for Your New Coupons', *Picture Post*, 26 February 1944, p. 22. Kurt Hutton/*Picture Post*/Hulton Archive/Getty Images (984851068).

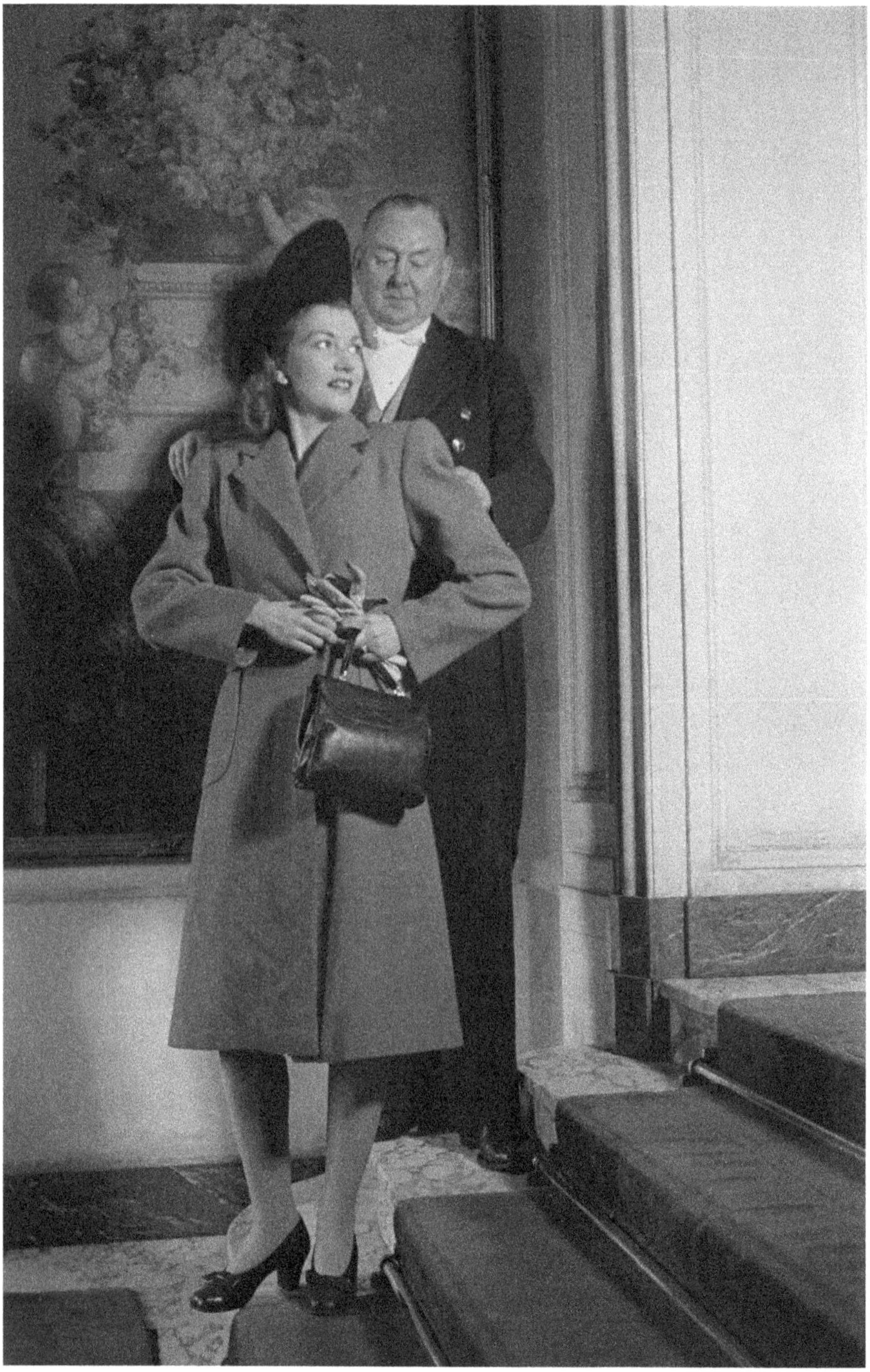

Figure 74 'The Unbelted Coat. A bright red coat has a tailored line, a minimum of trimming. Dereta Utility from Fenwick; £4; 18 coupons'. 'Some Clothes for Your New Coupons', *Picture Post*, 26 February 1944, p. 22. Kurt Hutton/*Picture Post*/Hulton Archive/Getty Images (984851388).

war. As seasonal fashion variations dwindled and the capacity for choice on the high street significantly contracted, women had to accept the controlled style templates emerging from Utility and Austerity. Fashion itself was now being re-fashioned. Instead of representing creative change it came increasingly to signify creative fine-tuning or re-working of existing designs and silhouettes. Meanwhile style continued to be synonymous with clothes that were cared for, well-turned-out and deftly accessorized.

Picture Post stories also reflected the decline in conspicuous consumption and trophy dressing associated with the wealthier classes. As prestige fashions became increasingly difficult to come by and, to a degree variable with setting and company, unpatriotic, the dress styles of the population increasingly began to look more similar. This was not an indication of real demographic shift. Evidence of class simply became less enshrined in clothing. Even after clothing controls were completed there were still more and less expensive clothing ranges and Anne Scott-James's columns often bore witness to the dearer end of Utility production. 'Practical Living' never, to my knowledge, for the period covered by this work, called at Marks and Spencer or any of the other chain stores, to see what could be picked up there for a much lower price. Wherever the clothing might come from, and at whatever price level it sold for, the style templates operating from mid-1942 not only reflected the need for efficient, controlled manufacture, but also delivered a relatively homogenized clothing aesthetic – a visual metaphor of sorts that furthered the cause of unanimity rather than difference under the current wartime conditions.

The subtle yet specific adjustments made to the beauty blueprint during the war years provide a final example of *Picture Post*'s value as an archive of dress and appearance. Women had increasingly been encouraged, either by their types of employment or the demands of their domestic lives, to become fitter and healthier. Information on creating a nutritious diet, exercising and resting all contributed now to an evolving beauty blueprint that endorsed and celebrated physical fitness, mental alertness and the look-alive energy and charm that was a result of both. An understanding of the need for better ways of living and the importance of a more holistic approach to health had both been formulated pre-war as we have seen. The conditions of war and the stress and strain that now affected so many people's lives as a result gave these concepts added significance and practical application. Maintaining the good health of the nation now became a major component of home-front war strategy, underpinning as it did the capacity to carry on. It was, for example, a prime incentive behind the rationing and fair-sharing of both food and apparel, on the basis that everyone was to have access to a nutritious diet and fit-for-purpose clothing. It is hardly surprising that the achievement of these goals set up new hopes for a brighter, healthier future that would continue to affirm the rights of all to social justice, work and well-being.

And finally

The signature, familiar styles of wartime enlivened – both capriciously as well as judiciously – by the addition of home-crafted items of the sort now familiar to us through 'Practical Living' continued to represent the wartime wardrobe. If they also provided intimations of a new spirit of democracy, these were both low key and, to a degree, illusory. That they were pointers of more significant shifts in public perception about the nature of and need for greater equality is, arguably, more admissible. Whatever the future might hold *Picture Post* charted the ways in which the changing face and fortunes of fashion reflected a broader reorientation of social forces brought about by the state of war and the demands it made on everyone.

Fashions and the fashionable, beauty parlours and cold perms; the trappings of privilege, the privation of poverty, *Picture Post* covered them all and more. In doing so it reflected the lives and livelihoods of so many women in so many stories. Today it continues to tell us about service women, blue-collar workers, women volunteers. It takes us on active duty, shows us the home front; we go down into air-raid shelters or help bring in the harvest. We visit old women in a Grandmothers' Club, join young women learning how to be mothers; witness country members of the Women's Institute preparing for the future, watch town women rebuilding their homes and lives. Here is a chronicle of war that is not only informative and thoughtful, but also has the capacity, still, to elicit a very real emotional response. One of the extraordinary strengths of the *Picture Post* photo-story at its best, and, arguably, its most important legacy of all, is the way in which it can facilitate a sense of empathy and connection with individual histories. Where this happens what we see leaves an indelible image and effect. The hardship and strain experienced by families in some of the poorest London neighbourhoods, a bombed-out mother being helped at a refuge centre, work and rest at a farming camp; injustice and distress, anxiety and relief, enjoyment and well-being. These stories, without doubt, create living histories. Each of us will engage with different stories for different reasons. They are all there, waiting to be rediscovered.

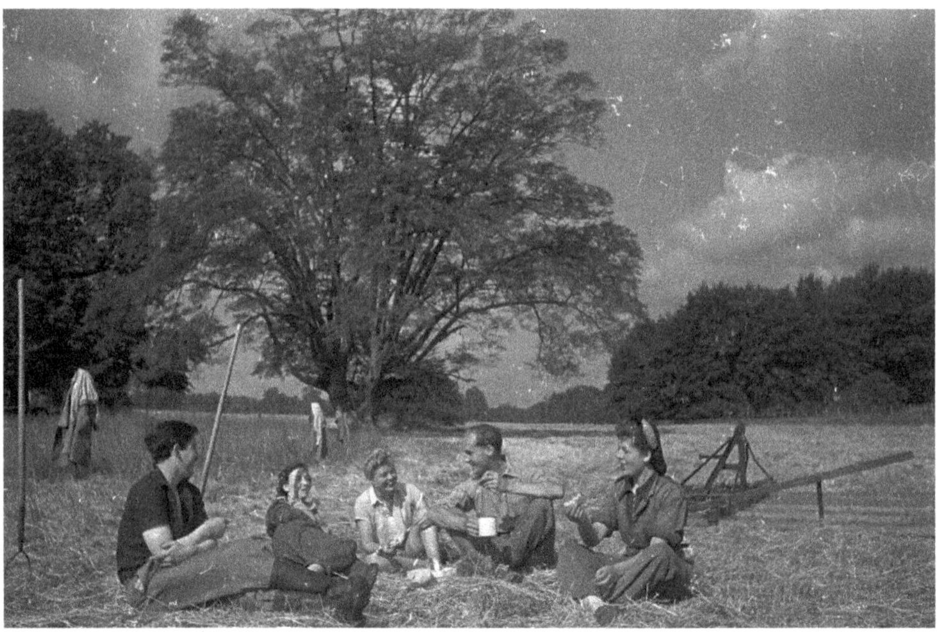

Figure 75 'Lunch-time for the Workers from Chesfield Park Farming Camp in Hertfordshire ... ', *Picture Post*, 17 July 1943, p. 23. Kurt Hutton/*Picture Post*/Getty Images (131419912).

NOTES

Introduction

1 The Editors of Time Life Books, *Photojournalism* (Time Life Books, 1971), p. 96.

2 There is a considerable body of information on this topic. Much of it derives from post–Second World War scholarship and from more recent material that also addresses the impact on photo-narratives of twenty-first-century digital medias. See for example: J. H. Newton, *The Burden of Visual Truth: The Role of Photojournalism in Mediating Reality* (Lawrence Erlbaum Associates, 2001); J. H. Newton, 'Photojournalism: Do People Matter? Then Photojournalism Matters', *Journalism Practice*, Vol. 3, No. 2, Routledge, Taylor and Frances, 2009, pp. 233–243; The Editors of Time Life Books, *Photojournalism*.

3 M. Hallett, *Stefan Lorant: Godfather of Photojournalism* (Scarecrow Press Inc., 2006), p. 70.

4 Stefan Lorant from the *Modern Photography Annual* 1938, as cited in Hallett, *Stefan Lorant*, p. 72.

5 Ibid.

6 K. Hutton, *Speaking Likeness* (Focal Press, 1947), p. 10.

7 Ibid., p. 10.

8 Ibid., p. 12.

9 Ibid., p. 14.

10 C. Osman (ed.), 'Kurt Hutton on Naturalness' (1935) in 'Fifty Years of Picture Magazines', *Creative Camera* (Coo Press Ltd., 1982), p. 594.

11 *Picture Post*, 7 February 1942, pp. 24–25.

12 Ibid., p. 25.

13 This may well have been because the editor, where appropriate, would include photographic stories or stills from photo agencies. Ties with the *American Time Life* archive, for example, were established early on.

14 See 'A Day with Gracie', *Picture Post*, 29 October 1938, pp. 12–16 and p. 70. This story on singer and actress Gracie Fields is a particularly good example.

15 J. Hartley and E. Rennie, 'About a Girl: Fashion Photography as Photojournalism', *Journalism Theory, Practice and Criticism*, Vol. 5, No. 4, 2004, p. 463. Gidal went on to say it was acceptable, however, to repeat a scene that had taken place, ibid.

16 In *Speaking Likeness* Hutton explained his dislike of flashlight as 'the arch enemy of naturalness' in some detail. See Hutton, *Speaking Likeness*, p. 17.

17 Robert Kee in *The Picture Post Album: A Fiftieth Anniversary Collection* (Barrie and Jenkins Ltd., 1994) remarked that *Picture Post* 'nominally… had no overall political stance, or rather no overall national party-political stance. It was certainly anti-Nazi from the beginning'. In Kee's view, Lorant and Hopkinson took a 'radical humanist approach to everything' and all politics became 'subordinate' to this philosophy within the paper. Anne Scott-James, Woman's Editor of *Picture Post* from 1941, believed Hopkinson 'made the paper increasingly political and controversial, gradually building up a campaign for a more equal Britain after the war'. A. Scott-James, *Sketches from a Life* (Michael Joseph, 1993), p. 79.

18 *Picture Post*, 19 November 1939, p. 4.

19 All these features will be returned to in future chapters.

20 *Picture Post* was not aligned to a specific political party. Although the majority of the staff professed themselves either Labour supporters or liberal in outlook, Edward Hulton – the magazine's proprietor and publisher – was a staunch member of the Conservative party and *Picture Post* journalist MacDonald Hastings was also right wing. *Picture Post* journalist Bert Lloyd was a communist as was guest writer Tom Wintringham.

21 While Lorant established the founding principles and orientation on which *Picture Post* was based, it would be Tom Hopkinson who would consolidate this approach as editor after Lorant's departure for America in 1940.

22 Hitler became German Chancellor on 30 January 1933. In August 1934, on the death of President Hindenburg, Hitler took his place and declared himself Fuhrer. Many books recount Hitler's rise to power during the 1930s. This work has specifically used: F. McDonough *Hitler, Chamberlain and Appeasement* (Cambridge University Press, 2002); P. Brendon *The Dark Valley: A Panorama of the 1930s* (Jonathan Cape, 2000).

23 Hallett, *Stefan Lorant*, p. 32. Hallett also cites Wickham Steed's suggestions in the *Observer* (28 April 1935) that the patriotism of the Catholic publishing company and the competition with Nazi media that their papers offered might account for Lorant's treatment. His rejection of funds from a Nazi sympathizer could also have caused him to be a target. See p. 55. For more on Lorant's life at this time see pp. 19–46. Hallett has made an extensive study of Lorant becoming his biographer at Lorant's request. He provides a comprehensive account of Lorant's life and career with detail not available elsewhere. This chapter is much in his debt.

24 Ibid., p. 39.

25 Victor Gollancz would start the anti-fascist Left Book Club in 1936. See R. Overy *The Morbid Age: Britain and the Crisis of Civilization, 1919–1939* (Penguin Books, 2009), pp. 304–307.

26 Hallett, *Stefan Lorant*, p. 33.

27 As quoted in M. Hallett, *Stefan Lorant: Godfather of Photojournalism* (Scarecrow Press Inc., 2006), p. 87. For more on Webb, see ibid., p. 67, footnote 4.

28 Lorant's story entitled 'Back to the Middle Ages' is a powerful example. It presented a sequence of photographs revealing the horrifying persecution of the Jewish people in Germany and Austria as a result of the shooting of a German official in Paris by a young Jewish man whose parents had been arrested in Germany. Tom Hopkinson saw the story as 'an attempt to dramatize photographically the monstrous crime which had been – and still was – taking place in the middle of Europe, in the heart of our Christian civilization'. Writing in 1970 he still regarded it as 'the finest example of the use of photographs for political effect'. See T. Hopkinson (ed.), *Picture Post 1938–1950* (Allen Lane, Penguin Press, 1970), p. 38, p. 11. The story appeared in *Picture Post*, 26 November 1938, pp. 14–19.

29 Kaye Webb in conversation with Alan Dien (Library of the National Sound Archive, Oral History and British Photography) as quoted in Hallett, *Stefan Lorant*, p. 87.

30 See P. Quennell (ed.), *Mayhew's London* (Bracken Books, 1984), p. 20. Sociological enquiry continued in works such as Seebohm Rowntree's *A Study of Town Life* published in 1901

(Macmillan 1901 and Policy Press, 2001) or access online at *www.archive.org*, and Charles Booth's study of poverty in London, *London Life and Labour* (Macmillan, 1902–1903, and RareBooksClub, 2012). Rowntree focused on the disadvantaged of York and later revisited the area from 1936 to provide a comparative study published as *Poverty and Progress* (Longmans, Greene and Co., 1941). For further information on Charles Booth visit *www.booth.lse.ac.uk* for access to archive material stored at Senate House. For an excellent overview of later sociological enquiry see M. Roiser, 'Social Psychology and Social Concern in 1930s Britain', in G. C. Bunn, A. D. Lovie, and G. D. Richards (eds), *Psychology in Britain: Historical Essays and Personal Reflections* (British Psychological Society Books, 2001), pp. 169–187.

31 John Thomson had already travelled widely in the Far East between 1862 and 1872. The photographs from these expeditions are now housed at the Wellcome Library and can be viewed via *www.wellcomelibrary.org.* Site accessed 4 April 2016: 15:46.

32 *Street Life in London* by Adolphe Smith and John Thomson can be read online at the LSE digital library. The complete collection of thirty-six images are also available here. See both at *wwwdigital.library.lse.ac.uk*. Site accessed 4 April 2016: 15:53. Thomson made the transition from taking anthropological photographs abroad to ones at home that pre-empts the same focus of Mass Observation. Also of interest is Jack London's *People of the Abyss* (Create SpaceIPP, 2013) illustrated, in this edition, with London's photographs of poverty in London in 1902.

33 Jacob A. Riis, *How the Other Half Lives: Studies among the Tenements of New York* (Penguin Classic, 1998).

34 Hine worked on his Ellis island photographs from 1905 to 1906 and for the National Child Labour Committee from 1908 to 1916; see H. Gernsheim, *Creative Photography: Aesthetic Trends 1839–1960* (Dover Publications Inc., New York, 1991), p. 111, p. 238. See also the New York Public Library Digital Collections, *Lewis Wickes Hine: Documentary Photographs, 1905–1938*, which provides examples of Hine's work at *www.digitalcollections.nypl.org*

35 H. Gernsheim, *Creative Photography: Aesthetic Trends 1839–1960* (Dover Publications Inc., New York, 1962), p. 216, p. 220. A collection of over two-and-a-half-thousand FSA photographs, including work by Lange and Evans, can be accessed via the New York Public Library at *www.digitalcollections.nypl.org*

36 E. Caldwell and M. Bourke-White, *You Have Seen Their Faces* (University of Georgia Press, USA, 1994). First published in 1937 by Viking Press.

37 The idea that social boundaries based on class caused gulfs between communities difficult to cross, and that within broad classes there were nuances of class distinction that also created divisions, becomes a theme in the work of writers such as George Orwell and J. B. Priestly, the material from Mass Observation and in the photography of Humphrey Spender.

38 T. Harrison and C. Madge as quoted by J. Mulford (ed.) in H. Spender, *Worktown People: Photographs from Northern England 1937–38* (Falling Wall Press, 1982), p. 7. A third founding member of Mass Observation was the film-maker Humphrey Jennings whose wartime work would include *Listen to Britain* (1942), *Fires Were Started* (1943) and *A Diary for Timothy* (1945).

39 Spender had undertaken the work in Stepney to help publicize the possible connection of juvenile crime with poverty. See Spender, *Worktown People*, p. 13. The Hunger Marches had been organized by the National Unemployed Workers' Movement to bring the plight of the unemployed to public attention. See S. Rose, *Which People's War? National Identity and Citizenship in Wartime Britain 1939–1945* (Oxford University Press, 2003), pp. 30–31.

40 Spender, *Worktown People*, pp. 15–16. Humphrey Spender came from a liberal, relatively privileged background, developing an early interest in photography and painting. He described himself as politically 'on the fringe', although he very much endorsed the liberalism of his father. For more on *Worktown People* and Spender's life see ibid., 'Interview with Humphrey Spender', pp. 11–24.

41 Ibid., pp. 23–24.

42 Ibid., p. 23.

43 Ibid., pp. 9–10. This was despite the fact that Spender remarked he 'felt very much a foreigner' in Bolton and that both here and in his previous work at Stepney he had always been confronted by 'class distinction, the fact that I was somebody from another planet, intruding on another kind of life'. Spender, *Worktown People*, p. 16. Many of the photographs can be found online in the *Worktown Archive* at Bolton Museum and accessed at *boltonworktown.co.uk*

44 Spender, *Worktown People*, p. 14. See 'Tyneside', *Picture Post*, 17 December 1938, pp. 23–31.

45 All quotations from T. Gidal, 'Modern Photo-Journalism', in C. Osman (ed.), *Creative Camera* (Coo Press, 1982), p. 575.

46 All quotations from A. Kaes, M. Jay, and E. Dimendberg (eds), *The Weimar Republic Source Book* (University of California Press, Berkeley and Los Angeles, 1995), p. 646. Up until 1927, when *The Jazz Singer* became the first talking picture to be released, film had been silent except for musical accompaniment. Visual narratives with captions were therefore a familiar form of media even if film was now moving on into sound.

47 Hallett, *Stefan Lorant*, pp. 3–26. For an excellent scholarly review, in depth, of how one particular issue of Lorant's *MIP* works and the intellectual complexity that underpinned Lorant's method of selection and layout for the magazine, see D. H. Magilow, *The Photography of Crisis: The Photo Essays of Weimar Germany* (The Pennsylvania State University Press, Penn, 2012), pp. 46–60.

48 Gidal, 'Modern Photo-Journalism – The First Years', p. 575, p. 579. These agencies made, in Gidal's opinion, a 'great contribution to modern photojournalism', p. 575.

49 *Kolnische Illustrierte Zeitung* (*Cologne's Illustrated Newspaper*).

50 Magilow, *The Photography of Crisis*, p. 51. Magilow suggests, however, that while not entering into an 'explicit' political arena Lorant was able to communicate 'an implicit politics' or political critique through elements of photographic selection and composition. See pp. 44–46.

51 Hutton was born Kurt Hubschmann in Strasbourg, Alsace, in 1893. Man was born Hans Felix Sigismund Baumann in Freiberg, Germany, also in 1893.

52 Magilow, *The Photography of Crisis*, p. 43.

53 Hallett, *Stefan Lorant*, p. 40. Lorant was released in October 1933 and edited the *Pesti Naplo* supplement from December to March 1934. See pp. 40–41; p. 46 footnote 33.

54 Ibid., p. 49.

55 F. Mann, 'Going North', *Man with Camera; Photographs from Seven Decades* (Secker and Warburg, 1983), unpaginated.

56 Ibid., 'England in the Thirties', unpaginated. Man was not Jewish.

57 Hutton was Jewish and therefore had additional reasons to leave Germany.

58 They would later be joined, if only until 1940, by another German émigré Tim Gidal (b. Munich, 1909) who similarly fled the increasingly hostile environment of Nazi persecution. He would contribute notable human interest photo essays to *Picture Post* such as 'Life of a Station', 'School for Beauty' and 'Unemployed – Industrial Transfers' (all from *Picture Post*, 11 February 1939) before moving on to India and Palestine. For more stories by Gidal see T. Gidal, 'Working For *Picture Post*', in *Creative Camera* (Coo Press, 1982), pp. 602–603,

p. 609. Felix Man and Kurt Hutton would both be interned in Britain but only temporarily, Man for three months in the Summer of 1940. See F. Mann, chapter entitled 'Picture Post', *Man with Camera; Photographs from Seven Decades* (Secker and Warburg, 1983), unpaginated. Hutton's internment details remain unclear.

59 Bert Hardy was born into a working-class home and had begun working life learning to develop and print photographs. He had moved naturally into taking his own photographs and experimenting with camera technology. Moving from agency work into *Picture Post* he would become particularly well-known for his shots of fire-fighting during the blitz for which he was credited by the magazine whose general policy was to publish photographs anonymously.

60 B. Hardy, *Bert Hardy: My Life* (Gordon Fraser, 1985), pp. 30–36.

61 With a sad irony this reputation for truth and credibility would render the German illustrated magazines useful vehicles for the spread of National Socialism with the photo-story being pressed into service promoting Nazi propaganda. For more on this see Magilow, *The Photography of Crisis*, pp. 60–61.

62 T. Hopkinson, *Of This Our Time: A Journalist's Story 1905–1950* (Hutchinson, 1982), p. 141. Hopkinson came to *Picture Post* from *Weekly Illustrated*, arguably Britain's first picture magazine also started by Stefan Lorant in 1934. Hopkinson's autobiography above provides comprehensive information on his early career.

63 Work by each of these writers will feature in the chapters ahead where their contribution to the paper's ethos will become clear.

64 See Scott-James, *Sketches from a Life*, p. 109, p. 17, p. 16.

65 Ibid., p. 79.

66 Ibid. The letters stand for 'It's That Man Again' the hugely popular radio comedy programme written by Tommy Handley and Ted Kavanagh and starring Tommy Handley. It ran from 1939 to 1949. Listen to selected back episodes on BBC IPlayer Radio, via *www.bbc.co.uk*, where the BBC also includes a brief introduction to the programme (accessed 22 April 2016).

67 Ibid. Scott-James goes on to talk about the 'Plan for Britain' issue of *Picture Post* (4 January 1941) which contained articles discussing new ideas for social security, full employment, planning of housing and education, and new health initiatives. Writers included the miner B. L. Coombs, scientist Julian Huxley, and novelist and social commentator J. B. Priestly among others. For a full list of contents see this edition of *Picture Post*, p. 5.

68 Ibid., p. 80.

69 Ibid., pp. 81–82.

70 A war reporter for the liberal paper *News Chronicle* during the Spanish Civil War and founder of the Plan International for child welfare, Langdon-Davies went on to help train the Home Guard during the war.

71 Macdonald Hastings married Anne Scott-James in 1944. See Scott-James, *Sketches from a Life*, p. 109.They divorced eighteen years later at which time she spoke of him as 'very right wing'. Ibid.

72 The first woman to become president of the Oxford University Liberal Club in 1934, she was subsequently active within the liberal party. Balfour's papers are held at the Bodleian Library Oxford.

73 J. B. Priestley was a novelist, playwright, broadcaster, socialist commentator and thinker. He became especially well-known for his series of talks for the BBC in 1940 called 'Postscripts'. BBC Radio 4's 'Archive on 4' marked the seventieth anniversary of these broadcasts with a documentary programme using some of the original sound recordings. These can be listened to via *www.bbc.co.uk* searching 'archives, Postscripts' (last accessed 12 April 2017). Priestly was an early contributor to *Picture Post*.

Michael Foot was a journalist for the left-wing paper *Tribune*, founded in 1937 by Stafford Cripps, and then for the *Evening Standard*. He was one of three writers (the others being Frank Owen and Peter Howard), using the pseudonym Cato, to publish *Guilty Men* (Gollancz, 1940), a denunciation of the supporters of appeasement.

Richie Calder was a socialist journalist and author of *Carry on London* (English Universities Press, 1941), an account of Britain during the blitz. Kingsley Martin joined the Fabian Society while at Cambridge University (1919–1922). After an early career in academia he became editor of the leading left-wing weekly the *New Statesman* (founded in 1913 by Beatrice and Sidney Webb and George Bernard Shaw among others from the Fabian group) in 1931. Post-war he was a founder member of the Campaign for Nuclear Disarmament (CND). The *Kingsley Martin Archive* is held at Sussex University. Richard Titmuss published *Poverty and Population* (Macmillan and Co., 1938) and, with F. Le Gros, *Our Food Problem: A Study of National Security (and its relation to our National Defences)* (Penguin, 1939). Post-war Titmuss wrote *Problems of Social Policy* (HMSO, 1950) for the *History of the Second World War* series. Violet Bonham-Carter was the daughter of Liberal Prime Minister Herbert Asquith. She was twice president of the Women's Liberal Federation (1923–1925, 1939–1945), a devoted friend of Winston Churchill and an anti-appeasement supporter. She was a governor of the BBC from 1941 to 1946. See *Liberal History*, the website of the Liberal Democratic History Group at *www.liberalhistory.org.uk*. H. G. Wells was a prolific writer, historian and social commentator and a committed socialist. See M. Taunton, 'H. G. Wells's Politics', accessed via the British Library at *www.bl.uk*

74 Hopkinson, *Picture Post 1939–1950*, p. 10.

75 *Picture Post*, 4 February 1939, p. 2.

76 The *Illustrated London News*, begun in 1842, has been credited with founding the illustrated paper format. By the 1930s it was still a successful paper but at a cost of one shilling it was arguably aimed at a more affluent readership. A history of the *Illustrated London News* can be accessed at *www.iln.org.uk*. See *www.newstatesman.com* for a brief history of this socialist paper and *www.archive.spectator.co.uk* for a complete digital archive of the conservative *Spectator* covering the period. Both these latter papers had a more intellectual rather than broad-church orientation.

77 Hallett, *Stefan Lorant*, p. 51 and footnote 5, p. 54. Experienced press photographer James Jarche also contributed.

78 Hallett, *Stefan Lorant*, p. 52.

79 Hopkinson, 'Weekly Illustrated – Photojournalism's Forgotten Pioneer', p. 581.

80 *Radio Times* (launched 1923) cost 2d and *Film Weekly* (launched 1928, merging with *Picture Goer* in 1939) 3d in the later 1930s. For more on the *Radio Times* see *radiotimesarchive.co.uk*; *Film Weekly* Archive 1928–1939 can be found via the British Library, *www.explore.bl.uk*. Robert Opie has amassed a fascinating collection of popular magazines; see R. Opie, *The 1930s Scrapbook* (New Cavendish Books, 2003), and the Museum of Brands, Packaging and Advertising via *www.museumofbrands.com*

81 *Woman*, launched in 1937, sold for 2d; *Woman's Own*, launched in 1932, cost 2d in 1938; An example of *Woman's Own* (1932 copy) can be found via the British Library at *www.explore.bl.uk*. *Woman's Pictorial, Woman's World* and *Home Chats* are all available for contextually appropriate dates at the British Library as above.

82 While *Picture Post* occasionally carried a knitting or craft pattern, it was not generally in the market for giving away dress patterns, embroidery transfers or other templates for home projects as did many of the women's magazines.

83 M. Grieve, *Millions Made My Story* (Gollancz, 1964), p. 90. Interestingly, Grieve remarks that at the onset of war women's magazines were the 'Cinderellas of the publishing industry' and that there were over fifty different titles. Ibid., p. 125.

84 Ibid., p. 125.

85 Hungarian-born Zoltan Glass had already had a successful career as both a picture editor on a German daily paper and, later, a freelance photographer specializing in automobiles. He also started two picture agencies. By 1938 the fact that he was Jewish had made continuing to work or run businesses in Germany impossible and he left for Britain. See J. Reynolds, 'Sharp Shooter', 20 February 2001 at *www.telegraph.co.uk*. Anne Scott-James was Beauty Editor at *Vogue* at this point. She would join *Picture Post* as Women's Editor in 1941. This story may be the one Scott-James refers to in her autobiography when she recalls inviting Stefan Lorant to come and do a feature on *Vogue*. See Scott-James, *Sketches from a Life*, p. 79.

86 See Chapter 1 'Beauty's Blueprint' specifically.

87 At this time Miller was a freelance photographer with *Vogue*. For more on Miller see the Lee Miller Archives at *leemiller.co.uk*

88 For more on Lee Miller and her modelling career, see ibid. Miller would become a front-line war photographer in 1944.

89 For more on the general decline of long, formal evening wear in the early years of the war, the effect on the fashion industry and the alternative styles that arose, see G. Howell, *Wartime Fashion Haute Couture to Homemade, 1939–1945* (Berg, 2012), pp. 57–62.

90 'The Taking of a Fashion Magazine Photograph', *Picture Post*, 26 October 1940, p. 25.

91 Ibid., p. 24.

92 American President F. D. Roosevelt signed the Lend-Lease Bill on 11 March 1941. It enabled America to provide aid in the form of war materiel to Britain and the Allied nations without the payment that had been required by the Neutrality Act of 1939.

93 Both Ibid., p. 25. The Getty images archive credits the whole photo-sequence to Glass.

Chapter 1

1 'The Making of a Mannequin', *Picture Post*, 10 December 1938, pp. 62–63.

2 All references, ibid., p. 62.

3 Ibid., p. 62.

4 Ibid.

5 'School for Models', *Picture Post*, 23 November 1940, pp. 26–27. In the same issue *Picture Post* also ran stories on the life of an East End Parson coping with the ravages of the blitz (which had begun in September 1940), the Nazis in Paris and the war on lice, as part of a series on epidemics, among other items. The contrast witnessed in lifestyle through the 'School for Models' reveals something of the *Picture Post* sense of balance as serious articles are counter-weighted by lighter more cheerful material.

6 Ibid.

7 'Where the Beauties go for Lunch', *Picture Post*, 3 December 1938, pp. 33–35.

8 Ibid., p. 33.

9 'A Glamour Girl's Day', *Picture Post*, 22 October 1938, pp. 12–15. The girls were young, four being sixteen and the average age being 'less than eighteen', p. 12. As girls in Britain regularly left school at fourteen or sixteen, the dancers' ages are not necessarily unusual.

10 A similar theme is developed in another article from *Picture Post* called 'The Last Thirty Seconds before the Curtain Goes Up' and featuring 'The Most Beautiful Girls in the World', a song and dance troupe selected by Broadway producer Earl Carroll. These girls had to be 5 foot 4 inches in height, have a 35 inch hip measurement and be weighed everyday 'on arrival and departure from the theatre' to make sure they retained the correct weight – which wasn't specified. The girls were to exude charm and good looks during their cabaret act for which they would be 'paid anything from £15- £70 a week' – a potentially very high salary. See *Picture Post*, 30 March 1940, pp. 26–27.

11 'The Making of a Glamour Girl', *Picture Post*, 6 May 1939, pp. 22–26.

12 There is no getting away from the fact that scantily clad women feature with some regularity in *Picture Post*. Girls in a state of partial undress, in swimming costumes or other similarly revealing items of clothing were clearly an accepted element of editorial policy. Hallett remarks that 'pictures of showgirls and other girls over the years became increasingly commonplace, while features on corsets and models, initially rather daring subject matter, began to make regular appearances. He [Lorant] long appreciated the advantages such exposure gave to circulation figures'. Hallett, *Stefan Lorant*, pp. 77–78.

13 'The Making of a Glamour Girl', p. 24.

14 Ibid., p. 25.

15 The article mentions typing as another job prospect. Interestingly Strachey tells us that there was plentiful work typing for girls leaving school at sixteen or seventeen which would earn them 'about 25s. a week' rising sometimes to £2. 10 or £3.00. Quite a contrast in pay scale. R. Strachey, *Careers and Openings for Women* (Faber and Faber, 1935), p. 117.The *Picture Post* article also suggests that girls with performance talents were generally offered stage opportunities by 'most managements', p. 25.

16 The *Vogue Beauty Book* (23 August 1939, p. 7 and p. 57) carried two articles on aspects of the ideal body, one advocating sport for a fitter, better body shape, the other considering body proportion and the ideal height to weight ratio which was delineated by use of a chart. For more on this see Howell, *Wartime Fashion*, Chapter 4 'The Healthy Body and the Politics of Fitness', pp. 31–40. The chart reveals the willowy figure as fashion-forward.

17 This subject is explored in detail in Chapter 8, 'A Fashion for Fitness'.

18 In the time frame of the immediate pre-war and early wartime period *Picture Post* ran five articles on or featuring corsetry: 'The History of the Corset' (1 October 1938), 'Grandmother's Corset Up-To-Date' (29 October1938), 'The Crinoline Comes Back' (5 November 1938), 'Modern Bustles' (23 September 1939) and 'Wartime Corsets' (2 March 1940). To what extent these articles were considered racy by readers of the time (see footnote 12) is difficult to assess today.

19 'The History of the Corset', Photographer Kurt Hutton, *Picture Post*, 1 October 1938, pp. 15–19.

20 Ibid., p. 16.

21 Ibid., p. 19. The follow-up story on 29 October entitled 'Grandmother's Corsets Up-to-Date' (pp. 50–51) revealed a new boned corselet designed to provide the support for a strapless evening dress, p. 16.

22 Laver with Pearl Binder had presented the first television series dedicated to fashion history in 1937 called *Clothes Line*. His interest in, and theories concerning, fashion history emerged at a time when the study of fashion and dress was not seen as an independent academic discipline.

23 Family size, particularly in middle-class homes, had indeed, been going down. See R. Titmuss, *Problems of Social Policy* (HMSO; Longmans, Green and Co., 1950), p. 416 and pp. 536–538. See also D. Beddoe, *Back to Home and Duty: Women between the Wars*

1918–1939 (Pandora Press, 1989), p. 20; and R. Samuel 'Suburbs under Siege. The Middle-class between the Wars. Part 111', *New Socialist*, Vol. 11, May/June 1983, pp. 28–30.

24 The Phoney War, or period during which Britain was at war but experienced almost no direct conflict, lasted from the declaration of war on 3 September 1939 to 8 April 1940 when the Allies violated Scandinavian neutrality by mining Norwegian waters against German use. See A. Calder, *The People's War: Britain 1939–1945* (Pimlico, 1994), p. 76.

25 'War-Time Corsets', *Picture Post*, 2 March 1940, pp. 26–29, p. 26.

26 Ibid., 'Elastic materials, firm lace and net, satin and batiste' are mentioned. From June 1941 the rationing of textiles and clothing would impinge on the production and quality of corsetry. For more information on wartime corsetry see E. L. Hargreaves and M. M. Gowing, *Civil Industry and Trade* (HMSO, 1951), pp. 446–447.

27 All quotations, 'War-Time Corsets', p. 26.

28 The film had not yet been released in Britain at the time this article was written. The book by Margaret Mitchell was published to huge acclaim in 1936. The MGM film premiered in America in December 1939 and in Britain on 18 April 1940. The story of *Gone with the Wind* began just before the American Civil War which lasted from April 1861 until May 1865. During this time affluent fashion on both sides of the Atlantic was reflected in opulent proportions and generous use of fabric in crinoline skirts.

29 'War-Time Corsets', p. 27.

30 See Introduction, 'The Taking of a Fashion Magazine Photograph'. Service women at the outset of the war were expected to wear their uniforms even while off-duty. This practice was relaxed early in 1940 by which time dress protocols on wearing full evening dress had already changed. See C. Harris, *Women at War in Uniform* (Sutton Publishing Limited, 2003), p. 31.

31 *Vogue Pattern Book*, January 1940, p. 3.

32 Horst P. Horst was *Vogue's* main fashion photographer by the middle 1930s. See *www.vam.ac.uk*, 'Horst: Photographer of Style', written to accompany the touring exhibition of Horst's work which appeared at the Victoria and Albert Museum from 6 September 2014 to 4 January 2015; accessed 11 May 2016.

33 All quotations, 'We make Corset History! Three AMBROSE Stars for your Approval.... says Mary Armstrong Chief Corsetiere', *Picture Post*, 10 December 1938, p. 80. Broche was a silk or rayon fabric with a patterned weave. Ambrose Wilson was promoted as variously 'the Largest Corset House in the Kingdom' and the 'World's Largest Mail Order Corset House' (see below). The advertisements featured here, and below, were both full-page spreads.

34 All quotations, '"One of these means new CHARM for you!" says Mary Armstrong', *Picture Post*, 25 March 1939, p. 70. The prices for all the corsets mentioned were not especially cheap and were not representative of chain store prices. They reflect a middle market for reasonably priced, quality items.

35 Some of the corsets advertised began at waist size 24 inches, generally considered petite today. The fact that corsets were made in this size suggests both that corsets were more generally worn than not at this time, and by smaller women, and that the artificial support and svelte shaping offered were considered attractive enhancements even for the naturally smaller figure.

36 These products were carried regularly in *Picture Post*. See, for example, in the first year of publication: '10 Years Slimmer Natex Tonic Slimming Food', 8 October 1938, p. 78; 'Slim without Starving' for Marmola, 26 November 1938, p. 76; a whole-page advertisement for Dermina 'Reduce Where You Want to Reduce', 4 March 1939, p. 7; 'Science Reveals *Genuine* Way to REDUCE FAT Safely and Permanently' for Vitamox, 3 June 1939, p. 9; and Silf Brand Obesity Tablets', 10 June 1939, p. 6.

37 'The School of Beauty', *Picture Post*, 11 February 1939, pp. 30–33.

38 'What Women Do for Beauty', *Picture Post*, 27 May 1939, pp. 43–45. Some of the narrative repeats material from the earlier February story whereas the photographs are all new.

39 For more on the role of sunlight as part of a wider philosophy of health see Howell, *Wartime Fashion*, pp. 156–157, and associated footnotes. *Picture Post* regularly carried advertisements for sun lamps.

40 'What Women Do for Beauty', p. 43.

41 *Picture Post* carried several more similar stories on this topic: 'A Girl Prepares for Spring' visited Helena Rubenstein's West End London salon, 6 April 1940, pp. 42–44; 'They Even Export Baths' revealed America now offering spa bath treatments no longer available in Europe, 15 February 1941, p. 27; and 'The Slim Rollers', 19 April 1941, p. 20, and 'The Hard Road to Beauty', 19 July 1941, p. 20, both revealed specialized machinery designed to help American women combat excess weight.

42 'What Women Do for Beauty', p. 45.

43 There are many of these in the first year and a half of *Picture Post* but see, for example, 'Exciting News for Humphrey', 20 May 1939, p. 4.

44 See, for example, 'Ann Seymour Editor of *Woman and Beauty* says ..."To Keep Your Skin Young" – follow Beauty Rule No. 1 Tone-Up Before Make-Up', *Picture Post*, 11 February 1939, p. 5.

45 'Beautiful Grandmothers', *Picture Post*, 8 April 1939, p. 6.

46 'Surface Beauty is Not Enough', ibid., p. 69.

47 For example: 'Have You This Air?' Vinolia, *Picture Post*, 4 February 1939, p. 77 and 'Lifebuoy Toilet Soap Prevents "B.O."', *Picture Post*, 22 April 1939, p. 9.

48 'What Women Do for Beauty', pp. 43–45. 'Between 1921 and 1936 the percentage of women using face powder rose from 20 to 95 ... [and] rouge and lipstick ... from 6 to 35', p. 45.

49 Toiletry products began to be restricted through a Limitation of Supplies Order in June 1940. See E. L. Hargreaves and M. M. Gowing, *Civil Industry and Trade* (HMSO and Longmans, Green and Co., 1952), pp. 531–536.

50 Antonia White was a novelist and journalist. She was married to Tom Hopkinson from 1930 to 1937. Her first novel *Frost in May* was published in 1933.

51 'Trouble about Hair', *Picture Post*, 8 October 1938, pp. 53–59, p. 53.

52 The free demonstrations were saving clients 'several guineas' (Ibid., p. 54). A guinea was 21/- or £1. 1s. The equivalent in decimal currency is £1. 10d.

53 A further article ('King of the Hairdressers', *Picture Post*, 11 March 1939, pp. 30–34) on the work of famous Parisian hairdresser Antoine, also shows 'The "Brushed-up" Theme', p. 33. The style complemented the current fashion for historical clothing.

54 'Trouble about Hair', p. 57.

55 Ibid.

56 *Pygmalion*, written in 1913 by George Bernard Shaw, concerned a flower girl who was trained to speak correctly and behave as a duchess. *My Fair Lady* was the screen adaptation.

57 'Charladies', *Picture Post*, 18 February 1939, pp. 59–62. Underneath a photograph of two charladies having a break (p. 62), one of them is quoted as saying, 'We ain't no glamour girls.'

58 'Charlady into Glamour Girl', *Picture Post*, 17 June 1939, pp. 52–55.

59 'Charladies', p. 59 and p. 62: 'Wages as a rule, range between 22s. 6d and 30s per week for about 30 hours work – sweeping, cleaning, dusting and scrubbing floors.'

60 'Charlady into Glamour Girl', p. 55. We are told Mr Nichols did like the permanent wave that remained. Perms clearly had currency in the hairdressing arena and *Picture Post* carried advertising from brands such as Jamal (26 November 1938, p. 75) and Christy (25 March 1939, p. 5) who licensed high street salons to offer their perming products, while Christy also offered a 'Special consultation treatment, value 5/-', to allow potential clients to see how a perm would take on a lock of their hair, 15 March 1939, p. 5.

61 Captions 1 and 12, ibid., p. 52 and p. 55.

Chapter 2

1 The only exception to this general rule for inclusion is the final brief look at the Women's Land Army uniform which was not bought but given to recruits. A Land Army story has been included because the uniform offered only trousers and follows on from comments made about the growing adoption of trousers by women both for leisure and service wear.

2 'The Queen's Dressmaker', *Picture Post*, 19 November 1938, pp. 26–29.

3 Ibid., p. 29.

4 Ibid., p. 27. The Queen's outfits for the state visit to Paris in July 1938, now known as the White Wardrobe, had been put together after the death of the Countess of Strathmore, the Queen's mother. Hartnell tells us that white was a royal prerogative for mourning clothing, an acceptable alternative to royal purple. The Queen left Buckingham Palace in traditional mourning black but arrived in Paris in white (see *www.royal.gov.uk* Queen Elizabeth's White Wardrobe, accessed 14 September 2005). For more on the origin and details of the White Wardrobe, see N. Hartnell, *Silver and Gold* (Evans Bros. Ltd., 1955), pp. 94–99.

5 Ibid., p. 29. In early 1937 and as inspiration for his future designs for the Queen, the King had taken Hartnell to see the paintings of Franz Winterhalter at Buckingham Palace. See Hartnell, *Silver and Gold*, p. 94.

6 Ibid., p. 27.

7 Ibid., pp. 27–28.

8 Ibid., p. 29.

9 Ibid.

10 'The Queen with a Little Girl', *Picture Post*, 25 November 1939, p. 40.

11 'On the Home Front: The Queen in Scotland', from 'Diary of the War – No. 26 The Twenty-fourth Week', *Picture Post*, 9 March 1940, p. 48.

12 'Design for Spring Time', *Picture Post*, 25 March 1939, pp. 38–39.

13 Ibid., p. 39.

14 Tim Gidal's photo-report on 'Bond Street' with text by Antonia White also provides abundant evidence of the fashion for fur coats in all lengths in this wealthy shopping district of London. See *Picture Post*, 20 May 1939, pp. 25–28.

15 'Fashion Show on Wheels', *Picture Post*, 25 November 1939, pp. 38–39.

16 Ibid., p. 38.

17 For more on the drop in clothing sales during the first few months of war, see Howell, *Wartime Fashion*, pp. 58–59.

18 'Fashion Show on Wheels', p. 38.

19 Ibid., p. 39.

20 'Backstage at a Paris Fashion Show', *Picture Post*, 15 October 1938, pp. 33–36 and p. 76.

21 Strachey reported that girls leaving school at fourteen who entered a two-year training programme in a field such as dress-making, tailoring or millinery could expect to earn 'from 18s. to 25s. a week' (Strachey, *Careers and Openings for Women*)which would be loosely on a par with the assistant tier mentioned here.

22 'Backstage at a Paris Fashion Show', p. 35.

23 The house models earned about £3 to £5 a week, while the special show mannequins could earn 'up to £30 a week during the brief "season"'. The latter was roughly equivalent to British and American general rates as noted in the previous chapter. Readers were told the vendeuse was well paid and took a commission on all garments she sold. White comments that the special relationship between vendeuse and client helped maintain the house and that should a vendeuse move on clients might well move with her. Male employees undertook the physically more demanding cutting and pressing required by 'hard' tailoring and elements of 'soft' tailoring and a chief pattern-cutter and fitter was quoted as earning '8 to 15 gns. [guineas] a week'. Other male employees were paid on 'an elaborate piece-work system called "on-the-log"'. Ibid., p. 76.

24 Ibid.

25 'The Crinoline Comes Back', *Picture Post*, 5 November 1938, p. 52.The article cited the removal of the ban on representations of Queen Victoria's life as the reason for this. The film *Victoria the Great* (RKO) had appeared in 1937 starring Anna Neagle and a sequel, *Sixty Glorious Years* followed in 1938.

26 The flapper dresses of the later 1920s were considered tube-shaped. The White Wardrobe brought prominence to the historic style, as we have seen, as did Hollywood costume drama. For a year-by-year resume of film releases of this type, see, for example, D. Shipman, *Cinema: The First Hundred Years* (QPD Orion Publishing, 1993).

27 See 'Modern Bustles', *Picture Post*, 23 September 1939, p. 43. On long-line corsets rather than bustles, the article compares the 'heavy, unwieldy, unwashable' 1889 corset with the 'two-way stretch elastic reinforced with slight boning' of its 1939 counterpart. The writer expressed the view that for the slim-line of the evening dress with bustle pictured 'a corset is quite essential'.

28 'Monk to Mannequin', *Picture Post*, 14 January 1939, pp. 53–55.

29 'The Wimple Returns', *Picture Post*, 11 February 1939, pp. 56–57.

30 Ibid., p. 56.

31 Ibid., p. 57.

32 'One Hundred and Thirty-five Feet of Veil to Make One Hat', *Picture Post*, 18 February 1939, pp. 54–55.

33 'Grandmother's Hat Comes back', *Picture Post*, 8 April 1939, pp. 52–53, p. 52.

34 'The Last Straws of Summer', *Picture Post*, 1 July 1939, pp. 61–62.

35 Ibid., p. 61.

36 Ibid., p. 62.

37 Ibid.

38 Frieze was a form of woven wool.

39 For more on these types of clothing see A. Settle, *Clothes Line* (Methuen and Co., 1937), p. 164, pp.168–169, or Howell, *Wartime Fashion* Chapter 3, 'Being Chic and Being British', pp. 27–29.

40 See J. Mulvagh, *Vogue History of the Twentieth Century* (Bloomsbury Books, 1992), pp. 122–179, for what remains one of the best annotated pictorial overviews of this period and which reveals the wealth of fashion themes and styles, season to season and year on year.

41 'Fashion Goes Wild', *Picture Post*, 15 April 1939, pp. 56–57.

42 Ibid., p. 56.

43 This move would bring the TA to a strength of 340,000 men. The government also announced plans to build 'more weapons factories, more camps' and provide 'vast supplies of boots and uniforms'. See D. Mercer (editor-in-chief), *Chronicle of the Twentieth Century* (JL International Publications, 1993), p. 509.

44 *Picture Post* had visited new recruits to the Women's Auxiliary Territorial Service at the Duke of York's Barracks, Chelsea in November 1938. See 'Mary Atkins on Parade', *Picture Post*, 19 November 1938, pp. 30–31.

45 See A. Mollo, *The Armed Forces of World War Two* (Greenwich Editions, 2000), p. 67; M. Brayley and R. Ingram, *World War 11 British Women's Uniforms* (Windrow and Greene Ltd., 1995), p. 22; Harris, *Women at War in Uniform 1939–1945*, pp. 10–15.

46 'Fashion Goes Wild', p. 56.

47 Ibid., p. 57.

48 They were the first reigning monarchs of Britain ever to take such a trip which lasted from 6 May until 22 June 1939. Its purpose was to extend Britain's friendship across the Atlantic. A fascinating record of the visit from the Canadian perspective exists at *www.cbc.ca* – the Canadian Broadcasting Company digital archives – where sound recordings of 'Their Majesties in Canada: The 1939 Royal Tour' can be heard (accessed 2 May 2017). The royal couple toured America at the invitation of President F. D. Roosevelt, and the FDR Library has an excellent summary of the visit which allowed Britons to be seen as 'no longer strangers or evil colonial rulers from the past but familiar friends and relatives with whom Americans could identify'. See 'The British Royal Visit' *@fdrlibrary.org* (accessed 2 May 2017). A *YouTube* short – 'New World Hails King and Queen' and various other contemporary newsreel reports are also available online.

49 Danzig had been made a free city under the sovereignty of the League of Nations after the First World War in 1919 and Poland had been granted the Polish Corridor by the Treaty of Versailles also in 1919. On 27 May 1939, *Picture Post* ran a story called 'Danzig, the Danger Spot' (pp. 32–34) which it called the 'storm-centre of Europe' (p. 32) and questioned whether the status of this city would be the 'cause of a world war' (p. 33). It reviewed the political and military importance of Danzig to both Poland and Germany and the deepening Nazi presence in the city.

50 'A Mayfair Girl Gets Married', *Picture Post*, 3 June 1939, pp. 52–55.

51 Ibid., p. 52, p. 55.

52 Ibid., p. 55.

53 Ibid., p. 52. Accumulating items for a marriage in a 'bottom drawer' in Britain or a 'hope chest' in America is a more modest interpretation of this. The practice of acquiring clothes, linens and other valuables in readiness for marriage arguably has links back to the tradition of dowry giving.

54 Ibid.

55 Ibid., p. 55. It is interesting to remember that a Norman Hartnell daywear dress at this time cost in the region of 45 guineas (see E. Wilson and L. Taylor, *Through the Looking Glass* (BBC Books, 1989), p. 91). For more on comparative prices during the mid- and later 1930s see Howell, *Wartime Fashion*, pp. 7–8 and p. 20.

56 Ibid., p. 55.

57 *Picture Post's* only other photo-sequence on a wedding within this work's time frame appeared in April 1942 when Kurt Hutton and Anne Scott-James visited a village wedding in

Berkshire. With food, petrol and clothes rationing all now an established part of daily life, the photo-story celebrated the fact that a traditional white wedding could still take place under wartime conditions with careful planning and cooperation. See 'A Soldier Gets a Bride', *Picture Post*, 25 April 1942, pp. 16–19. The outfits seen here preceded the style regulations that followed clothes rationing in the late spring and summer of 1942 and some of the restrictions on fabric production which had begun in the autumn of 1941 for cheaper fabrics. For more on clothing control and its affects, see this work Chapters 5–7.

58 A. White, 'Only Four Months to Summer', *Picture Post*, 25 February 1939, pp. 56–57. The word 'bikini' had not yet entered the fashion lexicon.

59 Ibid., p. 57.

60 'On the Beach – In Paris', *Picture Post*, 15 July 1939, p. 57. The photographs also featured a range of cork-soled and platformed beach shoes secured by crossover sandal and ankle straps.

61 'Play Suits for Summer', *Picture Post*, 1 April 1939, pp. 52–53.

62 All ibid., p. 53. Make-up colours could also be affected by the period styles. See for example 'New Powder Shades from Paris – To Go with Latest Fashions', *Picture Post*, 8 July 1939, back page.

63 'Holiday Camp', *Picture Post*, 5 August 1939, pp. 43–49. Writer Tom Wintringham was an established left-wing journalist who had been a member of the Communist party of Great Britain from 1923 until July 1938. He had been a commander in the International Brigade fighting against Franco during the Spanish Civil War and would later write on home defence for *Picture Post* (see 'Arm the Citizens', *Picture Post*, 29 June 1940, pp. 9–21)

64 'Holiday Camp', p. 49. There is no specific demographic mentioned for staying at a holiday camp, seaside hotel or with a seaside landlady. See p. 47. The range of activities at a holiday camp combined with private sleeping quarters would undoubtedly have had a wide demographic appeal.

65 Ibid., p. 46.

66 Ibid., p. 43. Skegness is a coastal resort on the east coast of England. A Butlin's still exists there today.

67 Ibid., p. 46. This price was per week. All on-site medical services were provided free as also four good meals a day (pp. 48–49). Campers could choose to spend money on things such as horse riding, cycling, drinks, cigarettes or purchases from the camp shop but had no need to (p. 47).

68 Statements like this are always fraught with uncertainty, of course, in that the demarcation of demographic can rarely be exact. Whatever the actual costs of buying or making these clothes, they remain a fair reflection of aspects of contemporary holiday style.

69 This term is well applied. The article shows outdoor dancing, team games, swimming, roller-skating, rowing and exercising all of which required comfortable, lightweight clothing that was easy to move in.

70 For more on the place of trousers in the female wardrobe, see this work, Chapter 5.

71 'A Day Awheel', *Picture Post*, 10 June 1939, pp. 19–22. Cycling, 'hiking, camping and exploration of the countryside' were all seen as contributing to an 'out-of-doors movement that has been developing steadily during the last twenty years'. Ibid., pp. 20–21.

72 Ibid., p. 19.

73 Cost of membership, if any, was not mentioned.

74 A baggier trouser was also shown (Ibid., p. 21).

75 'A Day Awheel', p. 19. The whole outfit appears to have been purchased for around thirty-five shillings (£1.15s) making this affordable for most young wage earners in regular employment even if over a period of time. While the price of the hire purchase payments for a bicycle was not given, readers were told that the low prices of bicycles dated from the modern low-built designs of 1926 and that a 1935 census revealed 'an increase of 95 per cent in the number of cycles between 1931 and 1935'. Ibid., p. 21.

76 For more on the YHA, see ibid., p. 21. For an account of the Women's League of Health and Beauty see P. Stack, *Zest for Life* (Peter Owen, 1988); an excellent, broader view of health and well-being across Europe during the 1930s can be found in C. Wilk (ed.), *Modernism: Designing a New World 1914–1939* (V&A Publications, 2006), Chapter 7, 'The Healthy Body Culture', C. Wilk, pp. 248–295.

77 'A Girl Goes Cycling', *Picture Post*, 17 February 1940, pp. 42–43. Petrol rationing was introduced at the end of September 1939, Calder, *The People's War*, p. 64.

78 Ibid., p. 42.

79 It is worth remembering that in the not too distant future specialist clothing would become limited by clothes rationing (1 June 1941) which would favour all-purpose trousers, jackets and coats.

80 'A Girl Goes Cycling', p. 43.

81 Turn-ups would become a subject of controversy when clothes rationing abolished them as an unnecessary waste of fabric. While this had no impact on women's clothing, it caused an outcry from male supporters of the style.

82 'A Girl Goes Cycling', p. 42. Larger pockets on outerwear became an early wartime fashion because of their practicality in blitz conditions.

83 Ibid., p. 43. Russia invaded Finland in December 1939 and Finland would be defeated in March 1940. Mercer, *Chronicle of the Twentieth Century*, p. 520 and p. 527.

84 Both quotations ibid., p. 43.

85 'Should Women Wear Trousers?' *Picture Post*, 1 November 1941, pp. 22–23. See this work Chapter 5.

86 'Girl Pilots', *Picture Post*, 22 October 1938, pp. 47–51.

87 Ibid., p. 50. There was also a weekly subscription of 6d.

88 Ibid., p. 48.

89 M. Brown, *Put That Light Out: Britain's Civil Defence Services at War 1939–1945* (Sutton Publishing, 1999), p. 55. Elements of civilian service uniform were in due course provided as were all military uniforms. See this work, Chapter 4.

90 D. M. Hastings, 'This was the Women's Land Army', *Picture Post*, 13 January 1940, pp. 33–37.

91 For further information about the uniform of the Women's Land Army, see A. de la Haye, *Land Girls: Cinderellas of the Soil* (Royal Pavilion and Museums, Brighton and Hove, 2009) published to accompany the exhibition of the same name. Headscarves were not part of the uniform. See de la Haye (above), p. 41.

Chapter 3

1 'Whitechapel', *Picture Post*, 15 October 1938, pp. 23–28 and p. 72.

2 'Life in the Lambeth Walk', *Picture Post*, 31 December 1938, pp. 47–53.

3 'Whitechapel, p. 23; and ibid., p. 47.

4 'Whitechapel', ibid., p. 28.

5 A loose term meaning the cotton button through overall worn for housework that provided greater cover than an apron.

6 'Whitechapel, p. 27.

7 Ibid., p. 28. Cameron referred to Whitechapel residents collectively as 'Jews and Cockneys' (p. 25) and reported that 'much, but not all, of the trade of the East End is carried on by Jews. It always has been' (p. 24). Hence Yiddish expressions. Cameron also pointed out that 'racial questions mean very little' in Whitechapel (p. 24).

8 Ibid.

9 Ibid., p. 23.

10 Ibid. p. 24.

11 'Life in the Lambeth Walk', p. 47.

12 'Whitechapel', p. 25.

13 Ibid., p. 27. These 'districts' are contrasted with Whitechapel so are presumably not part of it.

14 'Unemployed!' *Picture Post* 21 January 1939, pp. 11–19. The article was photographed by Kurt Hutton and written by Sydney Jacobson who had been appointed assistant editor at *Lilliput* (edited at the time by Stefan Lorant) in 1937. This was the first in a series of four stories on aspects of unemployment, two of which were written from the perspective of those experiencing unemployment and two looking at government initiatives to provide new routes back into work. The other articles were: 'Unemployed! 2 A Government Training Centre', 28 January 1939, pp. 49–51; 'Unemployed! 3 The National Unemployed Workers' Movement', 4 February 1939, pp. 31–37; 'Unemployed! 4 Industrial Transfers', 11 February 1939, pp. 43–48.

15 'Enough of All This!', *Picture Post*, 1 April 1939, pp. 54–57.

16 The actual figure quoted as registered unemployed in the article was I,830,000. A later figure of 2,000,000 quoted at the end of the article, and also the follow-up article in March might have included the 'many more' unregistered unemployed (p. 11). There had been several demonstrations over Christmas 1938–1939 organized on behalf of the unemployed by their union, the National Union of Unemployed Workers. See Rose, *Which People's War?* pp. 30–31.

17 The dole was a term for state unemployment benefit. The term has roots in both a dole as a gift of charity and as a share or part of something.

18 'Unemployed!' p. 14.

19 Ibid., p. 13.

20 Ibid., p. 14.

21 I have found nothing else about either. See 'Readers' Letters', *Picture Post*, 11 February 1939, p. 64.

22 'Unemployed!' p. 14.

23 Ibid., pp. 13–14.

24 For a more detailed account of Clothing Clubs at this time and of other ways in which those on limited budgets could obtain clothing, see Howell, *Wartime Fashion*, pp. 48–50.

25 'What Our Readers Say', *Picture Post*, 4 February 1939, p. 71.

26 'Unemployed!' p. 14.

27 Ibid., p. 13.

28 Evacuation was the process of sending vulnerable children and adults away from areas thought likely to be bombed in the event of war. School children, travelling without their parents, were required to have a full set of under and outer clothing suitable for the autumn and winter months ahead. For a significant number of children, this was simply not manageable on existing parental budgets.

29 'What Our Readers Say', *Picture Post*, 11 February 1939, p. 64.

30 The idea of adopting an unemployed family was raised by reader Ursula Thomas in the 4 February 1939 issue of *Picture Post* ('What Our Readers Say', p. 71); by 18 February Gracie Field's brother-in-law Bert Aza was also supporting the idea, while Ursula Thomas wrote again to offer help in connecting readers with unemployed families in the north ('What Our Readers Say', p. 52).

31 'What Our Readers Say', *Picture Post*, 18 February 1939, p. 52.

32 The Personal Services League, whose patron was Queen Mary, would later provide garments and hospital comforts for the armed forces alongside of several other service-associated organizations.

33 'Thanks to Our Readers', *Picture Post*, 25 February 1939, p. 77. Two other addresses were also given for readers. The first was for those sending clothing to struggling Tyneside families, after an article on the difficulties this once prosperous ship-building town was now experiencing ('Tyneside', *Picture Post*, 10 December 1938, pp. 23–31). The other was for the 'Silver Lady Fund' which supported a 'Night Travelling Café' offering a meal and hot drink to the homeless men and women of London. *Picture Post* had carried several advertisements for this mobile cafe around the Christmas period and ran an article on some of the men who had used it (see 'They Had No Work', *Picture Post*, 14 January 1939, pp. 50–52).

34 For an account of the first clothing schemes to assist evacuating children and subsequently help with the growing number of blitz victims, see Howell, *Wartime Fashion*, pp. 50–53.

35 *Picture Post's* coverage of these new mechanisms for making good shortfalls in wartime textiles will be returned to in Chapter 6.

36 'Employed!' *Picture Post*, 11 March 1939, p. 58. Mrs Smith is pictured wearing her gift coat next to Alf in his new-to-him suit (p. 59).

37 Both quotations, Ibid., p. 59.

38 'Enough of All This!', pp. 54–57. At least three of the photographs for this story – one of two children in a tenement and two of children waiting for their meal outside the Hoxton Market Mission (*Picture Post*, p. 54 and p. 56, respectively) – can be attributed to Bill Brandt. Information from *billbrandt.com*

39 Ibid., p. 54.

40 Ibid., p. 56.

41 Ibid., p. 57.

42 Both, Ibid., p. 56. The capacity of the natural and built environment to promote hygienic spaces for healthier living was an important component of contemporary modernist thinking during the interwar years. For further information on this topic, see C. Wilk, 'The Healthy Body Culture', in C. Wilk (ed.), *Modernism: Designing a New World 1914–1939* (V&A Publications, 2006), pp. 249–295.

43 'How the War Began': The Great Evacuation', *Picture Post*, 16 September 1939, pp. 14–20.

44 See 'What Our Readers Say' from *Picture Post* on: 30 September 1939, p. 44; 21 October 1939, p. 48; 4 November 1939, p. 53.

45 'What Our Readers Say', *Picture Post*, 30 September 1939, p. 44.

46 'What Our Readers Say', *Picture Post*, 21 October 1939, p. 48.

47 All ibid.

48 'Employed!', pp. 58–59.

49 J. B. Priestley, 'Britain's Silent Revolution', *Picture Post*, 27 June 1942, p. 21.

50 Ibid.

Chapter 4

1 Uniform would become a primary influence on styles for war clothing. Civilian clothing or mufti was allowed to be worn on home leave from early 1940. See Harris, *Women at War in Uniform 1939–1945*, p. 31. For an account of developing trends in clothing styles in the first year of hostilities, see G. Howell, 'Fashions for a Phoney War', in *Wartime Fashion: Haute Couture to Homemade 1939–1945* (Berg, 2012), pp. 55–73.

2 'Air Raid Warden to Glamour Girl', *Picture Post*, 4 November 1939, pp. 30–31. ARP stands for Air Raid Precautions. In February 1939 the government agreed that full-time ARP wardens should be paid at the rate of £3.00 per week for men, and £2.00 per week for women, although much ARP work was voluntary and unpaid. Later in 1939 part-time air-raid call out also became paid. See M. Brown, *Put That Light Out! Britain's Civil Defence Services at War 1939–1945* (Sutton Publishing Ltd., 1999), p. 7.

3 Brown, *Put That Light Out! Britain's Civil Defence Services at War 1939–1945*, p. 13.

4 Arguably one of the first fashions of war, the all-in-one cover-all siren suit had been designed for use in the air-raid shelter. When no air raids took place these practical and warm garments were marketed as cosy winter-wear for the home or when out and about on ARP work. For more on the sale of siren suits see Howell, 'Fashions for a Phoney War', pp. 67–69.

5 Such as a W for Warden.

6 These items were the first elements of 'uniform' that distinguished the ARP as a service. The badge had been produced since 1937 and 'for three years, along with the armband and helmet, remained the only uniform for most ARP workers'. Brown, *Put That Light Out! Britain's Civil Defence Services at War 1939–1945*, p. 13 and Introduction illustration, unpaginated.

7 Valerie's short sleeves might suggest a rather warmer time of year than the November publication date of the article. Whatever the actual date of the photograph Valerie was clearly not in ARP bluette. Her white bag with white shoulder strap might have been for blackout purposes.

8 E. Wilkinson M. P. 'Women in War', *Picture Post*, 9 March 1940, pp. 19–24.

9 Overalls could have their own departments in stores. See *Drapers' Record*, 23 September 1939, p. 19. As there were many variations on the overall when clothes rationing was introduced (1 June 1941), they were divided into heavy and light use and specified as to fabric and type of finish. Lighter weight overalls such as cambric or imitation linen, could be bleached, dyed or printed, while the heavier weights, such as cotton twill or denim, were either bleached or dyed. Standard colours were navy, brown or khaki. Full information on weaves can be found at British Library BS/BOT 24.

10 This article was written by J. B. Priestley.

11 H. Balfour, quoting a woman working on aircraft production 'Women at War, No. 5, A Girl Goes into War Industry', *Picture Post*, 10 January 1942, p. 16.

12 A. Scott-James, 'Women at War, No. 1, I Conduct a "Midland Red"', *Picture Post*, 15 November 1941, pp. 18–20.

13 Ibid., pp. 18–19. Clothes rationing required the surrender of a specified number of coupons for every item of commercially produced clothing.

14 Scott-James, 'Women at War, No. 1, I Conduct a "Midland Red"', p. 20.

15 Ibid.

16 Ibid., p. 18.

17 'Diary of the War: No. 4. The Second Week, The Changed Face of London', *Picture Post*, 30 September 1939, p. 27.

18 Ibid.

19 Ibid.

20 For more on the attempt to market gas mask cases as fashion items see Howell, *Wartime Fashion, Haute Couture to Homemade, 1939–1945*, pp. 63–65.

21 'February Fashions', *Picture Post*, 3 February 1940, pp. 44–45.

22 Ibid., p. 45. The fabric of this two-piece rain ensemble is not specified other than being waterproof. Visually it looks rather similar to PVC (polyvinylchloride), popular in the mid-1960s, which together with the slightly A-line styling also pre-empts sixties design. PVC had already been used in America during the 1930s for waterproofing fabrics (see 'History' @pvc.org) but whether this garment provides an example is unknown.

23 Ibid.

24 Ibid., p. 44.

25 Ibid., p. 45.

26 Holland surrendered on 15 May 1940, Belgium on 28 May.

27 Operation Dynamo began on 27 May. France surrendered on 22 June. For a comprehensive account of the fall of these three counties and Operation Dynamo, see M. Gilbert, *Second World War* (Phoenix, 1999), Chapters 5–7, pp. 61–102.

28 The LDV which became known as the Home Guard from July 1940 had been called into operation by Anthony Eden on 14th May 1940. Any man exempt from military service for whatever reason was eligible to join. See M. Smith, *Britain and 1940: History, Myth and Popular Memory* (Routledge, 2000), pp. 58–60.

29 'The New Swim-Suits Arrive', *Picture Post*, 18 May 1940, pp. 28–29.

30 Ibid.

31 While supplies of raw materials were plentiful at the outset of the war, early reductions in imported clothing to save currency meant that the 'growing need for war-related textiles' would see the high street competing 'for resources'. (See Howell, below, p. 77.) A comprehensive account of all wartime regulations and controls affecting trade and manufacture in this area can be found in E. L. Hargreaves and M. M. Gowing, *Civil Industry and Trade* (HMSO and Longmans, Green and Co., 1953). For a summary of the various controls and restrictions placed on textiles and clothing from 1939 until the advent of clothes rationing, see Howell, *Wartime Fashion: Haute Couture to Homemade 1939–1945,* Chapter 7, 'Calls for Rationed Fashion', pp. 75–87.

32 'The New Swim-Suits Arrive', p. 29.

33 'Something We Rather Missed This Summer', *Picture Post*, 14 September 1940, pp. 18–19.

34 Ibid., p. 18.

35 'Ideas for Next Summer: They Come from the South Seas', *Picture Post*, 25 January 1941, pp. 18–19.

36 Ibid., p. 18.

37 Ibid., p. 19.

38 Clothing manufacture would be controlled by both the Utility scheme and the austerity regulations. The various ramifications of these are explored in Chapters 5–7.

39 Raw silk for civilian use was prohibited in October 1940 by the Ministry of Supply while December 1940 saw 'supplies of pure silk stockings to home consumers ... prohibited except under licence'. The plentiful supply of yarn was to be redirected to more important use and stocking supplies exported. Hargreaves and Gowing noted, 'Thus came to the women of Britain the first strong foretaste of austerity'. See E. L. Hargreaves and M. M. Gowing, *Civil Industry and Trade* (Longmans, Green and Co., 1952), p. 106, both quotations.

40 'No More Silk Legs', *Picture Post*, 1 March 1941, p. 31 and p. 34. (See also J. Langdon-Davies, 'Silk's New Rival Nylon', *Picture Post*, 2 November 1940, pp. 23–24, discussing the invention of nylon in America.)

41 Ibid.

42 Ibid. The price range for rayon stockings was reported as starting at 2s. 3d, with mesh rayons from around 3s. 6d. to 8s. No prices were quoted for lisle or wool. Ibid., p. 34.

43 Ibid., p. 34. Lisle is a type of cotton thread.

44 Ibid.

45 Ibid. Scott-James suggested using an additional preparation like Deb. This was a 'tonic rinse' designed to prolong the life of stockings by keeping them 'supple and prevent[ing] ladders'. See *Picture Post* advertisement for 'Deb', 12 April 1941, p. 7.

46 'No More Silk Legs', *Picture Post*, 1 March 1941, p. 34.

47 In June 1940 the price of clothing within the cost of living index had risen by 37 per cent from the onset of war. By May 1941 that figure had risen to 75 per cent. It was in the context of these escalating prices and diminishing supplies that new controls over both the supply and cost of clothing had to be introduced. Clothes rationing, the Utility scheme and the austerity measures were the outcome, mostly introduced between June 1941 and early summer 1942. Together these controls ensured that enough affordable clothing, boots and shoes could be made available across the population as a whole. For a summary account of the run-up to clothes rationing see Howell, *Wartime Fashion: From Haute Couture to Homemade*, Chapter 7, 'Calls for Rationed Fashion', pp. 75–87 specifically p. 77 and p. 86.

48 A. Scott-James, 'Shopping for Spring', *Picture Post*, 29 March 1941, pp. 30–31.

49 Ibid., p. 30.

50 The setting of the ration had been kept secret. Shortly after the inception of rationing, a Mass Observation survey reported that many respondents did not think clothes rationing would affect them too much requiring just cutting down in 'a number of smaller ways'. Tom Harrison felt this could be 'partly explained ... by the fact that people had rarely planned clothing purchases with any rigour before and were therefore not used to doing it now'. Mass Observation, *Change 1–5 No. 1 Bulletin of the Advertising Service Guild, August 1941 'Clothes Rationing Survey: An Interim Report*' (Advertising Service Guild, 1941), pp. 14–15.

51 The skirt, hat and shoes appear to have been Thelma Gordon's own. The jacket might be the new one pictured on p. 31.

52 Bourne and Hollingsworth was a good-quality department store in London's Oxford Street. Digby Morton would design Utility wear for them. See Howell, *Wartime Fashion: Haute Couture to Homemade 1939–1945*, p. 169 quoting Mass Observation, MO-A TC / 18/4 /E, 5 March 1942.

53 Scott-James, 'Shopping for Spring', p. 30.

54 Ibid., p. 31.

55 Ibid., pp. 30–31. The Ghillies depicted were almost flat shoes laced across the in-step without a tongue. They are now largely seen as a dance shoe style. An article entitled 'Spring Shoes' that appeared three weeks later showed eight shoe styles from sandals and classic lace-ups to chunky sport shoes, all of which were flat. High heels were out and flat heels ranged 'from squares to wedges'. Good fit and maintenance were cited as essential for longevity. A. Scott-James, 'Practical Living, Spring Shoes', *Picture Post*, 19 April 1941, p. 30.

56 Full evening dress had been considered the first fashion victim of the war as discussed in the Introduction.

57 Ibid., p. 31.

58 Thelma Gordon spent a total of £14. 4s. 8d. For an average young woman earning around £3–5 a week this would have been difficult – on top of board and lodging – unless she was in better paid work, had savings or private money. Readers were told nothing about Thelma but might have inferred she was relatively well-off as she shopped in Bourne and Hollingsworth and continued to buy long evening dress when shorter styles would do.

59 For more on clothing control see this work, Chapter 5.

60 *Picture Post*, 8 March 1941, pp. 28–30.

61 Ibid., p. 28.

62 Ibid., p. 30.

63 Ibid.

64 The garden or Anderson shelter and the indoor Morrison shelter were the two types of domestic air-raid shelter for private homes. See 'History' at *andersonshelters.org.uk* for more on Anderson shelters, and 'Morrison "Table" Shelter' at *iwm.org.uk* for the Morrison shelter.

65 'Shelter Life', *Picture Post*, 26 October 1940, pp. 9–11.

66 Millicent Rose, 'Down in the Shelter There Is Life', *Picture Post*, 29 March 1941, pp. 16–17.This story, about a shelter in Bermondsey, focused on the number of organized activities that had been arranged by the Borough Shelter Council to provide shelterers with both entertainment and opportunities to acquire new skills.

Chapter 5

1 A. Scott-James, 'We Appoint a Woman's Editor', *Picture Post*, 8 February 1941, pp. 32–33.

2 Ibid., p. 32.

3 Ibid.

4 Ibid., p. 33.

5 A. Scott-James, 'Practical Living: Make Up and Cut Down', *Picture Post*, 15 March 1941, p. 32. Scott-James reported that the cosmetics industry now produced only 25 per cent of its original output.

6 Scott-James does not specify what these cosmetics were. She would later investigate the unregulated production of cosmetics for the black market ('I Take a Look at the Black Market', *Picture Post*, 27 September 1941, pp. 22–23) and the insanitary conditions and impure products emerging from such illegal manufacture.

7 All quotations, Scott-James, 'Practical Living: Make Up and Cut Down', p. 32.

8 For a full account of the need for, and delivery of, the clothes rationing scheme see Hargreaves and Gowing, *Civil Industry and Trade*, Chapter 14: 'Consumer Rationing', pp. 303–338. The

British Library holds a comprehensive collection of coupon listings across the rationing years within the yearly 'Clothing Quiz' booklets published by the Board of Trade which also contain questions and answers covering how the ration worked. See British Library BS 41/151. For a summary account of how the ration was set and recalculated during the war see Howell, *Wartime Fashion: Haute Couture to Homemade 1939–1945*, Chapter 8: 'Setting the Ration', pp. 89–98.

9 At this point the ration began to rise. See Howell, *Wartime Fashion: Haute Couture to Homemade 1939–1945*, as above, pp. 96–97.

10 A. Scott-James, *Picture Post*, 7 June 1941, pp. 25–27.

11 This story is likely to have been conceived and photographed prior to clothes rationing which was kept secret until its implementation.

12 Ibid., p. 25.

13 All ibid., p. 26.

14 Ibid., p. 27.

15 A. Scott-James, 'Practical Living: How to Run Your Dress Allowance', *Picture Post*, 21 June 1941, pp. 28–29.

16 Ibid., p. 28. At this date a fully lined woman's coat in wool, for example, was 18 coupons, a fully lined wool jacket 12 coupons and a woollen skirt 6 coupons, meaning a two-piece suit was also 18 coupons. See British Library BS 41/151 'Clothing Quiz', 1 June 1941, p. 5.

17 This was the initial allocation. Coupons could not all be spent in one go. The first twenty-six coupons were enclosed within the food rationing books as margarine coupons. Once these were spent the remaining forty had to be spent in two parts, the last twenty only after 1 January 1942. For further information on how coupons were released throughout the rationing years see Howell, *Wartime Fashion: Haute Couture to Homemade 1939–1945*, pp. 95–97.

18 Scott-James, 'Practical Living: How to Run Your Dress Allowance', p. 28.

19 Collars were valued at one coupon each. See BL BS 41/151 'Clothing Quiz' booklets up to rationing year 1944–1945.

20 Cloth was valued by type and in widths. Wool cloth, 33"–39" wide needed three coupons while for the same width any other fabric required two coupons. See BS 41/151 'Clothing Quiz', 1 June 1941, p. 9. Ribbon and strips of cloth below three inches wide were unrationed at this time, as was lace, lace net and curtain net (pp. 9–10).

21 Scott-James, 'Practical Living: How to Run Your Dress Allowance', p. 28.

22 All descriptions ibid., p. 29. To what extent these type of collars could have been bought on the high street is not mentioned and difficult to assess as is the extent to which any of these collars could be successfully created at home. Sewing and knitting skills were much prized during the war for just the sort of ration-stretching shown here (see this work, Chapter 7) and the public were encouraged to improve their home-crafting skills through local classes.

23 Ibid., p. 28. The following September Anne Scott-James showed readers how to convert a soft-brimmed, medium-crowned 'American Style' hat into five further hats by using ribbon, net, brooches, flowers and a quill: 'Practical Living: This One Hat Is Five Hats', *Picture Post*, 21 September 1941, p. 23.

24 A. Scott-James, 'Practical Living: Clothes for a Coupon Summer', *Picture Post*, 5 July 1941, front cover and pp. 26–27.

25 Ibid., p. 26.

26 Ibid.

27 Scott-James, 'Practical Living: Clothes for a Coupon Summer', p. 27. A further article 'News in Shoes' (A. Scott-James, *Picture Post*, 18 October 1941, p. 21) summarized the autumn shoe trends for practical leather shoes, in materials such as 'suede, sealskin, pigskin, elk, canvas and chenille', all of which were now 'more common than calf'. Styles ranged from classic medium-heeled pumps and laced town shoes to flat sports shoes in one or two materials – a good device that meant small pieces of leather did not go to waste. Crepe souls were durable against damp and broken glass – highly practical in blitz conditions – and wedge-heeled house-boots in felt or chenille lasted longer than 'the old flimsy slipper'. An advertisement early the following year for Clark's shoes carried in *Picture Post* on 28 February 1942, p. 2, reported, however, that crepe was no longer available for the civilian market: 'You Can't Say Crepe . . . But You Can Say Clarks.'

28 The inclusive philosophy of *Picture Post* did not affect the often middle- or upper middle-class tone and context of many fashion-lead features. This was arguably balanced out by other human-interest stories that captured different demographics both poorer and richer.

29 'Should Women Wear Trousers', pp. 22–23; p. 22.

30 This was certainly borne out by a Mass Observation survey taken in August 1941 where, after a considerable review of older and younger women across the class spectrum from both London and beyond, Tom Harrison summarized that 'slacks, which are the only new female garment of the war mentioned as in fairly general use, do not yet appear to be quite accepted as normal wear by those who have acquired them at all recently'. MO, *Change 1–5 No. 1 Bulletin of the Advertising Service Guild, August, 1941 Clothes Rationing Survey: An Interim Report*, p. 55.

31 All quotations, 'Should Women Wear Trousers', p. 22.

32 A comprehensive account of the Utility scheme and the associated austerity regulations can be found in Hargreaves and Gowing, *Civil Industry and Trade*, pp. 431–440 and for Utility fabrics in detail, pp. 440–464. Although the scheme had been started in August 1941 it took time to create the first Utility fabrics and garments so that it was not until the spring of 1942 that Utility clothing became more noticeable in high street shops.

33 Deborah Kerr was a young British actress who had come to public attention in two films the previous year, *Major Barbara* from a play by G. B. Shaw and *Love on the Dole* based on the book by Walter Greenwood.

34 A. Scott-James, 'Deborah Kerr Shows Off the New Utility Clothes for Women', *Picture Post*, 28 March 1942, pp. 18–19; p. 18.

35 Ibid., p. 18. It was not necessary, and therefore no longer economic to sustain, a luxury fabrics market or, at the other end of the quality spectrum, continue to manufacture the poorest textiles that could not produce clothing of the required quality. This was good news in so far as the worst fabrics were largely eradicated. The industry now focused on delivering a smaller number of good-quality fabrics in amounts that would allow the civilian clothing ration to be met.

36 Ibid.

37 Ibid.

38 All prices as quoted by Anne Scott-James, ibid., p. 19.

39 Ibid.

40 She reported that two-thirds of all clothes were Utility, leaving scope for some inappropriate extravagance, in her view, for the other third. Ibid.

41 Ibid.

42 The British Crown colony of Hong Kong had been lost to the Japanese on Christmas Day 1941. It had thus been occupied for three months. The British military base of Singapore fell to the Japanese on 15 February 1942. A massacre of Chinese people – believed hostile to Japan – followed, ending on 4 March 1942. Mercer (Editor-in-Chief), *Chronicle of the Twentieth Century*, p. 559 and p. 562; and see H. Hirofumi, 'The Battle of Singapore, The Massacre of Chinese and Understanding of the Issue in Post-war Japan', in *The Asia-Pacific Journal: Japan Focus* (13 July 2009) Volume 7 (Number 4) at *apjjf.org*, accessed 21 November 2016.

43 Scott-James, 'Deborah Kerr Shows Off the New Utility Clothes for Women', p. 19. Interestingly in an interview with Mass Observation also in March 1942 couturier Digby Morton revealed he was, in fact, now cutting new clothes with far less material. For the impact of the restrictions on Morton and the type of work he was currently doing as a couturier see Howell, *Wartime Fashion Haute Couture to Homemade 1939–1945*, pp. 150–151.

44 Scott-James hints at some restrictions that might be coming, ibid. The various new regulations would begin to appear in April 1942 with the final stipulations appearing in June. Together these would control the design and making up of all commercial garments as well as the degree of decoration or embellishment they could have and of what sort. For a full list of these see Hargreaves and Gowing, *Civil Industry and Trade*, pp. 436–439. A discussion of the austerity regulations and the Utility Prototype Collection, created by members of the Incorporated Society of London Fashion Designers who worked within the austerity controls, can be found in Howell, *Wartime Fashion Haute Couture to Homemade 1939–1945*, pp. 170–178.

45 The same interview with Digby Morton referenced above (footnote 43) also revealed that his house was still producing outfits from 'an increasingly small supply of expensive non-Utility fabric'.

46 A. Scott-James, 'American Fashions for Summer', *Picture Post*, 16 May 1942, pp. 22–23.

47 All ibid., p. 22.

48 Ibid., p. 23.

49 Ibid.

50 Ibid. All the garments were cotton except for a rayon crepe dress and a taffeta skirt. Prices hovered below or above the two pounds mark while the rayon crepe dress was more expensive at nearly three pounds, as also the more opulent frilled taffeta skirt and sash costing four guineas. By this time taffeta would almost definitely have been made from rayon rather than silk.

51 A. Scott-James, 'Austerity Clothes for the Fourth Year of the War', *Picture Post*, 29 August 1942, pp. 22–23.

52 Ibid., p. 22.

53 Ibid., p. 23. All commercially produced clothing, even if made with non-Utility fabric, had to abide by the austerity restrictions. See Hargreaves and Gowing, *Civil Industry and Trade*, p. 436.The austerity regulations effectively put an end to the extravagances Scott-James had complained about earlier.

54 Both jackets have a squared shoulder, a military line popular pre-war that was retained as part of the signature wartime style. It would finally be displaced by Dior's New Look sloping shoulder in the spring of 1947.

55 For a comprehensive account of the policy of industrial streamlining known as 'concentration' as it pertained to textile manufacture, see Hargreaves and Gowing, *Civil Industry and Trade*, Chapter 10: 'Concentration of Production', pp. 202–233. For more on the process of designating manufacturers to produce Utility cloth and clothing see Hargreaves and Gowing, *Civil Industry and Trade,* pp. 403–406 and p. 426.

56 Scott-James, 'Austerity Clothes for the Fourth Year of the War', p. 22.

57 Ibid., p. 23.

58 A. Scott-James, 'Fashions for Summer: All Under £3', *Picture Post*, 19 June 1943, pp. 24–25; p. 24.

59 Ibid., pp. 24–25.

60 Ibid., p. 25.

61 Ibid., pp. 24–25.

62 Ibid., p. 25.

63 While no mention is made of them, some of the most stringent austerity restrictions came in the form of style templates that limited the number of styles for any one type of garment. Dresses, for example, were restricted to 'fifty sets of basic style templates per annum' in May 1942. See Hargreaves and Gowing, *Civil Industry and Trade*, pp. 437–438.

64 The limited range of Utility fabrics, both woven and knitted, were specified according to a number of different criteria including the type of yarn used, the weave chosen and how washable, waterproof or shrink resistant they were. The various different qualities of fabrics used and the garments manufactured from them meant commodities sold at different price points. All Utility production, however, was fit-for-purpose and quality-controlled so that the public could make their coupon purchases with confidence, irrespective of the amount they were able to afford. For more on the tiered production of Utility see Howell, *Wartime Fashion Haute Couture to Homemade 1939–1945*, pp. 99–104.

65 Scott-James, 'Fashions for Summer: All Under £3', p. 24. In terms of creating different looks, *Picture Post* kept readers up-to-date with the latest inventive uses for accessories such as scarves or veils. See, for example, 'Scarf Tricks', *Picture Post*, 9 January 1943, p. 24; and 'Something New for Dinner', which explored the use of glamorous veils for evening wear, *Picture Post*, 31 July 1943, pp. 24–25.

66 'So That's What They Mean by a Leg Bar', *Picture Post*, 16 October 1943, pp. 21–22.

67 Ibid., p. 21.

68 Ibid. British women had begun to experience reduced supplies of stockings as far back as the summer of 1940. For a summary of the various Woven Textile Orders and Limitation of Supplies issued at this time that caused reduced high street supplies in Britain see Howell, *Wartime Fashion Haute Couture to Homemade 1939–1945*, pp. 77–78 and pp. 80–82. British women had also turned to leg make-up to save precious stockings or in their absence. See Howell above, pp. 158–159, including a photograph (p. 159) of a similar leg bar in Croydon, England (dated 1941), where legs could be 'painted while you wait'.

69 'A Crazy New Fashion from the U.S.', *Picture Post*, 11 December 1943, p. 25.

70 Ibid.

71 Ibid.

72 *Life*, 13 September 1943. *Picture Post*'s use of stories from *Life* was not without precedent. For the original relationship between Stefan Lorant and Henry Luce and *Life* see Hallett, *Stefan Lorant: Godfather of Photojournalism*, p. 52 and associated footnotes. A September date of publication, as opposed to December, made espadrilles more logical.

73 K. Yohannan and N. Nolf, *Claire McCardell: Redefining Modernism* (New York: Harry N. Abrams Inc., 1998), p. 68 and reference to wool jersey p. 75. For more on McCardell's development of the leotard see p. 69.

74 A. Scott-James, 'Some Clothes for Your New Coupons', *Picture Post*, 26 February 1944, pp. 22–23; p. 22.

75 Ibid., p. 23.

76 Colours and patterns were plentiful and unrestricted under the Utility textile scheme. See Hargreaves and Gowing, *Civil Industry and Trade*, pp. 433 and 442.

77 All quotations, ibid., p. 23. In the article 'Fashions for Summer: All Under £3', referred to earlier in this chapter, Anne Scott-James described the beret as 'the hat fashion of the war', p. 25. A further article, entitled 'Spring Hats: All for Under 45/-' (*Picture Post*, 25 March 1944,

p. 20), looked at fashionable millinery that could be purchased less expensively. The article included the school girl beret – this time with accessorizing 'foot-long quill' – several straw hats and a couple of soft felt hats, all of relatively modest size.

78 Ribbon had to be less than three inches wide to be coupon free.

79 Ministry of Information, *Picture Post*, 7 February 1942, p. 6.

80 Ministry of Information, *Picture Post*, 11 July 1942, p. 4.

81 Board of Trade, *Picture Post*, 29 August 1942, p. 28.

82 Board of Trade, *Picture Post*, 28 November 1942, p. 28.

83 Scott-James, 'Some Clothes for Your New Coupons', p. 22.

Chapter 6

1 The Blitz lasted from September 1940 until May 1941. This was followed in July 1941 by the sporadic 'Tip and Run' daylight raids which continued until January 1944. The Baedeker raids targeted historic centres in Britain from April to July 1942. The 'Little Blitz' lasted from January to March 1944, and in June 1944, the first V1 flying bomb was launched against Britain and the first V2 the following September. These seriously damaging attacks ended in March 1945. Summarized from Brown, *Put That Light Out', Britain's Civil Defence Services at War, 1939–1945*, pp. 15–18.

2 See this work Chapter 3 for previous references in *Picture Post* to the social concern raised by evacuation.

3 The scheme was slow and hindered by bureaucracy but did, nevertheless, establish a type of clothing scheme and a welfare precedent that could be built on. For the official history of the origins of clothing initiatives for the evacuated poor, and the arrangements made to apply for and receive necessary clothing, see Titmuss, *Problems of Social Policy*, pp. 116–120 and pp. 165–166. A summary account of how the clothing needs of young evacuees were met can also be found in Howell, *Wartime Fashion Haute Couture to Homemade 1939–1945*, pp. 50–53.

4 Apart from clothes rationing, utility production and the austerity regulations, other government interventions involving the production and distribution of apparel included providing demobilization attire and supplying relief clothing across areas of liberated Europe in the wake of Allied invasion. *Picture Post* raised the need for food and clothing for France several times, particularly as parts of the country appeared to be heading towards famine conditions. See, for example, E. Monroe, 'Famine in France: Does It Matter to Us?' 24 February 1945, pp. 11–13; T. Hopkinson, 'Famine in France: Readers Call for Action', 10 March 1945, pp. 22–23; 'Readers Write about Two Allied Nations', 24 March 1945, p. 10, p. 26. There was evidence from some of this material that independent organizations were acting to send clothing to France, including, for example, the Salvation Army.

5 For the amendments to, and fine tuning of, this system, see Howell, *Wartime Fashion Haute Couture to Homemade 1939–1945*, pp. 51–52.

6 This service had been officially launched on 18 June 1938 and had an advisory council made up of representatives from all the leading women's organizations already in existence, such as the National Federation of Women's Institutes and the National Union of Townswomen's Guilds among others. For more see M. McMurray, WRVS Archivist, 'The Formation and Founding of the Women's Voluntary Services for A.R.P', 10 March 2008, pp. 4–7, at *www.royalvoluntaryservice.org.uk*.

7 B. Morgan, 'Children's Hotel', *Picture Post*, 31 August 1940, pp. 25–28.

8 Ibid., p. 26.

9 Ibid., p. 27.

10 Ibid., p. 28.

11 Ibid.

12 Both quotations ibid.

13 The first hotel had been set up at Bedford College, ibid., p. 25.

14 Not, presumably, all at once! 'The Happy Knitters', *Picture Post*, 17 February 1940, pp, 28–29.

15 Ibid., p. 29.

16 The Order of St John is better known in Britain today through its St John's Ambulance medical services.

17 A. White, 'Mayfair's Own Sewing-Bee', *Picture Post*, 24 February 1940, pp. 40–43.

18 Ibid., p. 43. A caption noted that the ladies were 'neutrals but they may serve humanity' presumably an allusion to this work being considered consonant with neutral status. Ibid., p. 41.

19 Why this was so is not entirely clear as the inference later on (p. 42) is that materials were supplied to groups from the Mayor's Red Cross Fund. Ibid.

20 Ibid., p. 42.

21 Ibid., p. 41.

22 Ibid., p. 42.

23 Ibid.

24 'Bombed-out', *Picture Post*, 12 October 1940, pp. 9–11.

25 Ibid., p. 11.

26 Ibid.

27 Ibid., p. 10.

28 Ibid., p. 11.

29 Ibid.

30 Ibid., p. 10.

31 Bomb victims appear to have continued to suffer from a tiring round of visits to different locations for the money, coupons and alternative accommodation they needed to restart their lives. A much later article that appeared in *Picture Post* in September 1944 reported that 'after four years of groping and experiment', a Ministry of Health initiative in a southern town had brought all the relevant offices under one roof. From replacing clothing coupons to billeting help, the centralized service was suggested as a way forward for future 'Social Security plans for peace-time'. 'Social Service Centres: A Lesson of the Bombing', *Picture Post*, 16 September 1944, pp. 18–19.

32 'Bombed-out', p. 11. Other information on acquiring furniture and on house repair was also included.

33 A. Scott-James, 'We Adopt 100 A.B.s – and we want your help', *Picture Post*, 8 March 1941, pp. 32–33. A.B. stood for able-bodied. Unusually for *Picture Post* knitting patterns (for a sweater, gloves and sea-boot stockings) were included in the article. After the launch of rationing in June 1941, knitters wishing to provide garments for the services could join registered service working parties via which coupon-free wool could be received. See, for example, Imperial War Museum, Ephemera Box C 'Fashion', 'Knitting for the RAF'. Also in the 'Your Questions Answered' section of the *Clothing Coupon Quiz* booklet for 1941 (British

Library BS.41/151), the answer to question 75 on ways of obtaining wool for service comforts implies some coupon-free wool was available for service-affiliated organizations.

34 A hussif, or 'housewife', was and is a small material wallet containing a simple set of sewing items such as needle, thread, scissors and thimble.

35 All quotations, 'We Adopt 100 A.B.s – and we want your help', p. 32.

36 For an overview of the supplementary coupon allowances, see Hargreaves and Gowing, *Civil Industry and Trade*, p. 317 and in more detail, pp. 317–321.

37 Hargreaves and Gowing comment that such replacement coupons were 'based on assumptions by the Board of Trade about the coupon value of a minimum wardrobe'. See ibid., p. 317, footnote 2.

38 See Howell, *Wartime Fashion Haute Couture to Homemade, 1939–1945*, p. 115 citing PRO, BT64/3025, 17 July 1942, p. 1.

39 From 1941–1946, the cost of all second-hand clothing was based on a fixed price of two shillings which was then multiplied by the coupon value of the item if new. A dress at seven coupons, for example, could only be bought second-hand coupon free if it was priced at fourteen shillings or below. For more on the market for second-hand goods, see Howell, *Wartime Fashion Haute Couture to Homemade, 1939–1945*, pp. 134–135.

40 See *Clothing Coupon Quiz*, 1941 (British Library, BS.41/151), 'Your Questions Answered, No. 26. Are coupons required for charitable gifts of clothing?' The answer was yes. Charities had to surrender the coupons back to the Board of Trade 'if so directed'. Interestingly Question 60 in the same *Clothing Coupon Quiz* asks whether coupons were needed for 'new or other gift clothing distributed by the WVS to persons suffering from war distress?' While it was recognized that the WVS obtained supplies without coupons, when they gave clothing out it was 'only fair that they should collect coupons'.

41 *Picture Post*, 13 September 1941, pp. 17–19. The youngest child was two years old, the eldest twelve. There was no day nursery in the area to take the two-year-old, so going back to work was not a realistic option for Mrs Bicknell, particularly with a home and six children to look after.

42 Ibid., p. 19.

43 Ibid.

44 Ibid., p. 17.

45 Ibid., p. 18.

46 Ibid.

47 Readers' Letters, *Picture Post*, 11 October 1941, p. 3.Exactly how the clothes were gifted and whether coupons were surrendered is not raised. Money rather than coupons appeared to be the problem however.

48 Ibid.

49 For more on the number of coupons children of different ages and size were allowed, see Howell, *Wartime Fashion Haute Couture to Homemade 1939–1945*, p. 113 and p. 218.

50 'This Is a Clothing Exchange', *Picture Post*, 2 October 1943, pp. 24–25.

51 Ibid., p. 24.

52 Both quotations ibid., p. 25.

53 Both quotations ibid.

54 'The Store Where Everything Is Free', *Picture Post*, 3 March 1945, pp. 24–25.

55 Brown, *Put That Light Out! Britain's Civil Defence Services at War, 1939–1945*, p. 18. See this chapter footnote 1 for a summary of air attacks on Britain. V stood for Vergeltungswaffen – a weapon of retaliation or reprisal.

56 'The Store Where Everything Is Free', p. 24.

57 See I. Kikuchi, 'The Terrifying German "Revenge Weapons" of the Second World', at *iwm.org.uk*, accessed 5 December 2016.

58 See this chapter footnote 4. For a full account of textile production at this time, see Hargreaves and Gowing, *Civil Industry and Trade*, pp. 472–479.

59 Two wartime films highlighting the early work of the WVS are available on DVD. These are *Britannia Is a Woman: A Tribute to the War Effort of British Women* (British Movietone News, 1940), and *WVS* (Verity Film, 1941) both available on *Women and Children at War* (Imperial War Museum Official Collection, 2006).

Chapter 7

1 The price of clothing had been rising in tandem with a range of governmental Orders limiting supplies of clothing to the civilian market. A purchase tax introduced the previous October (1940) had also caused prices to rise. For a summary account of the wartime restrictions affecting the production and price of civilian clothing prior to clothes rationing see Howell, *Wartime Fashion: Haute Couture to Homemade 1939–1945*, Chapter 7, 'Calls for Rationed Fashion', pp. 75–87.

2 The high street had become increasingly affordable pre-war due to the chain stores and other retail outlets selling in the lower price ranges. See G. Howell, as above, pp. 7–22.

3 A. Scott-James, 'Make Yourself a Model Outfit', *Picture Post*, 31 May 1941, p. 30.

4 A. Scott-James, 'Make Yourself a Spring Hat', *Picture Post*, 15 February 1941, pp. 30–31.

5 Ibid., p. 30. By May 1941, clothing was 75 per cent higher in price than at the start of the war. See Howell, *Wartime Fashion: Haute Couture to Homemade 1939–1945*, p. 86.

6 Ibid.

7 Ibid., p. 31.

8 Ibid., p. 30.

9 Scott-James, 'Make Yourself a Model Outfit', pp. 30–31; p. 30.

10 All quotations ibid., p. 30.

11 Ibid., p 31.

12 For more on these regulations see this work Chapter 5.

13 Scott-James, 'Make Yourself a Model Outfit', p. 30.

14 The Viyella fabric was in 'soft, dusty shades of green, cinnamon brown and pink'. The dress accessories were all white. Ibid., p. 31.

15 Ibid., p. 30.

16 A. Scott-James, 'Old Clothes Make News', *Picture Post*, 26 July 1941, pp. 26–27.

17 Ibid., p. 26.

18 Ibid.

19 All ibid.

20 Ibid., p. 27.

21 The before and after pictures of the bedspread are the largest of all those included. If size represents importance, then these images may have been considered most representative of the storyline. The candlewick coat has certainly become a well-known picture since.

22 Scott-James, 'Old Clothes Make News', pp. 26–27.

23 A. Scott-James, 'Patchwork', *Picture Post*, 16 August 1941, pp. 24–25.

24 All quotations ibid., p. 24.

25 Ibid.

26 The Board of Trade provided information for making patchwork slippers from scratch in their 'Bits and Pieces' section in *Picture Post* on 13 February 1943, p. 4. Information on patching moth-eaten garments appeared in the same place.

27 Scott-James, 'Patchwork', p. 24.

28 Ibid., p. 25.

29 Sub-heading quotation from 'Next to No Coupons', *Picture Post*, 11 July 1942, p. 18.

30 Details of the regulations as they applied to the design, cut, making-up and finishing of different types of garment are available in the following editions of the trade magazine the *Drapers' Record*: 18 and 25 April; 2, 9 and 16 May; 13 June. A full list of these and further regulation orders can be found in E. L. Hargreaves and M. M. Gowing, *Civil Industry and Trade* (Longmans, Green and Co., HMS0 1952), pp. 436–438.

31 Scott-James, 'Next to No Coupons', pp. 18–19; p. 18.

32 One coupon had to be surrendered for every two ounces of wool bought. Sequins had already been banned from use in the commercial production of 'Infants' and Girls' ... Dresses, Day Gowns, Robes and Tunic Shorts ... ' and 'women's, maids' and girls' ... civilian dresses, blouses, jumper suits, cardigan suits and cardigan-cum jumper suits', as of Orders that came into operation on 1 June (for girls' and infants' clothing) and 20 June (for women's, maids' and girls' clothing), 1942. See *Drapers' Record*, 9 May 1942, p. 30 and 2 May 1942, p. 13, respectively. It is hard to know how easy it would have been to buy sequins on the high street. A category called hard haberdashery appears in the original 1941 clothes rationing manifest as coupon-free but does not reappear in subsequent wartime inventories.

33 As many patterns would be supplied as paper restriction allowed.

34 Scott-James, 'Next to No Coupons', p. 18.

35 Ibid., p. 19.

36 A reader responded to this article in the Readers' Letters section (*Picture Post*, 25 July 1942, p. 3). She said she had made herself 'two blouses on the lines suggested' and had 'nearly finished the jersey and cap set'. She thought she had saved '13 coupons' and thanked *Picture Post*. In general there was little published response from readers on the 'Practical Living' sections quoted here, although Anne Scott-James encouraged readers to contact her.

37 Hats had not been rationed, as mentioned elsewhere, nor, initially, material like lace or narrow ribbon that might be used in hats. Fashion hats were not, however, seen as essential by the Board of Trade, and in May 1942 it was announced that there would be no more coupons for milliners to obtain fabric. Only workmen's Utility caps and certain children's or infants' hats would now be allocated fabric. A ban was also placed on lace manufacture for the home market (see *Drapers' Record*, 23 May 1942, p. 9). This meant that milliners had to rely on existing fabric stocks and employ a good deal of ingenuity in the use of haberdashery – such as ribbon less than 3 inches wide – and of any other coupon-free materials they could find. For this variety of reasons commercial millinery had become very expensive.

38 'Not Much Cash, Not Many Coupons', *Picture Post*, 27 February 1943, p. 24.

39 'Clothes without Coupons', *Picture Post*, 28 August 1943, pp. 24–25, p. 24. The Merriam-Webster dictionary defines a skiver as a 'thin soft leather made of the grain side of a split sheepskin, usually tanned in sumac and dyed'. Found at *merriam-webster.com*.

40 I have come across little information on how popular sewing with pelts actually was. The fact that they were reasonably cheap and coupon-free could have made them attractive although wet laundering would have been tricky and dry cleaning – though still available – less economic. Readers were advised that 'a good sized skin, large enough for a hat or handbag, costs round about 12s. 6d.' Ibid., p. 24. A skin for an adult waistcoat would, arguably, have cost more.

41 Ibid., p. 25.

42 See for example: 'Do You Care for Clothes?' 29 August 1942, p. 28; 'The Raiders', 19 September 1942, p. 28; 'It Fairly Makes Me Bristle', 17 October 1942, p. 28. For care of fabrics: 'Rules for Rayon', 26 December 1942, p. 2; 'Look after Wool', 2 January 1943, p. 4; 'Cotton Clues', 16 January 1943, p. 27; 'The Secret of Long Wear in Rayons', 3 April 1943, p. 27. All Board of Trade notices published in *Picture Post*. Readers could also buy moth cubes to help store clothes safely. See 'Laid up in Lavender', advertising Sentinel moth cubes, *Picture Post*, 4 July 1942, p. 5 and 'The Moth Menace' advertising Mothaks, *Picture Post*, 4 March 1944, p. 5.

43 See for example: 'Bits and Pieces', 13 February 1943, p. 4; 'Longer Life for Your Towels', 13 March 1943, p. 27; 'Lacings and Buttons Were Great Grandma's Mainstays', 26 June 1943, p. 28. All Board of Trade notices published in *Picture Post*. The Board also advertised make-do and mend classes, many of which were now in action countrywide.

44 Ministry of Information, 'Shipping saved by rags', *Picture Post*, 19 September 1942, p. 2. The Ministry of Supply issued similar appeals for salvage in *Picture Post*. See for example: 'Me for the Royal Navy', 6 May 1944, p. 4 and 'Now I'm Going into Battle', 7 October 1944, p. 5.

45 'Darn and Mend Afternoon: A.T.S. Gives Soldiers a Lesson', *Picture Post*, 23 January 1943, pp. 12–13; p. 13. In a similar way sailors also had time each week for making running repairs on their 'rig'. See 'Do You Care for Clothes?', *Picture Post,* 29 August 1942 p. 28.

46 'I Teach the Baker's Wife a New Washing Method' by Home Front Correspondent, *Picture Post*, 29 March 1941, p. 8.There were many advertisements for *Rinso* which rang the changes in advertising technique but kept to the same essential formula of a no-boil wash that got clothes clean through soaking, washing and rinsing.

47 'New Fuel-Saving Way to Wash Clothes', *Picture Post*, 7 November 1942, p. 4.

48 'Rinso soaks clothes clean in 12 minutes', *Picture Post*, 10 July 1943, p. 27.

49 Later advertisements, dating from spring 1944 to early 1945, adopted a comic-strip format revealing how using *Rinso* allowed more time for valuable pursuits such as war-work of one sort or another or increasing time with the family.

50 'Prices Up: Clothes Become Precious', *Picture Post*, 24 August 1940, p. 36.

51 'Jumpers Jump in Price Again', *Picture Post*, 21 June 1941, p. 32.

52 'Make This New Style Magyar Blouse from an Old Printed Summer Frock', *Picture Post*, 18 July 1942, p. 28.; 'Summer Suits Spiked with White', *Picture Post*, 3 July 1943, p. 2 – both advertisements for Lux.

53 'Net Results ... Curtains into Brassieres', *Picture Post*, 30 October 1943, p. 28. Various brands that were either in shorter supply or no longer available kept some form of advertising going until they could resume normal production.

54 There are a good number of advertisements for both of these products but these examples from towards the end of the war show how rhetoric continued to prioritize the care and conservation of clothing. 'Persil for Extra Whiteness and Longer Wear', *Picture Post*,

17 March 1945, p. 5 and 'Busy Bubble's Helping Hand "We Condemn All Washtub Wear and Tear"', *Picture Post*, 14 October 1944, p. 5.

55 'How to Prolong the Life of Your Rubber-Proofed Coat … or Your Raincoat', *Picture Post*, 2 May 1942, p. 6; also similar on 6 June 1942, p. 6.

Chapter 8

1 Although this section is looking specifically at physical health and capacity, it is as well to remember how much of wartime life also revealed women demonstrating a mental acuity and emotional strength that their pre-war circumstances may never have demanded of them. Several of the *Picture Post* stories here infer that psychological strength was a necessary correlative of the physical strength needed for the job in hand, although the precise relationship, one to the other, was not defined.

2 See Hastings, 'This Was the Woman's Land Army', 13 January 1940, pp. 33–37 and p. 34, briefly mentioned in this work already (Chapter 2) in relationship to workwear.

3 Ibid., p. 34.

4 J. Morgan, 'Women at War, No. 3: The Land Girl', *Picture Post*, 29 November 1941, pp. 18–19; p. 18.

5 Ibid.

6 Ibid.

7 Ibid., p. 19.

8 Ibid., p. 18.

9 N. Shute, 'Women at War, No. 2: I Am a War Nurse', *Picture Post*, 22 November 1941, pp. 10–13.

10 All quotations ibid., p. 10.

11 Ibid.

12 Ibid., p. 12.

13 Ibid., p. 11.

14 Ibid., p. 13.

15 Ibid., p. 10.

16 'Our Nurses in Tobruk', *Picture Post*, 21 March 1942, pp. 18–19.

17 Ibid., p. 18.

18 Ibid., p. 19. The berets may have been 'neat' but this did not necessarily infer any nod to the feminine as berets were, of course, equally a component of certain male service uniforms.

19 Ibid.

20 Ibid., p. 18. This part of West Africa continued to be an active theatre of warfare throughout early 1942.

21 M. Lethbridge O. B. E. 'Women's Army for Britain', *Picture Post*, 17 February 1940, pp. 18–23; p. 21.

22 J. Head, 'Women at War, No. 4: A Girl Joins the A.T.S.', *Picture Post*, 13 December 1941, pp. 16–19.

23 Ibid., p. 18.

24 Ibid.

25 Both quotations ibid., p. 19.

26 'The WAAF Learn to Man the Balloons', *Picture Post*, 13 June 1942, pp. 9–11; p. 10.

27 Ibid., p. 11.

28 Ibid., p. 9.

29 Ibid., p. 11.

30 A. Scott-James, 'Rag-Doll Exercises', *Picture Post*, 23 August 1941, pp. 27–29.

31 Ibid., p. 27.

32 Ibid., p. 28 and pp. 27–28.

33 Ibid., p. 28.

34 Ibid., p. 29.

35 'Can You Do These New Summer Exercises?' *Picture Post*, 20 June 1942, pp. 22–23.

36 Ibid., p. 22.

37 Ibid.

38 Ibid., pp. 22–23.

39 Ibid., p. 23.

40 'Holiday Camp for War Workers', *Picture Post*, 26 September 1942, p. 16. Odney is an island in the Thames and the Odney Estate, including Lullebrook Manor, borders that of Cliveden. Today the Odney Club, which uses the manor house, is owned and run by the John Lewis Partnership for the benefit of their staff.

41 All quotations ibid.

42 'Off-Duty in the Farming Camp', *Picture Post*, 17 July 1943, pp. 22–23.

43 It was also noted that the British nation's 'output of food per man is probably the highest in the world'. Ibid., p. 22.

44 All ibid.

45 Ibid., p. 23.

46 His nationality is not specified.

47 Food rationing was introduced on 8 January 1940 limiting butter to 4 ozs. a week, bacon and ham also to 4 ozs. and sugar to 12 ozs. Meat was rationed in March 1940 to an amount of 1s. 10d. per week. Coupons for specific commodities in the ration book had to be cut out by the shopkeeper who would subsequently return them to the Food Office. For a comprehensive contemporary account of food rationing in Britain up until 1944 see 'Impresario', *The Market Square: The Story of the Food Ration Book 1940–1944*, originally published by the Ministry of Food, 31 March 1944 (reprinted as Historical pamphlet series; no. 6, Imperial War Museum, 1997). See also Calder, *The People's War*, pp. 71–72 on the start of food rationing.

48 Ministry of Food, 'Plan Your Meals the 4 Group Way', Government Announcement, *Picture Post*, 10 August 1940, p. 8.

49 All quotations, Ministry of Food, 'The Week's Food Facts No. 10', *Picture Post*, 5 October 1940, p. 4.

50 Ministry of Food, 'The Week's Food Facts No. 11', *Picture Post*, 12 October 1940, p. 7.

51 Ministry of Food, 'There's More in Them Than Meets the Eye', *Picture Post*, 8 February 1941, p. 39. See also Ministry of Food, 'Let's talk about Food', *Picture Post*, 22 March 1941, p. 8, for further 'health values' of food, potatoes and carrots in particular.

52 Ministry of Food, 'Spring Mood on the Food Front', *Picture Post*, 15 April 1944, p. 28.

53 Ministry of Food, 'When Can a Vegetable Eke Out a Meat Food', *Picture Post*, 20 June 1942, p. 28 and Ministry of Food, 'Dried Eggs Are My Eggs . . .', *Picture Post*, 2 October 1943, p. 4.

54 'Impresario', *The Market Square: The Story of the Food Ration Book 1940–1944*, originally published by the Ministry of Food, 31 March 1944 (reprinted as Historical pamphlet series; no. 6, Imperial War Museum, 1997), p. 61. For representative notices publicizing dietary supplements for pregnant women and babies see: Ministry of Food, 'Commando in Training?', *Picture Post*, 23 January 1943, p. 4; Ministry of Food, 'You Asked These Questions . . . ', *Picture Post*, 30 October 1943, p. 4; Ministry of Food, 'To Every Mother of an Under-6', *Picture Post*, 24 December 1943, p. 28; 'Welcome Little Stranger', *Picture Post*, 28 October 1944, p. 28. For a good contemporary summary of the vitamins available under the National Vitamins Scheme and relevant dates see 'Impresario', as above, pp. 61–62; for the same information on milk, shell eggs and dried egg for expectant and nursing mothers and children of various ages, see pp. 59–60 and pp. 60–61, respectively.

55 For a comprehensive account of both the milk and vitamin schemes as written shortly after the war, see M. Titmuss, *Problems of Social Policy, History of the Second World War United Kingdom Civil Series* (H.M.S.O and Longmans, Green and Co., 1950), pp. 511–514.

56 Ibid., p. 513. If family income fell below forty shillings a week '(plus an allowance of 6s. a week for each non-earning dependent)', milk, orange juice, vitamins and cod-liver oil were free (Ibid., p. 511 and p. 514).

57 Ibid., p. 514.

58 Ibid. The evacuation scheme had revealed evidence of just this type of inequality where poor diet was seen as another indicator of a broader social deprivation. In a much later article by Anne Scott-James called 'What Can We Do for Everyone's Child', the type of child welfare that the nation ought to have in place for the future well-being of children was considered. The article covered child clinics, community health care and appropriate day-care services. While this was a pre-Beveridge wish list, it put future hopes into the contemporary perspective of wartime thinking and expressed the view that 'the prospects of our getting a comprehensive children's health service within a reasonable time after the war are really favourable'. See *Picture Post*, 29 July 1944, pp. 14–17; p. 16.

Chapter 9

1 Taylor reports, however, that 'astonishingly, the British couturier Molyneux's house stayed open [in Paris]. . . operating on a small scale' during the Occupation while Molyneux was 'working with the Free French Army'. See L. Taylor, 'The Work and Function of the Paris Couture Industry during the German Occupation of 1940–1944', in *Dress: The Annual Journal of the Costume Society of America*, Vol. 22, 1995, pp. 34–44; p. 41.

2 'In Paris: Clothes for the 2,000 Wealthy Collaborators', *Picture Post*, 1 May 1943, pp. 10–11; p. 10.

3 Ibid.

4 All ibid., p. 11.

5 Ibid., p. 10.

6 Ibid., p. 11.

7 The first restrictions placed on jewellery occurred in June 1940 under S. R. and O. 1940, No. 874 Limitation of Supplies (Miscellaneous) Order issued by the Board of Trade.

The restrictions were by value over a period from June to November 1940 and quotas were reduced to two-thirds of the value of the goods in the same period the preceding year (the base period). For more information see the official history by Hargreaves and Gowing, *Civil Industry and Trade*, pp. 102–103. Jewellery was further restricted when, in addition to limiting supplies, the Board of Trade also implemented 'prohibitions' on certain unessential commodities. Hargreaves and Gowing noted these were wide ranging and included 'all goldsmith's and silversmith's ware, jewellery, and imitation jewellery except clocks, watches, gem diamonds, identification bracelets, cuff links, studs, watch chains and key chains that did not contain gold finer than nine carats, and plain wedding rings made according to Board of Trade specification'. See ibid., pp. 502–505. Perfumery along with other toiletry preparations had first been regulated in June 1940 under the same Order as jewellery above. The two-thirds quota was applied, although by December 1940 this had been reduced to 25 per cent of the output for the base period. See ibid., p. 531.

8 'In Paris: Clothes for the 2,000 Wealthy Collaborators', p. 11.

9 Ibid., p. 10.

10 Ibid., p. 10 and p. 11.

11 Ibid., p. 11. Subsequent histories would reveal, however, that couturiers who remained open had provided work, thereby protecting employees from possible removal to Nazi labour camps. Further information on the workings of the couture during wartime can be found in D. Veillon, *Fashion Under the Occupation* (Berg, 2002). Other texts providing information on the justification by the French couture for remaining open during the Occupation include: H. R. Lottman, 'As War Ended', and N. Gasc, 'Haute Couture and Fashion 1939–1945', both in S. Train (ed.), *Theatre de la Mode* (Rizzoli, 1991); D. Veillon, 'Haute Couture on German Time' and 'Conclusion', in *Fashion Under the Occupation* (Berg, 2002); L. Taylor, 'Paris Couture 1940–1944', in E. Wilson and J. Ash (eds), *Chic Thrills: A Dress History Reader* (Pandora, 1993); L. Taylor, 'The Work and Function of the Paris Couture Industry during the German Occupation of 1940–1944', pp. 34–44.

12 Ibid.

13 Allied troops first entered Paris on 25 August 1944.

14 Article title, *Picture Post*, 7 October 1944, p. 19.

15 All quotations 'Paris Fashions Are Quick Off the Mark', *Picture Post*, 7 October 1944, p. 19. The article mentioned that some designers had left Paris during the Occupation for America.

16 This centres on the representations made by *Chambre Syndicale de l'Haute Couture* president, Lucien Lelong, to the German authorities to maintain the couture in Paris as opposed to Munich, Vienna or Berlin. They were based on safeguarding the fashion houses – and the numerous smaller industries serving the couture – as French, thereby maintaining its indigenous workforce. Forced relocation to Nazi labour camps of redundant employees might then be avoided. See Taylor, 'The Work and Function of the Paris Couture Industry during the German Occupation of 1940–1944', p. 36 and p. 39. In a later *Picture Post* article Alison Settle remarked that the French fashion industry had retained 'all but 5 per cent of its highly trained workforce' while Britain, in comparison, had lost 'almost all trained needlewomen... to war work'. A. Settle, 'London: Can It Become A World Fashion Centre?' *Picture Post*, 6 January 1945, p. 21.

17 Christian Dior's New Look would launch in February 1947 affirming the renewed pre-eminence of Paris as the centre of couture fashion design.

18 'What a *Vogue* Photographer Sees in Paris', *Picture Post*, 25 November 1944, pp. 12–13.

19 Ibid., p. 12.

20 Ibid.

21 Ibid., p. 13. Captions revealed that hair was shampooed and set on the first day and styled on the second.

22 Ibid., p. 12.

23 Alison Settle was a writer on fashion and had edited British *Vogue* from 1929 to 1936. She became fashion editor at the *Observer* newspaper in 1937. The *Alison Settle Archive* is held at Brighton University. See *arts.brighton.ac.uk*

24 'What a *Vogue* Photographer Sees in Paris', p. 12.

25 Ibid., p. 13.

26 A. Settle, 'London: Can It Become A World Fashion Centre?', *Picture Post*, 6 January 1945, pp. 19–21.

27 The austerity restrictions on women's clothing were not removed until March to April 1946; see Hargreaves and Gowing, *Civil Industry and Trade*, p. 439. The civilian coupon-based ration continued to be cut until May 1946; see Howell, *Wartime Fashion: Haute Couture to Homemade 1939–1945*, p. 97.

28 Settle, 'London: Can It Become A World Fashion Centre?', p. 20.

29 Ibid. Settle noted in parenthesis that Paris was 'aghast because its designers must now have a collection of no more than 160 models'. She identified several problems besetting the British fashion industry across the article as a whole. In brief these were: fashion was not taken seriously enough either as a business or a philosophy; the Board of Trade was not being pro-active in fostering the development of 'prototype patterns of textiles' to ensure the textile industry's future; a perceived labour shortage for any further development in the textile industry; at least some of the austerity regulations needed to be lifted to allow the 'softer and more feminine line of after-war' to develop and new design ideas to emerge, p. 21.

30 Ibid.

31 On 21 July 1945, *Picture Post* ran an article entitled 'Britain's Best Clothes Are for Export' (p. 16), with photography by Kurt Hutton. The emphasis was still very much on tailored coats and suits but the text suggested that designers were now being allowed 'more scope', although no specific details of any leniency in the controls were given. Utility clothes were priced accordingly but couture clothing was 'very expensive' with models costing '£50 or £60'.

Conclusion

1 Scott-James, *Sketches from a Life*, pp. 79–80.These comments are made in the context of the editorial policies created by Lorant and expanded by Hopkinson.

2 'A Plan for Britain', *Picture Post*, 4 January 1941, pp. 7–40.

3 Ibid., 'Forward', p. 4.

4 Priestley, 'Britain's Silent Revolution', p. 22. This article is referred to at the end of Chapter 3.

5 Jennie Lee, 'A New Life Opens Out for Women', *Picture Post*, 1 August 1942, p. 21. Jennie Lee was from a Scottish mining background and had been the Independent Labour Party MP for North Lanark 1929–1931. Elected at the age of twenty-five, she had become the youngest MP. She married Aneurin Bevan in 1934. The Jennie Lee Collection can be accessed via www.open.ac.uk

6 Ibid. This was, arguably, a more discreet way of saying that only when all men were employed would women find any surety of work.

7 Ibid.

8 Ibid., p. 22.

9 'Special Issue: Changing Britain', *Picture Post*, 2 January 1943.

10 'Social Security: The New Ideal', The Hon. Frank Pakenham, ibid., p. 14.

11 It would be Hopkinson's desire to publish the politically sensitive truth concerning the ill-treatment of prisoners on both sides during the Korean War that would lead to his dismissal as editor in October 1950. See Hopkinson, *Of This Our Time: A Journalist's Story 1905–1950*, pp. 282–289.

12 'The Work of Ferry Pilots', *Picture Post*, 16 September 1944, pp. 7–10.

SELECT BIBLIOGRAPHY

Primary Source

Picture Post Historical Archive. Gale Cengage Learning, Mirror Group Newspapers and Getty Images.

My access to the *Picture Post* online archive was made possible through Westminster Reference Library, London.

Archives Used

British Library, Board of Trade Archives; *Clothing Quizzes* 1941–1947; Orders and Miscellaneous Circulars and Memoranda 1939–1945.

British Library, Newsroom: Magazines and journals (various, see below) 1938–1945.

Getty Images at www.gettyimages.co.uk

Mass Observation Archive, University of Sussex, Topic Collections (various) 1938–1945.

National Archives, Board of Trade Archives 1939–1945.

Westminster Reference Library: Using 24/7 online archive of Newspapers and Magazines.

NB All online archival resources and portals with detail of access routes through to specific topics appear in the relevant chapter footnotes.

Newspapers and Magazines

At British Library:

Berliner Illustrirte Zeitung 1927–1932

Drapers' Record

Illustrated London News

The Lady

Life

The Oracle

Woman's Own

Westminster Reference Library:

Vogue (*British*)

Books, Articles, Pamphlets

British Library Clothing Quiz booklets (BS 41/151).

Caldwell, E. and Bourke-White, M. (1994), *You Have Seen Their Faces*, Georgia USA: University of Georgia Press. First printed 1937, New York: Viking Press.

Hardy, B. (1985), *Bert Hardy: My Life*, London: Gordon Fraser.
Hargreaves, E. L. and Gowing M. M. (1952), *Civil Industry and Trade*, London: HMSO and Longmans, Green and Co.
Hopkinson, T. (1982), *Of This Our Time: A Journalist's Story 1905–1950*, London: Hutchinson.
Hutton, K. (1947), *Speaking Likeness*, London: Focal Press.
'Impressario' (1944, 31st March), *The Market Square. The Story of the Food Ration Book 1940–1944*, reprinted 1997 (London: Ministry of Information), Historical Pamphlets Series No. 6, London: Imperial War Museum.
Jephcott, A. P. (1942), *Girls Growing Up: A Study of the Lives of Young Working Girls*, London: Faber and Faber Ltd.
Man, F. H. (1983), *Man with Camera: Photographs from Seven Decades*, London: Secker and Warburg.
Mass Observation (1941, August), 'Clothes Rationing Survey, Bulletin of the Advertising Service Guild', *Change*, No. 1, London: Advertising Service Guild.
National Archive, Board of Trade, BT64, Industries and Manufacturers Department: Correspondence and Papers, Kew.
Priestley, J. B. (1940), *Postscripts*, reprinted 1941, London: Heinemann Ltd.
Priestley, J. B. (1943), *British Women Go to War*, London: Collins.
Priestley, J. B. (1943), *Three Plays* (Including 'They Came to a City'), London: Heinemann Ltd.
Scott-James, A. (1993), *Sketches from a Life*, London: Michael Joseph.
Settle, A. (1937), *Clothes Line*, London: Methuen and Co.
Spender, H. with Mulford, J. (ed.) (1982), *Worktown People: Photographs from Northern England 1937–38*, Bristol: Falling Wall Press.
Strachey, R. (1935), *Careers and Openings for Women: A Guide for Girls and Young Women in Settling the Choice of a Career*, London: Faber and Faber.
Titmuss, T. M. (1950), *Problems of Social Policy*, London: HMSO and Longmans, Green and Co.

Other Media

Britannia Is a Woman: A Tribute to the War Effort of British Women (1940), British Movietone News, Imperial War Museum Official Collection: Women and Children at War (2006), written by G. Sangerand and R. Landon.
WVS Women's Voluntary Services (1941), A Verity Film for the Ministry of Information, Imperial War Museum Official Collection: Women and Children at War, 2006, directed by L. Birt, commentary written by R. Howe.

Secondary Sources

Beddoe, D. (1989), *Back to Home and Duty: Women between the Wars 1918–1939*, London: Pandora Press.
Booth, C. (1902–1903), *Life and Labour of the People in London* (3rd Edition), London: Macmillan.
Brandt, B. (1936), *The English at Home*, London: Batsford.
Brayley, M. and Ingram, R. (1995), *World War 11 British Women's Uniforms*, London: Windrow and Greene Ltd.
Brendon, P. (2000), *The Dark Valley: A Panorama of the 1930s*, London: Jonathan Cape.
Brown, M. (1999), *Put That Light Out! Britain's Civil Defence Services at War 1939–1945*, Stroud: Sutton Publishing.
Calder, A. (1994), *The People's War: Britain 1939–1945*, London: Pimlico.
Cannadine, D. (ed.) (1989), *The Speeches of Winston Churchill*, London: Penguin.
De Courcy, A. (1989), *1939: The Last Season*, London: Thames and Hudson.

De la Haye, A. (2009), *Land Girls: Cinderellas of the Soil*, Brighton: Royal Pavilion and Museums.
Doss, E. (ed.) (2001), *Looking at Life Magazine*, Washington, USA: Smithsonian Institute Press.
Esquevin, C. (2008), *Adrian: Silver Screen to Custom Label*, New York, USA: The Monacelli Press, Inc.
Evans, H. with Buckland, G. and Baker, K. (1998), *The American Century: People, Power and Politics. An Illustrated History*, London: Jonathan Cape.
Gardiner, J. (1993), *Picture Post Women*, London: Collins and Brown.
Gernsheim, H. (1991), *Creative Photography: Aesthetic Trends 1839–1960*, New York: Dover Publications Inc.
Gilbert, M. (1999), *Second World War*, London: Phoenix Giant.
Grieve, M. (1964), *Millions Made My Story*, London: Victor Gollancz.
Hallett, M. (2006), *Stefan Lorant: Godfather of Photojournalism*, Maryland, USA: Scarecrow Press Inc.
Hardt, H. (1989), 'Pictures for the Masses: Photography and the Rise of Popular Magazines in Weimar Germany', *Journal of Communication Inquiry* (Vol. 13) via *journals.sagepub.com*, pp. 7–29.
Hardt, H. (1996), 'Sites of Reality: Constructing Press Photography in Weimar Germany 1928–1933', *The Communication Review*, Vol. 1, No. 3, pp. 373–402. DOI: 10,1080/10714429609388270, or via the British Library *ESTAR* in-house electronic journals system – BL Reading Rooms only.
Harris, C. (2003), *Women at War in Uniform 1939–1945*, Stroud: Sutton Publishing Ltd.
Hartley, J. and Rennie, E. (2004), 'About a Girl: Fashion Photography in Photojournalism', *Journalism Theory, Practice and Criticism*, Vol. 5, No. 4, pp. 458–479, Sage Publications, *SAGE Journals Online*, accessed via British Library.
Hartnell, N. (1955), *Silver and Gold*, London: Evans Bros. Ltd.
Head, E. and Calistro, P. (2008), *Edith Head's Hollywood*, California USA: Angel City Press.
Hopkinson, T. (ed.) (1970), *Picture Post 1938–1950*, London: Allen Lane, Penguin Press.
Hopkinson, A. and Lenman, R. (2005), 'Photojournalism', in R. Lenman (ed.), *The Oxford Companion to the Photograph*, pp. 488–492, Oxford: Oxford University Press.
Howell, G. (2012), *Wartime Fashion: Haute Couture to Homemade 1939–1945*, London: Berg.
Hudson, R. (1984), *The Best of Signal: Hitler's Wartime Picture Magazine*, London: Hamlyn.
Kaes, A., Jay, M., and Dimendberg, E. (1995), *The Weimar Republic Sourcebook*, Berkeley, LA, and London: University of California Press.
Kee, R. (1994), *The Picture Post Album: A 50th Anniversary Collection*, London: Barrie and Jenkins.
Kobler, J. (1968), *Henry Luce: His Time, Life and Fortune*, London: MacDonald and Co.
Lewis, J. (1984), *Women in England 1870–1950*, Sussex: Wheatsheaf Books.
London, J. (2007), *People of the Abyss*, Middlesex: Echo Library (First published 1903, New York, USA: Macmillan).
Magilow, D. H. (2012), *The Photography of Crisis: The Photo Essays of Weimar Germany*, University Park, Pennsylvania, USA: The Pennsylvania State University Press.
McDonough, F. (2002), *Hitler, Chamberlain and Appeasement*, Cambridge: Cambridge University Press.
Mercer, D. (editor-in-chief) (1993), *Chronicle of the Twentieth Century*, Farnborough: JL International Publications.
Mollo, A. (2000), *The Armed Forces of World War Two*, London: Greenwich Editions.
Mulvagh, J. (1992), *Vogue History of Twentieth Century Fashion*, London: Bloomsbury Books.
Murphy, K. (2014), 'A Marriage Bar of Convenience? The BBC and Married Women's Work 1923–39', in *Twentieth Century British History*, February 2014, pp. 533–561 (accessed via *tcbh.oxfordjournals.org*)
Newton, J. H. (2001), *The Burden of Visual Truth: The Role of Photojournalism in Mediating Reality*, Mahwah, NJ: Lawrence Erlbaum Associates.

Newton, J. H. (April 2009), 'Photojournalism: Do People Matter? Then Photojournalism Matters', *Journalism Practice*, Vol. 3, No. 2, pp. 233–243, London: Routledge, Taylor and Francis Group.
Opie, R. (2003), *The 1930s Scrapbook*, London: New Cavendish Books.
Oram, A. (1996), *Women Teachers and Feminist Politics 1900–1930*, Manchester: Manchester University Press.
Osman, C. (1982), *Creative Camera: Fifty Years of Picture Magazines*, pp. 570–617, London: Coo Press Ltd.
Overy, R. (2009), *The Morbid Age: Britain and the Crisis of Civilization, 1919–1939*, London: Penguin.
Pugh, M. (1992), *Women and the Women's Movement in Britain 1914–1959*, London: Macmillan.
Quennell, P. (ed.) (1984), *Mayhew's London*, London: Bracken Books.
Riis, J. A. (1998), *How the Other Half Lives: Studies among the Tenements of New York*, New York USA: Penguin.
Roiser, M. (2001), 'Social Psychology and Social Concern in 1930s Britain', in Bunn, G. C., Lovie, A. D., and Richards, G. D. (eds), *Psychology in Britain: Historical Essays and Personal Reflections*, pp. 169–187, Leicester: British Psychological Society Books, John Wiley and Sons.
Rose, S. O. (2003), *Which People's War? National Identity and Citizenship in Wartime Britain 1939–1945*, Oxford: Oxford University Press.
Rowntree, S. (1941), *Poverty and Progress*, London: Longmans, Green and Co.
Samuel, R. (1983), 'Suburbs under Siege. The Middle-class between the Wars. Part 111', *New Socialist*, Vol. 11 May/June, pp. 28–30.
Shipman, D. (1993), *Cinema: The First Hundred Years*, London: QPD Orion Publishing.
Smith, M. (2000), *Britain and 1940: History, Myth and Popular Memory*, London: Routledge.
Stack, P. (1988), *Zest for Life: Mary Bagot Stack and the Women's League of Health and Beauty*, London: Peter Owen.
Taylor, L. (1993), 'Paris Couture 1940–1944', in Wilson, E. and Ash, J. (eds), *Chic Thrills: A Dress History Reader*, pp. 127–144, London: Pandora.
Taylor, L. (1995), 'The Work and Function of the Paris Couture Industry during the German Occupation of 1940–1944', *Dress: The Annual Journal of the Costume Society of America*, Vol. 22, pp. 34–44.
Time Life Books' Editors (1971), *Photojournalism*, Virginia, USA: Time Life Books.
Train, S. (1991), *Theatre de la Mode*, New York, USA: Rizzoli.
Veillon, D. (2002), *Fashion Under the Occupation*, Oxford: Berg.
Wilk, C. (ed.) (2006), *Modernism: Designing a New World 1914–1939*, London: V&A Publications.
Wilson, E. and Taylor, L. (1989), *Through the Looking Glass: A History of Dress from 1860 to the Present Day*, London: BBC Books.
Yohannan, K. and Nolf, N. (1998), *Claire McCardell: Redefining Modernism*, New York, USA: Harry N. Abrams Inc.
Ziegler, P. (1998), *London at War*, London: Arrow Books.

INDEX

Note: Numbers in italics indicate references to pictures.